Burnham of Chicago

Burnham of Chicago
ARCHITECT AND PLANNER

THOMAS S. HINES

New York
OXFORD UNIVERSITY PRESS
1974

Copyright © 1974 by Oxford University Press, Inc.
Library of Congress Catalogue Card Number: 74-79625

A selection from the book *Leaves of Grass* by Walt Whitman (arranged by Dr. Emory Holloway, Everyman's Library Edition, E. P. Dutton & Co., Inc.) is used by permission of the publisher.

Printed in the United States of America

To my mother
Polly Moore Hines
and to the memory of my father
Thomas Spight Hines

Acknowledgments

It is a pleasure to acknowledge the stimulation and support I have received from individuals and from institutions during the various stages of this long but enjoyable enterprise. My first debts are posthumous ones to my earliest architectural heroes—Louis Sullivan and Frank Lloyd Wright—whose great buildings and writings made me curious about the "other side," as embodied in the work and person of Daniel Burnham. The two individuals who first encouraged me to write on Burnham were Nancy Boone, former architectural reference librarian at the Art Institute of Chicago, and the late Philip Blumenthal, a seminar colleague at the University of Wisconsin.

This study first took shape as my University of Wisconsin doctoral dissertation and my debts to friends and mentors in Madison are more numerous than I could ever list or perhaps even remember. Several individuals and organizations, there and elsewhere, stand out, however, as being particularly important to me as the work progressed.

Irvin G. Wyllie, now chancellor of the University of Wisconsin, Parkside, my first adviser and major professor in the department of history, was especially helpful during the early stages of research and conceptualization. William L. O'Neill, of the same department, furnished crucial support and encouragement during the later stages of the project. Alan F. Mast, my adviser in the Wisconsin department of art history, has continued to be a source of critical inspiration and fresh ideas. The department of history, the University of Wisconsin Archives, and the Ford Foundation furnished financial support during the early years of research and writing. Numerous friends at the University of California, Los Angeles, have been helpful during the project's later phases. A U.C.L.A. Faculty Fellowship and grants from the U.C.L.A. Academic Senate and the University of California Humanities Institute provided support for travel and research. Kate Howells furnished helpful bibliographic assistance, especially in the preparation of Appendix A. Yvonne Tuchalski and Kenneth Rasmussen assisted with the proofreading. The skillful and patient staff of the U.C.L.A. Stenographic Bureau typed and retyped the revisions of the manuscript. The most supportive of all has been my wife, Dorothy Hines, whose special contribution is the preparation of the index.

Members and friends of the Burnham family who furnished information are acknowledged in the Note on Sources. Special thanks are due to the librarians and staffs of the following institutions: the Library of the University of Wisconsin, Madison; the Library of the Wisconsin State Historical Society, Madison; the Library of the Art Institute of Chicago; the Archives of the Chicago Symphony Orchestra; the Newberry Library, Chicago; the Houghton Library of Harvard University; the New York Public Library; the Library of the New-York Historical Society; the Avery Library of Columbia University; the Research Library of the University of California, Los Angeles; the Bancroft Library of the University of California, Berkeley; and the National Library of the Philippines, Manila. Other versions of Chapters VIII and X first appeared as articles in the *American Quarterly* and the *Pacific Historical Review*, respectively. I am grateful to those journals for permission to reprint them in their present form.

Numerous individuals read this manuscript during various stages of its revision. All of them offered helpful suggestions, though none of them is ultimately responsible for any errors of fact or judgment. They include, among others: Nancy Boone, Fawn Brodie, George Collins, Merle Curti, Donald Hoffmann, Stanley Katz, Alan Mast, William O'Neill, John Pilkington, David Rodes, Ruth Schoneman, Stanley Schultz, and David Weber. These and others have helped me to find answers to the questions: Who was Daniel Burnham? What was the meaning of his life and work? How did he both reflect his milieu and affect the changing environment?

Los Angeles   T.S.H.
June 1974

Contents

List of Illustrations

Introduction

"MAKE NO LITTLE PLANS," his credo ran, "they have no magic to stir men's blood. . . ." And indeed Daniel Burnham's plans—and achievements—were big ones, not only in architecture and urban design but in the integrally related areas of philanthropy and cultural leadership. Still, for all his acknowledged power and panache, Burnham the man has somehow remained elusive. The lives, the institutions, and the projects he touched have long been considered historically significant and have frequently been studied with care and insight. Yet, throughout the study of the elements of Burnham's world—the Chicago School of architecture, the World's Columbian Exposition, the City Beautiful Movement, indeed the history of modern architecture—there has, to now, been no sustained analysis of Burnham's leadership and influence in a profession that has guided, reflected, and articulated American culture. This study attempts to illuminate that achievement.

Though Burnham was born in 1846 near the rural community of Henderson, New York, and died in 1912 while touring in Heidelberg, Germany, he spent most of his life in Chicago, Illinois. He grew up with the city that he would help build, a city that would reflect increasingly his own developing characteristics as a man: a restless, vigorous, commercial city, sometimes a bit unsure of itself, but obviously, and with convincing bravado, bent on a future of "growth," "progress," and "self-improvement."

It was to Chicago in 1855 that Burnham's parents brought their family after repeated business failures in the east. There, Daniel Burnham grew up and went to school, while his father achieved a success in business and civic affairs he had never known before and it was to Chicago that the young Daniel returned in 1870, after his own disappointing failures as a student, businessman, and politician. But if Chicago had been the promised land for the elder Burnham, it would prove to be even more beneficent and stimulating for the younger. During the 1880s and 1890s, innovations in skyscraper design by the firm of Burnham & Root constituted major contributions to the early Chicago School of architecture. The Chicago World's Fair of 1893 and the Chicago Plan of 1909 began and climaxed Burnham's efforts as a city planner.

His Chicago reputation, however, as an architect, planner, and organizer increasingly pulled him outward as his firm designed buildings in every section and major city of the country. As a city planner of the early 1900s, he, and others, saw his work in Washington, Cleveland, San Francisco, and Chicago as an architectural expression of the heterogeneous Progressive Movement. Concurrent with others' programs for attacking social, economic, and political malaise, Burnham and his followers in urban planning attempted to reform the physical environment. As an upper-class "Progressive" Republican, Burnham also, not surprisingly, defended the burgeoning American imperialism of the early twentieth century, and, in 1905, gave his architectural signature to the newly Americanized Philippines with city plans for Manila and Baguio. As president of the American Institute of Architects in 1894, Burnham's chief concern was the chaotic state of government architecture, which he helped to improve by a closer advisory liaison between A.I.A. experts and decision-making officials. In 1910, toward the end of his life, he approached the same problem from the other side when President Taft appointed him chairman of the National Commission on the Fine Arts.

As an architect, planner, and cultural leader, Burnham was alternately archaic and progressive. His artistic tastes were often conservative, making him sometime a ponderous and confident specimen of what historian Henry May has called the "custodians of culture."[1] Yet, at other times, he welcomed new ideas in art. In architecture and city planning, he understood and frequently exploited the newest technology and planned for a future technology then undreamed of. Burnham, the man, was a curious, though not incongruous, set of contrasts: a Swedenborgian mystic of sorts, less interested in theology than in the practice of Christian ethics; a tough and hard-headed businessman, whose natural kindness, poise, and sweetness of disposition tempered his machine-like efficiency and his materialistic goals. After a rather prodigal youth and bachelorhood, Burnham became a devoted husband and father, attempting, somehow, to relive through his children his own early life which he grew to regret as wasted, inchoate, and misdirected. Despite his firmness, however, as a father and as a businessman, he almost always won respect and affection from those whose lives he touched. Burnham believed strongly in the idea of free enterprise capitalism, shorn of its excesses and grosser injustices by "progressive" governmental controls, and he worked on the assumption that, with proper regulation, reform, and receptiveness to change, the system could somehow manage to coexist compatibly with political democracy. Burnham was always a mover, but he was decidedly not a shaker.

When he died in 1912, his reputation was international. President Taft thought him "one of the foremost architects of the world," but one who had more than merely professional skill. He had, Taft thought, a "breadth of views as to the artistic subject that permitted him to lead in every movement for the education of the public in art, of the development of art in every branch of our busy life without pay."[2] The architect Cass Gilbert praised his artistic contributions but believed that he "would have been successful in any walk of life, for the qualities which make for success were his to an unusual degree. . . . Easily a leader, his leadership gave prestige to every project that he undertook."[3] Former British Ambassador James Bryce remembered Burnham from his years in America and recalled an "impression of the power and range of his mind and ideas" and thought he would "be reckoned in his way and sphere of art one of the most remarkable men of the generation. . . ."[4] Even his professional detractors found much in him to like. Frank Lloyd Wright stated bluntly that Burnham "was not a creative architect, but he was a great man"—high praise in view of Wright's firm belief that there were few creative architects in 1912 other than Wright himself and Louis Sullivan! Still, Wright knew that Burnham "made masterful use of the methods and men of his time" and that as an "enthusiastic promoter of great construction enterprises . . . his powerful personality was supreme."[5]

Burnham's reputation at the time of his death was reinforced for many in 1921 with the publication of Charles Moore's *Daniel H. Burnham, Architect, Planner of Cities*. Moore was a friend and professional colleague of Burnham. The two had met when Burnham undertook the Washington Plan in 1901 while Moore was the secretary of the Senate's

District of Columbia Committee. Subsequently, they worked together
on most of Burnham's planning enterprises until his death. Moore's
handsomely printed, two-volume biography, written in close collaboration with the Burnham family and dedicated to Burnham's wife, was, in
reality, little more than a long and affectionate eulogy. Historian A. D. F.
Hamlin, writing in the *American Historical Review*, spoke for most re-
viewers in regretting that the book was a "one-sided account of the life
of a man whose career was so remarkable, and so typically American."[6]
Because Moore knew Burnham well, however, and was able to recall and
retrieve firsthand accounts of so many of his activities, the book is valuable as a primary source. Though it contains many errors of fact and
some questionable judgments, and though large parts of it are direct
quotations from Burnham's letters and diaries, the book's importance
has been second only to those letters and diaries as an aid in the reconstruction of his life.

Equally significant in molding Burnham's image for later generations
has been the writing of Louis Sullivan, especially *The Autobiography of
an Idea*, first published in 1924. Superseded only by his apprentice and
follower, Frank Lloyd Wright, as the greatest architect in American history, Louis Sullivan was also a brilliant, if often acerbic, critic of people,
architecture, and society. Long opposed to most of Burnham's aesthetic
judgments and later achievements, Sullivan, in his declining years, became especially piqued and dismayed by the prestige, reputation, fame,
and wealth that Burnham had so obviously acquired. Sullivan had admired John Wellborn Root, the major designer of the Burnham and
Root partnership, who deferred to Burnham on most questions of business, promotion, and relations with clients. Sullivan in his own firm had
held a comparable position to that of Root in Burnham's, depending
heavily on the practical wisdom of his own partner, Dankmar Adler.
Sullivan's erratic temperament, however, had led to a break with Adler
in 1895, after which his fortunes slowly declined. Despite the continued
brilliance of his designs, Sullivan simply lacked Adler's, or Burnham's,
ability and desire to get along with people, and during his last twenty
years, he grew increasingly destitute, depressed, and alcoholic.

In the *Autobiography*, Sullivan recalled briefly his first impressions of
Burnham: "a dreamer, a man of fixed determination and strong will . . .
of large wholesome, effective presence, a shade pompous . . . a man
who readily opened his heart if one were sympathetic." Sullivan saw
other occasional virtues in the make-up of his rival, but his feelings to-

ward Burnham were, at best, ambivalent. Usually, he was more damn-
ing: he "watched through the years the growing of Daniel Hudson Burnham into a colossal merchandiser," whose "megalomania concerning the
largest, the tallest, the most costly and sensational, moved on in its sure
orbit, as he painfully learned to use the jargon of big business." In a
world of "bigness, organization, delegation, and intense commercialism,"
Sullivan thought, Daniel Burnham "sensed the reciprocal workings of his
own mind."[7]

Sullivan's critique of Burnham contained much truth and insight.
Prompted, however, by his own state of poverty and neglect, the general
tone was one of bitterness and contempt. As Sullivan's reputation has
justifiably risen in the years since his death, Burnham's reputation has
declined in almost direct proportion. Most historians who have discussed them at all have rather glibly depicted Sullivan as a culture
hero and Burnham as the necessary villain, usually taking their text from
Sullivan, himself, and finding sufficient confirmation in the innocent
platitudes of Charles Moore's well-intended eulogy.

Burnham's relationship to Sullivan was suggestively similar to the relationship of William Dean Howells and his fellow novelist Henry James,
and even more comparable to that of the biologist Louis Agassiz and his
colleague Asa Gray. Though personally unable to accept the implications
of Darwinian evolution, Agassiz's reputation and influence, as an edu-
cator and promoter of science, remained strong with contemporaries until his death in 1885. Though, at times, defending increasingly obsolete
ideas, Agassiz's vigor and poise nevertheless allowed him a continuing
voice in the affairs of the scientific world. His Harvard colleague, Asa
Gray, on the other hand, accepted Darwinism and extended those
theories in his own work, but, as a more detached introvert, failed to rival
Agassiz's general influence over the greater part of the scientific community. Very much like Louis Agassiz, Burnham's importance and influence
was chiefly of a horizontal nature, spreading out during his own lifetime
to affect and direct contemporary thought and action in the arts. Like
Asa Gray, on the other hand, Louis Sullivan's influence has been of a
more vertical nature, exerting an impact on architects and designers of
succeeding generations, who, while never knowing the man, have justifiably appreciated the brilliance of his work. For a generation of Sullivan
admirers, however, to discount the importance of Burnham's very different achievement is to misunderstand the workings of history.

Burnham's direct and indirect relationship with Sullivan leads, moreover, to larger questions that are components of but that reach beyond the biography or the achievements of either man—questions that will, both explicitly and implicitly, pervade and inform this book. Sullivan produced very great work, but he was severely limited in the number and scope of his commissions and in his immediate architectural influence by his elitist disdain for the tastes and demands of those whom Frank Lloyd Wright, in his book on Sullivan, described, not as the democracy, but as the mobocracy. In Sullivan, artistic sensitivity carried over into a personal insularity that often found expression in a smug and snobbish arrogance. He was never particularly interested or gifted—his own contentions notwithstanding—in popular educational or promotional activities beyond the circles of the architectural cognoscenti. He was seldom willing to establish real or lasting rapport with the architecturally innocent public or to establish effective communications with difficult prospective "otherwise-minded" clients. Yet Sullivan believed that he knew, in an almost mystical way, the *needs* of the public and he consequently described his work as "the architecture of Democracy," while characterizing Burnham as "feudal," "imperial," and "Philistine."

As opposed to Sullivan, however, Burnham had greater patience and rapport with Americans of all classes, despite his own grand life style and his frequently pompous manner. Indeed while instructing and cajoling doubting laymen to his position, he also listened to and considered their own ideas, prognoses, and recommendations. By claiming that he responded more sympathetically to clients' conscious and expressed needs, Burnham believed that he, rather than Sullivan, was the kind of architect needed in a capitalistic democracy. A critical understanding and evaluation of that Sullivan-Burnham conflict and its relation to the problem of a "democratic architecture" are surely central to an understanding of the role of art and architecture in a capitalistic and democratic system.

As a major spokesman for, and promoter of, the arts in American society in the late nineteenth and early twentieth century, Burnham has been too long ignored, for different reasons, by social, cultural and architectural historians. Historians of art have favored the indisputably greater artists, Henry Hobson Richardson, Louis Sullivan, and Frank Lloyd Wright. Social and cultural historians have generally lacked the interest or the inclination to incorporate an architect of Burnham's nature into their reconstruction of the American past.

In this study, I will attempt to assess both the positive and the negative aspects of Daniel Burnham's contributions to American life. While characterizing and describing the essence of his architecture and his city plans, I will focus on his successes and failures as a cultural spokesman and entrepreneur. I am concerned here chiefly with Burnham's character and his personal make-up as a key to his achievements as a cultural leader because I believe that Burnham was more important and more interesting as a man and as a leader of men than he ever was purely as an architect, city planner, or aesthetic philosopher. His character, his personality, his enthusiasm, his forcefulness, as displayed in all his roles, did more to influence American artistic and cultural development than his buildings or his city plans ever have as individual works. His friendships and associations included people of many callings and from all social classes. At the highest level, those he knew and influenced comprised a galaxy and a cross section of American leaders in art, architecture, literature, education, business, politics, and social reform. He had, in the long run, a way of getting things done and of opening doors, not only for his own ideas and projects, but for those of others, even those other artists and architects whose views and values often differed from his own.

"Make big plans," his credo commanded, "aim high in hope and work, remembering that a noble, logical diagram once recorded will never die, but long after we are gone will be a living thing asserting itself with ever-growing insistency. Remember that our sons and grandsons are going to do things that would stagger us."[8] Most of Burnham's plans and projects were very big indeed, and, in something of a reversal of his own prophecies, have frequently "staggered" succeeding generations. Burnham failed often, but even his failures were instructive, providing large, tangible, and sometimes daring models from which others could draw inspiration or depart and move in new directions.

Burnham of Chicago

I
The Long Childhood

1846–1873

One may scan work after work on history, society, and morality
and find little reference to the fact that all people start as children and that all peoples begin in their nurseries. It is human
to have a long childhood. . . . Long childhood makes a technical and mental virtuoso of a man, but it also leaves a lifelong
residue of emotional immaturity in him.

ERIK H. ERIKSON
Childhood and Society

Daniel BURNHAM was conscious all his life of the effects on his
make-up of two ancestral influences: his Anglo-American antecedents
and his family's Swedenborgian religion. "It can do us no harm," he
once wrote, "to have Englishmen know that we honor their blood as we
do our own, which, as a matter of fact, is theirs." Indeed, Daniel Burnham, an eighth-generation American, valued and revered the contributions of Anglo-American ethnicity to his own and his country's background. For at least the first half of his life, the only world that Burnham
knew was Anglo-American. His family, his friends, and his early associates
in western New York, in middle- and upper-class Chicago, in suburban
Boston, and even in the Nevada mining camps were all like himself
descendants of Englishmen.[1]

Daniel's earliest American ancestor, Thomas Burnham, had emigrated
from Norwich, England, to Ipswich, Massachusetts, in 1635. The Massachusetts Burnhams became lawyers, farmers, mill owners, soldiers, and
ministers and several sat in the Massachusetts General Court. Successive
generations moved slowly westward and southward through Vermont
and Connecticut. Daniel's great-grandfather, John Burnham, became

3

a captain in the Revolutionary Army and later served in the first General Assembly of Vermont, which framed the state constitution. Through all this, the Burnhams, like most American colonists, considered themselves Englishmen. Their break with their motherland changed their political allegiance but not their cultural heritage.[2]

In 1811, Edwin Burnham, Daniel's father, moved with his parents to Henderson, New York. In 1832, at the age of twenty-eight, he married Elizabeth Keith Weeks, a granddaughter of the theologian Samuel Hopkins, colleague of Jonathan Edwards, and the cousin of Mark Hopkins, the noted nineteenth-century Williams College president. Her parents, the Reverend Holland Weeks and Harriet Hopkins Weeks, both had ancestral ties to the famous Puritan couple, John and Priscilla Alden. From both his maternal and paternal ancestry would be introduced into Daniel Burnham's heritage the work-oriented subculture of Anglo-American Puritanism. And from his maternal grandfather, in particular, the renegade minister Holland Weeks would come the morally demanding code of Swedenborgian Christianity.[3]

Ordained a Congregationalist, the Reverend Holland Weeks had become a leader among dissenting young clergymen early in his ministry. Daniel's mother in later years would describe her father's influence among the other young ministers who would come to him, as the saying went, "to have their horns put on." But the event that would alter the minister's life was his excommunication for condoning, among other things, the theological tenets of Emanuel Swedenborg.[4]

Swedenborg, the philosopher and theologian, had been the secular inspiration for the founding of the New Jerusalem Church in London in 1787. Born in Sweden in 1688 and residing there most of his life, he spent considerable time in England in his later years. Nominally a Lutheran and with no aspirations of organizing a new church himself, Swedenborg, through his writings, inspired a sect that spread rapidly, though sparsely, throughout Europe. Swedenborgian Christianity reached America around 1790. As the country moved west, congregations of this new sect sprang up along the new frontiers. Weeks, after his excommunication, moved to Henderson, New York, and set up his own "New Church" congregation, which Edwin Burnham soon joined. Burnham's marriage to Weeks' daughter confirmed his own and his future son's commitment to the new religion of his father-in-law.

Similar in its liturgy to Anglicanism and Lutheranism, the communicants of the New Church had little use for trinitarian theology. They recognized and worshipped "one divine Lord" as revealed and articulated in the person of Jesus. The Holy Scriptures, they believed, were divinely given revelations constituting, in essence, the true "second advent" of Christ into the world. The New Church would be therefore "a new divine dispensation," following the Christian church as that had followed the Jewish, and would welcome all who acknowledge "the divinity of the Lord . . . the holiness of the Word . . . and the life of charity." Swedenborgians emphasized the latter tenet of Christian love, believing that "all religion has relation to life, and the life of religion is to do good." Similar theologically to the more popular and pervasive Unitarianism of the nineteenth century, Swedenborgianism predicted the later movement in its subtle and implicit tendencies toward pantheism. It made less of an attempt, however, to rationalize religion or to deny the essentially mystical nature of divine revelation, past or present.[5]

Spiritually, ethically, intellectually, and socially, the Swedenborgian faith pervaded the Burnham household. After only moderate success as a merchant in Henderson, Edwin Burnham took a job with the Oliver Newberry Steamship Company and moved his family to Detroit. On August 25 of that year, Holland Weeks visited his daughter and son-in-law and helped them organize the first Detroit congregation of the New Church. Burnham, one of the members of the congregation later wrote, "who was also engaged in merchandise, was accustomed to place New Church books and tracts in boxes of goods sent out" and his customers "became the happy recipient[s] of these spiritual commodities." Edwin was elected leader and secretary of the Swedenborg Society and also served as an instructor in the small Sunday school.[6]

In May 1840, the Burnhams moved back to Henderson chiefly because Elizabeth felt a responsibility to care for her aging father. But storekeeping there proved even less lucrative than it had been before and the next year Edwin, "sick and unhappy," sold out and moved to Smithville, New York, about five miles from Henderson. Failure followed him there, however, and after a year in Smithville, they returned to Henderson and repurchased the store they had owned before. The family's religion sustained them in those years of financial troubles and their devotion to the New Church in return sustained and enlarged the Church's efforts and activities in western New York. The Reverend George Field, a New Church missionary, recalled their hospitality in the journal of his eastern travels of 1844: "I shall say . . . nothing of my visit to the Brook Farm phalanx, or of my introduction to the celebrities there," he wrote, "as all this would be foreign to my purpose, nor of my pleasant visit to New York City; nor any of my adventures until I again arrived at Henderson, the home of our brother in the church, Edwin Burnham." With the Burnhams' subsequent help and support, Field conducted a successful series of meetings and baptized their son Lewis. Other visiting churchmen were similarly impressed with the couple's hospitality and religious devotion. Indeed, though less renowned than Nathaniel Hawthorne and the other "celebrities" at Brook Farm, Edwin and Elizabeth Burnham became, over the years, quietly modest "celebrities" of the New Jerusalem Church, in Detroit, New York, and later in Chicago.[7]

Born September 4, 1846, in a modest, though comfortable two-story stone house, Daniel was the youngest of three sons and the fifth of six children. Though Edwin seems to have been a loving and attentive father, Elizabeth exerted the more dominant influence on the development of the children. Her youngest daughter Clara recalled that though her mother did not care for high society, she was friendly and "fun-loving" and "had a reserve fund of merry wit . . . to which she often resorted under trying circumstances 'to carry her through.'" She was a sympathetic listener and a reliable friend and many people came to her for counsel and advice. "To her dying day," her daughter recalled, "she showed a remarkable openness of mind, with readiness to welcome progressive thought in any direction."[8]

"Remember your health," she exhorted her children, "for without it you can do nothing comfortably"; and so Daniel became preoccupied with good health and health cures, a preoccupation he had all his life. She played the piano and introduced her children to music, an interest that Daniel in particular continued to cultivate. Both parents were concerned with the family's intellectual and religious development. In 1848, Elizabeth wrote her daughter Ellen that "Mary, Lewis, and Daniel have been having a play tonight with Pa and then were seated to hear some stories just before going to bed which made them quite happy." She was "glad to hear that you read your chapters regularly . . . and should like to have you read some of Swedenborg's writings also every day. . . ." On another occasion, she wrote to her oldest son, Edwin, asking him to purchase and send home a complete set of Scott's Waverly novels. "It is a great blessing to your parents," she told him, "to see you in this your first effort in business, pursuing the path of virtue and striving to gain a good reputation. Your future success in life will depend upon the course you take now. You must guard your every thought, word, and action and not let any unworthy thing have a dwelling place with you. The path to the mountain height is arduous," she warned, "7 and many times difficult," but "with Our Lord for your guide and a trusting and determined heart you will reach the top and dwell *forever there*." She thought his "sojourn in Boston was the best thing . . . ever done" for him, giving him "an opportunity to see what the New Church really is in Massachusetts and judge for yourself in regard to many things that are matters of controversy." There, she suggested, he was "within the sphere of those that started a 'middle course' several years ago," and had chosen to govern themselves without regard to the rules laid down by the church convention. She hoped that Edwin would choose her own position in the matter and "love to be governed by the law." In later life, her youngest son Daniel would echo those admonitions to obey and respect the law and to attempt to change society only as one could effect changes in the law that guided it. Elizabeth's legacies to Daniel were strongly moral, but they were cultural and intellectual as well. According to his respectful sister Clara, his traits of "courage, progressiveness, clear judgment, ready sympathy, sincerity, . . . trustfulness, [and] moral responsibility" were "characteristics inherited . . . from his mother."[9]

Daniel began his formal education at the District School in Henderson. One teacher, Harrison Montague, impressed him especially and Burnham corresponded with him as late as 1902. In 1854, Daniel's grandfather, Holland Weeks, died, relieving his daughter of the long responsibility of caring for him. Because Edwin's business ventures were still unproductive at that time, he suggested that the family move to the larger town of Rome, New York. Elizabeth Burnham, however, thought that a move to Chicago would be more beneficial, especially since Edwin's brother Dyer had become a successful lawyer there. From all that she had read and heard, Chicago in the 1850s seemed a healthy, promising, and exciting place to live and a good place to raise and educate children. By contrast she believed, Henderson simply did not "have a school and society suitable for their age." She persuaded her husband to go out alone, look over the city, and prepare for them to follow him. While there he bought an interest in a stone quarry in Joliet, near Chicago, but soon learned that his partner was dishonest and had defrauded him. "Quite desperate" he decided to "return to Henderson . . . to get a farm with the little money he had left and settle down in New York state." But Elizabeth was adamant. Chicago offered the opportunity for

Burnham at twelve. Courtesy Houghton Mifflin Company.

a fresh start, and, upon hearing of Edwin's plans, she broke up the house
and quickly sent the children west to prevent her husband's return.
Having little further choice, Edwin reluctantly agreed to the move
and soon thereafter entered a Chicago wholesale drug business. Somewhat to his own surprise, he quickly vindicated his wife's precipitous but
determined decision, for with William Sears, an honest and efficient
partner, he became financially prosperous for the first time in his life.[10]

Throughout the years in Chicago, the Burnhams lived an increasingly
comfortable life. The old religious ties continued, and the family took
an active part in Chicago New Church activities. Daniel began his Chi-

cago schooling at Snow's Swedenborgian Academy, a respected and socially prominent institution on Adams Street, and in his early adolescence attended the Jones and Dearborn public schools. In 1861, before his fifteenth birthday, he responded to the general patriotic fervor in the country and enlisted in the 19th Illinois Regiment of the Union Army. Daniel's father, however, citing his son's age, erased his name from the muster roll and kept him at home.[11]

At Chicago's Central High School, Burnham excelled in both athletics and artistic projects, but, as with many potential artists, not in scholarship. A contemporary colleague recalled that Daniel "rarely studied and was always censured for his negligence. He was a tall . . . fellow, much too large for his age" and was often called "the handsomest boy in school." Still, he never forgot "to be a gentleman in his manners. . . . He was never without a pencil in his hand and annoyed his tutors by drawing when his other studies lay neglected. . . . Toward the close of a session he always grew restless and longed for the freedom following dismissal. He was the athlete of the boys," his classmate remembered, "and was leader in all their efforts for physical improvement." His marks were often low, "but before holidays and upon all state occasions, Dan was in his glory—there were the boards to be decorated and he was the only one who could do it. He was then furnished with colored chalks and excused from all class recitations for about a week." Contending that he needed assistants for such projects, he was able to get his less artistic teammates excused from class. Apparently, Burnham was, even then, an "operator" of considerable managerial talent. Throughout his school years he took private drawing lessons, which he later considered of signal importance to his career and to his life. In his adulthood, he sent a check for $100.00 to his old drawing teacher's caretaker, promising more whenever needed. "Let me know about dear Miss Starr from time to time," he wrote. "I know what I owe her. It cannot be paid."[12] As with other people who had influenced him, Burnham appreciated and kept in touch with his drawing teacher until her death.

In 1865, Edwin Burnham climaxed his successful career as merchant and business leader with his election as president of the Chicago Mercantile Association. Formed in 1860 in an effort to "purify the commercial atmosphere" and to work "to establish the currency upon a sound basis," the organization was a forerunner of the numerous businessmen's organizations that would proliferate in Chicago and other American cities during the late nineteenth and early twentieth century. Edwin Burn-

Burnham at nineteen. Courtesy Houghton Mifflin Company.

ham's financial and social mobility and now his public recognition made more realizable the Burnhams' aspirations for their children, at least for the younger ones.[13]

With the hope that Daniel would ultimately gain admission to Harvard, his parents sent him east in 1863 to a preparatory school in Waltham, Massachusetts. His younger sister Clara also attended school there and his older sister Ellen accompanied them to keep house. Daniel spent two years at the Waltham New Church School under the Reverend Joseph Worcester, another instructor who would become a life-long friend. The years at Waltham also included non-academic respites—the adolescent Burnham became interested in girls. He wrote to his family about Anne Hyde, who he was certain was destined to become his bride. She had many virtues, he believed, and "but one fault, which I think she will overcome. She is quick-tempered. But that must give way before her sense of duty. . . . She has no boldness or roughness, which you so much dislike and which I think is equally detestable to me. She has education and cultivation and withal a very engaging address and impresses everyone as being lovely." Daniel left no further record of his relationship with Anne. It would be another eight years before he found the ideal mate and settled into married life.[14]

Burnham then began a period of intensive study in nearby Bridgewater with a private tutor, the Reverend Tilly Brown Hayward. As the time of the awesome college entrance examinations approached, however, a growing awareness of the gaps in his knowledge and his increasing regrets over his earlier academic lapses created in Burnham doubts and anxieties—compounded by parental expectations. For it now seemed extremely important, especially to his mother and father, that he matriculate at Harvard and vindicate his earlier academic failures. But, despite his mentor's confidence in both his intelligence and his preparation, Burnham failed the entrance tests, attributing his failure to a form of "stage fright." "I went to Harvard for examination," Burnham later asserted, "with two men not as well prepared as I; both passed easily, and I flunked, having sat through two or three examinations without being able to write a word." His paralysis at these exams stemmed perhaps from the conflict between his desire to please his parents and enter Harvard, and his own unconscious reaction to the imagined trials and fantasized horrors of academic life in general. Perhaps he knew instinctively that he simply was not a scholar at heart and that early elimination due to nervous stage fright was preferable to the possibility of even more traumatic intellectual failures in his later college career. In any case, the Harvard experience unsettled and depressed him. He likewise failed to gain admission to Yale.[15]

Burnham's emotional maturation had been considerably slower than either his physical or his intellectual development, and in a figurative sense, his emotional childhood lingered on into his adolescence and his young manhood.[16] In 1867, discouraged and restless, he returned to Chicago and became a salesman in a mercantile house, but he found the work unsatisfying and quit after four months. He then attempted to collect his thoughts and define the kind of career he truly wanted. He recalled with special pleasure the earlier discussions with his tutor, T. B.

Hayward, about the history and practice of architecture, discussions that had been reinforced by the handsome volumes in his mentor's well-stocked library. He had also been stimulated during his Massachusetts years by conversations with a Hayward "family friend, W. P. P. Long-fellow, a nephew and ward of the poet," later to become professor of architecture at M.I.T. He therefore decided to give architecture a try, and began a draftsman apprenticeship in the Chicago office of Loring and Jenney. There, with William L. Jenney, the great architectural pioneer, he had his first experience and training in architecture.[17]

"I was at Lincoln Park this morning," he wrote his mother in 1868, "taking sketches and dimensions of bridges, and for a few days I shall be occupied in making designs to cover them with rustic work. It is very engaging work and I enjoy it." Later in the year he wrote even more optimistically about his career. "I shall try to become," he resolved, "the greatest architect in the city or country. Nothing less will be near the mark I have set for myself, and I am not afraid but that I can become so. There needs but one thing. A determined and persistent effort." In addition to his regular work with the firm, he began designing a few houses of his own. But in 1869, despite his determined rhetoric, Burnham admitted to continuing mixed feelings about architecture, about Chicago, and about himself. Still too restless and uncertain to settle down to steady work, he was ripe for a friend's proposal to head west for the Nevada mining country.[18]

In 1869 and 1870, Burnham sought his fortune in the great silver area of White Pine County, the lesser rival of the Comstock Lode. He and his friend Edward C. Waller, however, staked claims that were not geologically typical of the region's richness and failed to secure the fortune they had expected. Finding the area exciting and promising, though, Burnham decided to enter local politics and with the aid of an older politician, Pish Kelly, ran in 1870 for the state senate on the Democratic ticket as the representative from White Pine County. The *Daily Inland Empire* praised one speech of Burnham's, though it failed to mention the particulars of his platform. According to the editor, the speech did him great credit and convinced his audience that he was "the right man in the right place." Further details of his campaign have not survived the years and his close defeat in the election turned him away from political activity. Later, he gravitated to the Republican party.[19]

Political and financial defeat had met him in the West. Academic failures had colored his experiences in the East. Burnham, at twenty-four, returned to Chicago to take another hard look at himself and at his future. "There is a family tendency," he wrote years later, "to get tired of doing the same thing very long." Although he had let himself give in to that weakness, the Nevada adventures and mis-adventures had sobered him considerably and had helped to temper the vagrant side of his restlessness. He was now impatient to get on, to succeed at something, to do something well. As he thought about himself and reviewed his development, he recalled the few things that he *had* done well. He did like to draw and had succeeded in his adolescent art enterprises. For the most part, he liked people and, despite his own failures, had been able to attract them and get along with them. The social and aesthetic facets of architecture, the most public of the arts, still attracted him. His positive memories of his first architectural job now outweighed his earlier reservations.[20]

The answer seemed clearer—even if the ideal master did not appear at once to train him and to make him an architect. He worked briefly in the Chicago offices of John Van Osdel, H. B. Wheelock, and Gustave Laureau, picking up here and there bits of technique, germs of ideas, and enough enthusiasm for the trade to keep looking for the "right situation." In 1872, Burnham found work in the office of Carter, Drake and Wight, a firm busily engaged in helping to rebuild Chicago after the fire. In the young Peter Wight, Burnham found a sympathetic mentor. "It was to Wight," he later wrote, that he "owed most." "He was introduced to our firm," Wight recalled, "by his father, who was very desirous that Dan should be cured of his roving disposition." Wight helped develop his drawing skills, recharged his imagination, and taught, by example, the way in which an architect performed. Burnham built on his assets and cautiously began to play the new role. His activity, if not his progress, was enough to allay self-doubts. As he began to find himself, his motion found a direction, and his role became more than play-acting. His truncated education and his resulting insecurity about his ability to apply himself would return to plague him later, but his practical education delighted him for the moment and he knew that he was honing the natural talents he possessed.[21]

Wight had the trained intellect that Burnham saw lacking in himself. It was Wight's "scholarly quality," Burnham later noted, that had a "deep effect" upon him. Indeed the college rejections had marked him more than he knew. His failure to experience academe and to learn its limitations gradually instilled in him too great a reverence for academic

Burnham rendering of Stewart Bentley Building for Peter B. Wight,
ca. 1872. Courtesy Art Institute of Chicago.

authority. Exalting the qualities he thought he lacked, he mistrusted and underestimated his own developing assets. When he believed a good mind to be on his side, the resulting confidence served to release the flow of his own particular and considerable gifts. Temporarily, Peter Wight filled such a need, and in Wight's office Burnham met John Root, his future partner, who later on would do the same. Burnham was finally moving. The long childhood was fading before a period of uncertain but exciting promise.[22]

II
The Large Partnership

Burnham and Root, 1873–1891

When the materials are all prepared and ready, the architects
*   shall appear.*
I swear to you the architects shall appear without fail,
I swear to you they will understand you and justify you. . . .
You shall be fully glorified in them.

WALT WHITMAN
Leaves of Grass

IN THEIR EIGHTEEN YEARS together, Burnham and Root built over $40,000,000.00* worth of buildings, including residences, office buildings, railroad stations, hotels, schools, churches, warehouses, stores, hospitals, and miscellaneous structures from barns and convents to casinos and ceremonial monuments.[1] Their finest work brought them acclaim and earned the reputation among their contemporaries that later generations would more than sanction. During those same years, both men married and began families, rising to social as well as professional prominence in Chicago and beyond. By the time of Root's death, they had become major architects and respected citizens. The beginning of their relationship, however, in the Chicago of the early 1870s, hardly differed from the beginnings of countless other business and professional associations of the same time and place that would end, somehow, less auspiciously and productively.

Before his introduction to Burnham in Peter Wight's office, John Root, in contrast to his future partner, had already known a life of considerable fullness and promise. Born in 1850 into a prosperous family in

---

* For a discussion and tabulation of comparative building costs, 1870–1970, see Appendix B.

Lumpkin, Georgia, Root spent the Civil War years at school in Liver-
pool. There, he studied music with William Best, the greatest organist
in England, and passed entrance examinations to Oxford University. He
would have matriculated in 1866, but with the end of the Civil War, his
parents sent for him. They had moved to New York and after he joined
them there he entered New York University to study engineering. He
graduated with honors in 1869. Music and architecture were his greatest
loves, and, while music remained a lifelong avocation, he determined,
upon graduation, to become an architect. For slightly more than a year
he worked in the New York office of James Renwick, the builder of St.
Patrick's Cathedral, and for an equal period under J. B. Snook, the designer of Grand Central Terminal.[2]

In 1872, he went to Chicago, attracted by the promising possibilities
for architects in the burned-out city. Because he had impressive credentials and practical experience, he was able to secure the job of head
draftsman in the established firm of Carter, Drake, and Wight, where
he met and soon formed a close friendship with Daniel Burnham, a
draftsman four years his senior. Though well educated, quick-witted,
and comfortable with friends, Root was shy and reserved among stran-
gers. While talented and sensitive, his varied interests and abilities often
became distractions and excuses for procrastination. Burnham, on the
other hand, had grown increasingly aggressive, persuasive, and determined, and though sensitive and perceptive, he was less the artist than
was his cultivated young friend.[3]

Sensing mutual ideals and values as well as contrasting and reciprocal
qualities of temperament, the two men began to think out loud over
their drawing boards about the possibilities of an eventual partnership.
The times could not have seemed better for such a venture and, in early
1873, with promises of several jobs that Burnham had secured from
friends, they left Peter Wight and set up their own office. The poet and
editor Harriet Monroe, a friend of both partners and the sister of Root's
second wife, believed that Root's rich artistic genius would have come to
little "without persistence and opportunity, and Mr. Burnham was the
plasmic influence which he needed at this time." Root, she believed,
"lacked personal ambition" and "considered his own career of little importance," while Burnham, on the contrary, "resolved from the first that
the new firm should lead the profession and never flinched from his purpose through the years of waiting. He was always noting or making opportunities, evolving large projects, which the younger man smiled at

but fulfilled." Burnham, she observed, "had initiative, strength of will, and a certain splender of enthusiasm which captured men and held them while his partner was amply content to sit in the inner office, aloof from the boresome talkers, and do his work." Indeed, she concluded, Burnham's influence "during these formative years saved Root from dilettantism, held him to a definite purpose, and helped to keep him confident in spite of tardiness of fortune."[4]

The "tardiness of fortune" was never more obvious than in the first summer of the firm's existence when the Panic of 1873 canceled commissions and wiped out the promise of the earlier building boom. The only compensations the two young partners received during this period were two badly needed "suits of clothes of unwonted splendor paid them by one of the collapsed capitalists to whom a tailor owed some money." The winter of 1873-74 was especially hard. "Office rent was twenty dollars a month," Burnham remembered. "In the office was a fireplace and a large brick vault. We must have burned a ton and a half of soft coal that winter in order to keep our fingers warm enough to work! Paper we bought a few yards at a time, just enough by the most economical handling to lay out the immediate plan and an elevation or two. Then with a couple of pencils, a piece of rubber, a few boards, two stools and a dozen thumb tacks, we did business. Between us, we had a full color box and one stick of India-ink. We did all our work ourselves." To supplement their income, both men worked part time in other older, more established architectural offices and Root played the organ at the First Presbyterian Church. Optimism, odd jobs, and youthful buoyance carried them through. "Work gradually came our way," Burnham recalled, "and when it did we used to dive down to the next floor below, burst in on Dr. Woodyatt, a crony of about our age, and tell him about it. He on his part used to come up three steps at a time whenever a leading citizen became a patient of his."[5]

The first jobs were for small residences and barns, enough for the moment to support the two young bachelors, whose social life continued to blossom despite financial woes. "John and I make a good many calls of one sort or another," Burnham wrote to his sister in June 1874, "and, of course, we enjoy life as much as hot weather and an exceedingly scanty treasury will permit. We think of a trip to Grand Haven Saturday night." A young lady friend named Amy had asked him to see a performance of Mr. Russell, her "comedy cousin" and Burnham was sure that "John Wellborn and I shall therefore escort them all this evening to see the interesting young gentleman give his entertainment of face making." "We have an entire rest," he then reported wearily, "from Theatricals, and the like for the summer; for which we are sincerely thankful." The letter ended, as usual, with more family trivia and with an indication of Burnham's constant concern for health and appearance in the lament that sister Clara was "getting fleshy in face and arms."[6]

The firm's turning point, the first big commission, came in 1874 with a contract to design a house for the stockyards magnate, John B. Sherman. Burnham and Root met Sherman through one of his protégés, George Chambers, a young real estate agent and friend of Root's. Sherman was living on Michigan Avenue, and when he decided to build a new house on ultra-fashionable Prairie Avenue, Chambers persuaded him to give some young architects a chance, in particular, his friends Root and Burnham. The idea appealed to Sherman and he told Chambers to send them to see him at once. Root was out of the city, however, and Chambers introduced only Burnham to his older friend. Sherman liked the young man instinctively, and, pleased with his building proposals, asked him to submit drawings for further consideration. Burnham and Root designed a house which the Shermans and their daughter Margaret accepted with delight. The house and barn together cost Sherman the sumptuous sum of $30,000.[7]

The three-and-a-half-story mansion was built of brick and sandstone with ornamental columns of blue granite. An impressive, though delicate outside stairway rose above the cellar to the small porch and large entrance hall. On the main floor, parlors, diningrooms, and sitting rooms opened spaciously to the hall and into each other. The upper floors contained bed-, bath-, and sitting rooms for the family, guests, and servants. Numerous dormers from the steeply pitched roof and small balconies along each side opened onto the street, giving the house a pleasant airy ambience. The usual array of Victorian turrets and bric-a-brac did, in fact, suggest an effect of unnecessary clutter that the firm would sublimate or eschew altogether in its later, more austere residences. But in 1874, the house seemed chic and urbane and Chicago society began to inquire as to its designers. Even more important, the Sherman commission led to another development that capped for the young firm the social and economic benefits of the architectural achievement: Daniel Burnham married Margaret Sherman.[8]

Margaret recalled that she fell in love with Daniel the first time she saw him and "used to hang around the new work in order to see him."

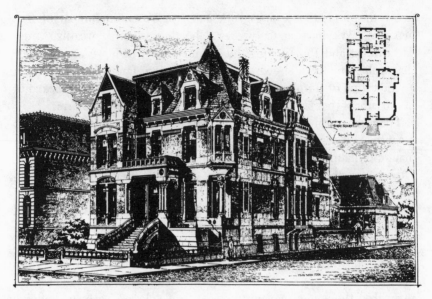

Sherman House, Chicago, 1874. *American Architect and Building News.*

Her friend Della Otis lived on the opposite side of the street, which gave her a "good excuse to be in the neighborhood frequently." Fortunately, the attraction was mutual, and Burnham soon decided that he would propose to Margaret after "the building was completed and his business finished" with her father. Actually, the couple became engaged shortly before the house was completed.[9]

In September 1875, Margaret felt obliged to spend several weeks away from Chicago vacationing with her ailing mother, but she wrote to her fiancé telling him she missed him and was homesick. She wanted to return to Chicago, but Daniel wrote to her and encouraged her to stay, espousing beneath the heavy love-letter rhetoric both the Swedenborgian ethic of love and unselfishness and his personal self-help credo of forbearance and self-control. "We live to overcome selfishness," he asserted. "Our compact is to help each other do it. And lasting love will only grow between us as we succeed in this struggle. Here is a chance for self-denial, which calls for a strong effort and living well in this, will add greatly to our own chances of overcoming, when the next struggle comes," when maybe, "some deeper principle will be involved." But he finished the letter on a lighter note: "What do you think we are up to at home here?" he asked. "Discussing the subject of dining room furniture. It may be all ordered and half made when you arrive. So you had better have a care how you leave us to our own devices, or we may commit irreparable mischief."[10]

Despite rumors as to the "convivial propensities" of his prospective son-in-law, rugged John Sherman gave his blessings to the engagement. A minor tragedy in the Burnham family, however, temporarily darkened the wedding plans. Daniel's brother, Edwin, Jr., had entered the family's wholesale drug business and had forged his father's name to several large checks. The business was hurt and "a very ugly scandal" developed close to the time of the wedding. Daniel immediately went to Sherman and suggested, despondently, that Sherman break the engagement as it did not seem to him "fair and honorable that it should continue under the circumstances." Sherman, however, refused to take the matter seriously, told Burnham that he was proud of him for making the gesture, and consoled him with the adage that there was a "black sheep in every family." The wedding took place with Prairie Avenue splendor on January 20, 1876.[11]

With the success of the Sherman commission and the influence of the Sherman family with important Chicago socialites and business magnates, the young firm's "starving time" would quickly end. New clients led to social invitations to attend parties and join clubs, which led, in turn, to more clients—wealthier, perhaps, and more demanding than before. Daniel and Margaret rose socially as Burnham and Root rose professionally, the movement of both inevitably and inextricably entwined. Commissions for houses soon came from Chicago's great and near-great: the journalists Victor Lawson and Henry Demarest Lloyd; the composer and music critic Reginald de Koven; the painter George P. A. Healey; General Philip Sheridan; and such prominent businessmen as William T. Baker, Charles L. Hutchison, Edward Ayer, and Joseph Sears. With business booming in Chicago and in other cities the firm became larger and its organization better defined.

"We have a student in the office," Burnham had confided earlier to his fiancée. "Sounds nice, doesn't it? But [it] makes one feel rather shaky, for fear he may wake up and know more than his employers in the course of a year. Another goad to study, a thing I have been a stranger to except in a desultory way, since last spring." The first draftsman was Tom Wing, from whom little more was ever heard, but the second and third, William Holabird and Clinton Warren, were to go on to great careers as distinguished architects in their own right. The firm soon took a "front room on Washington Street, and finally a room across the hall. There we stayed seven years," Burnham recalled, "finally paying over seven hundred dollars a year rent. At first the rent item made me lie awake nights, but before seven years were over fortune had smiled on us."[12]

The often-noted differences in the two men's characters and personalities were apparent from the first, but the exact division of labor and professional contribution of each appeared only as the firm's work increased in volume and in scope. Most interpretations of the work of Burnham and Root have contended simplistically that John Root was "the only real architect" in the firm, that in reality, the buildings were *his* conceptions and *his* achievements and have dismissed Burnham with the standard acknowledgment of his "administrative ability." The main text for such treatment was, of course, Louis Sullivan's writings, but in accepting so uncritically Sullivan's myopic biases of the 1920s, historians have forgotten Harriet Monroe's earlier, more contemporary memoir. Though her special adulation of her brother-in-law Root caused Monroe, perhaps, to overpraise the firm's total accomplishment, it did not prevent her from observing and noting the contributions of Daniel Burnham to the life and work of her esteemed relative.

Obviously and admittedly, Burnham became the public relations partner, sniffing the Chicago air for new jobs and clients: meeting, greeting, shaking hands, talking, lunching, explaining, convincing, and reassuring. Once, when Burnham was on an extended leave from the city, Root lamented his partner's absence because it forced him "to do much more of the 'jaw' work than I enjoy, and tends also to keep down something of the efficiency of my proper work." Root considered his "proper work" to be that of pure design, though even there, Burnham's hand was not absent.[13]

"Burnham was skillful in laying out a building," Monroe contended in her biography of Root. "Root did not enjoy this part of the work, and rarely assumed it. . . . When a building came to the office, Mr. Burnham, as a rule, laid out more or less roughly ground and floor plans. Frequently he made many such studies, the partners deciding together upon the best one, which Root would use as the first element of his problem in designing the exterior. The senior partner," she asserted, "influenced strongly Root's exuberant imagination both as a stimulus and a check." This occurred, she believed, because "Root often felt a certain reluc-

Daniel Burnham in the 1880s. Courtesy Chicago Art Institute.

tance in initiative. His mind was of the Shakespearean type: it could build temples, towers, and palaces on a hint; but it craved the hint as Shakespeare craved the plot, for the starting point of his dream." Often the hint would come "from one or more conditions inherent in the problem: such as shape of ground, proportions of building, kind of material to be used," or the "amount to be expended." Sometimes clients suggested the larger plan or idea, she conceded, but more often than not it was Burnham who produced the raw conceptions that Root needed to get started. Burnham also drew inspiration, of course, from the same

basic elements of site, materials, cost, and client's needs, but he pulled
them together in initial sketches "drawn from a few rough lines" from
which seed "the plant would grow and flower in Root's brain as swiftly
as a magical mango tree."[14]

It was indeed Burnham's willingness to "think big" that evoked ambivalence in his antagonist Louis Sullivan. While deploring Burnham's
tendencies toward "megalomania," Sullivan appreciated his largeness of
vision, one quality in Burnham's make-up that, with characteristic ego,
he identified with himself. It was a quality he found lacking, not only in
his own partner, but also in Burnham's. "Unquestionably," he thought,
"Adler lacked sufficient imagination; so in a way did John Root—that is
to say, the imagination of the dreamer. In the dream imagination lay
Burnham's strength and Louis' passion." Root, Sullivan admitted, had
not "one-tenth of his partner's settled will, nor of said partner's capacity
to go through hell to reach an end."[15]

Burnham's contribution, however, did not end with securing commissions and conceiving the larger plans. Harriet Monroe also attested that,
on matters of specific design, his "judgment and taste were good, and as
a critic, he was very suggestive." She quoted a "gentleman long in their
employ" to the effect that Burnham "would lean over John's drawing
board . . . and say 'John, I don't like that very well.' 'Well, what's the
matter with it?' John would say. And then Dan would point out something: tell him to fix up that corner, or change the grouping of those
windows, or strengthen the skyline, or do something else with the drawing. And John would reply that he thought it was pretty good as it was.
But invariably after Dan had left, he would fall to studying over the
drawing, and would end by strengthening the weak places as Dan had
suggested."[16]

Indeed, the alliance of Root and Burnham represented one of the first
important confrontations of the older, more traditional, more fully
rounded architectural craftsman with the newer architectural entrepreneur and business executive. Under Burnham's direction, the large office staff and efficient organization became a prototype for all great modern architectural firms. Much as contemporary university presidents
—Charles Van Hise at Wisconsin; William R. Harper at Chicago;
Daniel C. Gilman at Johns Hopkins; Nicholas M. Butler at Columbia;
and Charles W. Eliot at Harvard—were drawing principles of organization from the world of big business, Burnham did the same for architecture. In fact, as Louis Sullivan so accurately observed, "the only architect

in Chicago to catch the significance of this movement was Daniel Burnham, for in its tendencies toward bigness, organization, delegation, and intense commercialism, he sensed the reciprocal workings of his own mind."[17]

If there was ever a source of even temporary friction between the partners, it was in the very conflict between the architectural craftsman and the entrepreneurial architect. Once when Sullivan dropped by their office, he recalled that "John was in his private room at work designing an interesting detail of some building. He drew with a rather heavy, rapid stroke and chatted as he worked. Burnham came in. 'John,' he said, 'you ought to delegate that sort of thing. The only way to handle a big business is to *delegate, delegate, delegate.*' John sneered. Dan went out, in something of a huff."[18]

Yet, in general, their relationship was remarkably cooperative. Harriet Monroe marveled at the lack of harshness or suspicion as the work of each man became more dependent on the other. It was incorrect to speak of a building "by John Root" or "by Daniel Burnham." The buildings were "by Burnham & Root," collaborative efforts in the truest sense of the word. Unlike Sullivan, who underestimated his dependence on Dankmar Adler and met professional ruin after he cavalierly severed the partnership, Burnham and Root appreciated the nature of their great dependence on each other. When speaking to clients or friends, each man praised lavishly his partner's special talents. In part, perhaps, each took this tack to promote the firm without himself seeming egotistical. In general, however, there was no doubt as to the sincerity of the admiration or the degree of mutual respect that the two friends and partners maintained through eighteen years of increasingly complex achievements.

While Burnham's practical contributions to conception and design were important, Root's work was paramount in creating the ultimate artistic form. Often following Burnham's initial suggestions as to general visual configuration and over-all room arrangement, Root perfected the spatial relations and proportions, harmonized the plan to materials and site, and in his modulation of line, color, texture, and ornament, gave the building its ultimate architectural personality.

Both partners were generally acquainted with the "organic" theories of such aesthetic philosophers as John Ruskin and William Morris in England, Gottfried Semper in Germany, Viollet-le-Duc in France, and Ralph Waldo Emerson and Horatio Greenough in America. Both also appreciated the organic integration of Richard Wagner's music dramas.

John Root in the 1880s. Courtesy Chicago Art Institute.

And, like most advanced artists of the late nineteenth century, they saw
the aesthetic relevance of Charles Darwin's momentous theories of natural evolution. Long before young Frank Lloyd Wright would claim to
have discovered "organic architecture," Root urged that architects "continually return to nature and nature's methods . . ." and asserted that
"the greatest works of great artists must be studied with nature for a
handbook." Nature taught the architect, he believed, that "no reason is
good, no answer worth giving that does not spring from the present

question and is not inherently connected with it." Even before Sullivan had pronounced his famous credo that "form follows function," Root wrote that "as far as natural conditions permit it to be possible, a building designated for a particular purpose should express that purpose in every part. . . . Ascertain first," he argued, what conditions were "essential to the function which a house is to perform; and the force with which that function is expressed measures its value as a work of art."[19]

Strongly attracted to the architectural vocabularies of the great Romanesque period (particularly their expression in the buildings of southern France) and the Queen Anne idiom (the Victorian revival and combination of Renaissance forms in evidence in England and Holland), Root took his cue from the two contemporaries most associated with those modes—the American Henry Hobson Richardson and the Englishman Norman Shaw. Like Richardson with the Romanesque and Shaw with the Queene Anne, Root borrowed selectively from other eras and traditions, but seldom allowed other styles to dominate his own. Pedantic, archeological copying appalled him. As historian Oliver Larkin has said so aptly of Sullivan's later Wainwright Building: his best work followed no "style"; it *was* style.[20]

Speaking in 1890 to the architecture class at the Chicago Art Institute, Root re-emphasized his belief that "to be true, architecture must normally express the conditions of life about and within it, not in a fragmentary and spasmodic way, but in the mass and structure. . . . As yet," he contended, "the search after a national or new architectural style is absolutely useless for this purpose. Architectural styles, national or new, were never discovered by human prospectors however eagerly they have searched. Styles are found truly at the appointed time, . . . but solely by those, who, with intelligence and soberness, are working out their ends by the best means at hand, and with scarce a thought of the coming new or national style. Architecture is, like all other art, born of its age and environment," he said. "So, the new type will be found by us, if we do find it, through the frankest possible acceptance of every requirement of modern life in all of its conditions, without regret for the past or idle longing for a future or more fortunate day."[21]

Root believed that successful design demanded stretches of undecorated surface offset with ornament applied with accent and rhythm. Strive for plain surfaces, he urged, "and when the fates place at your disposal a good generous sweep of masonry, accept it frankly and thank God." Root also presaged Wright's later veneration for the distinctive qualities inherent in each building material and argued that it would "be found upon a careful study of the most successful buildings of the world as well as the most impressive natural creations, that there is in every building an effect of power produced by the use of a single material as against the combinations of many."[22]

Root could also criticize and satirize his own designs. In a short survey called "Architects of Chicago," he praised his partner Burnham's aesthetic restraint, his "keen artistic perception," and his "remarkable executive ability," but remarked, of himself that "Mr. Root, upon whom has largely devolved their designing, seems to have been too facile always to carefully reconsider his designs and to have been, to a large extent, the victim of his own moods." His droll sense of humor did not spare his own occasional architectural foibles. Speaking in 1886 to the Western Association of Architects, he ridiculed the proliferation of the " 'Tubercular Style,' sometimes called by the facetious 'Queene Anne,' " as well as the "Romanesque which might often be more properly called the Dropsical." On another occasion, he castigated the antiquarian fussiness, not wholly absent in his own earlier work, of much of the contemporary architecture and rebuked the architects who fought their battles "behind bulwarks made of stays and ruffs, laces and ribbons, baggy and tight trousers, snuff-boxes and smelling salts; 'Queene Anne' gables and 'Neojacobean' bays and 'Romanesque' turrets; battlements behind which we risk our professional lives today, and which, tomorrow, we blow into oblivion with a sneer. For our own self-respect," he urged, "for the dignity of our own position, for the sake of an architecture which shall have within it some vital germ, let us come out from our petticoat fortress and fight our battles in open field."[23]

Indeed, while Burnham took the firm to the marketplace, espousing its philosophy and its plans of action in anonymous offices and over endless lunches, John Root became its orator and its literary spokesman, taking the same message to another public via speeches and magazine articles. Written or spoken in Root's clear and engaging style, with a literary and oratorical flair that Burnham did not possess, the speeches and articles comprised a treasury of general architectural wisdom that preceded and rivalled the later, more famous writings of Louis Sullivan and Frank Lloyd Wright. But the philosophy that Root defined owed much to the Burnham association. Each consulted the other on all the essential questions and each criticized and gave ultimate sanction to the other's official statements and activities. Though Burnham in later years would move away from some of his old commitments, Root's pronouncements, in most cases, represented the contemporary rationale of both.

The residential projects of Burnham and Root that followed the Sherman mansion of 1874, moved gradually away from an eclectic "Victorianism" toward a newer aesthetic of greater purity and simplicity. However much later generations might lament the trend away from a "messy vitality" toward a more "obvious unity," the late nineteenth century, and much of the twentieth, favored and followed that inexorable imperative. Though it suggested "French Renaissance" influences in matters of detail, the Sidney A. Kent house, on South Michigan Avenue, 1882-83, marked for example, an important progression from the work of the 1870s in its relative simplicity. The ornament, for the most part, was in low relief. The dominant accent was on the wide undecorated expanses and unusually large areas of plate glass windows. The move to greater simplicity was sustained in the Romanesque-inspired houses Burnham and Root built in 1885 for J. E. Hale, on Drexel Avenue, and for Edward E. Ayer, on East Banks Street. Though rippling throughout with heavy slightly jutting stonework in the Richardson manner, the wall surfaces were bolder than before and were composed of fewer materials, giving to the houses an effect of strength and directness that had not always characterized the firm's earlier efforts.

Four juxtaposed townhouses for J. L. Houghteling on Astor Street, 1887-88, contained echoes of French and Flemish Gothic, and Renaissance motifs but continued the firm's general movement in the direction of beautiful but simpler, more cohesive structures. The house for the composer and music critic, Reginald de Koven, 1888-90, also contained Queene Anne accents but moved toward the same end in its convenient room arrangement and conservation of space. The Houghteling and de Koven houses, indeed, reflected the tastes of the owners who sought the surface exquisiteness the firm had suppressed in the Hale and Ayer residences. The V. C. Turner house, however, on Schiller Street and Lake Shore Drive, 1887-88, echoed the plain, stone-faced, sometimes curving surfaces of the Hale and Ayer houses, with their slight but impressive details of original ornament and balanced, asymmetrical, wide-opening areas of large, plate windows.

Most of the great Chicago houses of Burnham and Root were pleasantly original variations, slimmed-down abstractions and sometimes radical extensions of the late "Victorian" idioms of Chicago's 1870s and

Kent House, Chicago, 1882-83. Donald Hoffmann.

1880s. Though they never made enough break with the past to an-
nounce a real revolution in house design, they marked both the end of
an older order and, in several late houses, a transition to the revolutionary work of Wright and his contemporaries. Significant not only for
their increasingly austere and simplified exteriors, but also for their "organic" openness and fluidity of inside plan, such later houses included
the J. L. Lombard home in Kansas City, 1887-88, and the magnificent
Chicago houses of Edward H. Valentine, State and Goethe streets,
1888-89, and William J. Goudy, Astor and Goethe streets, 1889-91. Except for plain blunt arches of Romanesque descent, the last three
houses were almost totally lacking in literal, historical architectural references. Each rose two and a half stories above a basement. The Lombard house presented some ornamental brick work on the gables and
porch railings, but the Goudy and Valentine houses showed entirely

plain and elegantly proportioned surfaces of pressed stone and brick, punctured only by plain, large light-receiving windows.

In a larger "sculptural" sense, therefore, the houses of Burnham and Root progressed from derivative and imported "styles" of considerable clutter and fussiness to the relatively cleaner and starker new aesthetic of simplicity and functional fitness. Inhabited, for the most part, by middle- and upper-class Midwesterners, the dwellings both molded and reflected a style and quality of life. The spacious, formal areas of hall, parlor, and diningroom provided ample stages for the playing out of the social drama. The cozy, intimate spaces of "den," breakfast room, or fireplace inglenook enhanced and articulated the quality of family life and informal social activities. Socially and personally sustaining and nourishing, especially during the long, cold Midwestern winters, the houses, at their best, displayed the gift of all successful building art—the integration of architecture and life.[24]

"Yours is a good concern to do business with," a satisfied client J. H.

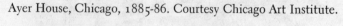

Ayer House, Chicago, 1885-86. Courtesy Chicago Art Institute.

de Koven House, façade, Chicago, 1888-90. Monroe, *John Wellborn Root*.

de Koven House, hall. Monroe, *John Wellborn Root.*

de Koven House, Fireplace Inglenook. Monroe, *John Wellborn Root.*

Lombard House, Kansas City, 1887-88. *Inland Architect*.

Turner House, Chicago, 1887-88. Courtesy Chicago Art Institute.

Valentine House, Chicago, 1888-89. *Inland Architect.*

Goudy House, Chicago, 1889-91. *Inland Architect.*

Nolan wrote to Burnham and Root. "You not only can make a good picture of a house, but you can also build a good one, make specifications that keep out the wedge of extras, give the whole business good supervision, secure an owner his money's worth from the various contractors he is brought in contact with, and in the end, when it comes to delivering up the keys make a man happier . . . than he expected he would be. . . . You might, without straining anything, gather the suspicion that I rather like you people. Well, I own up that I do. Why shouldn't I?"[25]

On a physical scale between its residences on the one hand and its later tall office buildings on the other, the firm built numerous structures such as small hotels, small businesses, small railroad stations, clubhouses, and churches—buildings which were functionally related to larger cultural and commercial contexts but which were structurally closer to the firm's residential idiom. Built to house many different types of functions, the buildings, as a group, lacked the same degree of progressive continuity that had characterized the growing modernity of the houses.

Calumet Clubhouse, Chicago, 1881-83. *Inland Architect.*

Montezuma Hotel, Las Vegas, New Mexico, 1883-85. Monroe, *John Wellborn Root.*

The Calumet Clubhouse, at Michigan Avenue and Twentieth Street, 1881-83, was a three-and-a-half-story structure of red brick and terra cotta. In design, it illustrated the aesthetic dichotomy between the older and newer modes of the growing firm. With its fancy dormers, turrets, and roof-top ornament, the top half of the building echoed the Sherman house, while the two bottom floors suggested the later bolder, cleaner mode of faintly Romanesque effects. It housed what contemporaries considered the most aristocratic club in Chicago.

The same years that saw the building of the Calumet also witnessed the rise of another retreat for the leisure classes. Far to the west in Las Vegas, New Mexico, the great Montezuma Hotel, 1883-85, rose above hot springs at the entrance to the Rio Gallinas canyon. Resembling a sumptuous, oversized country residence, as opposed to the firm's urban hotel towers, the rustic retreat hugged the mountainside in a horizontal sprawl. Built of shingle, wood, and sandstone, the building's dominant feature was a round tower that had a conical, shingle roof and stood at the axis of the two long wings. Though its residential ambiance made it seem much smaller than it was, the hotel could accommodate as many as five hundred guests. A leading architectural journal of the time remarked that its "interior fittings are as elaborate as those of any in the West, and it has the distinguished quality of being the only hotel in the United States that is entirely lighted by electricity, there being not even a provision made for the use of gas lamps. . . ." It concluded, in

fact, that the Montezuma was "one of the finest conceptions ever executed in hotel designing in this country."[26]

Another of the firm's most interesting minor genres in the 1880s included the small railway station, usually built away from Chicago's
busy railroad nexus. The stations at Fort Scott, Kansas, 1885-87, Kewanee, Illinois, 1887, and Aberdeen, Mississippi, 1888, typified the mode.
Low-slung and hugging the ground, with wide over-hanging eaves and
simply decorative supporting brackets, such stations were usually of
painted wood or red brick and had slate or shingle roofs. Crisp and unpretentious provincial train stations in an era of railroad opulence, they
would seem to later generations refreshingly "modern" precursors of
much that Wright and the Prairie School would develop and extend to
other types of buildings, especially houses.[27]

No small building of Burnham and Root's evoked more contemporary praise than their original Art Institute on Michigan Avenue,
1886-87, later modified to house the elite Chicago Club after the institute's activities were moved up the street to larger quarters. The most
obvious of all the firm's major buildings in its debt to Richardson and
the Romanesque, the small three-and-a-half-story structure suggested,
in its stonework and fenestration, the larger and more famous Marshall
Field Wholesale Store only a few blocks away, completed by Richardson the previous year. "It may be significant with reference to the tendency of western architecture," wrote the noted contemporary critic
Montgomery Schuyler, viewing the building among its taller neighbors,
"that this admirable building, admirable in the sobriety and moderation that are facilitated by its moderate size, is precisely what one would
not expect to find in Chicago, so little is there evident in it of an in-

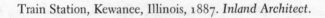

Train Station, Kewanee, Illinois, 1887. *Inland Architect.*

Art Institute, Chicago, 1886-87. *Architectural Record.*

tention to 'collar the eye' or to challenge the attention it so well
repays."[28]

The history of American church architecture includes few structures
that are finer or less well known than Burnham and Root's St. Gabriel's
Catholic Church on South Lowe Street, 1886-87, and Lakeview Presbyterian, Church, Broadway and Addison, 1887-88. Simple and unpretentious, eloquent and enigmatic, each expressed the spiritual transcend-
ence and organic rootedness that has been the aim of church and
temple builders everywhere. In the original plan for St. Gabriel's the
tower originally rose above the intersection of nave and transept, but
church members had the important feature moved to the front and side
to the detriment of the original design. With early Romanesque accents

St. Gabriel's Church, Chicago, first design, 1886-87. Monroe, *John Wellborn Root*.

St. Gabriel's Church, second design, 1886-87. Monroe, *John Wellborn Root*.

Lakeview Presbyterian Church, Chicago, 1887-88. *Inland Architect.*

in the tower and front portals, a contemporary critic referred to it as being without a doubt "the most interesting church in Chicago."[29]

The Lake View Presbyterian Church was a brilliant essay in the popular "shingle style" of the period. Rising from a stone base several feet above the foundation, grayish-brown shingles completely enveloped the walls, roofs, porches, and gables. It was probably the most mysterious, brooding, and "otherworldly" edifice the firm produced. Yet, in its monochromatic singleness of material and texture, it seemed, more than most buildings, to grow out of the ground. Its shingled, conical tower seemed to suggest both a futuristic "modernism" and a peculiarly Nordic medievalism. Even more than the contemporary St. Gabriel's, the church

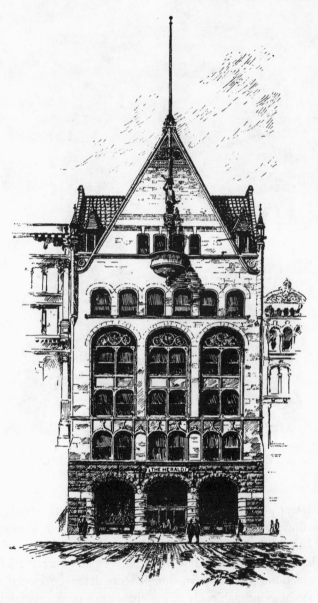

Herald Building, Chicago, 1890-91. Monroe, *John Wellborn Root.*

seemed a perfect blend of ethereal mystery and earthly organicism.[30]

The most "house-like" commercial buildings the firm produced in its later period were for two Chicago newspapers. The *Herald* building on West Washington Street, 1890-91, showed a steeply pitched roof and a highly ornamented façade pointing back to the smaller but similar de Koven and Houghteling residences. Schuyler did "not know of a more successful work in its own kind." It would be hard, he thought, "to find a more picturesque street front, or one in which picturesqueness has been attained with less sacrifice of practical requirements." Built the same year, the façade of the *Daily News* building on North Wells Street eschewed all ornament except one small finial at the peak of the gable. Four stories tall with a steep roof and a high gabled street front, its utter plainness of surface and of fenestration recalled the atmosphere of the famous Valentine House.[31]

Building chiefly for the upper and middle classes, Burnham and Root reached a large, anonymous public by publishing their work in newspapers and magazines. Ultimately their published designs found a national and an international audience, which adapted and absorbed them into common usage. Had Root lived beyond 1891 and into the decades that welcomed the work of Wright's Prairie School, the residential canon of Burnham and Root might have complemented that famous movement and stretched far beyond the functional and aesthetic modernity of their own later houses and house-like structures. Root, especially, enjoyed his work on the smaller, more personal, buildings and might have become an old-guard mentor of the Prairie School, as, indeed, he became an indirect reference. Yet, Burnham had long before confided to Sullivan that he was "not going to stay satisfied with houses; my idea," he had said, "is to work up a big business, to handle big things, deal with big businessmen, and to build up a big organization, for you can't handle big things unless you have an organization."[32]

And, despite the excellence and importance of their houses and smaller buildings, it was, indeed, the big things that counted most in the ultimate contribution of Burnham and Root: the big buildings for the big businessmen that critics would soon begin to label "skyscrapers," a term originally tinged with varied connotations of fear, suspicion, derision, and contempt. Along with a handful of other Chicago architects, Burnham and Root rose up in the 1880s to help dispel such notions and to vindicate the skyscraper as a national phenomenon of far reaching social and cultural significance.

III
Building in the Sky

Burnham, Root, and the Rise of the Skyscraper
1881–1891

"You want to see Lincoln Park," he said, *"and Michigan Boulevard. They are putting up great buildings there. . . . Chicago is getting to be a great town."*

THEODORE DREISER
Sister Carrie

T HE WORK of Root and Burnham in the 1880s became a paradigm of the development of the skyscraper. Their earlier and smaller work, while usually excellent and often prophetic, had progressed, nevertheless, from older traditions that were not of their making. As beginning architects in 1873, they had joined a procession long in progress. If they and others had continued to build only small and conventional structures, they still no doubt, would have maintained positions of importance and of leadership on their own brilliant terms. Yet within that more traditional success story of personal achievement by older standards, the rise of the skyscraper constituted a new architectural movement of which Root and Burnham were founders, creators, and decisive makers of policy—a redirection of their own thinking that affected their later work with smaller forms. But, even so, they did not work apart from others or create in a vacuum. Their accomplishments were great because the possibilities were great and because they exploited them and learned from their equally innovative contemporaries.

The years between the Civil War and the end of the century were years of enormous and often-noted change in American life. The population of the country increased from 40 million in 1870 to 76 million in

1900. Migrants from the country and immigrants from abroad radically altered the rural-urban ratio. In 1870, approximately 60 per cent of the American labor force worked on farms; by 1900, that figure had dropped to 37 per cent. Concomitant with urbanization, America's industrial revolution was creating new problems as it solved old ones, restricting and depressing life for some while opening and expanding it for others. A dominant force in redirecting American life, the railroad was stimulating both the economy and the American imagination, connecting isolated sections with urban centers and helping to break down provincialism. Between 1870 and 1900, railroad mileage increased from 30,000 to 170,000. With increased population and material wealth, moreover, education improved, cultural awareness quickened, and thinking Americans began seeking solutions to their new dilemmas: political, social, economic, intellectual, and aesthetic.[1]

While pondering the dichotomy of concurrent poverty and progress, many Americans also asked questions concerning the nation's image abroad, its character in general, and its contributions to civilization. Some critics argued that the United States had no identity or national culture. Furthermore they saw few prospects of lasting American contributions to international thought and culture. Yet, as America writhed in its new commercial and industrial adolescence and lamented and apologized for its apparent cultural poverty, a significant response to the new forces began to awaken in American art.

Particularly in the realm of architecture, the skyscraper emerged to meet a number of the problems, and the opportunities, presented by the forces of industry and commerce. The skyscraper was, at the same time, a result of and a reaction to the new forces. Symbolizing much of the American experience in the late nineteenth century, it became one of the country's first significant cultural exports. Identified quickly as a purely American phenomenon, the skyscraper became the new cathedral of modern international business society and provided abroad, as well as at home, the practical and artistic solution to sheltering and projecting the new urban empires of industry and commerce.

Though the skyscraper had become, by the last decade of the century, a widely recognized American success story, it had had to emerge from the frequently depressing doldrums of American aesthetic eclecticism. Public and domestic architecture following the Civil War had become increasingly suggestive of American affluence and aggressiveness, but in its tendency toward derivative display, it had, in most cases,

H. H. Richardson, Marshall Field Wholesale Store, Chicago, 1885-87. Courtesy Chicago Art Institute.

gone little further than that. To such general conditions, there were, of course, exceptions, including, on the one hand, the work of such architects as Richardson and Frank Furness and, on the other, such sensitive engineers as John and Washington Roebling—men whose work and ideals would endure. The problem lay, however, with the less gifted followers of those few original giants and with the resulting proliferation of eclectic mediocrity. Failing to come to terms with the machine and its related social changes, most architects sought escape into the past, imitating historic styles or combinations of styles in pathetic attempts to answer, or avoid, the nation's new and demanding architectural needs.

It was from that milieu that the Chicago School emerged and it was against that background that it made its contributions. Although its achievements and its influence extended far beyond the problem of the tall building, the skyscraper was the most typical and significant of its accomplishments, the apogee of its aspirations, the end result of the initial stimulus provided by the problems and possibilities of technical and commercial society. Ultimately, at its best, the skyscraper unified the divergent worlds of commerce, technology, and art.

The architects of the Chicago School did not, of course, originate the ideal commercial building, full-blown in their great skyscrapers of the late 1880s and 1890s. Other designers, notably H. H. Richardson, had recognized the need for a marriage of art and technology in building a proper house for commerce. Though only six floors tall, the Marshall Field Wholesale Store (1885-87) epitomized for Louis Sullivan the blending of those essential elements: "Four-square and tall it stands," he wrote, "a monument to trade, to the organized commercial spirit, to the power and progress of the age, to the strength and resource of individuality and force of character. . . ."[2]

In most European cities, the heights of buildings had been officially limited, but early American efforts in the same direction had been attacked as an invasion of property rights. As a result, the limitations in American cities were the physical ones of insufficient technological advancement and the degree of human willingness or unwillingness to climb steps. If, however, the American traditions of laissez faire made the tall building legally possible, the new complexities of a competitive business society made it necessary.

The growing city, the scramble for commercially attractive building sites, and the resulting rise in land rents constituted the greatest general long-range stimulus for tall buildings. In the 1880s, for example, the greatest decade in the building of the early skyscrapers, Chicago's population increased from 503,298 in 1880 to 1,098,570 in 1890. The average value of land per quarter acre in the Loop district increased in the same period from $130,000 in 1880 to $900,000 in 1890 and $1,000,000 in 1891.[3]

The trend was not unique to Chicago. Expanding business operations all over the country, growing office staffs, and greater demands for housing new equipment necessitated the creation of substantially more building space on substantially less land surface. The only answer was, somehow, to build higher. Resulting chiefly from competition for choice sites and from increasing land costs, the proliferation of taller buildings with more and more rentable space contributed to the further upward spiraling in land values, to the consequent need to build on smaller and smaller areas of land, and in turn to the call for even higher buildings.

In addition to such demanding commercial considerations, technological advances had meanwhile been developing to enable the tall building to become a structural reality. The development of the elevator was, of course, essential to the feasibility of the tall building just as the electric streetcar was to the expanding suburbs. The idea was not

new. Elevating freight by horsepower was common in Chicago and New
York even before the Civil War, and in the mid-1850s, the horse gave
way to steam power, especially in the great grain elevators of the Midwest. The first successful passenger elevator was the hydraulic machine
of Elisha Graves Otis, demonstrated at the New York Crystal Palace
Exhibition of 1853. The hydraulic elevator soon became a great prestige
symbol for businesses, and hotels especially were proud to advertise it as
one of their extra luxuries.[4]

The first electric elevator of 1889 was another leap forward, as momentous for the utility of the skyscraper as were the earlier developments of the electric light bulb, patented by Thomas Edison in 1879,
and the telephone of Alexander Graham Bell, first demonstrated in
1876. By 1877, there were 1300 commercial telephones; by 1880, there
were nearly 50,000. In 1884, the first long-distance line was completed
between New York and Boston, and cross-country connections followed
soon thereafter. By 1881, two years after Edison's patent, there were
5000 electric lamps in use, one-tenth the number of telephones. Yet the
number had doubled by 1882, and by 1886 there were 200,000 electric
lamps in use. Throughout the 1880s, both telephones and electric lights,
like the elevator before them, were considered "good business" in the
sense of demonstrating the modernity and sophistication of an enterprise. More important, they contributed strongly to the utility and via-
bility of tall buildings, often built in juxtaposition too close to receive
sufficient light and yet, at the same time, separated by height from the
rest of the community so as to necessitate a substitute for personal face-
to-face communications. The skyscraper without the elevator, telephone, and electric light would have been unthinkable—a dark, remote,
and inefficient prison, negating the very concept of propinquity that had
been among its greatest stimulants.[5]

Cast-iron framing had been known and used sporadically throughout
the nineteenth century. It relieved lower walls of having to support the
entire structure and distributed the weight more equally along all parts
and levels of the metal skeleton. Iron's limited tensile strength, however, and its extreme vulnerability to fire had inhibited general enthusiasm for its application as the dominant strength factor in erecting tall
buildings. Still vivid were the memories of the Chicago Fire of 1871,
when "hundreds of tons of pig iron in the McCormick Reaper yards
had melted and flowed in rivulets." Yet the increasing quest for space
and mania for height even in the 1870s had pushed buildings higher by

simply expanding as far as possible the old techniques of "wall-bearing" construction, implemented occasionally with partial iron supports insulated against fire by heavy masonry proofing. Under such construction, the outside walls had to bear not only their own upward weight but the weight of the intervening floors as well. Despite the possibilities of the elevator, the height of buildings was still limited by something like a structural law of diminishing returns. Each additional floor constituted more weight that had to be supported. Each new increment of space and weight necessitated a thicker wall from the base upward. As the lower part of the wall grew thicker, it had to have fewer, smaller, and less efficient windows. It was obvious, as Sullivan put it, "that the very tall masonry office building was in its nature economically unfit as ground values steadily rose. Not only did its thick walls entail loss of space and therefore revenue, but its unavoidably small window openings could not furnish the proper and desirable ratio of glass area to rentable floor area."[6]

Despite such restrictions, New York had by 1875 several office buildings of wall-bearing construction that reached a height of nine or ten stories. Between 1873 and 1875, for example, George Post built the 260-foot Western Union Telegraph Building and Richard Hunt designed the 230-foot edifice for the *New York Herald-Tribune*. Both were nearly equal in height to the dome of St. Peter's in Rome, but each building appeared little more than a succession of horizontally oriented floors laid atop each other. Neither building gave any feeling of unity or any or any real indication of the building's heightened verticality. Similar tall buildings also appeared in Boston, Philadelphia, and Chicago, exploiting the elevator to obtain more rental space with additional floors but contributing little in structural or aesthetic innovations.[7]

Burnham and Root's seven-story Grannis Building, built in Chicago in 1880-81, illustrated many of the problems that business architecture inherited from the 1870s. Though indeed relatively free of historical references, the building's interior contained large amounts of unprotected wood, which later led to its destruction by fire. But in 1882, a revolutionary building appeared—in the same city by the same architects. The ten-story Montauk Building, at the corner of Monroe and Dearborn streets, was probably the first building ever to be called a skyscraper.

The construction of the Montauk revolved around the personalities of its five chief principals: its architects, Burnham and Root; its owners

George B. Post, Western Union Building, New York, 1875. Courtesy Museum of the City of New York.

and commissioners, the Boston capitalists Peter and Shepherd Brooks; and their Chicago real estate agent, Owen F. Aldis, who translated the Brooks' desires to the architects. Root, and especially Burnham, learned a great deal from Peter Brooks' shrewd analysis of needs and architectural possibilities for immediate and later reference. Brooks urged that the "preliminary plans be on a small scale and not expensive . . . a plain structure of face brick . . . with flat roof." Unconsciously adumbrating much of the later aesthetic of the Chicago School and of the

Montauk Building, Chicago, 1881-82. Courtesy Chicago Art Institute.

"modern movement" in general, Brooks demanded that "the building throughout is to be for use and not for ornament. Its beauty will be in its all-adaptation to its use."[8]

Brooks gave specific directions as to heating, fireproofing, and elevator installation. He was also cost-conscious, not only with regard to building expenses but to later maintenance costs. "No projections on the front (which catch dirt)," he wrote, and "the less plumbing, the less trouble. It should be concentrated as much as possible, all pipes to show and be accessible, including gas pipes. It might also be advisable," he said, "to put in wire for future electric lights. It is not uncommon to do it in Boston now." After looking at the architects' subsequent proposals, he wrote again to his agent: "The most is certainly made of the lot, to the credit of the architects, but I have no idea it can be built well for the sum proposed. . . . Tile is expensive and bothersome to keep clean," he asserted, "it is good on the first floor only—nowhere else." There seemed to be a "needless amount of plate glass," he thought, and to reduce replacement costs, "the panes should be divided horizontally in halves." He was sure that "colored glass is mere nonsense, a passing fashion, inappropriate in a mercantile building and worst than all it obstructs the light. Strike it all out." His objections indeed ranged from the highest to the most basic details: "What is the object," he asked matter-of-factly, "in glass at the front of the urinals? The best I see . . . are made of slate with trickling water and a simple slate gutter at the bottom . . . in the streets of Paris." He also noticed with dismay that "all the wash bowls are to be boarded up with a door underneath, a good receptable for dirt, mice too. . . . This covering up of pipes is all a mistake, they should be exposed everywhere, if necessary painted well and handsomely." Brooks' pragmatic frame of mind appealed to the same qualities in Daniel Burnham, who continued to complement, especially in the years with Root, such practical suggestions of frugal clients with similar contributions of his own.[9]

In explaining his new interests in Chicago real estate, Brooks had prophesied: "Tall buildings will pay well in Chicago and sooner or later a way will be found to erect them." In his "sooner or later" reservation, he was referring chiefly to the soggy, shifting soil of the area which posed foundation problems even for smaller buildings. Burnham and Root's solution was a "floating raft" foundation, a slab of concrete about twenty inches thick reinforced with layers of steel rails to withstand shearing and bending forces. The steel rails, encased in concrete to add stability and to prevent rusting, allowed the weight of the building to be uniformly distributed over an area larger than that beneath the footing of a single wall or column. The invention was a significant one. The floating raft foundation formed the base of most of Chicago's greatest buildings until later in the decade, when improved drilling and drainage techniques permitted builders to sink foundations to bedrock.[10]

The Montauk was structurally unique in other ways as well. It was the most nearly fireproof tall building to date, its builders encasing its interior supporting columns with protective masonry. Another innovation occurred in the actual building process: it was the first building in Chicago to be constructed on a year-round basis without halting work during winter. To combat the snows and winds, the builders erected a large canvas to cover the entire operation, the interior space being heated from within.[11]

Brooks liked the final result even though, at times, the architects had exceeded his instructions and the building ultimately cost over $200,000.* The Montauk rose ten stories, all identical above the second. It had two "first floors," the entrance to the ground floor shops at sidewalk level with a flight of stairs leading through an open archway to the main floor and the elevators. The ground floor, however, contained the building's chief defect. Its ceilings were too low to accommodate the necessary utilities and the architects had to provide a small, separate building for them in the rear. The Montauk's functional aesthetic, however, led architect Thomas Tallmadge to call it the "father of . . . the commercial style." "What Chartres was to the Gothic cathedral," he contended, "the Montauk Block was to the high commercial building."[12]

While Burnham concurred in and contributed to the building's new austerity, Root had later doubts about the structure as a work of art. Harriet Monroe quoted a conversation Root had with a client about a prospective commission that preserved Root's feelings and his wit: It was "a very polite gentleman" who came in.

> "Now, Mr. Root," he said after their talk, "you will give me a beautiful building, won't you?"
> "We shall try to, Mr. X.," replied the architect.
> "Much of your work I like very much," continued the polite gentleman, "but—will you permit me to be quite frank?"
> "I desire it above all things."

* For a discussion and tabulation of comparative building costs, 1870–1970, see Appendix B.

> "Many of your buildings are remarkably successful; but—
> there are one or two I do not like quite so well."
>
> "Very natural, I am sure," said Root.
>
> "I suppose my taste is at fault, but—may I venture upon a
> criticism?"
>
> "You could not do me a greater favor."
>
> "Well, then, Mr. Root,"—it was difficult for so polite a
> gentleman to confess his trouble—"I like most of your build-
> ings immensely, but—I do not like the Montauk Block."
>
> Root put his hand on his critic's shoulder and shocked him
> . . . by exclaiming, "My dear Mr. X., who in H - - - does?"[13]

But Root and the "polite gentleman" client had underestimated the
building and its effect upon the larger public. Recalling his arrival in
Chicago as a young immigrant from Germany, the building contractor
Henry Ericsson wrote that, "On ahead, the street was solidly built up
with four and five story buildings with here and there a structure reaching six. . . . Breathlessly, I turned West into Monroe Street where, beyond Dearborn . . . I beheld the miracle being wrought. Facing south
on Monroe Street . . . the Montauk was rising to its third story. Seven
stories more were to pierce the sky—the highest building so far undertaken. I pondered long upon what my eyes beheld, and I became conscious that Chicago had already begun to Americanize the Goth within
me. . . . I wondered where I could take hold. What place there was
for me in a city such as this?"[14]

During the next three years, Root and Burnham produced numerous
structures with minor technical and aesthetic variations. The office
building for the Chicago, Burlington and Quincy Railroad (1882-83)
appeared one year later at Franklin and Adams streets. Containing the
better features of the Montauk in its relative austerity, fireproofness,
and business efficiency, the lower, six-story building could hardly be
called a skyscraper. It contained other elements, however, that Root and
Burnham would employ in later, taller buildings. The quadrangular
plan of four connected wings, enclosing a large central light court allowed the architects to increase considerably the size of the building
without diminishing the amount of light each office received. Each
suite in the building, moreover, led onto the open interior hallway balconies overlooking the court which made interoffice transit convenient.

The nine-story Calumet Building (1882-84) on La Salle Street had
the distinction of being Chicago's second skyscraper and the first tall
building in the new Board of Trade district. A handsome structure of

Counselman Building, Chicago, 1883-84. *Inland Architect*.

red brick and terra cotta, the Calumet gained its vertical accent from five balanced rows of large, front windows, articulated by impressive spandrels containing Root's original ornament. The contemporary Counselman Building (1883-84) at La Salle and Jackson was only one story higher than the Calumet, but it rose from a smaller base and thus appeared to be much taller. As chaste ornamentally as the Calumet, the Counselman also had dramatic window arrangement as its chief means of articulating character, with 2-1-2/1-2-1 patterns on its two, corner street elevations.

Rialto Building, Chicago, 1884-86. *Inland Architect*.

In the Rialto Building (1884-86) on Van Buren Street the excellence of Burnham's general layout and the clean lower façade clashed with Root's overly exuberant ornamental topping. Significant aesthetically for the strength and simplicity of its deeply recessed spandrels and its corner piers, the Rialto's chief importance lay in its general H-shaped plan, partially enveloping two large courts that provided more natural light and ventilation to the four hundred offices. Root damaged the building's over-all excellence, however, by lapses into irrelevant ornamentation and clumsy, rooftop pinnacles.

Though marked by traces of the horizontality of the firm's own neighboring Insurance Exchange (1884-85), the famous Rookery (1885-88), at La Salle and Adams, also managed to retrieve something of the distinctly skyscraper verticality of the earlier and smaller Montauk, Calumet, and Counselman buildings. Larger and taller than any skyscraper before it, the eleven-story Rookery repeated the quadrangular form and enclosed light court of the older six-story C.B. & Q. Railroad Building. The Rookery, wrote architect Thomas Tallmadge, was another "epochal" building. "In style, it appears to be Romanesque," with traces of "East Indian or Hindoo" influence—"a wayward child of Root's seething brain, an architectural *tour de force*. It is the first 'modern' office building plan. . . . The problems of arrangement of light courts, of corridors, of stairs, and the divisions of offices were here for the first time intelligently solved."[15]

Indeed, the Rookery's most important features were largely Burnham's contributions, displaying his talent for conceptualizing large, general plans. In the Burnham and Root partnership, the critic Montgomery Schuyler observed, "the administrative faculty is not less conspicuous than the power of design. The Rookery, for example, is not artistically so successful, either in mass or in detail, as some other buildings of the firm, but, at the time it was built, it was perhaps the most impressive of all by dint of the Roman largeness of its plan and of the thoroughness with which this was carried out to the last detail, as a matter not alone or mainly of artistic elaboration, but of practical administration. If it is not so uniquely impressive [in 1895], it is because such a project, when it has once been successfully executed, becomes common property, and may be reproduced and varied until, much more than in purely artistic successes, the spectator is apt to forget the original inventor and the fact that the arrangement he takes for granted was not always a commonplace but was originally an individual invention."[16]

The Rookery was a nearly square structure hollowed out in the middle. Bounded on its two front sides by Adams and La Salle streets and by Quincy Street and a large alley on its rear, it looked inward to a large interior court. Its four, eleven-story connected wings received natural light from all sides. While the front sides rested on the heavy and aesthetically appropriate stone work, the interior court walls and parts of the rear outside walls were true curtain walls of the incipient new mode, supported by wrought- and cast-iron skeleton frames. Another project of Peter and Shepherd Brooks of Boston, managed again by Owen Aldis and built by their favorite Chicago architects, the Rookery iterated the commercial and architectural prowess that had made the Montauk such a many-sided success. Supplied with ideas and suggestions from his business friend, Edward Waller, Burnham reviewed what he had learned since the Montauk and produced a plan so efficient and

The Rookery, Chicago, 1885-88. Author.

The Rookery, upper façade. Author.

so "liveable," that the Rookery would continue into the late twentieth century to be one of Chicago's most prestigious and sought-after office locations.

The Phoenix Building (1886-87), at Jackson, Clark, and La Salle streets, and the Midland Hotel in Kansas City (1886-88), their next two major buildings followed the same aesthetic idiom and employed the combination metal skeleton and wall-bearing constructions. Both buildings, however, followed cleaner and smoother lines than those of the Rookery, continuing with more explicit emphasis, the skyscraper esthetic of ever-sharpened verticality.

Meanwhile, in the middle of the 1880s, another series of developments coalesced to form an even greater achievement: the simultaneous perfection and demonstration of the metal cage concept of weight support and the first use of steel as a structural metal, with its superiority to iron, especially in matters of compression, tension, and resistance to heat, impact, and fatigue. The earlier use of steel for structural purposes had been prohibited chiefly by its exorbitant costs. In 1865, Alexander Holley had introduced into the United States the Bessemer

The Rookery, stairway. Author.

method of refining metal by blowing air through the molten pig iron that flowed from the blast furnace, but the capacity of the method was still limited and the price remained beyond the reach of most builders. In 1865, however, Abram Hewitt introduced the Siemens-Martin open-hearth process, wherein pig iron mixed with steel scrap allowed eventually for greater production. By the late 1870s the price had fallen to a level that made the new metal economically feasible on a large scale. Yet, like a majority of individuals in other fields, conservative builders and architects were hesitant to discard familiar methods, regardless of their liabilities, and slow to educate themselves, and their clients, to the advantages of the new. Other external factors, such as problems of shipment, also weighed heavily in the relatively slow acceptance of steel construction.[17]

Since the middle of the nineteenth century, architectural theorists, from the Frenchman Viollet-le-Duc to the American James Bogardus had advanced tentative and partial solutions to the problem of iron-supported construction. But not until 1885 with William Le Baron Jenney's Home Insurance Building in Chicago did anyone demonstrate practically the metal cage theory of weight support for tall buildings. A Minneapolis architect, LeRoy S. Buffington, had apparently perfected the idea before and independently of Jenney and had even obtained a patent on this theoretical conception. But Jenney, unaware of Buffington's ideas, was the first to apply the metal cage theory to the problems of the skyscraper, a system in which the weight-bearing responsibilities were taken away from the slightly pyramidical walls and moved to the now familiar cage of metal piers and beams.[18]

Jenney began the Home Insurance Building with plans to use the

William L. Jenney, Home Insurance Building, Chicago, 1883-85, with Burnham and Root's Calumet Building, 1883-84, to the left. Courtesy Chicago Historical Society.

Rand McNally Building, Chicago, 1888-90. Courtesy Rand McNally Co.

traditional cast iron as his basic supporting metal, enclosed by fire-proofing envelopes of masonry. Yet, "Jenney's approach to the design of the Home Insurance Building, typical of so much building of the nineteenth century, was to an extent empirical and pragmatic," a later critic noted, changing "in detail several times as design and construction progressed." With the arrival in Chicago of the first shipment of structural steel, Jenney, halfway through the building process, sought and obtained permission to substitute the new metal for the inferior iron products with which he had begun the building. Produced by the Carnegie-Phipps Steel Company of Pittsburgh, the rugged metal had after two decades of slowly declining cost finally reached a level where incorporation into ordinary buildings had become economically practicable.[19]

The ten-story structure that Jenney produced was a revolutionary step in technology and building art, making possible the final forging of the modern skyscraper form. Yet aesthetically and conceptually, the Home Insurance Building was still a dowdy, horizontally oriented "stacking" of floors atop one another. It failed to achieve even the aesthetic success of Root and Burnham's earlier wall-supported Montauk and Calumet buildings. But Jenney was primarily an engineer, not an artist, and a combination of both of those talents was essential for forging great architecture.

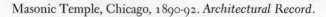

Masonic Temple, Chicago, 1890-92. *Architectural Record.*

Burnham and Root were quick to sense the importance of Jenney's accomplishment, and their handsome, ten-story, Rand McNally Building (1888-90) on Adams Street was the first tall building in the world to be completely supported by an all-steel frame. It was also the first skyscraper with an all terra cotta façade. Based on Burnham's similar floor plan for the Rookery, with natural light coming from the interior court and from three open sides, the building looked exactly like what it was, a masonry curtain stretched across a steel frame. The great size and width of the building, as compared to its height, justified, moreover, the horizontal articulation that had seemed so dowdy in the hands of less skillful architects.[20]

Woman's Temple, Chicago, 1890-92. Courtesy Chicago Art Institute.

Mills Building, San Francisco, 1890-91. Monroe, *John Wellborn Root*.

Similarly competent integration of form and function in steel-framed skyscrapers continued in Root and Burnham's Great Northern Hotel (1890-91), the Mills Building in San Francisco (1890-91), and the Equitable Building in Atlanta (1890-92). The Woman's Temple (1890-92), at Monroe and La Salle, was a tall but ultimately fussy attempt to make a skyscraper seem "feminine." Though it may have pleased its female subscribers as a W.C.T.U. tribute to Frances Willard, it failed, somehow, to measure up as architecture to the firm's other contemporary masterpieces. The Masonic Temple at State and Randolph com-

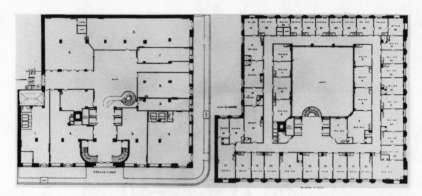

Mills Building, ground and fifth-floor plans. *Architectural Record.*

Monadnock Building, Chicago, 1889-92. *Inland Architect.*

Monadnock Building, Jackson Street façade. Author.

pleted in the same year, was the first twenty-story building in Chicago. Had its first eighteen floors been capped by a flat roof and an appropriately bold cornice, the Masonic building might have been the firm's greatest skyscraper, but instead the partners placed a steeply pitched, densely dormered, and wholly irrelevant gabled roof at the summit of the "tallest building in the world."

Though perhaps the most perfect specimens of the mature, steel-framed skyscraper would appear in Sullivan's buildings of the 1890s and in the 1894 Reliance Building of D. H. Burnham and Company, there has seldom been any doubt that Burnham and Root's most elegant and prophetic structure was the great Monadnock Building at the corner of Dearborn and Jackson, begun in 1889 and completed early in 1892. In 1884, before the building of the Rookery, Peter Brooks, through Owen Aldis, had commissioned Burnham and Root to design a building for his corner lot at Jackson and Dearborn. He did not actually intend to begin the building for several years, awaiting the incipient southward movement of the business district to envelop the spot and enhance its value. A rumor, however, to the effect that the city planned a forthcom-

Monadnock Building, Dearborn Street façade. Author.

ing ordinance to limit the heights of buildings caused Brooks to ask the architects to submit a proposed design to be used immediately in securing a building permit and thus to evade the prospective law, at least for one more building. The structure, like the Montauk, was to be as plain as possible. Burnham and Root completed preliminary studies in 1885, suggestive of, but less grandly austere than, the final product.[21]

The city did not pass a height-limiting ordinance, however, and Brooks lost interest in the building until 1889. Intrigued with Indian names, like Montauk, he had earlier suggested the "Quamquisset" as the name for the new structure, but as Root and Burnham conceived the building, its proposed height suggested something greater and Brooks renamed it for Mount Monadnock in New Hampshire. Later revisions in the original plans raised the structure to sixteen stories and called for an all-steel edifice "without one round arch or any ornament." Shepherd Brooks, however, Peter's more conservative brother, still questioned the financial worth of steel-framed construction, and the Monadnock rose finally in 1889 on the traditional wall-bearing formula. Despite the structural anachronism, produced only on Brooks' orders, the Monadnock was in all other ways the perfect model of skyscraper architecture. Sixteen stories of dark brick, with gracefully undulating bays and an outward curving cornice, the building was ultimately an abstract combination of certain classic pre-Greek Egyptian forms that had long fascinated Root. The dramatic outward sweep of the bottom walls also emphasized the structural basis of the last, great wall bearing building. To Louis Sullivan, the Monadnock was "an amazing cliff of brickwork, rising sheer and stark, with a subtlety of line and surface, a direct singleness of purpose, that gave one the thrill of romance."[22]

Indeed, along with Sullivan and Adler, and a handful of other Chicago architects, Burnham and Root had produced in the skyscraper a unique response to a rapidly urbanizing business society. Forging a new building aesthetic from converging technical and commercial developments, they synthesized and articulated much of the American urban experience in the last decades of the nineteenth century. The appeal of the skyscraper, as Sullivan expressed it, lay in its "soaring quality," in its "rising from the earth as a unitary utterance . . ." much as America, itself, in the 1890s, was obviously rising among the nations of the world. The Chicago skyscraper, soon exported elsewhere, became the new cathedral, the votive symbol, of turn-of-the-century American culture—an architectural offering created of and for the time, that unified the worlds of science, of commerce, and of art.

In addition, moreover, to the work of their own firm, Root and Burnham also involved themselves with the general problems of the profession. Believing that the American Institute of Architects had become too eastern-oriented and therefore "neglectful of the interests of the architectural profession in the middle west," Burnham and several Chicago colleagues led a movement in 1884 to organize the Western Association of Architects. While fostering common interests and confronting such general problems as professional ethics and maximum and minimum architects' fees, the Western Association also provided a Chicago-based forum or sounding board upon which western architects could communicate with each other on various aspects of the new architectural revolution. With Burnham and Root as early leaders, Peter Wight recalled, the new organization "grew with great rapidity, so that . . . the authorities of the Institute learned to appreciate that the absorption of a sectional body was a necessity for the success of a national body." In 1889, accordingly, the two groups were consolidated.[23]

After the completion of the Grannis Building in 1881, Burnham and

Burnham and Root in their office, The Rookery, ca. 1890. *Inland Architect*.

Root had moved the firm's offices there. In 1885, they moved to their newer and higher skyscraper, the Montauk Building, and in 1888, it seemed fitting to move again to the top of their even taller and greater Rookery Building. Professional success also allowed Daniel and Margaret to engage themselves further in Chicago social pursuits, to begin raising a family, and to enjoy life to its fullest. After their marriage in 1876, the couple had lived in part of the huge Sherman mansion on Prairie Avenue, but in 1880, John Sherman gave his daughter a house on South Michigan Avenue. The 1870s and 1880s saw the birth of Burnham's five children, John, Ethel, Hubert, Margaret, and Daniel, Jr. But by the late 1880s, Burnham could "no longer bear to have my children run in the streets of Chicago" and succumbed to the suburban impulse. He consequently bought and restored an old farmhouse on Lake Michigan in Evanston, a home which through the years became an increasingly active center both for lavish entertaining and for a rich and pleasant family life. As Root and Burnham entered the decade of the 1890s, life seemed good. They were building their greatest buildings, from houses to skyscrapers, and they were soon to embark on what promised to be their greatest collaborative effort—the building of the World's Columbian Exposition.[24]

Yet Root's sudden death in 1891 diverted that forward movement in a number of ways as it became Burnham's task to shoulder the firm and the fair alone. Historians espousing the virtues of Root have rightly pointed to the unevenness and the contradictions in Burnham's work after Root's death. Many of their objections have been valid, but in criticizing the later Burnham, they have failed to understand his complex make-up and his accommodation to the Root relationship. The worst and later work of D. H. Burnham and Company was not, as some have implied, the "real Burnham" finally exposed after Root no longer lived to cover up and carry on. It was a different Burnham, with both negative and positive manifestations, a Burnham changed not so much by Root's death as by his partner's life and by their close association of eighteen years. With John Root, Burnham had found himself. With Root as a kind of intellectual "authority," Burnham had felt secure to combine his vision and his practicality in a large, aggressive way without fear of ultimate academic, artistic, or intellectual "error." His failure after Root's death to find the same kind of lasting *human* authority forced him, for the most part, into a gradual dependence upon "the book," upon the abstract academic authority of the "classics." Often noted factors of time, place, and historical taste and fashion indeed had a great effect upon the process, but the old insecurities inherited from childhood were equally important factors.

Burnham's uneven achievements after Root's death confirm the importance of the earlier collaborative partnership. But historians have failed to speculate from the other direction: If *Burnham* had died in 1891 and Root had lived another twenty-one years, how would the loss have affected *Root's* work? Would he have been more successful than Burnham in finding the total replacement for the other essential member of the team? The answer is probably no. Yet, the facts are that Root did die and that Burnham lived until 1912, growing, expanding, and contributing much of value to American life, while sometimes, also supporting forces of reaction and regression. But Burnham owed much of the best of himself to the eighteen years of the large partnership. And he knew it.

IV
The Big Dream

Planning the World's Columbian Exposition

1889–1891

*If the people . . . actually knew what was good when they
saw it, they would some day talk about Hunt and Richardson,
La Farge and St. Gaudens, Burnham and McKim, and Stanford
White when their politicians and millionaires were otherwise
forgotten . . . Chicago asked in 1893 . . . the question
whether the American people knew where they were driving.
Adams answered, for one, that he did not know, but would try
to find out . . . he decided that the American people probably
knew no more than he did; but that they might still be driving
or drifting unconsciously to some point in thought . . . and
that possibly . . . this point might be fixed. Chicago was the
first expression of American thought as a unity; one must start
there.*

HENRY ADAMS
The Education of Henry Adams

DANIEL BURNHAM'S alliance with John Root was the first major
turning point in his life, his marriage to Margaret Sherman was the second, and the Chicago world's fair was the third. The World's Columbian Exposition of 1893 was the fifteenth and largest of the world's fairs
of the second half of the nineteenth century. In its scientific, industrial,
and artistic displays and in the picturesque exotica of its Midway Plai-
sance, the exposition mirrored many of the values and accomplishments
of the nineteenth century and suggested some of what might lie ahead
in the twentieth. The millions of people who visited the fair saw things
that informed, perplexed, inspired, and titillated: the great dynamos in

73

the Hall of Electricity, the foreboding Krupp guns in the German exhibit, the mysterious horseless carriage, the paintings of the French Impressionists Degas and Monet, and the "shameless hootchy-kootchy" belly dancing of Little Egypt.[1]

Ultimately, however, in both positive and negative ways, the most significant aspect of the age's greatest show was the showcase, itself, the temporary but immortal "White City." It was appropriate and prophetic that one of the common laborers who silently worked to build the fantasy was a man named Elias Disney, the father of Walt.[2] Though it was the product of many minds and hands, the exposition, as an achievement of unified social and aesthetic planning, owned its greatest debt to Burnham, its Director of Works. While the influence and the legacy of the fair's predominantly neoclassical architecture would become a favorite controversy among later cultural historians, few contemporaries questioned its powerful effect upon them and their fellows. The challenge of organizing and building the exposition inspired and equipped Burnham ultimately to become one of modern America's first great city planners. For its visitors, the fair provided a model, against which they might compare their own urban centers. However insidious its architecture might seem to later critics of Beaux Arts neoclassicism, the fair, in general, helped to condition Americans to accept and then to demand the later suggestions for urban improvement that Burnham and his followers would present.

The White City was a microcosm of the later "City Beautiful" movement that Burnham fathered. Though its significance and its implications became apparent only as the work progressed and the plan unfolded, the fair provided for Burnham and his fellow planners and architects a laboratory for testing ideas and turning dreams into realities. Never before in the United States had so large a "city" been built all at once that went so far to provide for the intellectual, esthetic, social, and physical needs of its temporary citizens. It was, in fact, even before its builders realized it, a controlled experiment containing the seeds of a larger urban planning movement. Many of the grander and more permanent ideas that Burnham later employed in Washington, Cleveland, San Francisco, Chicago, and the Philippines had their origins in the 1890s in the make-believe city that housed the world's fair.

The movement to hold a world's fair in Chicago to commemorate the four hundredth anniversary of the discovery of America began informally and somewhat anonymously in the mid-1880s. Similar ideas found independent expression in several cities, notably Washington, D.C., where in 1886, citizens proposed an exposition to extend over three years beginning with the centennial of the adoption of the Constitution and continuing through the anniversary of Columbus' discovery of America. In 1886, the American Historical Association met in Washington and appointed historian George Bancroft to chair a committee "to urge upon Congress the desirability of celebrating the . . . discovery of America by Columbus." Senator Hoar of Massachusetts spoke for a New England group advocating the same cause. By the late 1880s, a lively competition had developed among the cities of Washington, St. Louis, New York, and Chicago for the honor of hosting the exposition.[3]

In July 1889, Chicago mayor DeWitt Cregier, upon the instructions of the city council, appointed a committee of 250 leading citizens to work toward holding the fair in Chicago. The committee conducted a vigorous campaign to arouse interest throughout the city and state, to secure promises of adequate financial support, and to convince Congress and the nation at large that Chicago was the best place for holding the exposition. The committee cited several reasons for approval of Chicago's bid. The city was very near the country's center of population. As the terminus of thirty-eight major railroads, it offered better facilities than any other city for transporting visitors from all parts of the continent. In traveling to Chicago, furthermore, Europeans and East Coast Americans would have an opportunity to see a lot of the country and to become better acquainted with the great American Midwest. Nothing, they argued, could better "typify the giant young nation whose discovery the projected fair is to commemorate" than "the marvelous growth of Chicago from a frontier camp to the active city of more than a million souls, with a corresponding advance in commercial, industrial, and intellectual activities. . . ."[4]

In confident anticipation, the committee directed E. T. Jeffery, the well-known railroad manager, and Octave Chanute, the noted engineer, to examine and report on the various technical, aesthetic, and administrative aspects of the French Universal Exposition, which was being held in Paris in 1889. The information brought back in their subsequent reports suggested how to proceed and what to avoid. After presenting evidence that Chicago could come up with a sufficient number of corporate investors to finance the building of the fair, the committee worked toward developing grass-roots sympathy for Chicago's claims throughout the country. Chicago finally won the support of Congress, and on April 25, 1890, President Harrison signed an act providing for an "international exhibition of arts, industries, manufactures, and the products of the soil, mine, and sea" to be held at Chicago. The act called for a national commission of representatives from each state of the union to assume, theoretically, general responsibility for the exposition, for the installation and management of exhibits and attractions, and for all communications with state and foreign governments. It then created a Chicago corporation to work in close cooperation with the commission in the building and operation of the exposition. Each organization had its own officers and committee systems.[5]

On April 4, 1890, the stockholders of the Chicago corporation met and elected a board of directors of forty-five leading Chicago businessmen, names that were or would become known throughout the business world. The group included, for example, Charles H. Wacker, Charles H. Schwab, Edward T. Jeffery, Charles T. Yerkes, James W. Ellsworth, Lyman J. Gage, Charles L. Hutchinson, Martin A. Ryerson, Cyrus J. McCormick, and Andrew McNally. The *Inland Architect and News Record* ridiculed the "remarks in different parts of the country by the small boys that Chicago cannot raise $5,000,000 for the World's Fair" when, "by a careful estimate the wealth represented by the directors aggregates about $70,000,000."[6]

Early disagreement developed, however, among the national commission and the Chicago city authorities over the choice of a site for the exposition. Hoping that professional advice would help settle the controversy, Lyman Gage, president of the Illinois corporation, invited the famous landscape architect Frederick Law Olmsted and his partner Henry Codman to Chicago to survey the situation. Olmstead had, in fact, previously studied the park system of Chicago some twenty years earlier and had recommended the conversion of the Jackson Park area into a public pleasure ground, a recommendation that had been only partially implemented. Returning in 1890, Olmsted made a survey of seven possible locations with Daniel Burnham, who had been retained as an unofficial adviser to the corporation. With Burnham's advice, Olmsted narrowed his preferences to two lakeshore sites north and south of the city's center. When railroad officials refused to provide the needed transportation to the preferred northern area, Olmsted, strongly in favor of a waterfront location, reluctantly turned to the undeveloped marshes of Jackson Park on the south side.[7]

After prolonged discussion and a resulting loss of valuable time, the corporation accepted the recommendation of its architectural advisers and subsequently rewarded them with permanent appointments. It retained Olmsted and his associate Codman as consulting landscape architects, Abram Gottlieb as consulting engineer, and Daniel Burnham and John Root as consulting architects. Discussion continued for months on the possibility of utilizing a dual site to include Jackson Park and a smaller area nearer the center of the city. Ultimately, however, the southern site became the single, unified location.[8]

In the fall of 1890, Burnham, Root, Codman, and Olmsted combined their talents and jointly produced the first tentative, unified plan for the exposition. In an effort to exploit the naturally low and soggy stretches of Jackson Park, Olmsted and Codman envisioned a completed landscape of both land and water courses. Root and Burnham suggested sizes and locations of buildings. All four men agreed tentatively that the plan should center on a large, architectural court which would enclose a body of water and serve as the focal point of the exposition. A canal should lead northward from the east-west axis of the court to a series of broader, less sharply defined lagoons. The specifications for dredging the lagoons called for leaving a "wooded island" in the center to remain free of large buildings and to serve as a natural, open horticultural preserve. The complex of waterways penetrating the entire site would make all of the major buildings approachable by water as well as by land and would give a distinctive quality to the exposition that it would not otherwise possess.[9]

Though Root had had an earlier "leaning to variety in style and color," the four architects finally agreed in their autumn discussions that the buildings around the basin and central court should be formal, impressive, and generally of the same stylistic mode, while those on the lagoons north of the court might be of a lighter and more varied nature, depending on the preferences of their individual designers. It was Root who usually had a "pencil in . . . hand" and who served as a kind of graphic stenographer committing to a plat of rough brown paper the combined ideas of the four men. Though Root "held the pencil" and had, on his own, already sketched a few possible exposition building schemes, the initial over-all report and diagram of tentative plans were the result of a four-way dialogue among the original consultants. Rushed through quickly to comply with the terms of the congressional act, a tentative draft was submitted to the National Commission. Despite its sketchiness the plan placed most of the buildings and other features in their actual, ultimate locations. The proposal also touched generally on matters of steam, electricity, gas, water supply, and sewage. In short, it anticipated most of the future needs of the proposed city's temporary occupants.[10]

While still conceptualizing the general plan and long before the combined corps of architects would determine a definite style, Burnham wrote to a friend with previsions of the ultimate result. "Dominating the entire Exposition," he predicted, "there will be some great monumental design to give to the mass of the buildings that architectural interest and splendor which an exposition of this magnitude demands. The space at the disposal of the commissioners and directors is so ample (being all told considerably over 1000 acres) that every department of the Exposition will be provided for in ideal fashion," and yet, "at the same time great care will be exercised that the various departments are so concentrated as to be easily accessible and to present an impressing and picturesque ensemble." Whatever the ultimate stylistic orientation, the four consultants had early determined that the fair would not be a mere repeat of previous expositions with mammoth glass sheds merely covering the exhibits. Neither would the architecture connote only a frivolous carnival gaiety. The fair would indeed "abandon the conservatory aspect of the older expositions and . . . suggest permanent buildings—a dream city." Each building, it was hoped, would not only be a brilliant specimen in its own right, but, more important, would become a part of the larger scheme of the fair. On November 25, 1890, the National Commission approved the general plan. The next task was to work it out in detail and select designers for the individual buildings.[11]

In October 1890, Burnham had become chief of construction, later to be called director of works, with Root remaining in his original capacity of consulting architect. The chief officers were theoretically responsible to the Committee on Grounds and Buildings, which had "jurisdiction in all matters pertaining to grounds, leases, engineering, designs, plans, construction of buildings and works, maintenance of buildings and grounds, organization of guards, police, detective, and fire departments, gas, electric lights, water supply, medical services, application for space, telegraphy, insurance, etc." Owing, however, to the architects' eminent reputations and to their apparent competence, the committee allowed them considerable independence, flexibility, and power. Believing strongly in the necessity of centralized management, E. T. Jeffery, president of the Illinois Central Railroad and chairman of the committee,

drew the terms of Burnham's commission so that all other building officials and heads of departments would have to report directly to him. "It
was urged," Burnham recalled, "by men who knew more about organization than I did at that time, that it was absolutely necessary to have a
chief." He then literally became head of construction and, subsequently
gained a reputation as a demanding but benevolent dictator.[12]

Many had assumed after Burnham and Root's initial appointment,
that they would design most of the major buildings, and, indeed in the
very early stages, Root had sketched a few tentative designs. But while
it was virtually impossible for one firm to perform the feat in such a
short time, Root and Burnham also recognized that such a course would
be bad for them and for the morale of other architects who "were bit-
terly suspicious of exclusion." Harriet Monroe remembered "how Root
came home one evening, soon after his appointment, cut to the quick
because one of these, always hitherto a friend, had apparently refused to
recognize Mr. Burnham when they met at a club. 'I suppose he thinks
we are going to hog it all!' he exclaimed, disheartened." Hogging it all,
even if technically possible in the short time available, would, moreover,
have seriously diminished the intended national character of the enterprise, and Root and Burnham began discussing privately the most likely
and appropriate architects among the country's leading firms. "We tried
to shove on as fast as we could," Burnham recalled, "and carried the
plan as far as we could without having anything definite as regards the
various buildings; then late in the year, in December, I believe, I grew
very impatient and told my committee I must have action, get together
a force of men and start the work."[13]

On December 9, therefore, Burnham, by then the chief of construction, sent a memorandum to the Grounds and Buildings Committee on
possible selection processes. Signed and concurred in by Root, Olmsted,
and Gottlieb, Burnham's note proposed four possible methods of procedure: first, the unlikely possibility of selecting one architect to conceive
and design all buildings; second, unlimited competition, open to any architect who might wish to submit plans for any or all of the buildings;
third, competition on the same basis among a smaller, specially selected
group of architects; fourth, direct selection by the committee of a few
leading designers who would constitute a board of consulting architects,
divide the work among themselves, and consult each other during the
various stages of building. For reasons of time and ultimate efficiency,
Burnham eschewed the more democratic proposals and recommended

the fourth method. "The honor conferred on those so selected," he suggested, "would create in their minds a disposition to place the artistic quality of their work in advance of the mere question of emoluments" and "could not fail to be productive of a result which would stand before the world as the best fruit of American civilization."[14]

After a heated internal debate, a majority of the committee accepted Burnham's recommendation for direct selection and asked him to make actual nominations of architects for their consideration. Both he and Root were especially concerned that the fair be a national rather than a merely regional affair. After careful reflection and more discussion with Root, Burnham recommended for the central buildings the great architectural firms of Richard M. Hunt, McKim, Mead, and White, and George B. Post, all of New York; Peabody and Stearns, of Boston; and Van Brunt and Howe of Kansas City. Several members of the Board of Directors, however, "were in political life," Burnham recalled, and resented the recent majority decision to permit direct selection. On the matter of approving the nominations, they were still attempting to hold out, and could not come to an agreement, "the politicians desiring to keep me from making the selections. Finally, [Chairman] Gage put the motion and four of them voted for me and three against me. The next morning I had a letter prepared to the men in the East, asking them to come participate in the work." He had actually written them confidential "inquiries" earlier, he confessed to his friend Charles Moore, "feeling confident I would carry my point. My plan was to bring together the men of greatest experience. I . . . knew who *the* men were."[15]

Burnham's formal and official letter of invitation, December 13, 1890, insisted that he and the committee "would leave the matter of designing to the five architects" to "determine among yourselves whether to make a joint design of the whole as one, or each to take up separate parts to be modified to meet such views as shall be expressed in your conferences from time to time." His explanation defined sharply his own intended relationship with all the participating architects. His office, he assured them, would "supply you with all data about materials, sizes, general disposition and costs of buildings . . . have charge of the constructional features, and finally of the execution of the entire work, but with the understanding that the artistic parts are to be carried out with your approval, and that you are from time to time to visit the work either in a body or separately. . . . Our consulting architect Mr. Root would act as your interpreter when you are absent without imparting into the work any of his own feelings." In explaining his operating procedures, he realized "the hesitancy you may feel in assuming responsibility for design when you do not fully control the execution of it." He and the committee had adopted that policy in the belief that "strict economy of the two essentials, time and money, will be best subserved by keeping the actual control of the work in the hands of one man and his bureau." He could assure them, however, "that your intents and purposes of design, once agreed upon by the committee, shall be carried out as you wish and that they shall not be altered or meddled with, and when exigencies arise, making any important change necessary, you shall be consulted. . . ."[16]

Despite his formal invitation and his earlier informal enquiry, Burnham's letter evoked a prompt answer of acceptance only from Henry Van Brunt of Kansas City. He then decided to go to New York to talk personally with the eastern architects. To his great disappointment, however, he found them hesitant about the whole project, doubting seriously if the temporary nature and ultimate significance of the Exposition would be worth the time-consuming inconvenience it would cause them in the midst of busy and already prosperous careers. Burnham listened, but he also talked, and when he explained his own vision of the fair as a potential model and inspiration for later American architecture, he won the easterners over. They decided to accept his invitation and soon became enthusiastic.[17]

When Burnham originally presented his list of nominations, there had been growling within the committee that since Chicago was paying for the fair, more of the work should go to Chicago architects. The local sentiment grew stronger and when Burnham returned from the east, the Committee on Grounds and Buildings authorized him "to select five architects from Chicago to design the other great structures of the Exposition." Burnham approved the idea and nominated the firms of Adler and Sullivan, Burling and Whitehouse, Jenney and Mundie, Henry Ives Cobb, and Solon S. Beman. After getting committee approval, he then personally called on each of the individual firms and obtained immediate acceptances from all but Adler and Sullivan. In later recalling the incident, Burnham made no mention of Sullivan's response but he was sure that, at the time, Adler was a bit jealous of him and indeed "had hoped to be in the position I was in. He was rather disgruntled and 'did not know.' Later he decided to come in. It was all right except there was a little feeling of disappointment there."[18]

When all of the architects had arrived, Burnham called them together

and asked them to go with him to look at the site. Root, who had not
been feeling well, remained in the office. "We went to Jackson Park in
carriages," Burnham recalled. "It was one of those cold winter days. The
sky was overcast with clouds and the lake covered with foam. We looked
the thing over. Peabody got up on a pier and said, 'Do you really say
that you expect to open this Fair by '93?' I told him yes. He said he did
not think it could be done. I told him it was settled." That evening the
Grounds and Buildings Committee gave a dinner at which Burnham
argued that the success of the whole thing "depended upon team work.
If they worked for the thing as a whole, it would be a great success. . . .
From that time on this spirit never failed." The architects then organized themselves into a board with Richard Hunt as chairman and Louis
Sullivan as secretary.[19]

On Sunday afternoon, the following day, John and Dora Root invited
the visiting architects to call at their home on Astor Place. Root had not
felt well for some time and as the visitors left he foolishly escorted them
outside into the winter air without a coat. The next morning he appeared to have a cold, but the doctor diagnosed pneumonia. While the
architects continued their discussions waiting for news of Root's improvement, Burnham went out and stayed most of the week at Astor
Place. On Thursday, Burnham remembered, "John was breathing very
rapidly and said, 'You won't leave me again, will you?' I said, 'No, John,
I will stay.' I went in to see his wife, who was very ill. His aunt came
into the wife's room and told me that he was dead. . . ."[20]

Nellie Mitchell, the aunt who informed Burnham of his partner's
death, later told her niece Harriet Monroe that she had "sat on the dark
upper curve of the stairway which led directly from the living room" and
observed "Dan Burnham's pacing out the hours and talking to himself
at times under the room where his partner lay dead. He seemed to be
rebuking supernatural powers: 'I have worked, I have schemed and
dreamed to make us the greatest architects in the world. I have made
him see it and kept him at it—and now he dies—damn! damn! damn!'
His snatches of soliloquy through that night of despair, before he emerged
to new dreams, took the form of wrath," she recalled, "and he shook his
fist and cursed the murderous fates as he paced back and forth between
intervals of comfortless sleep on the living room couch." Perhaps he had
never before understood so clearly how very much both he and John Root
had depended on each other. If, however, Burnham's private reaction

in an unguarded moment seemed callous and bitter to his unseen observer his expressions to others left no doubt as to his sense of loss.[21]

Speaking later before the American Institute of Architects, Burnham insisted that Root "possessed a mind remarkable for its artistic insight, quickness and clearness of apprehension, and deep sympathy with everything of value about him. Though filled to running over with his own suggestive thoughts, he never failed to grasp another's, and it was his everyday custom to coordinate the elements of discussions with a rapidity and finish that seemed marvelous. . . . He saw comprehensively and exactly; both through his natural eyes and those of his spirit, and his power of expression to the ears, the eyes or the hearts of others kept pace with his own vivid impressions." Though Burnham could not frankly "believe that the Exposition would have been better had he lived . . . it certainly would have been modified and stamped with something of his great individuality. My own loss," he concluded, "I cannot speak of." Indeed, as Daniel Burnham, Jr., recalled some forty years later, his father "never got over the shock" of Root's tragic and untimely death.[22]

The other architects of the exposition, even those who knew him slightly, grieved Root's death and lamented his loss to the fair. They continued their discussions, however, for yet another week, making a number of important decisions about the fair's architecture. First, they studied and approved the general scheme set forth by Burnham, Olmsted, Codman, and Root. Second, they determined the size and exact location of the court, the canal, and the major buildings of the exposition. Third, they agreed upon a uniform cornice line for the buildings around the court and the approximate height of the corresponding terraces.[23]

After talking and listening for a week to the various architects and reflecting on their indicated preferences and predilections, Burnham assigned five of the six Court of Honor buildings to the non-Chicago architects, following the earlier plan that he and Root had tentatively determined. Richard Hunt would design the central Administration Building at the head of the court and the basin. Immediately south of Hunt's building, Peabody and Stearns would design Machinery Hall. Directly east toward the lake would rise the Agriculture Building by McKim, Mead, and White. Facing McKim's building on the northeast side of the basin would be George B. Post's mammoth building for manufactures and liberal arts. North of the Administration Building, the

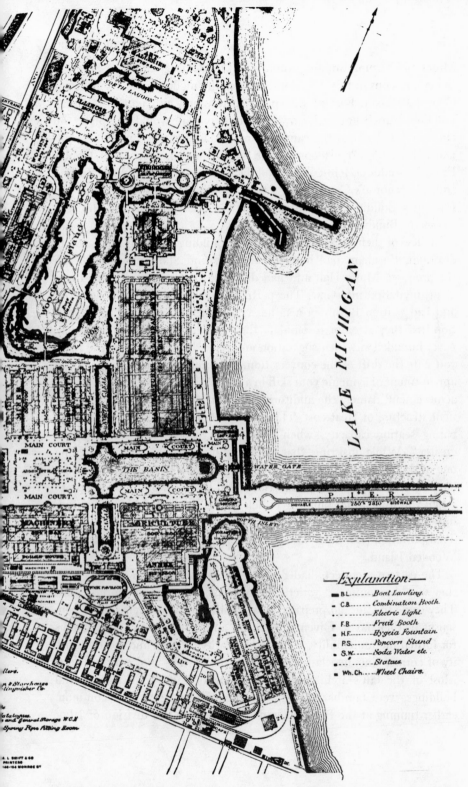

Map of the World's Columbian Exposition, Chicago, 1892-93. Courtesy Chicago Art Institute.

Mines and Mining Building would go to the Chicago architect Solon S. Beman, famous in the 1880s for designing the model workers' village for George Pullman. East of Beman's structure and also north of Hunt's building, Van Brunt and Howe's Electricity Hall would complete the circle and look across the canal to Post's Manufactures Building. Informally situated on the lagoons to the north would be Henry Ives Cobb's Fisheries Building, Jenney and Mundie's Horticulture Building, Burling and Whitehouse's Casino, and several buildings yet to designated: the Fine Arts Building, the United States Government Building, and the Woman's Building.[24]

In view of their earlier achievement in building the great Chicago auditorium, Burnham had hoped that Adler and Sullivan would design the proposed Music Hall and had discussed that possibility with them in his invitation interview. The partners had thought it over, however, and had written Burnham a rather crisp letter questioning his suggestion that they attempt to emulate their earlier triumph. Burnham had never intended any such suggestion and replied that "while in the main you state the drift of the conversation, I did not 'urge you to accept this appointment of evincing your skill in a manner parallel with your greatest achievement, namely the auditorium building,' because that is a permanent structure of great cost. The only mention made of it was in comparing seating capacity, when I said that of the temple would be greater." While insisting that they could make the music building one of the most significant at the fair, Burnham acknowledged their unhappiness with his proposal and concluded that he would "be happy to assign you some other building in lieu of the Temple of Music but cannot do so until the matter develops further." He later assigned them the Transportation Building to face east across the lagoon toward the Wooded Island.[25]

The eastern architects had decided before the Chicago meeting that they would recommend varieties of neoclassicism for the central court. They came to Chicago prepared to argue their case and left with a consensus in their favor. Given the general and agreed-upon specifications for formal monumentality, for basic similarity of style, and for uniformity of cornice line, neoclassicism seemed the obvious choice at the time. Most of the fair's architects, including all of those to design central buildings, were familiar with the classical idiom from their common, earlier training at the Paris Ecole des Beaux Arts. The division of labor

Charles McKim. Courtesy Chicago Art Institute.

and the shortness of time demanded that they agree on a unified theme and produce it quickly and conveniently. With other builders and over-seers in charge of executing their instructions so rapidly and at such a distance, it seemed important to work with an easily understood archi-tectural vocabulary. While choosing a period style as a frame of refer-ence, however, Burnham insisted that "all buildings were to be as dis-tinct from each other as they could possibly be." Criticism of the stylistic option would proliferate in the years that followed, but in 1891, even Louis Sullivan was silent. Most participants grew more enthusiastic with every week. "I feel this to be the greatest chance for architecture ever known on the continent," Burnham wrote to James Windrim, the United States government architect.[26]

For the next month, the architects worked on preliminary building plans with instructions to return to Chicago in February to discuss their initial schemes together. "This will be a meeting," Burnham prophesied, "memorable in the annals of architecture." And indeed it was. The easterners brought with them the noted sculptor, Augustus St. Gaudens, who so impressed Burnham that the chief of construction insisted on retaining him as a permanent exposition arts consultant. On their first day in Chicago, Burnham had all of the visitors to breakfast. "They were filled with enthusiasm," he recalled. Peabody suggested that the north-

Frederick Law Olmsted. Courtesy Chicago Art Institute.

Meeting of the Board of Architects and the Grounds and Buildings Committee, February 24, 1891. Burnham and Millet, *World's Columbian Exposition, The Book of the Builders.*

ern canal connecting the court and the lagoons be extended southward between his Machinery Hall and McKims' Agriculture Building. "Next, St. Gaudens took a hand in the thing. He thought the east end of the composition [on the edge of the lake] should be bound together architecturally. All agreed; and he suggested a statue surrounded by thirteen columns, typifying the original thirteen states. We all hailed this as a bully thing."[27]

The following day, the Grounds and Buildings Committee joined the architects for a meeting in Burnham's office. "Gage presided. All the fellows, including the Chicago men, were there, each with his sketch or sketches, and they put them up on the wall one at a time. The scheme as a whole began to take hold of us," Burnham noted. "The day went on, we had our luncheon on the table, then came in the large committee, and I think it got to be quite dark and we lighted up before the meeting was through. It was still as death except for the low voice of each speaker. You could feel the thing as a great magnet. . . . St. Gaudens had been in the corner all day, never opening his mouth, and

Group of World's Fair Architects, Artists, and Officials, May 1891. *Left to right:* D. H. Burnham, George B. Post, M. B. Pickett, Henry Van Brunt, Francis D. Millet, Maitland Armstrong, Colonel Edward Rice, Augustus Saint-Gaudens, Henry Sargent Godman, George W. Maynard, Charles F. McKim, E. R. Graham, and Dion Geraldine. Courtesy Chicago Art Institute.

scarcely moving. He came over and took me by both hands and said: 'Look here, old fellow, do you realize that this is the greatest meeting of artists since the 15th century?' "[28]

As the architects left Chicago to complete their designs, Burnham completed his building force. Olmsted and Codman remained as consulting landscape architects and Gottlieb as chief engineer, but finding Root's replacement—for the firm and for the fair—was a serious problem. "John's death," Burnham wrote to a friend, "has left a hole into which not one, but several strong men must be flung. . . ." He considered several different men for the post, but finally settled on Charles Atwood, a New York architect especially recommended by friends of Burnham at Columbia University. McKim had doubts about Atwood's personal stability but Atwood impressed Burnham, and he assumed Root's old position, both as consulting architect and later for a short time as the chief designer in Burnham's firm. The engineer Dion Geraldine became Burnham's chief administrative lieutenant as general superintendent. The sculptor Augustus St. Gaudens, and later the painter Frank Millet, became the chief artistic advisers.[29]

While choosing his staff in the spring of 1891 and waiting for the architects to perfect their plans, Burnham must have known that both he, and the exposition, were entering an important period. The basic planning was over. The dream seemed clearer. Now he had to build it, to face the thing, itself. Root was dead, and the larger, further future, without Root, must have sobered Burnham when he thought of it. Perhaps it was good that he had so little time for his private thoughts. Yet, for the immediate future, for the fair, itself, the plan was there. At least Root had lived to help him get it started. So without Root's help for the first time in eighteen years, without his presence and his calm, good humor from the back room, without his reciprocally steady and reassuring support, Burnham plunged in alone to build the exposition.

V
The Make-Believe City

The Building of the Fair
1891–1893

*Stunned by the majesty of the [exposition] my mother sat in
her chair, visioning it all yet comprehending little of its meaning. Her life had been spent among homely small things, and
these gorgeous scenes dazzled her, overwhelmed her, letting in
upon her in one mighty flood a thousand stupefying suggestions
of the art and history and poetry of the world.*

HAMLIN GARLAND
A Son of the Middle Border

IN THE SPRING of 1891, Burnham moved his exposition headquarters from the Rookery to Jackson Park, erecting a temporary structure
with drafting rooms, an office, living quarters, and a small gymnasium
for exercise. "He had a forty-foot room with several beds," his son recalled. "He seldom went to the big cafeteria below, for his old colored
servant Jackson looked after him and served his meals. The room had a
huge fireplace, for he loved an open hearth; and there, he often gave
suppers to his co-workers, to talk over plans." Perhaps it was Sullivan's
view of Burnham at Jackson Park that led him later to suggest that
Burnham had "feudal" inclinations.[1]

Burnham's commission as chief of construction charged him with
"the construction of buildings, the supervision of designs therefor, the
preparation of the grounds and engineering incident to proper erection
of the entire work . . . supervision of buildings erected by outside parties and . . . maintenance of all buildings belonging to the Exposition
Company," the power to "examine all bids and propositions for work
and recommend to the committee on buildings and grounds for approval

Caricature of Burnham as Director of Works, by Theodore L. Wust, ca.
1893. Courtesy Chicago Historical Society.

such as command themselves to his judgment . . . organize bureaus of architecture, engineering, and landscape gardening, sanitation, etc. and . . . subject to the approval of the committee, hire and dismiss all employees . . . and fix the compensation for their services."[2]

In fulfilling those duties, Burnham divided his time and his energy in several major directions: dealing with the Grounds and Buildings Committee on matters of policy, communicating with the architects about their individual buildings, dealing with subordinates in Jackson Park regarding administrative, personnel, and construction problems, personally overseeing and inspecting the actual construction process, receiving and answering the myriad enquiries of job seekers and the press, and entertaining the hoards of distinguished and curious citizens who wished to view the work in progress.

Burnham's correspondence with the participating architects alternately revealed his pleasure and his impatience with the progress and problems of each building at the fair. In a letter to Henry Ives Cobb asking him to make minor adjustments in his plan for the Fisheries Building, Burnham wrote that "these little refinements will be most telling things and in them more than in any other will perfection come or fail. . . . Come over if you can and help me scheme on this line." In the same cordial spirit, he advised Cobb to keep his structure simple. "I wish you would leave the statues off your building," he wrote, "I think you will hurt the effect by using them. I sincerely admire the design . . . and don't want you to make what seems to me will be a mistake."[3]

He was even more buoyant in suggestions to Henry Van Brunt. The Electricity Building, he thought, "should be exquisite. No other adjective fits the purpose. . . . It should possess utmost refinement and delicacy . . . and, I hope, be sumptuous, and in a quiet way, both rich and gay. It is the one spot where we should give way to fancy and make it sparkle by day or by night. The poetic spirit grows apace among us here," he exulted, "as you may guess from my frame of mind while writing this. It is perhaps a good thing, as practicality will doubtless elbow us enough before we get through."[4]

Practicality indeed elbowed him frequently. Olmsted was attempting to supervise much of the landscaping from his Massachusetts office and Burnham had to make numerous requests before he or Codman agreed to come out. Burnham wrote tenacious, tough-minded letters to all the designers—letters which contradict the later contentions of Sullivan that the chief of construction was overly apologetic, deferential, and sub-

servient to the eastern architects. "Your work is badly behind," Burnham wrote Stearns and Peabody in June 1891. "The delay you are
causing us by not forwarding scale drawings is embarrassing in the extreme. You had better send what you have and we will put on a force of
men night and day ourselves. We cannot wait any longer. . . ." Ten
days later, having failed to receive their plans for Machinery Hall, his
wrath increased. "We are completely put out with the delay on your
building. All drawings of other men, East and West, are delivered here
long ago, and some of them are more complex than yours. Please send
on at once everything."[5]

Though he admired Richard Hunt's work, and ultimately appreciated
his design for the Administration Building, Burnham frequently argued
with Hunt over occasional extravagances in his design. In one set of
drawings by Hunt's artist, the design and arrangement of the building
was totally fantastic. His rebuke to Hunt belied another of Sullivan's
later contentions—namely, that Burnham had no sense of humor. "The
water color of your building is just received," he wrote in June, "and I
am sorry to say that it will be of no use." Burnham could not "understand why Mr. Smith has created an imaginary environment, instead of
following the facts. None of the surrounding objects shown in the picture are even approximately correct. They are concepts of his own brain.
If, therefore, we publish the picture, it will be to invite derision, and to
undoubtedly get it. . . . There are no columns designed for the esplanade in front of your building. The Machinery Hall design as made by
Peabody is entirely ignored by Mr. Smith. There is not to be a vista of
eastern domes, towers, and minarets, back of your building toward the
railway. On the contrary, there will be a railway station, and this should
be shown. Your building does not come down to the water, but stands
on a broad esplanade several hundred feet in depth. . . . All of this is
left out. . . . Generally nothing is at all like reality except the building
itself." His annoyance seemed to justify a delicious bit of sarcasm: "The
surroundings are not Aladdin's, as conceived by his architects, the genii,"
Burnham mused, "who temporarily had possession of the building and
moved it a few thousand miles off into some garden . . . for the nonce.
We would like it moved back where it belongs and given its proper
background of activity and enterprise, as designed by the commission of
which you have the honor to be chairman."[6]

In addition to supervising the construction of the official exposition
buildings, Burnham also had the power to establish guidelines for the

special pavilions of foreign governments and the individual American states. He had only advisory relations with the buildings of foreign governments, but rules required that both he and the fair's director-general approve the design of state pavilions before construction could proceed. His guidelines in 1892 specified that all state structures "be designed in the form of pavilions, with symmetrical and rectangular plans except in cases where the site . . . seems to require a polygonal or irregular figure for the ground plan. . . . The architecture should be dignified in style, formal rather than picturesque. Oriental designs should be avoided as such motives will naturally be employed by the oriental nations in the erection of their own buildings. The earlier styles that prevailed in this country," he wrote, "such as the architecture of the old Spanish missions in Lower California and Mexico can with propriety furnish the motives for the buildings of the western and southwestern states." Indeed, if the larger architecture of the court suggested the "classical revival" at the turn of the century, Burnham's instructions to the states encouraged the coeval and apparently endless vogue for American "colonial" architecture. "For the eastern and southern states," he suggested, "buildings of the old colonial style would be appropriate, and reproduction of historic buildings would prove an interesting feature. These buildings should have more the character of club houses than buildings designed for exhibition purposes. Refinement and sobriety of treatment is to be preferred to anything that is sensational or startling in its appearance. The natural resources of each individual state can be drawn upon to furnish the material for its own building. . . ."[7]

Whether or not the criteria were valid, several states received strong rebukes when they tried to flaunt them. Delaware's building, for example, was "too domestic in its character," he wrote the state's representative, "there is a great superabundance of gables, particularly on the roofs of the verandas, and the proportions of the columns . . . are very ugly . . . and should be properly based on a classic formula. The fancy shingling of the exterior walls will give a trivial and undignified aspect to the exterior treatment and certainly will prove inconsistent with the dignity of the surrounding buildings."[8]

Burnham strongly opposed the unusual scheme of the state of Montana to erect as its pavilion, an artificial mountain, "which at the best," Burnham wrote, "will be an exceedingly ugly thing and which will be objectionable to everyone in the neighborhood of it, if built. It will also take up much more ground than we have to offer them, and though it might represent their industries, which I very much doubt, it will be a monstrosity considered from an artistic standpoint."[9]

He was equally conservative on a South Dakota proposition to erect its building in the shape of a Sioux tepee. "While it might in a measure be representative of your state," Burnham replied, it would, "I think present a rather startling effect from an artistic and architectural standpoint." He recommended that the tepee roof be eliminated and "one in harmony with the surrounding architecture be prepared." Sullivan would probably have agreed with Burnham in saying no to the Indian motif, whereas Sullivan's disciple, Frank Lloyd Wright, might have smiled and said yes. Though he probably never heard of the aborted South Dakota scheme, Wright designed a building in the shape of a much more abstract tepee some fifty years later for the Nakoma Country Club in Madison, Wisconsin. But it was also rejected.[10]

Indeed, Burnham's attitude toward the state pavilions mirrored and re-enforced his inclination toward conservative traditionalism. "There can be no question," he wrote the Pennsylvania representative, "but that Independence Hall would be the proper thing for your headquarters. The historical interest should settle this . . . as no modern design can be so fitting or suit our scheme so well." As the building progressed and the various structures began to take on character, Burnham grew increasingly attracted to "classical" architecture. He had greatly admired the better work of Richardson, Sullivan, and Root, but had he ever really understood how much *besides* the "Romanesque" each had forged into his art? Maybe so, maybe not. He had seldom ever designed the details of a building. In any case, the Romanesque was *their* idiom, not his own, and besides, he thought, it had run its course. In his generation, on the other hand, there had been little neoclassical architecture in America, and almost none in Chicago. For these, and other reasons, he liked what he saw rising up before him in Jackson Park. He liked it because it seemed different, because, in Chicago, at least, it seemed new, and because it seemed somehow now to be his metier. His exuberance of discovery blinded him increasingly to the sad fact that the "fresh," orderly, and incipiently fashionable neoclassical mode would be as unsatisfactory to modern American needs as the incipiently unfashionable genres of Victorian electicism.[11]

In addition to the buildings of the central court, the United States pavilion, designed by government architect James Windrim, was also neoclassical, as was the Horticulture Building on the Lagoon, by Wil-

Fisheries Building, World's Columbian Exposition, by Henry Ives Cobb.
Glimpses of the World's Fair.

liam L. Jenney, the "father of the skyscraper." Finally designed by
Charles Atwood, the Fine Arts Building rose in the north end of Jackson Park as another neoclassical structure. Atwood also used neoclassical
modes in his designs for the train station, the music hall, the casino, and
the lake-shore peristyle connecting them. In the only architectural competition of the fair, the Woman's Department, led by Mrs. Potter
Palmer, selected for the Woman's Pavilion a neoclassical design by
Sophia Hayden of M.I.T. Only Sullivan's Transportation Building and
Cobb's Fisheries Building eschewed the neo-classical motifs.[12]

Harriet Monroe thought that Cobb's building came closest to representing Root's original idea of what the fair should have been, but few
contemporaries echoed her view. The Transportation Building of Louis
Sullivan was somewhat more appealing, both to laymen and to architectural critics, owing largely to its sensational "golden door" as its central
entrance way. Though it would later become a symbol among Burnham's detractors of what the entire exposition *should* have been architecturally, one contemporary expert noticed structural and planning de-

fects. "The plan of the . . . building," wrote Director-General George Davis, "while lending itself to some excellent effects in a decorative way, is such as to make proper installation exceedingly difficult. It is, for instance, impractical to place the largest exhibits under the highest roof and many of the most important and in everyway most attractive exhibits must be relegated to the least desirable portions of the annex." Sullivan had, in other words, violated his famous credo that form should *follow* function. While contending that he had followed his principle by making the building decorative and gay as the carnival atmosphere of the exposition dictated, in reality he had totally ignored the building's interior function—housing for vehicular and transportation exhibits. Sullivan's admiring and sympathetic contemporary critic, Montgomery Schuyler, believed moreover that "the color treatment is not successful" and the elegant doorway "suffers from being an isolated fragment" stuck in front of a large shed. Indeed, the most discerning critics, then and later, agreed that the building's better attributes were its comparative simplicity of profile, its voluptuous organic ornament, and its famous "golden doorway." Though the ornament was Sullivan's

Transportation Building, World's Columbian Exposition, by Sullivan and Adler. *Glimpses of the World's Fair.*

The "Golden Door" of the Transportation Building. Courtesy Chicago Art
Institute.

own, the incipient neoclassicist Daniel Burnham ironically had much to
do with the building's other two major features.[13]

After submitting their original proposals, Adler and Sullivan had then
decided to use large amounts of sculpture on their structure's façade.
The committee had, however, already approved their budget and would
not allow the additional expenditure. But Burnham stated other reasons
as well when he instructed the firm to eliminate the extra sculpture from
its drawings. "Simplicity of treatment, where your structure will go, is
essential," he wrote, "you should reconsider the disposition and extent
of figure work." But even earlier, he had a more important recommendation. "My dear Louis," he wrote, after seeing the initial plans, "the best
possible method for handling the axis trouble we discovered the other
day will be for you to have one grand entrance toward the east and make
this much richer than either of the other you had proposed. Let this be
on the main axis running through the center of the Manufactures Build-

ing. It is the natural place for an entrance anyway. . . . Am sure that
the effect of your building will be much finer than by the old method of
two entrances on this side, neither of which could be so fine and effective as this one central feature." Burnham, therefore, conceived and encouraged two of his building's most distinctive features—the relatively
plain profile and the single grand entrance—though Sullivan, of course,
could never have acknowledged these contributions in his later denun-
ciation of Burnham and the fair.[14]

Sullivan's building was, in fact, the only major structure at the exposition to follow a varied color scheme. William Pretyman, the fair's first
"director of color" in charge of decoration, had suggested an ivory tint
for the major buildings, but Burnham recalled that the eastern architects "came out when Beman's building was nearly finished" and suggested an alteration that became one of the exposition's leading trademarks. "I was urging everyone on," Burnham later recalled to Charles
Moore, "knowing it was an awful fight against time. We talked about
colors and finally the thought came, 'Let us make it all perfectly white.'
I don't recall who made the suggestion. It might have been one of those
things that occurred to all minds at once, as so often happens. At any
rate, the decision was mine. At the time, Pretyman was in the East, and
I had Beman's building made cream white. When Pretyman came back
he was outraged. He said that so long as he was in charge, I must not
interfere. I told him that I did not see it that way; that I had the decision. He then said he would get out and he did." Frank Millet assumed
his duties. The whiteness of the buildings ultimately punctuated the
neoclassical ambiance of the fair, adding yet another element that
evoked the far-away, long-ago marble of Italy and Greece.[15]

The fair was, indeed, a stimulus to both sides of the growing schism
in Burnham's professional make-up, for if his movement toward classicism augured ill for his aesthetic future, the practical administrative
skills he was developing honed his executive talents. Among his subordinates, Burnham communicated most often with Superintendent
Geraldine and Chief Engineer Gottlieb. Most of his instructions were
oral and hence, unrecorded, but occasionally he gave written notices,
for the record. "Please let me have each Saturday at noon sharp, a written report of progress of your works, since preceding Saturday noon," he
wrote to all his department heads. "Include no recommendations in
these reports (these should be written separately) but simply describe
what has actually been done in seven days." He constantly urged econ-

omy and reprimanded Geraldine for purchasing items that had not been approved. He appreciated his superintendent's aggressiveness, however, and wrote to him in September to "make no apology for your persistence. It is approved and appreciated." When Geraldine suggested that Burnham petition the Grounds and Buildings Committee for a particular request, however, Burnham replied that he preferred to do what he could on his own and did "not wish to ask anything of any committee that can be avoided. I am committee-ridden now."[16]

"We are very far behind on the foundations . . . for the Fisheries Building," he wrote to Gottlieb in the spring of 1891, and suggested that "the men be worked at night in order to get this work through on time. . . ." Though Burnham delegated much authority to his staff officers, he also, when necessary, overrode decisions, analyses, and recommendations they had made. He had, for example, recently inspected the Agriculture Building, he wrote Gottlieb in July 1891, and did "not feel completely satisfied with the test made at the N.W. corner for bearing weight of ground." In suggesting a remedy, he displayed the technical acumen acquired in his early skyscraper days. "In order to test the weak spots found in the sites for Manufactures and Agriculture Buildings," he advised, "you will please at once proceed as follows: Cover a space 4 feet square with 3 inch plank, laid cross-wise, and place thereon 16 tons of RR iron, being one ton to the square foot. Before doing this, soak the ground with water and ram solid. Take levels and watch closely for four days, and then increase the load to 24 tons, or 1½ tons per square foot. Take levels and watch closely as before, and make a careful report to me of the result in each case."[17]

In August 1891, personal friction between Gottlieb and Burnham resulted in the engineer's resignation. Edward Shankland, from Burnham's own firm, took Gottlieb's place. "Your glory in this work," Burnham told Shankland in early 1892, "will be of the utmost value to you and to me for you. It must count as in my case against the larger earning I might make by myself." Except for Gottlieb and Pretyman, Burnham got along well with all his department heads and indeed had professional respect for them all, including the two defectors. "The force today," he wrote in July 1891, "has not a piece of dead timber in it, but is working with unusual vigor and unity." And "the force" reciprocated his respect. Shankland spoke for most of his colleagues when he told the American Institute of Architects that Burnham was a "tower of strength" for all of them. "His grand courage has always been an inspiration to us," he asserted. "If we had doubts, if we were discouraged; if, as often happens in any great enterprise we felt like throwing up the sponge, we had only to turn our eyes to him and gain new strength and new encouragement from his undaunted spirit. He always led as a true leader should. If he asked us to work until two in the morning he was sure to be at work with us, and worked longer and harder. His loyalty to his staff was so consistent and so unchanging that each of us felt he had the perfect trust and confidence of the chief. This loyalty has been our greatest stimulus and our greatest support at all times and in all difficulties."[18]

Despite the fair's temporary nature and its uniqueness as a building enterprise, it nevertheless was subjected to some of the agony of the Chicago labor strife of the late 1880s and early 1890s. Building trade organizers attempted to make the building of the exposition a complete "union job," but the directors refused, agreeing instead to a kind of company union in which "all disputes should be settled by arbitration." They agreed to hire union men on an individual basis, but they would not agree, until 1893, to a minimum wage, exposing the enterprise to continuing outside attack from the more determined and militant unionists. By no means hostile to organized labor, Burnham felt that the timely and temporary nature of the exposition warranted the directors' decisions to avoid dealing with organized unions and risk, thereby, the possibility of a totally destructive strike.[19]

Burnham, as a matter of fact, knew more clearly than anyone else the time pressure he was working under. As a result, he had little sympathy for the labor agitators who attempted to subvert his operation either from the outside or by infiltrating the labor force or visitors' contingent. He wrote to President Gage, for example, as early as February 14, 1891, that McArthur Brothers, Contractors, "have come to demand that some action be taken at once for the protection of their forces employed in the peaceful work of dredging and filling Jackson Park. There is a large crowd of persons who seem to have no employment but who are intimidating and driving away their men from their business, and the proper authorities ought to be compelled to gives Messrs. McArthur . . . relief from this annoyance at once." Burnham asked Gage to "give this matter attention" and to let him know "what measures are taken." Usually "the measures taken" involved a tighter policing of the Jackson Park area.[20]

Answering an enquiry as to "whether or not our draughtsmen were hired in Europe as reported," Burnham replied that "such [a] report was entirely erroneous. All our draughtsmen have been employed here, irrespective of nationality, or any other consideration except ability." Indeed many draftsmen and other workers on the more artistic endeavors were of recent European origin, but in choosing men for positions as watchmen and security guards, Burnham was more conservative. "Select native-born Americans [as] far as possible," he told Geraldine. "Take no man without very strong references and avoid placing any labor agitator of any description on the work." But there were equally important physical qualifications. "We have to be very particular about our watchmen," he argued. "Their work will soon be very heavy and we are selecting strong men bodily." If a man could "endure and is strong, send him to me and I will try him. . . . Don't send him if not in good shape."[21]

Burnham would not hesitate to fire workers, remove pass privileges, or eject visitors from the grounds if he thought they endangered his operation. He returned to the issuing committee a pass for a man "who proved when inside to be a walking delegate, showing a card of his union on which he claimed he could do as he liked. . . . He was making trouble and delaying men at their work, and was put out of the grounds without force; but only after having been warned to behave himself and he had not done so." In January 1892, Burnham asked for the authority to control the pass section. "The experience of the past few months," he argued, "has shown to us that many objectionable characters have gained entrance to the Park and . . . have been a great source of annoyance, if not of absolute danger to us."[22]

If Burnham sensed any unwarranted prejudice or discrimination in the hiring or treatment of individual workers, however, he took steps to correct the situation. He wrote to Geraldine in late February 1892 that "Mr. Samuel Gompers, representing the American Federation of Labor, has called at my office and tells me that discrimination is being made against [hiring] union men at Jackson Park." If such was the case, Burnham wanted corrective action. He asked Geraldine to "take the matter up at once, make a careful investigation, and advise me fully regarding the matter." The only preferential hiring that Burnham sanctioned was in the case of applicants who owned stock in the Exposition Corporation. Hoping that the fair would be a financial success, he believed that stock and profit sharing among the working force would stimulate interest and efficiency. He therefore wrote to all the contractors "requesting that they give preference, other considerations being equal" to exposition stock subscribers.[23]

Aside from his cautious approach on the union question, Burnham was generally sympathetic to workers' needs and problems. The large number of accidents caused him to take all possible safety precautions and to insist on compensation for injured workers or their families. At one time, he thought, the workers' food was "below par" and he demanded changes. He also ordered that "all water drunk or used in food preparation must be carefully boiled and stored." Though workmen were "to be paid only for time actually served," he would be glad to give special attention to "cases of absence for any cause where it would be humane to allow for time lost. . . ." When budgetary problems and the fluctuating and temporary nature of the construction work made it necessary to release some workers, he asked Geraldine to reconsider his dismissal actions in certain special cases. One John McRae, for example, had been led to believe that his job would last longer, had "resigned another position and had moved his family into the Jackson Park neighborhood." He was very "hard up," and Burnham asked that he be rehired.[24]

Burnham also had to deal with rumors and erroneous newspaper stories of alleged disasters on the site with implicit predictions of ultimate doom for the exposition. James Dredge, an English journalist and friend of Burnham's, warned him periodically of such reports. One erroneous report contained the prediction that the entire site would soon be flooded by a rise in the level of Lake Michigan. Other rumors abounded. "Your agent," he wrote to Dredge in November 1891, "mentioned that our friend, the secret enemy (whoever he may be), is still sowing rumors to our detriment, and especially is using the old tale of insecurity of the buildings. You were fully acquainted with the fact on which this was founded, as the matter occurred in the summer before your visit. The engineer in charge of construction [Gottlieb] was found not to have figured for wind pressure. Though he left us at that time because I ordered strength added to meet this possibility, he still maintains that the structures were strong enough, and some good engineers agree with him. I could not, however, take his view and had all the drawings refigured for strains due to this cause. None of the buildings were then above the foundations and therefore the work now going up is revised to this point. . . . This may be going to extremes, but to me it seems wise and prudent in view of the great interests involved. . . .

The solidity of our buildings," he concluded "as compared to those of previous fairs is commented upon by every travelled guest." False rumors and garbled reports of his work bothered Burnham greatly. After various members of the staff had leaked ultimately incorrect information to the press and a wandering Chicago *Inter Ocean* reporter was caught stealing sketches from the drafting room, Burnham tightened up his press policy. Only his office would give statements to and deal with the press.[25]

In addition to the big problems, there were always the tedious and often menial details. Businessmen and manufacturers besieged Burnham asking that he use their products in building the fair. The budget forced him to be frugal, and Burnham, stoically, investigated the ramifications of each new expenditure. Even in smaller matters, however, he seemed to enjoy his position and always proceeded as seriously as he did on large policy decisions. "I would like," he wrote gravely to one business house, "to have you state to me in strictest confidence what lawn mowers stand highest in your consideration and for what reasons? I am sure you will inform me without being prejudiced by your interests in any special manufacture as I need to get at the exact truth." The design of such items as gate passes, the exposition seal, and the various medals and diplomas also concerned Burnham greatly. The seal, he argued, would "be largely distributed throughout foreign countries and is one of those trivial things by which people will judge the artistic standard of the fair. It should be carefully designed," he thought, "both from the artistic and popular standpoint and should be made by the very best sculptors either here or in Vienna."[26]

Burnham was never reluctant to engage in political gamesmanship if he could not reach his ends by more conventional means. He needed an experienced and professional military officer to become the chief of the exposition's Police Department and Fire Department and after careful screening he found the man for the job, Edmund Rice, an Army colonel, then stationed in Chicago. His selection, Burnham argued, "brings us in perfect harmony with all Army people here and generally eases things up more than would be the case with an officer from outside the military district." But having an officer's assignment changed in the middle of a tour for such a unique and basically nonmilitary assignment was neither a quick nor an easy task. Seeking immediate action Burnham asked his old friend, William E. Curtis, the secretary of war, as well as the secretary of state, James G. Blaine, to ask the President to order the transfer. Rice promptly became chief of police and firemen in November 1891. Burnham was also careful always to meet and talk with the right people at the right times and places if such encounters could enhance or promote a particular goal or project. Though refraining from specifying the exact reasons for the particular request, Burnham wrote, for example, to the manager of an important exposition dinner meeting that "it would result in much good could Mr. H. B. Stone and I be placed at the same table very near General Newberry and Mr. Durbarrow [members of the national Commission] at the banquet Monday evening." Such maneuvers were not unique in Burnham's promotional enterprises, then or later.[27]

A tour of the site was *de rigueur* for all celebrities passing through Chicago. In May of 1891, for example, Burnham replied to the inventor Thomas Edison that he would "be glad to have you give this bureau the honor of a call. It will give me pleasure to explain to you the general scheme of the grounds and buildings and especially the electrical parts, on which latter we very much desire to have your general views." He received from time to time members of the diplomatic corps but it was European and especially English approval of the exposition that counted most with him. "Two colonels of the English Army were here last week," he wrote his London friend James Dredge. "I had the pleasure of showing them through the Park. One was Col. Larking, an agency of the Queen . . . who was very enthusiastic about the enterprise. He took upon departing, a number of photographs with him, stating that he would show them to the Queen and to the Prince of Wales." To Burnham's delight, "he seemed to feel that they would be greatly pleased."[28] But the most important visitors, Burnham knew, were leading members of the American Press.

He thoroughly approved of the suggestion "by several very prominent eastern men, our friends, that we should get the leading man of every New York, Philadelphia and Boston newspaper out here and entertain them at the very earliest date." It was very important, he believed, that "good feeling . . . be engendered before Congress comes to the question of appropriations and to influence some of the legislatures in a legitimate way by informing leaders of the press thoroughly as to the work done here and the scope of the Exposition."[29]

Burnham's decisions on all matters were not based only on expediency and sound business principles, however. Like his fellow Chicagoans, Burnham was aware of Chicago's regional inferiority complex as a "cultureless" city. In his request for extensive improvements in the music facilities he used this self-doubt to defend his proposed expenditures. "Outside peoples already concede our material greatness and that we are well nigh supreme in manufactures and commerce," he wrote. "They do, however, claim that we are not cultivated and refined to the same extent. To remove this impression, the thought and work of this bureau has been mostly bent from the start. In architecture, painting, sculpture, and landscape, I am confident of success, but above all things in art, music should be considered, and the most favorable conditions for it insured." The committee granted his request.[30]

The numerous frustrations that Burnham faced often made him long to get away. In November 1891 he wrote to an old friend, with whom he had hunted in northern Wisconsin: "Since I was up there with you, I have thought of the place very often and have wished myself back again. I think that a friend of mine and myself may go up for awhile, and I write to ask what the outlook is for deer. . . . Is there a good chance to shoot a buck on the run in the daytime?" He was able to spend little time with his family in Evanston though he often had them, especially his sons, down to his cabin in the park. He found occasional relief on trips to New York to confer with the eastern architects. On one such occasion, Charles McKim gave a festive dinner at Delmonico's. Burnham recalled many years later that "it was quite an affair." Not that life at Jackson Park was ever really dull. Burnham began his work at daybreak with an inspection of the grounds and ended it with a daily staff meeting. The after-dinner hours, however, usually gave way to less formal and rigorous pursuits. He liked to invite old friends and personal acquaintances to come and "camp out," warning them that they would get only "straw beds and hard tack, of course." Led by the earthy raconteur, Frank Millet, the evenings were often quite jovial affairs, and occasional stories reached the city of the nocturnal "revels" at Jackson Park.[31]

The winter of 1891-92 was relatively mild and Burnham's construction force made considerable progress through the summer of 1892. In that year another major problem was finally solved. When Burnham, Olmsted, Codman, and Root had originally planned the exposition they all agreed to reserve the wooded island in the center of the lagoon as a natural horticultural preserve, free of buildings and other impediments. This choice spot, however, appealed to many exhibitors and Burnham received numerous petitions asking for a building permit. He refused an early petition from the Japanese government and another from the United States government for an "ethnological exhibit of Indian industries," but he had considerably more trouble with the persistent young Theodore Roosevelt, "a member of many sporting clubs, among others, the Boon and Crockett," who wanted to establish a model "hunters' camp" on the island. Burnham, himself a hunter, thought the camp might not be so bad "snuggled in among the trees purely as an exhibit provided it shall be concealed only to be noticed casually by those on the Island and not at all from the shore." Olmsted refused to allow this, but agreed that Burnham could offer Roosevelt one of the smaller islands south of the larger wooded island. Writing to Roosevelt's intermediary, W. I. Buchanan, chief of the exposition's Department of Agriculture, Burnham approved the idea "provided there will be no buildings connected with same, and that it not be made in such an expensive manner as to indicate a permanent arrangement. Messrs. Olmsted and Company do not object to having a few tents, some horses, camp-fire, etc. placed there." The conditions did not satisfy Roosevelt, however, who continued "agitating the subject of a hunters' camp." Burnham's last suggestion in the spring of 1892 was for a hunters' camp in connection with the "anglers' camp" near the Fisheries Building, but Roosevelt wanted only the choice spot and the world's fair hunters' camp died before it was born.[32]

Finally, in 1892 Burnham urged Olmsted to accede to Japan's proposal to locate its small and elegantly simple pavilion on the island. If any building was to go there, the Japanese "ho-o-den" was it. "They propose to do the most exquisitely beautiful things," Burnham wrote Olmsted, "and desire to leave the buildings as a gift to the city of Chicago." Olmsted finally agreed. Few observers regretted placing the Japanese building on the wooded island. It was there that young Frank Lloyd Wright got his first taste of the type of Japanese architecture that would so influence his later thought and work. Indeed, besides Sullivan's Transportation Building, the only building at the fair that Wright admired was the Japanese structure with its low, horizontal lines, its cubistic intersections of surface planes, and its low-pitched roofs with wide, overhanging eaves.[33]

Though the exposition would not open until May 1, 1893, the dedication of the buildings was to take place on October 21, 1892, four hundred years to the day, given the historic calendar variation, after Columbus sighted land. The dedication ceremony was one of the many details

to which Burnham turned his attention. He spared no feelings in criticizing the proposed official format. "I notice," he wrote to the chairman of the "ceremonies committee," that "a programme is out this
morning. It is the old perfunctory one, lacking originality, and entirely
commonplace. If we are to do what the world fairly looks for from Chicago, it will be necessary to at once call on the men best fitted to work
out the problem you have in hand, and not allow this important matter
to slip into the worn grooves." Such proceedings, he argued, illustrating
his concern for the "Chicago image," were "familiar to everyone and in
which Europeans beat us badly and render our utmost efforts tame and
uninteresting except for profusion and glare." Though usually Burnham
effected great rapport and sympathy with the business community, he
told Chairman Lawrence that without expert professional advice, his
committee's "men of business . . . cannot expect to evolve new ideas,
which alone should be tolerated. How can you expect to reach any but
familiar stock conclusions?" he asked. "Are you going to rest at these,
and let this, which should be the greatest ceremonial of all time, lack
the very element needed to make it a great historical event?"[34]

In the following months, the Ceremonies Committee, with Burnham's advice, improved its program in the hopes of effecting "a great historical event." If the result was not the "greatest ceremonial of all
time," it was impressive. An elaborate procession of carriages and military units paraded from the center of the city to the mammoth semi-
completed Manufactures Building in Jackson Park. Theodore Thomas'
Chicago Orchestra played the specially composed "Columbian March."
Chicago Mayor Hempstead Washburn delivered an address. The Columbian Chorus sang, and a New York elocutionist, Sarah LeMoyne,
read portions of Harriet Monroe's "Columbian Ode." Burnham's
speech as he "tendered the buildings" to the exposition President, illustrated both his curious syntax and his freedom from understatement.
"When this day shall stand in the long perspective of the past and your
children read the story, it will be called an epoch—one of those rare moments which can only with intervals of centuries come. I congratulate
the city upon the devotion and the generosity of her sons, which have
made this day possible. I congratulate the company upon the success it
has attained by its wise course in suffering its expert advisers to lead it
on and in supporting them so nobly with its millions and its perfect
faith. I congratulate the whole country in the possession of such a pop-
ulace, whose spirit has risen to such an occasion. And I congratulate the

world upon the result." "You have freed the allied arts," he told his audience, "you have bidden architecture, sculpture, painting, and music to be free . . . and the allied arts have repaid your devotion and have produced this result." Burnham then presented the artists and architects who had designed the fair, awarding them with "commemorative medals . . . struck for the occasion." The chorus sang Mendelssohn's "To the Sons of Art." Mrs. Potter Palmer spoke for the Board of Lady Managers. Exposition President Harlow N. Higinbotham "tendered" the buildings to the national commission president Thomas W. Palmer who spoke and tendered them in turn to the Honorable Levi P. Morton, Vice-President of the United States. Morton finally ended the grand procedure by dedicating "the buildings and their appurtenances to the world's progress in arts, in science, in agriculture, and in manufacture." Lastly, he concluded, "I dedicate them to humanity." The few cynics who may have been present must have wondered at the discrepancy between the oratory and the yet unfinished buildings, still covered with scaffolding and surrounded by rubble. Much, obviously, remained to be done before the public opening in May 1893, and neither nature nor organized labor smiled on the final months of construction.[35]

Typical of the frustrations Burnham faced in building and completing the fair was the series of exigent alterations in the construction of Post's Manufactures and Liberal Arts Building, destined to become in its short life the largest building in the world. Shortly after the beginning of construction, it had become apparent that the space which the building provided would be totally inadequate for the required exhibits. The original plan, roughly in the form of an angular figure eight, had called for two interior courts, each surrounded by exhibition rooms and a large dome over the center section dividing the courts. The demand for more space had required the conversion of the courts into exhibition halls, the elimination of the dome, and the construction of a gigantic glass roof supported by steel-trussed arches to cover the great open inner spaces of the building. The "rapidity of action, and the fertility of resource, coupled with boldness and audacity," observed exposition President Higinbotham "were the notable characteristics of the Construction Department. The radical change in this structure . . . was determined upon and designed in a very few days after the conditions which required it were fully understood, and unlike most radical changes in architectural design, the change was successful from both an artistic and a practical point of view." Though Higinbotham's assess-

Manufactures and Liberal Arts Building, World's Columbian Exposition, by
George B. Post, after storm damage, winter 1892-93. Courtesy Chicago Art
Institute.

ment was ultimately correct, the extremely inclement winter of 1892-93
created its own intermediate complications. That winter, it snowed
heavily in Chicago. Several sections of the glass roof collapsed and damaged numerous exhibits in the process of being installed. After the building's contractor failed to stop the leaking, the Construction Department
added hundreds of extra roofers to complete the job. Burnham's interest
in the building continued to the last detail. "Its severity and great size,"
he decided, "demands livening up," and he proposed that "five or six
small restaurants be placed on the promenade . . . gay in color and yet
refined and severe in design."[36]

By the beginning of 1893, the completion of most of the work seemed
probable, but several buildings, including Stearns and Peabody's Machinery Hall, were far behind schedule, necessitating increased construction crews working overtime. "Doubts as to the possibility of completing
the Exposition were freely expressed," Higinbotham later admitted, but
"the great organized army, charged with the duty of completing the Exposition, was sustained by faith and the indomitable energy of the of-

ficers of the several departments. The director of works seemed omni-present. No hour was too early, no weather too severe for him to be abroad, inspecting and directing the progress of the work and urging on his lieutenants." In early April, a strike of all men belonging to the car-penter's union caused even graver doubts that the deadline could be reached but the carpenters soon returned to work when the exposition company guaranteed them "equal consideration with nonunion labor . . . and 'at least the minimum rate of wages' prescribed by their union."[37]

As the work neared completion, the encomiums began, and shortly before the exposition's formal opening, Burnham received a splendid tribute for his key performance as the fair's chief builder. On the eve-ning of March 25, 1893, his fellow artists and architects from the Ex-position and several hundred other leading citizens of New York and the nation honored Burnham with a spectacular banquet in the lushly bedecked Madison Square Garden. Carried off with a flair and a muted extravagance long since associated with Gilded Age society, the affair was chiefly the conception of architects Richard Hunt and Charles McKim, sculptor Augustus St. Gaudens, painter Frank Millet, and *Cen-tury* editor Richard Watson Gilder.[38]

Among the more than two hundred guests were the classical art his-torian Charles Eliot Norton; the novelist William Dean Howells; Johns Hopkins President Daniel Coit Gilman; the music conductor Walter

Work in Progress, Court of Honor, World's Columbian Exposition, June 1892. Courtesy Chicago Art Institute.

Damrosch; the sculptor Daniel Chester French; *Nation* editor E. L. Godkin; the actor Joseph Jefferson; the designer Louis C. Tiffany; the painters Edwin Blashfield, John La Farge, and J. Alden Weir; the architects William L. B. Jenney, Frederick Law Olmsted, and Henry Van Brunt; and the businessmen-art patrons Charles Hutchinson, P. A. B. Widener, James Ellsworth, Henry Villard, Marshall Field, Abram Hewitt, and Lyman J. Gage. President Cleveland expressed by letter his regrets that he could not attend the banquet and added his appreciation of Burnham's work.[39]

"The occasion was one of uncommon interest," observed the *New York Times*, "and the enthusiasm it evoked was infectious. It brought together some of the most eminent men in New York, and the gallery of the beautiful hall was thronged with women in evening dress. Music in abundant variety by the Hungarian band enlivened the two hours or more which passed while the dinner was being served . . . and while the diners were enjoying their coffee and cigars, the lights were turned down and a score or more of superb stereoscopic views of the exposition buildings were displayed on a large screen."[40]

To commemorate the occasion and to serve as a lasting tribute to Burnham's achievement, "a massive loving cup of solid silver, fully one foot in height, was presented to Mr. Burnham by Chairman Hunt," the *Times* noted "in phrases so complimentary and appreciative that they evoked unbounded enthusiasm." Burnham, himself, then filled the cup with wine and had it passed "from lip to lip around the room, each distinguished man being warmly cheered as he drank." Hunt then proposed a toast to Burnham and "each member of the company rose to his feet and drank with hearty good will." With obvious delight and appreciation Burnham responded to the tribute and acknowledged the contributions of his fellow artists and builders, especially Frederick Law Olmsted. Toasts and short speeches followed by Charles Eliot Norton, Richard Watson Gilder, and Lyman J. Gage. Other speakers alluded with uncommon levity to the long and often heated rivalry between New York and Chicago. Indeed the New Yorkers' gracious recognition of Burnham and the Chicago fair contrasted starkly with the initially cool reception he had gotten two years earlier when he first came to make proposals and to solicit their support in building the exposition.[41]

Always respectful of academic "authority," Burnham especially appreciated the remarks of Harvard Professor Charles Eliot Norton. Saluting and encouraging the incipient classical revival in American ar-

Court of Honor, looking west to the Administration Building, by Richard M. Hunt. Courtesy Chicago Art Institute.

chitecture, Norton spoke to both sides of Burnham's recently cultivated biases—his new enthusiasm for monumental classicism and his awakening interest in area planning. "The general design of the grounds and the arrangement of the buildings," Norton stated, "was in every respect noble, original and satisfactory, a work of fine art. . . ." The Court of Honor, he thought, made "a splendid display of monumental architecture. They show well how our ablest architects have studied the work of the past; and the arrangement of buildings according to the general plan produces a superb effect in the successful grouping in harmonious relationships of vast and magnificent structures."[42]

Burnham believed, indeed, that Norton's toast "was the most important address of the night," and upon returning to Chicago requested a copy to reread carefully and to show as well to "the several men here who wish to see it." He was also much impressed, he confided to Norton, with William Dean Howells, the "Altrurian Traveller" whom Burnham would soon host in Chicago at the fair. "I fear he thought me rude," Burnham admitted, "because I used my short time well in look-

ing him over; but if he did, it pays me well. I never saw such a face before and everything about the man fitted into my way of thinking and
liking at once." Howells and Norton soon reciprocated Burnham's
compliments in their warm enthusiasm for the completed "White
City."[43]

After two and a half years of planning and building, the fair opened
on May 1, 1893. The final result was more successful than its builders
had expected, but the amazement of the uninitiated was even more
pronounced. It seemed to most visitors that, indeed, a vision had "appeared on the shores of Lake Michigan, springing full bloom like a sudden summer flower." Despite the Depression of 1893, a later description read, "the public rubbed its eyes and came in thousands. Flags
waved in the hot midwestern sun, and the air was filled with the rush
of water from fountains and the murmur of admiring crowds."[44]

All of the buildings around the Court of Honor and most of the ma-

Court of Honor, looking south to Agriculture Building. *Left:* McKim, Mead,
and White, and Engineering Building; *right:* Peabody, and Stearns. Courtesy
Chicago Art Institute.

Court of Honor, looking northeast to Manufactures and Liberal Arts Building, by George B. Post. Courtesy Chicago Art Institute.

jor structures on the lagoons were variations of Roman and Renaissance adaptations of classical Ionic and Corinthian orders. The basic materials of the major buildings were steel, wood, glass, and plaster painted white. Murals by the American painters Edwin Blashfield, Kenyon Cox, Alden Weir, and Gari Melchers graced the walls of the various interiors. Sculpture by such notables as Karl Bitter, Lorado Taft, and Paul Bartlett adorned the buildings and promenades. The two most colossal pieces were the fountain of Frederick MacMonnies in front of the Administration Building and the statue of the "Republic" at the eastern end of the basin by Daniel Chester French. Augustus St. Gaudens had supervised the sculpture of the exposition as Frank Millet had the painting and interior decoration. The spectacle was especially impressive when floodlighted at night, using in the process three times as much electricity as the entire city of Chicago did in the same period.[45]

Visitors came from every part of the world, and from the Chicago area, at least, from every stratum of society. The total paid admissions of 21,480,141 brought in gate receipts of $10,336,065.75. The Duke of

Court of Honor, looking east to the Manufactures Building. *Left:* Peristyle center; *right:* Agriculture Building. *Glimpses of the World's Fair.*

Peristyle, World's Columbian Exposition, by Charles Atwood. Courtesy Chicago Art Institute.

Veraqua, a lineal descendant of Columbus, and the Infanta Eulalia, representing the King of Spain, were the undisputed guests of honor and the centers of attention in Chicago society. The Archduke Ferdinand, heir to the Austro-Hungarian throne also came, but preferred to prowl, unnoticed, around the streets of Chicago. President Cleveland was on hand for the opening. The congressional and diplomatic corps, society leaders from the East and West, and the plain people, especially of the Midwest, thronged the grounds and buildings. Hamlin Garland recorded the dumbfounded awe of his simple frontier parents. Henry Adams came and was sufficiently impressed to devote a chapter of his autobiography to the fair. William Dean Howells was Burnham's personal guest and later used the fair as a utopian symbol of the planned society in his *Letters of an Altrurian Traveler*. Indeed, Burnham's duties and pleasures as host increased as the summer progressed. He remained on the scene much of each day, entertaining visitors and keeping an eye on the buildings and the grounds.[46]

Several months after the fair had opened, Frederick Law Omsted, the inveterate traveler, wrote to Burnham of the exposition's impact on provincial America. Just that spring and summer he had "travelled in sixteen states" and had "seen a great variety of people." "Everywhere," he noted, "there is a *growing* interest in the Exposition. Everywhere I have found indications that people are planning to go to it. In country papers accounts of visits are now appearing adapted to increase the desire to see it. Clergymen who have been to the Fair are referring to it in their sermons. . . . On the platform of a small railway station in Kentucky, a farmer-looking man asked me: 'Been to the Chicago Fair, sir?' 'Yes.' 'Is it as fine as they tell of?' 'Yes, I think so. Are you going to it.' 'Reckon I shall have to; seems like everybody round here means to go, and I don't suppose I can stay back.' "[47]

When Burnham finally resigned in the fall of 1893, the Board of Directors presented him with a memorial of praise and appreciation of his work. "The world will pass on its merits," the testament began, "but none can know so well as ourselves how much of the success of this great Exposition has been due to you." Indeed, when the project began, "no man had any proper conception of what it was to be. It was to be grand and beautiful, but how vast its grandeur and beauty was to be, or what form it was to take, no one had ever dreamed. You were . . . charged with the duty of choosing the designers and artists of the great undertaking and of harmonizing and carrying out their great conceptions. You possessed that rare knowledge of men and their capabilities that enabled you to call to your assistance those best suited to the great work; that breadth of mind to blend their creations into a harmonious whole, and that energy and force to carry the work to an end so glorious and successful as to excite the pride and merit the gratitude of all the people." Even Louis Sullivan agreed that "Burnham performed in a masterful way, displaying remarkable executive capacity. He became open-minded, just, magnanimous. He did his great share."[48]

In the days and decades that followed the fair, the world would, as the board predicted, continue to discuss the exposition and to "pass on its merits." Most people who saw it were ecstatic from the first and usually embroidered their memories as the years passed. No contemporary expressed a completely negative reaction. Only a few artists and intellectuals voiced reservations. While amazed and bewildered on the one hand by the heterogeneous "babel" inherent in all world's fairs, Henry Adams appreciated the relative sense of unity and direction that the White City demonstrated. William Dean Howells was more generally enthusiastic, seeing in the central planning of the exposition a hopeful microcosm of an incipiently socialistic society—a society that would move away from destructively competitive capitalism toward a planned state coordinated for the common good. Burnham must have loved Howells' initial compliment but shuddered at some of its political implications. The muckraking journalist Henry Demarest Lloyd sensed the fair's impact on the ordinary visitor. It "revealed to the people, possibilities of social beauty, utility, and harmony of which they had not been able even to dream. No such vision," he wrote, "could otherwise have entered into the prosaic drudgery of their lives, and it will be felt in their development into the third and fourth generation."[49]

The critic Montgomery Schuyler also approved of the fair's general effect as appropriate to a festive, temporary exposition, but only so long, he emphasized, as no one mistook it for real architecture pertinent to the needs of modern America. In giving even such reserved approval, however, Schuyler failed to heed the acknowledged claims of the builders, especially Burnham, that the fair should not be forgotten in later years and should become, in fact, a model for reforming urban America. Though a willing participant in creating and supporting the great production, Henry Van Brunt agreed with Schuyler that the future relevance of the enterprise should not be misunderstood and went on to suggest that the White City should be received chiefly as an educa-

Spectators looking down on the Court of Honor from the top of the Manufactures Building. Courtesy Chicago Art Institute.

tional exercise. "It is not desired or expected," he asserted, "that this
display, however successful it may prove to be in execution, should make
a new revival or a new school in the architecture of our country or interfere with any healthy advance on classic or romantic lines which may be
evolving here." There were, however, "many uneducated and untrained
men practicing as architects, and still maintaining, especially in the remote regions of the country, an impure and unhealthy vernacular, in-
capable of progress; men who have never seen a pure classic monument
executed on a great scale, and who are ignorant of the emotions which
it must excite in any breast accessible to the influences of art. To such,
it is hoped that these great models, inspired as they have been by a profound respect for the masters of classic art, will prove such a revelation
that they will learn at last that true architecture cannot be based on undisciplined invention, illiterate originality, or indeed, upon any audacity
of ignorance." Van Brunt appreciated and condoned the classical exercise that the fair embodied, much as Schuyler did, but for different rea-

The peristyle columns, looking east to Lake Michigan. Courtesy Chicago Art Institute.

sons. Both agreed, however, on the essential limits of the exposition's architecture. Perhaps they were both confident that the nation would ultimately respond as they had done and would see the fair from their own perspectives as an interesting but temporary phenomenon. Or perhaps they whistled louder because they somehow feared a "classical" inundation.[50]

No one, however, in 1893—not even Daniel Burnham—predicted the effect that the exposition would ultimately have on American architectural taste. If Louis Sullivan harbored such fears, his criticism at the time was relatively restrained. Only in 1924 would he publish his scathing attack on the exposition, whose influence, he believed had "penetrated deep into the constitution of the American mind, effecting there lesions significant of dementia." The unsophisticated crowds, Sullivan argued, had "beheld what was for them an amazing revelation of the architectural art, of which previously they in comparison had known nothing. . . ." The naïve beholders of the spectacle had then "departed joyously, carriers of contagion, unaware that what they had beheld and believed to be truth was to prove, in historic fact, an appalling calamity." Though often guilty of both omission and overstatement, Sullivan's perceptive indictment of the fair's neoclassical legacy contained a great deal of truth. However justified and appropriate it may have seemed at the time, the "classical" White City and the "classical" revival that it introduced were retrograde forces in American culture.[51]

Failing to heed Van Brunt and Schuyler's contemporary strictures on the dangers of a classical revival, Burnham and his devotees continued to exploit both the worst and the best of the exposition's legacies. Had they built on its practical essence only, on its great suggestion of a planned community, the effects of the White City would have been largely positive. That, of course, they did abundantly, but in the process, they also fell willing slaves to the White City's antique "style," the proliferation of which Louis Sullivan so deftly castigated. While Sullivan, however, saw and brilliantly analyzed the fair's decadent legacy to America, he failed to comprehend the paradox of its double role. Burnham misunderstood it too, but from the other direction, having failed to realize that he had taken the chaff with the wheat.

While Sullivan slipped gradually into alcoholism, poverty, and professional neglect, Burnham rode the crest of a wave that would not break until long after his death. In doing so, he exploited both sides of the exposition's influence, while never discerning the dichotomy of its heritage. In the years that followed, Burnham became an important city planner and coordinator of the arts while spreading concurrently the stylistic "virus" of irrelevant "classicism." Indeed, coupled with the death of Root, the Columbian Exposition was the pivotal moment in Burnham's career. In a number of curious and important ways, it dominated his thought for the rest of his life and in so doing affected profoundly the cultural landscape he was striving to transform. In his own mind, he came to see the White City of 1893 as his life's most significant watershed. Ultimately, both for him and for American architecture, it was even more important than he realized.

VI
Legacies of the Fair

1894–1901

*People are no longer ignorant regarding architectural matters.
They have been awakened through the display of the World's
Columbian Exposition of 1893. . . .*

DANIEL BURNHAM
1894

THE WORLD'S FAIR did many things for Daniel Burnham. It enhanced his already eminent reputation as an architect, organizer, and promoter. It enlarged his circle of close friends and professional associates—many of whom would continue to work with him on other projects and would influence and be influenced by him the rest of his life. It satiated, for the moment, his unrelenting quest for advancement, and allowed him to punctuate stretches of exhausting work with moments of leisure, recreation, and worldly pleasure. Finally, the fair brought him long-sought intellectual and professional honors.

In 1894, in recognition of his achievement, Yale and Harvard, the universities that had failed to admit him as a student some thirty years earlier, conferred on him honorary master of arts degrees. Harvard appropriately praised his great "classical" enterprise in the recognizable academic Latin of the day: "*Danielem Hudson Burnham,*" the citation read, "*spectaculi omnium gentium Columbians' administratorum qui, ingeniorum inventorumque, aestimator acutus, res maximus ab aliis mente conceptas ad exitum feliciter produxit. Artium Magistros.*" In 1894, Northwestern University gave Burnham his first honorary doctorate.[1]

Burnham relished these academic honors, but he took even greater pride in the official recognition given him by his professional peers. In 1893 and 1894, the American Institute of Architects elected him its president. In his inaugural address, Burnham dealt with professional ethics and standards and the obligations of individual architects to their fellow practitioners. How far, he asked, should the A.I.A. press its members to conform to the institute's prescribed rules, especially to its fee schedule of a percentage commission on a building's total cost? The influence of the organization over individual architects, he stated, should be largely moral, not legal. Members should be "moved more by a desire to conform to the established standards of professional life than by any fear of discipline." While he hoped, indeed, that all worthy and competent architects would join the institute, he insisted that the A.I.A. refrain from pressuring reluctant candidates. "I think every man must be left to be independent," he said. "There may be plenty of practitioners who don't desire to join any society; whose . . . theories of life are opposed to society life; a stigma has already been cast upon this society," he stated, as it has been "said that we were a trades union. . . . We do not want to be a trades union. We do not want power in the sense of having all the architects united under us to force a certain conclusion of ours, except through moral influence."[2]

He then directed his audience to another matter, one that would consume the major portion of his time and energy as president of the A.I.A. —the means to improving the quality of federal government architecture. Architects and interested citizens across the country had long noted the inferior designs for government buildings emanating from the office of the Supervising Architect in Washington, D.C. Irrelevantly and anomalously sheltered in the Department of Treasury, the low-paying, overworked, post had not been held, at any time since the Civil War, by an official with talent comparable to that of the nation's leading independent architects. The heavy burden of work, moreover, both administrative and technical, further demanded that the actual designing of buildings be passed on to assistants and apprentices of even less talent than their supervisor. The result was a succession of eclectic Victorian failures that most acknowledged arbiters of taste regretted and rejected.[3]

The A.I.A.'s opposition to continuing under this arrangement had long been on record. During the early 1880s, in fact, Burnham and Dankmar Adler, representing the Chicago-based Western Association of Architects, had made an unsuccessful attempt to solicit congressional interest in reform. In early 1893, however, the long years of lobbying finally appeared to have achieved success when Congress passed the Tarsney Act for the regulation of governmental architectural projects.

Approved by President Benjamin Harrison near the end of his administration, the measure authorized the supervising architect to hold design competitions and to solicit plans from outside professional architects. The winning architect would oversee the construction of the
building although ultimate administrative and supervisory authority
would remain with the government architect. Shortly after the passage
of the act, a delegation from the A.I.A., including Hunt and McKim,
called on Secretary of the Treasury John G. Carlisle of the new Cleveland Cabinet to discuss implementation of the bill. Carlisle assured
them of his intention to begin to carry out its provisions forthwith.[4]

Burnham, therefore, began his presidency with guarded optimism.
The bill provided for a commission of five to judge competitions and
select winning designs, three members of whom were to be architects appointed by the President. He urged the institute members to accept such
an assignment conscientiously if and when they were appointed, since
the commission members would be largely responsible for the success or
failure of the program. "If an American would serve his country in any
public capacity," he exhorted them, "it must nearly always be done at
great personal cost. . . ." He was certain that the President would tend
to appoint the kind of "men who can least afford to give their time to
the work. But they must accept, because in their hands will lie the fate
of this glorious opportunity."[5]

Burnham's call for cooperation and implementation, however, was
somewhat premature since eight months elapsed after the passage of the
bill without action from the secretary or the supervising architect. On
November 6, 1893, Alfred Stone, A.I.A. secretary, wrote to Supervising
Architect Jeremiah O'Rourke on behalf of the institute reminding him
of Secretary Carlisle's earlier statement of support and inquiring as to
why there had been no action. O'Rourke replied briskly that there had
been no reason for the delay "beyond the fact that the Secretary's time
has been so fully occupied by public business of the most pressing character. . . ." While, indeed, the national financial problems of 1893 gave
credence to O'Rourke's alibi for the secretary of the treasury, Burnham
had other reasons to believe that the two men were, in any case, less than
enthusiastic about implementing the act.[6]

After years of activity in the cause of better government architecture,
Burnham determined that the matter should drift no longer. With the
legal lever of the Tarsney Act and the strong, wholehearted backing of
his A.I.A. constituency, Burnham resolved to use his position to force a

confrontation. The controversy that ensued raised anew a number of hoary questions about government and the arts, about government architecture, in particular, as a symbol of the nation's cultural achievements, and more obliquely, about the variance between centralized, bureaucratized "mediocrity" and the allegedly more excellent products born of creative, free enterprise capitalism. It also revealed the increasing vigor and temerity of Daniel Burnham as conservative reformer, the steadily developing sense of self-assurance that his work at the fair engendered, and the smooth, straightforward manner of a man with increased conviction, authority, and determination.

In his original interview with the architects, Secretary Carlisle mentioned the proposed federal building in Buffalo, New York, as one which well might be designed under the provisions of the new act. But in January 1894, the government published a finished sketch of the Buffalo building, as designed by the supervising architect. Although the institute had been led to expect that competitive designs would be sought for the building, it would most likely not have raised a protest, Burnham wrote to Secretary Carlisle, "but for the fact that the design was unanimously considered to be inferior and unworthy for the purpose."[7]

Carlisle referred Burnham's letter to Supervising Architect O'Rourke, and O'Rourke's acerbic reply further intensified the conflict. Writing to A.I.A. secretary Alfred Stone, he noted that Carlisle had referred to him "a rather clumsily folded communication, without official heading, accompanied by a design cut from a Buffalo paper, of 'Proposed Federal Building for Buffalo' . . . purporting to be a protest of the Board of Directors of the A.I.A. adopted at a meeting held in New York . . . against the adoption of the said design, signed by D. H. Burnham, President, and several other members of the A.I.A. This communication," he protested, "is of such an unusual and extraordinary character, based on ex parte and indefinite information and so at variance with professional courtesy and good breeding that in justice to the A.I.A. I hesitate to believe in its legitimacy and request that you kindly advise me by return mail if it has really emanated from the Board of Directors of the A.I.A."[8]

Offended by both the substance and the tone of O'Rourke's letter, the A.I.A. protested to Carlisle. Burnham did not, however, allow himself to be caught in an aesthetic fight he might not win. Instead, he argued hard economics. "The government paid out in 1893, for its buildings and repairs, apart from purchases of ground, about $3,200,000. The total expenses of the Supervising Architect's Office for 1893 were $198,000 or six per cent of the cost of the work actually done." Compared to the 6 per cent government expenditure, Burnham asserted, "the price for the same service by the best men in the country in private life is five per cent, or one per cent less than the actual cost to the United States for the same thing in 1893. This one per cent ought to very much more than cover the cost of the services, which, under the bill, the Supervisory Architect would still have to furnish, i.e., that of estimating, inspecting of accounts, auditing, and such superintendence as would be needed to supplement that done by the architects themselves. . . . Instead of its costing the government more for architectural service if private practitioners be employed," Burnham believed, "the cost will be reduced and there will be a considerable saving." He made clear to Carlisle that members of the architectural profession in Buffalo as well as many interested laymen wanted the matter thrown open to competition. There and elsewhere, he argued confidently, people "are no longer ignorant regarding architectural matters. They have been awakened through the display of the World's Columbian Exposition of 1893, where it was generally remarked that the Government Building was inferior to any of the other large structures."[9]

In answer to the government's argument that immediate construction, to supply jobs, had made necessary the suspension of the time-consuming outside competition, Burnham argued that the government "was mistaken about the urgency of the Buffalo people to have the building started at once, because of the need of furnishing employment to laborers." In fact, he "had a number of clippings from the Buffalo papers, some of them being editorials, in which this position is strongly controverted." Indeed, Burnham reassured Carlisle, "it is felt there that it would be poor economy to push forward an improper design, in order to furnish work a few days earlier for the small number to be employed, and although there is sympathy for the unemployed, this course would ultimately cost the city a price it is not willing to pay. The competition can be carried through in an exceedingly short time, if you will order it. . . . We are also ready to assist the government in arrangement of a code for the competition." A.I.A. members would compete without pay, except for the architect whose design was chosen. In closing, Burnham cited a statement in the press from the supervising architect "that it will take three years and a half for his office—as now constituted, to design the buildings already authorized. If this be approximately true," Burnham argued, "the retaining of a number of the most able architects of the country to assist him is imperative—and urgent."[10]

Carlisle's evasive reply annoyed Burnham intensely. The A.I.A.'s suggestions, the secretary noted vaguely, had not yet solved all the problems at hand. Whenever all technicalities could be worked out and translated into law, his department would be happy to "experiment" with the competitive method of employing outside architects. Meanwhile, the plans to build the Buffalo building from existing plans would proceed uninterrupted. In conclusion, Carlisle found it "unnecessary to have another conference, unless you are prepared to suggest such additional legislation as will accomplish the purposes you desire."[11]

Carlisle's recalcitrance provoked a final letter from Burnham that climaxed the long dispute. "I am astonished," Burnham wrote, "by the contents of your letter. . . . Its statements are very inaccurate. . . . The proposed change is not the action desired by the Institute of Architects alone. It is one in which the country is deeply interested." There was no reason, he argued, "why the law may not be put in force at once, nor has there been, that I am able to discover. The working of the Supervising Architect's office . . . is a simple organization which any good businessmen, with a knowledge of building can understand and operate and I venture to assert that if the good will to do so were present in your department, the organization of the office on the basis of the present law, which gives you the right to employ the best designers in the country, could be brought about in a few weeks, and that it would be better than the present one."[12]

Burnham reminded Carlisle that he had not forgotten "the protestations of the Supervising Architect, of his readiness and anxiety to do all in his power to forward this important matter," and that "you yourself stated to the gentlemen of the Institute that you were in hearty accord with them on the subject; I am also aware that twelve long months have since passed, during which nothing whatever has been done in your department looking toward the carrying out of this law. . . . The obstacles are not real ones and never were. . . . You now inform us, in effect, that the law must be amended before you can act under it. I can see but one amendment which is needed to insure the satisfactory working of the measure, i.e., the introduction of a clause ordering the Secretary of the Treasury to carry out its plain intent and purpose and not leaving it to his discretion." Carlisle's reply was short and seemingly final: "Your very offensive and ungentlemanly letter . . . is just received," he said,

Cartoon from *Life* magazine, 1894, on the Tarsney Crisis. Courtesy Chicago Art Institute.

"and you are informed that the Department will have no further correspondence with you upon the subject to which it relates, or any other subject."[13]

The affair then exploded before the country as Burnham made public the long and loaded correspondence. "The disreputable practices of municipal politics rule in the Treasury Department," Burnham told the *New York Times*. "Secretary Carlisle has lied and juggled with the facts. He furnishes a striking example of the result of installing a small man in a large place. It is most unfortunate for the country that he should have under his direction all the architectural work of the government. It is a national misfortune that the men who have charge of the Government architectural work have little or no knowledge of their profession. Secretary Carlisle has utterly ignored the statute which provides for competition in designs for all government buildings." So strong were Burnham's feelings in the matter, moreover, that he proposed that the A.I.A. expel O'Rourke from its membership. Charles McKim, however, while agreeing in principle that "expulsion . . . has been righteously earned by him," persuaded Burnham for tactical reasons to withdraw his plea.[14]

In responding to Burnham's attack, unidentified Treasury officials suggested to the *Times* that Burnham and the A.I.A. were concealing hypocritically beneath their rhetoric, a plain desire to get lucrative government commissions, contending that "this nice little plum . . . can reasonably be supposed to have quite as much weight with the architects as their patriotic desire to improve the character and style of the public buildings." Yet, while the national exposure tended to harden the position of the Treasury Department, most outside observers sided with Burnham, especially those from the world of architecture. The *Inland Architect* praised "President Burnham" for "assuming the tone which he did," and noted that it was "only after these years of disappointment and after learning the hollowness of the pretences of the officials at Washington that he was forced to speak the plain and unmasked truth." It also believed that "the wisdom of the course is now evident to the whole country, as editorials are pouring in from every section approving not only the arrangement of the statements in his letter, but its tone. Outside of two or three strong eastern administrative 'through thick and thin organs,'" it noted, "the press is united in upholding Mr. Burnham in the action he took. . . . Disliking personally to enter a controversy, as president of the Institute and representative of the profession he had no other choice, and has come into the work, as he enters everything he undertakes, with his whole soul, and the same spirit which made the history of his private practice and later the construction of the Columbian Exposition a marvel. . . ."[15]

The *New York Sun* also thought Burnham's rhetoric to be "entirely justifiable" and deplored "the damage done to the public taste by the vile standard established and maintained by the Federal architects." Furthermore, it contended, "the money wasted in the construction of the hundreds of costly post offices and custom houses, drearily commonplace, or startlingly repulsive, according to accident, is nothing in comparison with the permanent injury inflicted upon this generation and succeeding generations by the constant contemplation of these degrading objects."[16]

Despite the high degree of public opinion in his favor, however, Burnham realized that having forced a confrontation, he had also personally reached an impasse with Carlisle and O'Rourke. While continuing to work in the background, therefore, he allowed A.I.A. vice-president George B. Post to press the matter further with government officials.

Secretary Carlisle argued that further legislation was necessary before he *could* take action. Post and other members of the A.I.A. Executive Committee, therefore, attempted to work with him and congressional leaders for this additional legislation. Burnham suspected that Carlisle's new-feigned interest was only a façade for his basically conservative attitudes in the matter, but he supported Post's efforts to achieve the goal both during his own presidency and after Post succeeded him as the institute's chief.[17]

Congressional turnover, political realignment, and various other disparate factors, however, resulted in the congressional defeat of the ensuing McKaig and Aldrich bills for reform of the government architectural system. Carlisle refused to act without them, and the A.I.A. under Burnham and Post refused to keep quiet. Before the end of his two-year presidency, Burnham's fight and position on the matter had been well-published and supported. Especially responsive were many old friends from the Chicago Fair, not least of whom was Lyman J. Gage, the former exposition official. It surprised no one, therefore, in 1896 that when the recently elected McKinley appointed Gage secretary of the treasury, he began at once to enforce the Tarsney Act. Confirming Burnham's contention that the office needed no additional legislation, Gage and the new supervising architect began to implement the four-year-old Tarsney legislation. With the help and advice of the A.I.A., Gage created a program that would operate without drastic change until after World War I. Although some critics would protest the increasingly neoclassical cast of government architecture throughout that period, it was clear that within the stylistic limits the quality of designs showed a marked improvement. For the rest of Burnham's life, at least, the government architecture problem did not reappear. He felt proud of his part in the solution.[18]

Gage was not the only friend from world's fair days to influence Burnham's later life. The list was long, but several names were especially noteworthy: Stanford White of the McKim, Mead, and White partnership remained a favorite artistic arbiter and conferee of Burnham's, especially in matters of interior design and decoration. Theodore Thomas, the fair's director of music and later conductor of the Chicago Symphony became one of Burnham's closest associates. Francis Millet, one of Burnham's chief exposition artistic advisers, remained a lifelong ally, especially in Burnham's public projects. The closest of Burnham's friends from the days of the fair, however, were undoubtedly Charles McKim

and Augustus St. Gaudens, both of whom continued to work with Burnham on other large projects including the later Washington Plan and
the American Academy in Rome. As the years progressed, those friendships deepened. Indeed, the exposition alumni played a role in Burnham's
life after 1893 as significant as his in theirs.

After the long hiatus of the fair and of Root's death, Burnham spent
considerable time visiting his clients, friends, and building projects
around the country. Railroads fascinated him and he never seemed to
tire of riding trains. On the road and in Chicago, Burnham enjoyed an
increasingly active social and cultural life. Though he had never subscribed to the gospel of work to the total exclusion of worldly pleasure,
he began now to allow himself real time for play. In addition to strictly
business notations, his diary came to include more and more personal
and social references. He played golf at the Glenview Country Club
whenever business and weather would allow, often working overtime at
night in his downtown office to justify spending a full day on the Glenview links. He played with his sons and business friends, including Edward Ayer, Will Brown, Martin Ryerson, and Owen Aldis; and seemed
to derive genuine pleasure from the game. "Come out to Glenview," he
wrote a business acquaintance in Pittsburgh. "You have no idea how
beautiful it is out there. There is nothing like it in the country." In addition to the game itself, he also enjoyed the dinners and parties in the
clubhouse with Margaret and other friends.[19]

His lifelong passion for music was enriched by his friendship with the
Thomases and his membership on the symphony Board of Trustees. He
loved Thomas' emphasis on selections from the German masters from
Bach to Wagner, but his music and theater tastes were versatile. In Chicago, he and Margaret enjoyed *Cyrano* and Sarah Bernhardt; in Philadelphia he heard *Die Meistersinger von Nürnberg*; and in Washington
he relished with no less interest the charms of Lillian Russell. He also
enjoyed the social aspects of his business trips—the lunches with the
steelmaker Charles Schwab in Pittsburgh, the reunions with John La
Farge in Philadelphia and Charles McKim in New York. He and Margaret entertained festively and graciously. On January 20, 1901, their
twenty-fifth wedding anniversary, Burnham recorded matter-of-factly
that "50 friends came in and listened to the program of the quartette
of the Chicago orchestra." On February 1 of the same year he and
Margaret gave a sumptuous dinner to the pianist Ignace Paderewski
and to Theodore Thomas at the music hall. During the same years,

Burnham also belonged to all the "right" clubs, the Chicago Club, the Union League Club, and the literary "Little Room," and sat for a portrait by the noted and fashionable Swedish painter Anders Zorn. Although he never became a great political activist, he always voted and supported the Republican ticket and enjoyed attending its local functions, especially its rallies and parades.[20]

Burnham loved to entertain grandly and lavishly, but he took equal pleasure in simple occasions. He and Margaret, with close friends and relatives, especially enjoyed the new card game "bridge." They also took winter sleigh rides with old friends—the Ayers and a younger Oak Park couple, Catherine and Frank Lloyd Wright. Burnham took even greater delight in being with his family, strolling and playing on the lawn with his children and taking long walks and swims with them along the lake. He loved the huge, old farmhouse he had bought in the 1880s, delighting in constant changes and improvements in its design and decoration. He enjoyed shopping for rugs and furniture at Marshall Field's. He especially valued, however, the quiet moments to himself on the back lawn, sketching, painting, or just looking at the lake. Although he was never the active churchgoer or worker in Swedenborgian circles his parents had been, Burnham continued to study the Bible and the writings of Swedenborg and often on Sunday conducted services at home for his family and his friends of the Swedenborgian persuasion.[21]

Burnham's love of travel was not restricted to business affairs. In 1897, with the Ayers and the Gages, he and Margaret spent a short holiday at the Grand Canyon. In 1898 they enjoyed a similar outing in Mexico. Their greatest adventure of the late 1890s, however, was a trip to southern Europe, the Middle East, and northern Africa—the first time Burnham went abroad. Its effects upon his psyche and his classical artistic predilections were profound. His diary preserved the impressions of that Mediterranean world, impressions that both confirmed and redirected his earlier aesthetic values. As opposed, in fact, to the more routine calendar notations in the regular diaries he kept at home, the notes Burnham made in the separate travel pocket diaries were much more richly and exuberantly detailed. Both relaxed and intoxicated by the exotic new experiences, Burnham revealed himself in his travel diaries with unprecedented verve and candor.

The Burnhams sailed on the *Fürst Bismarck* on January 28, 1896, accompanied by Margaret's parents. Reaching Funchal in the Madeira Islands on February 4, Burnham recorded his admiration of the pale, venerable buildings and the contrasting "mountains with their superb seal browns and rich greens, all laid over an undercolor of red ochre, mingled with the deep blue of sea and sky. If Europe can beat this," he mused, "it will be too much for me!" On February 7 they entered the Mediterranean through the pillars of Hercules and the next day they sailed along the southern shore of Spain. "For hours we ran by the Spanish Coast," Burnham noted in his most romantic vein, "while dreams swelled big by imagination blotted out the present and many centuries of the past, and the Roman fleets swept by, plainly in view, only to melt in the distance and so give place to the lateen-rigged Moorish ships carrying the dark-skinned warriors of Africa to Andalusia. On board the routine life went on, but the deck and the people were vague, unreal things." His reactions on February 9 were even more exuberant. "Up early and out on deck. The African coast in view, more giant mountains and most reverently welcomed they were." And then he wrote, with perhaps inadvertent candor, words that may have said more than he intended about Chicago and about much of the United States: "How noble and dignified this world is after all."[22]

They toured the French Riviera and Italian Riviera, saw the site of Carthage, and visited the Isle of Malta, "and the splendid Church of St. John. A grand mass was going on." Then they sailed to Alexandria and rode on to Cairo, where they met old friends: the Ayers; Charles McKim; the railroad magnate Alexander Cassatt and his sister, the impressionist painter Mary Cassatt. From Cairo, they toured the Nile Valley, reveling in the architecture of the pyramids. It was there that Burnham felt that "the past came and enveloped me fully and wholly, and I lived as if in the twenty-fifth century before Christ. Not a thing of the present, except our dress and the words we spoke to each other. . . . The view of the Pyramids and Ghezeh . . . was wonderful," he wrote. "The architects chose that high bank of sand, the Commencement of the Lybian Desert, because it formed a natural architectural base or terrace for the mighty monuments, and because they would not here be in competition with the mountains themselves. So they quarried the limestone from the Arabian side, hauled it across a plain, the Nile, then another plain and up the sandy beach instead of building where the stone was found." Neglecting for the moment to take into account the laborers who had quarried and hauled the massive stones, the autocrat in Burnham honored "the designer who chose the location and the king who let him do it. They have enabled men forever to feel the greatness of their conception and execution. Would that moderns could follow this example!"[23]

Sailing north from Egypt, Burnham admitted his impatience with "Beyrouth," which should, he thought, have been "the most delightful place on the east coast." But it was "under Turkish dominion and that settles it," he wrote. "It is very dirty and uninteresting, and the people are dull [and] apathetic. . . . They don't seem to have any energy or any hope, but just let the fleas bite them. . . ." Jerusalem and Istanbul he liked much better, but he reserved his greatest enthusiasm for Greece.[24]

He loved Athens, especially for its crispness and its cleanliness, noting, significantly, that "even its modern buildings are lovely." But he was even more impressed with the fact that "the spirit of Old Greece has not departed. It clings yet to nearly everything. . . ." They visited the Acropolis and stayed until after the sun set. "It was a perfect evening," Burnham wrote, and they "sat entranced, speechless on the rocks, amid fallen columns. . . . I have the spirit of Greece once and forever stamped on my soul. It is the blue flower, the rest of life must be the dream and this land of Greece the reality. . . . It has all seemed very familiar . . . the shapes of the hills and the colorings of everything. I imagine this is due to my old residence in the mountains of Nevada, but at times I have felt sure that I was here before." Rome seemed less mystical and less atavistic, but no less exciting. "Rome! To be in it, to wake up in it!" he wrote, "What a delight! Every nerve in one's body seemed to take a separate delight in the fact." He enjoyed visiting the classical monuments but he also took special pleasure in the American Academy in Rome, another recent offspring of the Chicago World's Fair, that he had done so much to found and to engender.[25]

The trip, indeed, opened new worlds to Burnham and made real for him what had formerly existed only in a world of dreams and picture books. From the time they headed home in April 1896, until his death some sixteen years later, Burnham sought to bring to American soil much of the power, grandeur, mystery, and monumentality he saw and imbibed in his Old World travels. Somehow, he thought, there must be in America the same sense of wonder for Americans who would never be able to travel abroad. And it was a noble dream, even if partially confused and misdirected. Sullivan scoffed at Burnham's antiquated "imperialism." But he failed to appreciate the paradoxes in his vision.

Despite his firm's losses during his tenure with the fair and his own personal investment losses in the depression of the mid-1890s, Burnham was thriving again before the turn of the century. On February 27, 1899, he wrote in his diary that he had repaid the note on a loan of $20,000 made to him in 1894. "This is the last of any notes out," he exulted, "and leaves no personal debts owing except small current bills." Even in 1894, however, Burnham's generous nature and sympathy for others was already becoming manifest. "You have been very faithful and valuable to me for many years," he wrote to an employee, William Sturgis, "and in recognition of your wedding day, I hereby cancel your indebtedness to me." His care and contributions to needy friends and relatives, moreover, as well as larger philanthropies, would increase and continue all his life.[26]

In addition to the fame, the leisure, the expanded social life, and the new professional responsibilities that Burnham experienced after the Chicago Fair, the White City of 1893 had other significant consequences for him and for the country. Besides confirming his and the nation's incipient inclinations toward a classical revival, it also triggered yearnings for new directions in urban planning. It extended, in fact, Burnham's vision of a temporary city in Jackson Park to the older, darker, and more challenging city of Chicago to the north and west. Whatever else Daniel Burnham might do in the years ahead, wherever he might go and win acclaim, reforming and replanning his own home city would remain his lifelong obsession and major interest. He spoke often in the late 1890s of his plans for the Chicago waterfront and the city beyond, but he never rallied real support in Chicago until near the end of his life. Meanwhile, he had to venture elsewhere and to practice his planning skills among more sympathetic and aggressive patrons.

Indeed, as the nation entered the new century, it and Daniel Burnham became aware of an inchoate development that would later be labeled the "Progressive Movement," a many-sided crusade of uplift and reform, often inconsistent, often naïve and innocent, and sometimes palpably conservative. As an upper-class Progressive Republican and an old admirer of Theodore Roosevelt, Burnham began to identify with that movement, and to consider himself to a large extent, its architectural and aesthetic arm. The Washington Plan of 1902 was, after the fair, the first manifestation of his new progressivism and of his newly developed planning talents. It bridged, in fact, the seminal planning of the White City with the maturer projects of his later years, reordering in the process the historical character of the capital of the United States.

VII
The New Capital

The Washington Plan of 1902

Washington . . . struck me from the first as presenting two distinct faces; the more obvious of which was the public and official, the monumental, with features all more or less majestically playing the great administrative, or, as we nowadays put it, Imperial part. This clustered, yet at the same time oddly scattered, city, presented a general impression of high granite steps, of light grey corniced colonnades, rather harmoniously low, contending for effect with slaty mansard roofs and masses of iron excrescence, a general impression of somewhat vague, empty, sketchy, fundamentals, however expectant, however spacious, overweighted by a single Dome and overaccented by a single Shaft. The back of the scene . . . might have been but an immense painted, yet unfinished cloth. . . .

HENRY JAMES
The American Scene

THE TWO MOST comprehensive and significant plans for the development of Washington, D.C., were promulgated during great transitional periods in the nation's history, periods in which Americans were especially conscious of accelerating internal development and of increased power and prestige in the affairs of the world. In 1791, with the counsel and support of President Washington and Secretary of State Jefferson, the French-American architect Pierre L'Enfant conceived a grand design for the new capital city of the young American Republic. One hundred and ten years later, in 1901-2, under the patronage of Senator James McMillan, chairman of the District of Columbia Committee, and with the subsequent backing of other officials, Daniel Burnham and the commission he directed produced a plan for a major renewal of the city, reviving much of L'Enfant's original scheme and enlarging the plan to fulfill new needs.

The new plan's quest for order and efficiency complemented the growing concern of the nation at large for correcting abuses in the social, political, and economic aspects of American life. The monumental scope, moreover, of the plan's architectural and landscaping proposals, significantly suggestive of Rome and Paris, provided for Washington an imperial splendor that the planners deemed fitting and proper for the capital of the emerging American empire.

L'Enfant's original Washington plan had provided a base of rectilinear streets, superimposed with diagonal avenues radiating from the proposed Capitol and President's house. Nineteenth-century planning, or lack of planning, however, had allowed extensive departures from L'Enfant's original recommendations, especially his provisions for great open vistas and promenades. The old eyesores of unfinished Capitol and truncated Washington Monument had finally reached completion, but the key element in L'Enfant's plan—the great mall between the two structures—had become, among other things, a common pasture, a lumber yard, and the railroad center of the city, dissected and cluttered by railroad tracks and depot buildings. As if to symbolize America's age of steam and iron, the terminal of the Baltimore & Potomac Railroad, sprawling beneath Capitol Hill, constituted one of the area's most prominent landmarks. Well-meaning attempts to retrieve and "beautify" certain sections of the mall throughout the century had not improved the situation. In 1850, for example, at the instigation of President Fillmore, the prominent landscape architect Andrew Jackson Downing had produced for the area a romantically picturesque "English Garden," with "natural" plantings and meandering walks and roads, a formula he had used with great success elsewhere but which, in L'Enfant's Washington, had merely added to the aesthetic cacophony. Faded remnants of Downing's work were still obvious in 1901. The vagaries, moreover, of nineteenth-century architectural romanticism had planted the turreted Smithsonian Institution and the mansarded "Second Empire" State, War, and Navy Building in the midst of an otherwise neoclassical format. The Capitol, lamented the novelist Henry James, in itself "a splendid building, unfolds its repeated colonnades and uplifts its isolated dome at the end of a long vista of saloons and tobacco shops."[1] Though later generations would again come to appreciate such eclectic and textured heterogeneity, Burnham and his contemporaries valued and strove for a more

Model of the Mall area, Washington, D.C., showing conditions in 1901.
Report of the Senate Committee.

homogeneous uniformity. In the early twentieth century, unity, not variety, was the ruling imperative.

Indeed, the railroad in the Mall seemed to suggest, in microcosm, the
darker, less fortunate by-products of the nation's recent, rapid industrial-
ization. But by the turn of the century many Americans had become impatient with such conditions and had come to believe that reform
should take place on the face of the land as well as in the deeper social and political fabric, that change must occur in the physical environment and in the architectural configuration of the cities themselves. The
City Beautiful Movement was a product of that impulse, an impulse
that had received its greatest stimulus from the White City of 1893.
Whatever reservations professional critics may have had, most visitors

to the fair had been aroused by its example and had returned to their home cities to work with renewed vigor in the movements for parks and "municipal art." Yet, the long, crippling depression of the mid-1890s had dampened the immediate prospects of a real city planning movement. Only with the increased prosperity that followed the Spanish-American War did the legacy of the White City exercise its anticipated influence on American urban development. The renewal of Washington furnished the impetus for the delayed unfolding of the City Beautiful idea. No American city was better suited to encompass and to illustrate its concepts.[2]

In 1900, the Federal Government, in cooperation with the citizens of the District of Columbia, held a celebration to commemorate the one hundredth anniversary of the removal of the capital to Washington. Federal officials, state governors, and representatives of foreign powers were invited. The theme of the celebration was the need for a physical renewal of the District "in a manner and to the extent commensurate with the dignity and the resources of the American Nation."[3]

While the celebration of the centennial was in progress, the American Institute of Architects was also meeting in Washington, its members discussing in more specific terms the potential development of Washington's park system and the ideal location of future public buildings. Encouraged by the promising possibilities of their tentative ideas, the institute appointed a legislative liaison committee to consult with the powerful Senate Committee on the District of Columbia. Michigan Senator James McMillan, chairman of the committee, proved warmly receptive to the architects' suggestions and on March 8, 1901, obtained Senate approval of a resolution permitting his committee "to consider the subject and report to the Senate plans for the development and improvement of the entire park system" of the District. The resolution empowered the committee to "secure the service of such experts as may be necessary for a proper consideration of the subject," and provided for the financing of the investigation from contingency funds of the Senate.[4]

Acting upon the suggestions of the A.I.A. and Senator McMillan's secretary and architectural adviser, Charles Moore, the committee appointed Burnham head of a three-man planning commission, which was also to include the young landscape architect Frederick Law Olmsted, Jr., the son of the famous landscape architect who had worked with Burnham at the World's Columbian Exposition. Burnham and Olmsted were to name the third member of the commission, and they selected the New York architect Charles McKim, also an important figure at the Chicago Fair. Later, deciding that the Commission should include a sculptor, they arranged for the appointment of Augustus St. Gaudens, yet another veteran of the exposition staff. The four commissioners gave their time and talent as a public service, accepting reimbursement only for expenses. Though not officially a member of the commission, Charles Moore served as full-time secretary and administrative assistant for the project. In addition, he became the commission's unofficial reporter and historian, contributing numerous articles and memoirs on the Washington work as well as writing early firsthand biographies of both Burnham and McKim. Moore's "power is very great," Burnham wrote to a friend, "although he keeps in the background."[5]

Moore's characterization of himself and his commission colleagues, revealed a keen perception of their personalities and the part of each in the total enterprise. "Daniel Burnham . . . never hurried and never rested," he later recalled. His "mind worked on a grand scale. He saw things in the large." McKim, on the other hand, "always acquiesced; he never contradicted; but when his logical mind began to work, quite hesitatingly he would offer suggestions which seemed only an expansion of the original idea, or perhaps a little better way of arriving at the intended result. Olmsted, being younger and possessing a brain fertile in expedients, offered many variations on the themes." Describing himself in the third person, in the Henry Adams–Louis Sullivan manner, Moore, "at the outset . . . ventured to suggest that the ideas were too overpowering to receive consideration in Congress, but he was silenced if not then convinced by Burnham's downright assertion that it was the business and duty of the Commission to make the very finest plans their minds could conceive. The future, he maintained, would prove even those plans all too small; and that the time (if ever) to compromise was after the large plans had been made."[6]

Burnham's convictions epitomized his credo to "make no little plans," but they also embraced a high Republican class consciousness that would likewise pervade his later thought. "My own belief," he wrote to "Rick" Olmsted, "is that instead of arranging for less, we should plan for rather more extensive treatment than we are likely to find in any other city. Washington is likely to grow very rapidly from this time on, and be the home of all the wealthy people of the United States."[7]

Throughout the spring of 1901, Burnham made numerous trips to

Washington to prepare for the study, to survey the city's conditions and
needs, and to confer with his commission colleagues. Often he combined
these visits with stops in New York, Boston, Philadelphia, and Pittsburgh, where he continued to conduct the business of his own firm.
Around and around the District he rode in March and April 1901, satu-
rating himself with the Washington atmosphere. "Breakfasted early and
drove on the obelisk-capital axis," a typical diary entry ran, "visited capitol and met Moore. Then took cars for Anacostia." On another typical
day, he spent the morning on the Potomac River, had lunch at the Congressional Library, and passed the afternoon in conference with Secretary of War Elihu Root and other government officials. McMillan had
arranged for a temporary study and working area for the commissioners
in the Senate press gallery, where they surrounded themselves with maps
of Washington and of foreign capitals. Burnham worked with enormous
gusto.[8]

He was greatly encouraged by the initial reception of most government
officials to the possibilities and potential of the commission's work. He
ignored for the moment the growling of Representative Joseph Cannon
of Illinois who opposed the spending of the people's money for such
things as art and architecture, a voice and an influence that would later
cause him trouble. For the moment, it seemed more important that
President McKinley and Secretary Root were enthusiastic. The first part
of the commission's work had been "most successful," Burnham wrote
to a business acquaintance. "The few days work there was not work at
all, but on the contrary a delightful past time." He believed confidently
that "a fine thing is developing and how practical it is going to be to
carry it out." He wrote his old friend Secretary Gage that he could not
think of "anything that has come into my life since the World's Fair"
that promised such excitement. Thus far it had been "a big absorbing
dream . . . and for all I can see, it will be constantly growing bigger
and more absorbing as well." He wrote to his son-in-law Albert Wells in
a tone even more ecstatic: "The Washington work is a stupendous job,"
he said, "full of the deepest interest and it appeals to me as nothing else
ever has. I have the best fellows with me and the sympathy of all the officials in Washington. It is going to make this summer a period of intensely hard work, but it is going to pay from every point of view. . . ."[9]

Before drafting a report, Burnham insisted that the commission spend
several months traveling and studying the city's architectural precedents,
both in America and in Europe. Many of the inspection sites Burnham

proposed were sites L'Enfant had either observed personally or studied via the maps of European cities Thomas Jefferson had acquired in France. These sites, Burnham felt, would serve to acquaint and imbue the commissioners with the general aesthetic atmosphere that surrounded L'Enfant and the architectural traditions that influenced him. Others would offer interesting solutions to building and landscaping problems similar to those the Commission expected to encounter in Washington. ". . . How else can we refresh our minds," Burnham wrote to McKim, "except by seeing, with the Washington work in view, all those things done by others in the same line?" The government, he quipped, "and especially our great Uncle George, have the right to expect the very best we can give."[10]

Believing strongly in Washington's and Jefferson's influence on L'Enfant's ideas, Burnham arranged for visits to the sites and environments that had shaped their thinking, including Stratford, Carter's Grove, Berkeley, and other great estates along the James and Potomac rivers. The commissioners took special note of the ruined and decaying town of Williamsburg, the old colonial capital, whose general plan had constituted an outline in miniature of the Washington Mall. The capitol building and the College of William and Mary stood at opposite ends of the main axis and the Governor's Mansion stood at one end of the cross axis in a position analogous to that of the White House.[11]

Even more important in the evolution of the commission's thinking, however, was their visit to Europe in June and July. Burnham suggested the general itinerary but left most of the actual travel arrangements to Moore and Olmsted. The schedule, he wrote to Albert Wells, "will cause us to travel very rapidly. . . . I do not dare take Mrs. Burnham along, because I am sure I could give her little if any of my company. We are going for very hard work and everything will have to bend to the necessities we are to be under." American diplomatic representatives in the respective countries would "lay out our time for us beforehand in each case so that on every stop we shall have to go on a run in order to accomplish anything near like what we are hoping to do." Sincere as always in his determination to seize each day, Burnham's lavish tastes and his appetite for recreation must also have told him that the trip would not be quite so arduous as he had predicted.[12]

Despite the pleasures and the epicurean diversions, however, Burnham set a serious tone for the mission from the day they embarked on the *Deutschland*: ". . . No sooner had the pilot gone over the side,"

Moore remarked, "than Burnham piped all hands to conference and work began. . . ." They worked and talked and planned throughout the voyage. Arriving in Paris on June 20, the commissioners took special note of the Tuilleries Gardens, the Bois de Boulogne, and the street and plaza system of central Paris, especially the Champs Elysées and the Place de la Concorde. Paris, as modified in the 1860s by Louis Napoleon and his architect Georges Haussmann, would become the central historical reference point in Burnham's later work, culminating by 1909 in his plan for Chicago. But in 1901, he was drawn less to the French capital as a model for Washington than to Rome itself, the greatest of all urban influences on the planning of Western cities.[13]

Arriving in Rome on June 24, the Americans not only studied the city's magnificent classical base, but its equally significant Renaissance, Baroque, and modern alterations. Rome affected Burnham deeply, Moore observed. "Thought of the strength, power, and mastery of imperial Rome made him walk erect. All day he kept putting Latin words to S.P.Q.R. . . ." Imperial Rome indeed appealed to the imperious aspects of Burnham's own nature. Determined to press on and cover the city, despite the heat of the scorching June days, he also chose to do so with the maximum amenities. "Tomorrow we must have two carriages with large light colored umbrellas," Moore remembered his telling their Roman factotum Raffaelo Vanelli. "Vanelli protested that there were no such combinations in Rome. 'That,' said Burnham, 'is not the question. We shall expect to have just those carriages at the door of the Quirinal Hotel tomorrow morning at nine o'clock.'" And at the appointed time, "there they were; and in them the party navigated Rome in comfort." Near Rome, at Tivoli, the setting and the landscaping seemed especially captivating. "The Temple of Vesta was one of Mr. Burnham's delights," Moore recalled ironically, "and his fondness for its form was not disturbed by the fact that it was reproduced for a chocolate booth at the Chicago Fair." Burnham, in his enthusiasm, poured a bottle of wine over the cliff into the great chasm as "a libation to the gods," and when Olmsted, "with true New England thrift expostulated on the waste of good wine, Burnham quickly answered, 'What's the matter with another bottle?'"[14]

The group toured Venice with S. A. B. Abbot, director of the American Academy in Rome. On July 4, ". . . We all wore red, white and blue flowers in our button holes," Burnham noted in his Diary, "had a run up [the] small canals back of the Grand Canal, . . . and finally and reluctantly down the canal, thinking Tintoretto, Carpaccio, del Sarto Titiano. . . ." In Vienna and Budapest the commissioners studied the ancient landmarks and the noted, more recent improvements in the cities' parks, streets, and river quays. By July 10, they were back in France revisiting Paris and examining the gardens at Versailles and Fontainebleau. The day at Versailles was "a long, hot day," Moore recalled, "with Burnham's vitality enjoying itself in leading the procession of four completely around the basin to the bitter, unfinished end. It was a fatigued party that sat down to a well selected dinner under the trees."[15]

Leaving the party in France, Burnham spent July 15 in Frankfort-am-Main, where he carefully examined the new train station, believed by many to be the finest and most advanced in the world. With only a few hours of the following day to spend in Berlin, Burnham visited Tiergarten Park and the grand avenues leading to the Brandenburg Gate. On July 17, he traveled across Holland and crossed the English Channel to join his companions. With London as a base, he and his colleagues then studied Hyde Park and Hampton Court and made excursions to Eton and Oxford. They sailed on the *Deutschland* July 26, and as in the earlier crossing, used the time aboard ship to work and to reflect on the over-all project. "McKim worked on the plan of the Mall," Burnham recorded on July 29, "and returned to D. H. B.'s suggestion, viz. a great court and fountain, the monument being on the edge of the terrace." While McKim sketched, Burnham worked on the commission's report. On August 1, they reached New York.[16]

There were ironies, of course, in the Old World references that somehow escaped both L'Enfant's and Burnham's eras. "From all these legacies of aristocrats and nobles," a late critic observed, "from all these seemingly tireless survivals of departed or decayed societies, they hoped to fashion on the banks of the Potomac an expression of the Republican ideal, a city honoring men who had revolted against a tyrant, others who had fought to preserve a Union, and still others who had more recently humbled a Spanish monarch." But these reservations seemed not to have crossed Burnham's mind. "We have much to learn and much to live out before we can equal old England or *any* place in Europe," he wrote to his wife. "I have not seen a sterile or barren spot in all our travels." Indeed, all agreed that the trip had been a great success. They had had a "glorious time," Burnham wrote to Augustus St. Gaudens, "breaking loose . . . and dreaming to the top of our heart." "Olmsted's tin case of Washington maps and plans was always at hand," Moore remembered, "his ever ready Kodak missed no important object; and his file cards recorded heights and breadths with method and without end. Everywhere the party took their meals together in their common room, where they would sit late into the night discussing the lessons of the day. Paris revealed itself as a well-articulated city—a work of civic art. Versailles, Fontainebleau, Hampton Court, examples of the use of a long stretch of water, tree-lined, furnished ideas for the basin. . . . Vaux le Vicomte, Compiègne, Schonbrunn . . . gave inspiration for the treatment of the mall. A close study of Le Nôtre's work in France," Moore observed, "together with reflections of it in other countries revealed subtleties and perfections applicable to the American work." Despite the indirect influences of Paris, however, "some things seemed to them self-evident: that the problems in Washington must be worked out along Roman rather than Parisian lines; that simplicity, directness and the subordination of ornament to structural uses should prevail. . . . More than this," Moore concluded, "it was determined that the fountain and not the man on horseback is the proper ornament for Washington and that the heat of our capital requires that the city should be filled with running water . . . as in Rome."[17]

One of the biggest obstacles confronting the commission from the very beginning was the B. & P. Railroad works that lay astride the Mall. To make matters worse, Congress, in February 1901, granted the railroad a larger and more central piece of the Mall on which to build its new and larger terminal. The railroad had been considering Burnham as the architect for this new station and shortly after accepting the chairmanship of the Park Commission, Burnham was offered the assignment. He accepted, not only for professional and financial reasons, but also because he felt that he might be able to exploit his double role and persuade the railroad to leave the Mall. Alexander Cassatt, president of the Pennsylvania Railroad, which controlled the B. & P. through stock ownership, was reluctant to give up the central location, and move his holdings elsewhere, however. In the early stages of Burnham's importunate arguments, in fact, Cassatt reminded him that he was "employed to design the station, not to locate it." The mind of the railroad magnate proved not to have been closed. Brother of Mary Cassatt, he had aesthetic inclinations. His chief problem stemmed from a very sensible reluctance to relinquish so choice a site, not to mention the exorbitant costs he would incur in moving the entire operation to a new location. Burnham, nevertheless, continued his efforts to convince Cassatt that the presence of the railroad on the Mall would mean the ruin of any plans the commission might present. The fear that Cassatt might not give in cast one of the few shadows on the European tour.[18]

It was during the latter part of the commission's European trip that Cassatt met Burnham in London and explained that, for a variety of reasons, he had decided to give in. In addition to nonmaterialistic motivations, the Pennsylvania Railroad had just acquired a controlling interest in the Baltimore & Ohio, formerly its chief competitor in the Washington area. If the government really intended to improve the Mall, Cassatt stated, he would be willing to give up his present location and build a union depot north of the Capitol provided that Senator McMillan obtained an appropriation of $1,500,000 in partial payment of the tunnel under Capitol Hill. The tunnel would be necessary for maintaining rail connections with the South.[19]

The commissioners believed that Cassatt's proviso would be acceptable to the government and were ultimately influential in persuading Congress to enact the necessary legislation. It also resolved the tension in Burnham's mind between his earlier commitment to Cassatt and his personal commitment to the commission's plan for the Mall. He began at once to plan Union Station looking south to the Mall and Capitol Hill, intensely concerned that it complement and ornament the larger commission plan as a "great and impressive vestibule to Washington."[20]

When, on August 20, 1901, the commissioners met for dinner with various Senators and government officials to discuss the results of their European trip and the further development of the plan, Senator McMillan introduced Burnham as "General Burnham." Later in the evening, Moore recalled, McMillan turned to Senator Allison of Iowa, saying, "Senator, perhaps you have noticed that I have persisted in calling Mr. Burnham 'General.' He doesn't like it; but—a man who could persuade President Cassatt to take the railroad out of the Mall deserves to be a general."[21]

With the railroad problem solved and the inspiration of the European examples still fresh in their minds, the commissioners turned their thoughts to specific proposals. Throughout the summer, they continued to appraise the needs of the situation and to entertain new ideas. Be sure, Burnham answered the Washington Citizens Relief Association and Associated Charities, "that the sentiment of the citizens of Washington as expressed in your series of suggestions will prove to be a helpful guide in the deliberations and final recommendations of the committee."

Burnham commuted often between Washington, New York, and his Chicago office, where he supervised the work on the design of Union Station. In Boston and New York, Olmsted, St. Gaudens, and McKim supervised the completion of the over-all drawings and models. George C. Curtis of Boston prepared the actual models; William T. Partridge, a young draftsman in McKim's firm, prepared most of the final drawings. Olmsted's office in Boston had general advisory responsibility for final landscaping details, especially in the outlying parks throughout the District. Burnham himself blocked out the rough draft of the report with the help of a Chicago writer, W. H. Harper. The report, he wrote to Olmsted on September 9, was "now in skeleton form, and will be ready to fill in when we meet" later in the month. He then turned it over to Moore for emendation and final editing.[22]

There was constant communication and interaction among the various members over many aspects of the project. Usually the criticism was friendly and constructive, and the work went smoothly, despite its geographical fragmentation. Occasionally, however, honest disagreements appeared, some caused by the peculiar financial pressures of the undertaking. Accustomed to operating in the grandest manner in all their other pursuits, and feeling justified because they were charging no fees, Burnham and McKim, in particular, failed to accept the scarcity of resources in the Senate Contingency Fund, raising further the ire of penurious congressmen. "We have out of our pockets now furnished Three Thousand Dollars toward paying Curtis" for the models, Burnham wrote to Moore in late August, "and this sum has been expended. Cannot you from this time on pay his bills? Mr. McKim is worried over the matter. . . ."[23]

Burnham also had words with Moore over the style and editing of the final report, revealing again his peculiar mixture of dreamy romanticism and tough-minded pragmatism. "I do not think the report should be elaborate," he wrote to Moore on August 30, 1901; "it should depend for its acceptance on the accuracy of its statement, and the good sense of its recommendations." He trusted "that the final draft will be shorn of every unnecessary word." Moore's tentative final draft, however, displeased Burnham not for its superfluity of words but for what he deemed to be its excessive aridity and austerity. Much of the commission's original excitement and enthusiasm, Burnham argued, had been sacrificed in the acknowledged desire for clarity and directness. Writing to Moore in early 1902, Burnham, the promoter, the man of the marketplace, questioned the artistic and intellectual biases of his colleagues: "You have taken the color out of the report and made it a dead level statement of facts," he complained to Moore. "While I sympathize with you and the Harvard dislike of highly colored statements, I doubt very much whether you are entirely right in this case."[24]

The ensuing argument revealed the conflict in Burnham's make-up of democratic values and elitist *noblesse oblige*. "A skillful lawyer," he suggested to Moore, "appealing to a judge in chambers does not care to go beyond unadorned statements of precedence and does not feel that his case is helped much by argument, especially of a sentimental kind, but would not the same man before a jury take the other tack? When appealing to the ordinary untrained mind, he would know that legal argument, standing by itself, would avail him little, and he would be wise therefore to deal . . . not on his own but on their plane of thought and understanding. If you expect this report to be copied in part or in whole by the newspapers of this country, as I supposed was your intention, should it not dress the statements up in colors that will appeal to the ordinary citizen who is not much moved by cold facts, but is carried forward by feelings." He believed, indeed, that "we should not write this report in a style that would appeal to us as individuals, if by taking the other course we can awaken a much needed sympathy, a sympathy which will be the parent of all that can be brought to support the objects we have in view." If they were trying "to raise the enthusiasm of the people, very few of whom are trained to appreciate cold statements of facts, it should have plenty of color." The final report contained the necessary balance between the "color" and the "directness" Burnham desired—as well as a compromise between his personal preferences and those of his colleagues. Certainly the section of the final report that dealt with Arlington cemetery was not lacking in "color" or emotion: "The interest excited by the drills at the cavalry post," it read "the superb view from the heights, and the feelings of patriotism awakened by the vast field of the hero dead, known or un-named, all call for such a treatment of the entire reservation as shall not diminish but rather enhance the effect produced on the visitor."[25]

The plan as finally submitted was generally a reinstatement, reiteration, and enlargement of the L'Enfant Plan of 1791. The original plan had called for a T-shaped arrangement with the Capitol at the eastern end of the main axis and the White House at the northern end of the cross-axis. The two main axes were to cross at right angles at the pro-

Bird's-eye view of proposed Washington improvements. *Report of the Senate Committee.*

posed Washington Monument. Due to soil and foundation problems, however, the nineteenth-century builders of the monument had failed to adhere to the plan and had placed it slightly east and south of the proposed point of axial convergence. Unlike the Treasury Building, which interrupted the sweep of Pennsylvania Avenue, and which seemed to the commission an irrevocable violation of the plan, the "monument problem" was not insoluble. The commission's plan, therefore, recommended that the north-south cross-axis, aborted by the dislocation of the monument, be redrawn to extend from the White House through a new central point slightly west of the monument, marked with fountains and other sculptural features, southward to the curve of the Potomac. It also called for redrawing the main axis from the Capitol dome through the actual location of the monument, extending west all the way to the Potomac and terminating on the plan's proposed site of a future memorial to President Lincoln.[26]

Beyond the Lincoln Memorial was to be an impressive bridge leading to Arlington National Cemetery. Public galleries and museums were to line the Mall above the Smithsonian Institution. Executive office buildings were to surround Lafayette Square, completing the circle already begun by the Treasury and the State, War, and Navy buildings. Structures relating to judicial and legislative matters were to border on the Capitol grounds. A reflecting pool was to lie between the Washington Monument and the proposed Lincoln Memorial. Rows of elms in columns of fours were to line the Mall for a distance of over two miles from the Capitol to the Lincoln site on either side of a plain strip of grass three hundred feet wide.[27]

Noting that the "dearth of the means of innocent enjoyment of one's leisure hours is remarkable in Washington," the commission recommended the conversion of the vast area between the south side of the Washington Monument and the Potomac into recreation grounds to include ball parks and facilities for summer and winter water sports.

Proposed treatment of the Mall from the Washington Monument to the Capitol. *Report of the Senate Committee.*

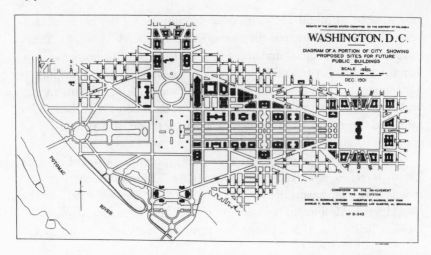

Plan of the proposed treatment of the Mall. *Report of the Senate Committee.*

Boulevards and parks were to encircle the city from Anacostia in the
east to the Soldiers' Home in the north and the Rock Creek complex
in the northeast, and were even to stretch as far into the surrounding
area as Mount Vernon and Great Falls, Virginia. The plan in its final
form was indeed the work of many hands and minds, but Burnham's direction assured its unity of scope and its over-all consistency.[28]

On January 15, 1902, the commission presented its proposals in exhibit form at the Corcoran Gallery of Art. The focal points of the display were the two large models of the Mall area, one showing existing
conditions; the other presenting the commission's vision of the area
after the fulfillment of the current proposals. Burnham and Senator
McMillan received the official guests, the ubiquitous Moore recalled:
"There came President Roosevelt, interested, curious, at first critical and
then, as the great consistent scheme dawned on him, highly appreciative." Secretary of State John Hay "was especially interested in the
location and design of the memorial to Lincoln. . . ." Hay also approved of the plan to surround Lafayette Square with buildings of the
various executive departments even though it meant the surrender of
his own double house, which he shared with Henry Adams. Secretary
of Interior E. A. Hitchcock was "particularly interested in the fountains, the play of waters recalling Versailles and Peterhof." Following
the senators and members of the House, the general public came to in-

spect the exhibits. Numerous popular periodicals reproduced the drawings, carrying the commission's concepts to the nation as a whole and
to foreign countries as well. Members of the commission also helped
to publicize the plan with articles, lectures, and interviews. Burnham
discussed it at the Chicago Art Institute and wrote an article for *Century Magazine* linking the plan to the incipient Progressive Movement,
a reform of the landscape, he suggested, to complement the burgeoning
reforms in other areas of society.[29]

Although the plan elicited a generally favorable and often enthusiastic response in both official and popular circles, the scheme was not
without its critics and opponents—both at the time of its submission
and throughout the first half of the century as it slowly attained fulfillment. Some congressmen thought the plan overly visionary and had
serious doubts concerning the accuracy of the cost estimates, which
ranged from $200,000,000 to $600,000,000. Others objected to specific
proposals, such as one removing the Botanical Gardens from the Mall
at the foot of Capitol Hill, where greenhouses had stood for more than
sixty years. Since the focus of the plan involved a westward extension
from the Library of Congress, east-side Washingtonians objected that
their section would continue to be slighted. Strong opposition existed
for years to locating the Lincoln Memorial in what then was only a
marshy backwater of the Potomac, where as one wag suggested, the
structure "would shake itself down in loneliness and ague." Representative Joseph Cannon, the arch-conservative from Illinois, was the plan's
most vicious and enduring critic. "So long as I live," he told Elihu Root,
"I'll never let a monument to Abraham Lincoln be erected in that God
damned swamp."[30]

Influenced indeed by the hostile Cannon, the House of Representatives officially ignored the plan, since Senator McMillan had earlier
made the "politically egregious error" of failing to obtain House con-
currence before appointing the Burnham Commission. For that reason
the commission could obtain no further funds and officially ceased to
exist shortly after it presented its work in 1902. With the death of Senator McMillan in the summer of that same year, moreover, the plan
lost its most important government supporter. Encouraged by the interest of Presidents Roosevelt and Taft, however, Burnham and McKim
continued making unofficial contributions of time and interest. Charles
Moore also retained his important affiliation with the Senate District of
Columbia Committee.[31]

Despite the continued opposition in the lower house, Congress took prompt action on the Union Station project and the removal of the old terminal from the Mall. It also provided for a number of important new structures including House and Senate office buildings, a new building for the Department of Agriculture, and an imposing series of structures by McKim, Mead, and White to house the Army War College. The attempt to disregard the commission's plan in the placing of the new Agriculture Building led to an especially bitter fight and test of strength. Only by winning President Roosevelt over to their position were Mc-Kim and Burnham able to save their scheme for the Mall. The Washington plan, Burnham wrote to Moore, would "persist in spite of all the Joe Cannons in the world."[32]

The formal landscaping aspects of the proposals received little attention until 1910 when President Taft created a permanent Fine Arts Commission and appointed Burnham as its first chairman. Under the leadership of Burnham and his successors, the commissioners became "virtually the executors of the Plan of 1901," and despite repeated skirmishes with Congress, the commission had, by the end of World War I, "made itself the arbiter of public taste in the Capital." The Lincoln Memorial reached completion in 1922, designed and located virtually as the Burnham Commission had intended it. Further building and landscaping programs in the spirit of the plan reached significant fulfillment in the administrations of Calvin Coolidge, Franklin D. Roosevelt, and Lyndon Johnson. Indeed, despite the slowness of execution, the Plan of 1902 had made far too strong an impact upon Washington and the nation for it ever again to be ignored or forgotten.[33]

The Plan of 1902 helped restore and create a monumental façade for the nation's capital as the United States became an increasingly important power in the twentieth century. While echoing the neoclassicism and the Old World values of both L'Enfant's time and of the recent Chicago Fair, the Washington plan also enforced the effects of the exposition in awakening the American public to the need and value of urban planning. It conditioned Americans, like the fair before had done, to accept and then to demand the type of planning that Burnham and his followers produced. Further, it grounded Burnham in the art of city planning that he would later practice in Cleveland, San Francisco, Manila, and Chicago. Burnham received no professional fees for any of his government work—he gave his time and his talents entirely as a public service. Due largely to his own attempt to revive much of the original plan and emphasize the memory of Pierre L'Enfant, Burnham's own contribution to Washington's historical development has remained an essentially anonymous one.

"The total result of Burnham's work," a later observer noted, "was to restore Washington to a plan that gave it spaciousness and its buildings a chance for dignity." As the century grew older, it would slowly fulfill the vision of the planners themselves as expressed in the 1902 report: that the city which the founders "planned with such care and with such prophetic vision will continue to expand, keeping pace with national advancement, until it becomes the visible expression of the power and taste of the people of the United States."[34]

VIII
The Paradox of
Progressive Architecture

The Cleveland Group Plan of 1903

I had an architectonic vision of what a city might be. I saw it as a picture. It was not economy, efficiency, and business methods that interested me so much as a city planned, built, and conducted as a community enterprise. . . . It was a unit, a thing with a mind, with a conscious purpose, seeing far in advance of the present and taking precautions for the future. . . . And I saw cities as social agencies that would make life easier for people, full of pleasure, beauty, and opportunity. . . . Especially in a city like Cleveland . . . . that was flanked on one side by a lake front which could be developed with breakwaters into parks and lagoons and with natural parkways extending about it far back into the country.

FREDERIC HOWE
The Confessions of a Reformer

THE CITY BEAUTIFUL Movement and Burnham's rise as an urban planner coincided with the coming of age of the heterogeneous reform spirit later known as the Progressive Movement. Yet, like many of the era's political and economic reforms, Burnham's planning was often ambiguous and contradictory. Sometimes his ideas were truly "progressive"; at other times, they were dismayingly conservative. The paradox was evident in the Cleveland Plan of 1903. It would become more obvious later.

After the completion of the Washington plan, the first urban reformer to exploit Burnham's talents was Cleveland's controversial mayor, Tom L. Johnson. Though Senator Mark Hanna attacked him as a "socialist-anarchist-nihilist," Johnson appeared to the liberal journalist Lincoln Steffens as "the best mayor of the best governed city in the United States." Beloved by his constituents for lowering public transport fares, Johnson worked tirelessly and, for the most part, sucessfully as a "light and water socialist" for municipal ownership of public facilities. He also fought corruption through firm but sensibly enlightened policing policies. In one daring and controversial move, for example, he agreed to exempt from prosecution all brothel keepers who promised not to steal from their customers, not to attempt to bribe policemen, and to remain orderly and hygienically circumspect. He instituted city meat and dairy inspections and, on the national scene, he advocated such relatively unpopular causes as woman suffrage and public ownership of railroads. In a fast-growing city, with a population of over 500,000, he constantly worked to educate his constituents and to stimulate interest and participation in civic affairs.[1]

He realized the extent to which state laws hampered urban reform and his long campaign for "home rule" was instrumental in 1910 in forcing an amendment to the constitution which gave Ohio cities "large immunity from control by the state legislature in the management of their purely municipal and domestic concerns." In addition to instituting such reforms as equalizing the city's tax structure, he also strove to increase the comforts and amenities of urban life, including, among other things, the erection of public baths and the enlargement of the city's park and recreational facilities. Through public architecture and landscaping, he and his advisers hoped to symbolize and articulate the metropolis' riches, stimulating Clevelanders to love and enjoy their city and thereby identify with its problems, assets, needs, and goals.[2]

Johnson was neither first nor alone, however, in promoting the city's face-lifting. Calls for various architectural and landscaping projects had sounded throughout the 1890s—chiefly in response to the various needs of Cleveland's cultural and governmental institutions for new physical facilities. Typical of the city's plight and suggestive of its promise was the fact that federal, county, and municipal governments were each in need of large new buildings in the very near future. Such a coincidence of needs and possibilities seemed encouraging to the city's more far-sighted citizens, especially to a young attorney named Frederick C. Howe, later to become one of Johnson's closest and most influential advisers. Around 1894, Howe and several equally enthusiastic friends began working to arouse public interest in a unified grouping of public buildings such as they had observed in older European cities and at the World's Columbian Exposition in Chicago.[3]

Their enthusiasm reached the newly created Cleveland Architectural Club, many of whose members had also been "inspired by the fine groups of buildings displayed at the Chicago Exposition." In 1895, the club arranged for a contest in which members competed with plans for a grouping of Cleveland's proposed public buildings. Similarly inspired, the Cleveland Chamber of Commerce set up a "Grouping Plan" committee, brought in a number of prominent experts to speak on the subject, and launched "a vigorous program . . . to interest the citizenship in the Group Plan advantages."[4]

One interested Clevelander, Herbert B. Briggs, lamented his city's long-standing conservative tendencies and strongly urged concerted municipal action. "The commercial value to Cleveland of the grouping of her public buildings," he wrote in 1899, "is an element unknown in its possibilities . . . for no one can estimate the number of people who would visit the city to see and enjoy the wonderful picture of municipal enterprise and beauty. Today Cleveland is known the world over, I doubt not, as a city of rioting, bloodshed, and anarchy by reason of her streetcar troubles. How would she be known," he asked on the other hand, "if she were to so plan her coming public buildings—as to present the eye of the traveller a reality, in imperishable material, of the past Court of Honor at the World's Fair. She would be known as the only city in the United States, having such an opportunity to grasp its import, to so wisely read the signs of the times, to see the necessity of solving the problem in no other way to meet the progress of the world."[5]

Tom Johnson endorsed the Group Plan proposal and after his election as mayor in 1901, incorporated the idea into his program. The Chamber of Commerce and the local chapter of the American Institute of Architects continued their promotion propaganda and in 1902 prepared and presented a bill to the Ohio legislature that would allow the governor to appoint a commission of three experts, financed by the state, to advise Ohio cities on questions of urban planning. Though worded in general terms, the measure was proposed at the instigation of the citizens of Cleveland and was ultimately destined to apply primarily to that city. The legislature promptly passed the bill, and on June 20, 1902, Governor Nash announced the appointments recommended by Mayor Johnson and close advisers such as Howe. The choices seemed too logical to be surprising. Commission chairman was

Daniel Burnham, whose work at the fair had done much to inspire the Cleveland movement. The other two commissioners were the New York architects John M. Carrère and Arnold W. Brunner. Carrère had planned and directed the 1901 Pan American Exposition in Buffalo and with his partner Thomas Hastings had designed distinguished buildings throughout the country. Brunner had recently been named by the national government to design the large, proposed Federal Building in Cleveland.[6]

Following their appointments, the commissioners began an intensive series of conferences with interested citizens and public officials. "We discussed with them," Brunner later recalled, "the needs and character of their individual projects and after we had mastered their requirements we spent much time studying the topography of the land and considering the problem on the field." In the consultation period, Burnham again betrayed his suspicions of participatory democracy and his preference for dealing with key representatives by contesting the city's suggestion of a large and open public hearing. "I do not think a public meeting had better be held," in the early planning stages, he wrote the city clerk, Edward Roberts. "I think we should meet there . . . and go over the general scheme, making our estimate perhaps on two or three different bases of costs and when we are thoroughly ready, then a public meeting might be called to which these things might be submitted, although I am not a believer in town meetings. They do not seem to have any permanent effect at all. I believe the best way to go about it would be . . . to place the whole matter in the hands of the mayor and ask him to consult with the proper officials and proper citizens and then advise us." Then as always, Burnham insisted on dealing with the big men and with the sources of power.[7]

Unlike his own more conservative city of Chicago, where he seemed to be too often alone in his calls for urban planning, Cleveland seemed overly demanding at times for quick decisions and results. The enormity and complexity of the problems, especially that of the train station and the rail connections, worried John Carrère, who feared that civic and commercial pressures might force the commission into hasty and ill-conceived compromises. Burnham reassured him, however, in his characteristically calm and determined manner: "I do not think that we should feel hurried in this matter," he wrote. "It is very important that we take plenty of time and study the matter down to the bottom of it before going any further. If the people wish to make a snap judgment and to get an opinion without considering all the elements, I, for one, would refuse to go any further and would prefer to resign on the spot because it is most evident to me that we cannot do justice to the situation in a hurry. I do not see my way clear to making even a tentative report. I think you will find that our best supporters in Cleveland will take the same view, viz. that we should be deliberate in this matter. It won't do for us to be too hasty and then make mistakes. . . . We will not have to carry out any preconceived idea of any individual or set of individuals. We are there to handle the problems in the broadest and most comprehensive manner for the people. I write this," he concluded, "because you have repeatedly said . . . that you are nervous and wish you had nothing to do with the scheme. We will do the most reasonable thing in the end and don't let us allow anybody to disturb our equilibrium or in the slightest degree harry our horses."[8]

There were times, however, when even Burnham seemed discouraged. Being financially independent and dedicated to contributing his planning talents whenever and wherever possible, Burnham would have preferred not to accept a fee beyond his expenses. But Carrère and Brunner depended on an honorarium and to avoid embarrassment, Burnham joined the other two in accepting a salary of $5000.00 a year, plus expenses. Despite its enthusiasm for the project, however, the city was often slow in paying the commissioners and on behalf of his two associates, Burnham was often forced to insist upon payment. It was "rather hard on the others," he wrote, "although it does not affect me very much." As for himself, he confided to a city official in temporary exasperation that the job was not the sort of thing "that one cares to hold except long enough to do his duty. The time I spend on it is a heavy loss to me and I shall be very glad indeed to be through with the work."[9]

The city's delinquencies and the commissioners' discouragements were relatively short-lived, however, and the project proceeded on all sides with a sureness and a confidence unusual for such enterprises. After the initial period of study and consultation in the summer and fall of 1902, Burnham, Carrère, and Brunner spent approximately one year discussing and refining the project. In New York, they set up a special office where drawings were made. Brunner and Carrère supervised the New York work and the mobile Burnham made frequent visits for inspection and criticism. "For over a year," Brunner later recalled, "we worked at the drawings and constantly conferred about the details of the plan, Mr. Burnham always adding fresh inspiration. . . . In writing the report,

which contained reproductions of our drawings, Mr. Burnham contributed largely to its presentation."[10]

The Burnham commission presented its report to Mayor Johnson and
the city of Cleveland on August 17, 1903. In essence the report recommended, as a civic center, a formal grouping of the six to eight proposed
buildings to be built in the near and distant future to house the city's
various governmental and cultural institutions. It placed the center, on
the shore of Lake Erie slightly to the northeast of the older commercial
and institutional hub known as the "Public Square." In close proximity
to the city's chief commercial and transportation nexus, the group plan
would facilitate a more efficient and convenient interchange of patrons
and staff members of the cultural and governmental agencies. The surrounding and connecting open spaces would offset the densely built-up
urban mass and would serve as a central park and recreational center
for visitors, citizens, and civic employees. It was hoped that ultimately
the complex would articulate and symbolize Cleveland's civic pride and
character. Similar schematically to the World's Fair Court of Honor, the
Cleveland proposal required, however, the acquisition, demolition, and
clearing of over a hundred acres of densely built-up urban land. Burnham had built the White City of 1893 in the open, unimpeded wastes
of Jackson Park. In Cleveland he faced, not surprisingly, a much more
real and formidable set of conditions.[11]

The area marked for reclamation formed in 1903 the core of a miser-
able and crime-ridden slum. The waterfront dives, bordellos, and tene-
ments had long embarrassed the city's progressive up-lifters and had
formed prime targets for their reforming zeal. Implementation of the
Burnham proposals would therefore serve quintessentially progressive
goals: the elimination of Skid Row, the revitalization of the lake front,
and the primary aim of attaining the much-needed civic center. There
was, unfortunately, little apparent concern on anyone's part for helping
to relocate the displaced persons made homeless by the demolition
project.[12]

The main axis of the proposed complex was to run north and south
along Wood Street from Superior Street toward the Lake. A green,
park-like mall would be developed on both sides of that line. The secondary axis, accordingly, ran east and west along the Lake front. "To
give absolute symmetry to the head of the Mall and to form an adequate
and imposing termination," the Public Library and Federal Building
would be of nearly identical exterior design, complementing each other

Paris, Place de la Concorde, a major reference for the Cleveland Civic Center. Author.

Plan of Cleveland Civic Center. *Report on a Group Plan of . . . Cleveland.*

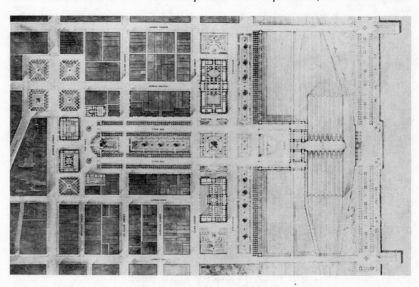

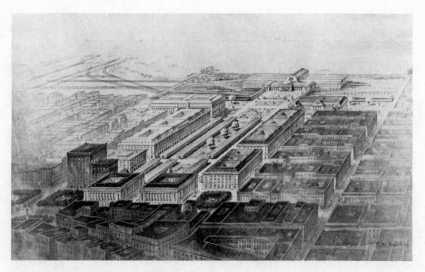

Cleveland Civic Center, looking north. *Report on a Group Plan of . . . Cleveland.*

Cleveland Civic Center, looking south. *Report on a Group Plan of . . . Cleveland.*

on either side of Wood Street. Inspiration for that element, as in much City Beautiful planning, came from abroad and from the past, combining the concern for modern, practical functionalism with paradoxically conservative allegiance to older forms and stylistic solutions. The Library and the Federal Building were to be "too near each other to be dissimilar, except in minor details," Brunner later explained, "and we intended them to be twin buildings alike in composition, treatment and scale. We took for our inspiration the Place de la Concorde and recalled the two beautiful buildings with which we are all so familiar. Wood Street is about the same width as the Rue Royale, which separates Gabriel's masterpieces and we included in our report a photograph of them with our views of Paris."[13]

The opposite or north end of the proposed mall called for a different treatment and the planners placed the City Hall and the County Court House in key positions across from each other as anchors for the whole composition. Separated by approximately 600 feet of mall, it was not necessary, the planners thought, "for them to be identical in design like the Federal Building and the Library, only the general mass, height, and treatment were to be the same. . . ." The façades "that now face the central axis," Brunner later noted after the actual completion of the buildings, "will be seen to balance extremely well notwithstanding some difference in treatment and the fact that one has an Ionic order and the other Doric." Other spaces on the main axis of the Mall, reserved for future civic administrative buildings, were ultimately occupied by such institutions as the Board of Education and the Public Auditorium.[14]

The location of the proposed Union Railway Terminal caused much discussion in the early planning sessions. Burnham's Chicago architectural firm had received a tentative commission to design a station if the several roads and the city of Cleveland could ever agree to get together and contribute the necessary funds. His position, therefore, vis-à-vis the railroads and the planning commission, was similar to his earlier position in Washington, where he was also chairman of the planning commission and architect-designate of the future Union Station. In both situations he expressed concern that his relationship with one group should not compromise his position with the other. On the contrary, he hoped that his dual position of planner and architect would allow him to mediate conflict and coordinate mutual interests. Planners should recognize, he felt, the dominant position of the railroad in the life and imagination of modern American society and should acknowledge that phenomenon with appropriate architectural symbols. There were also compelling practical factors. Existing railway tracks and traffic already ran along the lake shore. Moving them inland, even if desirable, would cost the city and the railroads dearly. It therefore seemed appropriate and to the best advantage of the railroads, the public, and the proposed Group Plan to locate the new station squarely in the center of the northern edge of the composition, facing southward to the mall and northward to the landscaped lake shore. In convenient proximity to both civic and commercial hubs, the social dynamics of the continually busy station would provide the diversity and the mixture of land use so essential to the vitality of the civic center area. Indeed the proposal spoke to both functional and aesthetic needs.[15]

Again harking back to the White City's Court of Honor, Burnham recalled that there had been a similar lakeside closure to complete the Chicago composition in the form of a colonnade to connect the wings of the primary axis. He felt that the Cleveland plan called for a similar treatment. "With our modern civilization," he then argued in the report, "the railroad has practically replaced the highway, and the railway station in its function at least has practically replaced the city gate." Indeed, in 1903, the promise of the automobile and of the airplane seemed too remote to justify any other view. Only a clairvoyant could have prophesied the demise of the railroad a half-century later when the crowded highways resumed their prominence and the equally crowded airways made the railways obsolete. "If the railroad station," Burnham continued, "can be made really imposing—a dignified and worthy monument, a beautiful vestibule to the town—it seems to us that this is a splendid opportunity of achieving great results. In bringing the visitor to Cleveland through a magnificent section of the city," he argued in a vein reminiscent of the Washington report, "his first impression, which is usually the most lasting, would be a favorable one." So large a mass, if placed off-center, would jar, he contended, the balance of the whole composition.[16]

Like other aspects of the Burnham report, the railroad's placement met with tentative, general approval. Unlike the plan's other major features, however, it was fated never to be realized. Its absence deprived the mall of much of the vitality and centrality its planners had envisioned. In the 1920s, long after Burnham's death, the machinations of businessmen and avaricious real estate speculators ultimately placed the station in the area southwest of the older Public Square, "a state of affairs," Arnold Brunner regretted, "that would probably not have existed if Mr. Burnham with his splendid enthusiasm, his force and personality, were here to plead for the execution of the plan on which he had set his heart."[17]

While acknowledging the limitations inherent in the original commission to confine themselves to the plans for a civic center, Burnham and his colleagues could not resist making a peroration on the virtues of broader-scaled comprehensive planning, recommending strongly that "the outlying parks, which are being made about the city of Cleveland and the other parks and squares within the city itself, should be developed with as much harmony as possible, and that a study should be made with a view to utilizing the most important avenues connecting these parks. . . ." The commission hoped, indeed, that the civic center would become a model for improving the architectural quality of the entire city.[18]

It also continued to identify "order" with "uniformity." "Your commission," the report concluded, "believes that all the buildings erected by the city should have a distinguishing character, that there is not a gain but a distinct loss in allowing the use of unrelated styles, or no styles, in schools, fire, police, and hospital buildings; that it would be much better to hold the designing within certain lines for these buildings—and that uniform architecture be maintained for each function, which shall make it recognizable at first glance. The jumble of buildings that surrounds us in our new cities contributes nothing valuable to life; on the contrary, it sadly disturbs our peacefulness and destroys that repose within us that is the true basis of all contentment. Let the public authorities, therefore, set an example of simplicity and uniformity, not necessarily producing monotony, but, on the contrary resulting in beautiful designs entirely harmonious with each other. The city and county buildings cannot all be monumental," the commissioners realized, "but they may have a distinguishing character that shall at once mark their purpose and relate them to the main structures of this group. Only in this way, as is so clearly established by a record of centuries throughout the older cities of the world, can a great city also become a beautiful city." In conclusion, the commissioners insisted that their report should not be considered final in scope or conclusive in detail but rather an indication of the direction the city might follow through the years.[19]

The plan was widely publicized in exhibits and in the local newspapers. Mayor Johnson liked it and so did most of his constituents. The favorable response from the press, the public, and city officials pleased the commissioners immensely. In discussing the plan before the A.I.A., John Carrère acknowledged that the commission's "labors have been made unusually easy because the people of Cleveland have been so sincerely interested in the project. They have been public spirited and enthusiastic," he noted. "We have received little or no criticism, and no end of suggestions, all of which have been very helpful." He could, in fact, "hardly conceive of circumstances under which the citizens of a large city like this could possibly lay aside every personal and other consideration to a greater extent than they have done here, simply with the one object of helping the commission and suggesting what they want as to the best possible grouping of these buildings." *The Inland Architect* was also complimentary of the commissioners and of the city stating that, next to the recent report of the Washington commission, the Cleveland work was "the most considerable effort to group the public buildings of a great city. . . . With the project in charge of the highest authorities in the United States and a well defined purpose on the part of the city to provide the proper setting for its public buildings," the report, it believed, was "well worth general consideration. Its lines, though local in purpose, are general in their adaptability to the problem of municipal improvement that confronts every city in the light of modern enterprise and art culture."[20]

Suggestive of the permanent and more comprehensive city planning commissions that all major cities would develop later in the century, the city of Cleveland extended as early as June 18, 1902, the duties of the Group Plan commissioners to include "the supervision and control of the location of all public, municipal, and county buildings to be erected upon ground acquired within the limits of said city, and . . . have control of the size, height, style, and general appearance of all such buildings for the purpose of securing in their location and erection the greatest degree of usefulness, safeness, and beauty. . . ." Burnham, Carrère, and Brunner, therefore, were not only consulted in subsequent years about the designs for the buildings of the Civic Center itself, "but also of many minor public buildings, schools, branch libraries, markets, bath houses, etc., and projects such as the treatment of several miles of Lake Front, the terminus of the high level bridge, and a proposed Lake Shore Boulevard. In fact," Brunner admitted, "we performed in part the function of an Art Commission to the City." After presenting their report, each of the three commissioners continued in an advisory capacity at a salary of two thousand dollars a year as long as they lived.[21]

The friendship and mutual respect of Chairman Burnham and Mayor Johnson continued over the years. On November 7, 1907, Burnham wrote to the mayor that he had noted his re-election "with much satisfaction," and believed, "as everyone does, this will open the way for continued work on the improvements which were so well begun by you and which have received such favorable comment all over the country."[22]

Later progress in realizing the plan was not always steady or certain, however. Brunner recalled, for example, that there was "a period . . . when the progress of the work was interrupted by what seemed to us inexplicable legal obstructions, but after much loss of time these obstacles were removed. Then there were suggestions, prompted by false economy, to make the Mall smaller and reduce the scale of the undertaking; but they were rejected by the City authorities. . . . The delays incidental to a great city enterprise were sometimes discouraging," he concluded, "and there were periods of depression due to postponements and inactivity, but on reflection the scheme has progressed as fast as could be expected."[23]

In 1911 and 1912, the Federal Building and the County Court House were completed and dedicated. Arnold Brunner designed the neoclassical Federal Building, setting the tone that the three-man commission had been so eager to establish. Not only did the civic center and its individual buildings recall the aura of the Chicago World's Fair, but exposition alumni reappeared, not surprisingly, to decorate the buildings' interiors. In the federal and county buildings there were paintings and murals by Edwin Blashfield, Kenyon Cox, and Francis Millet, as well as sculpture by Karl Bitter and Daniel Chester French. In 1911, Burnham sent his regrets that he could not be present for the laying of the cornerstone of the city hall, "the third great governmental building to be erected in conformity with the Group Plan adopted years ago. Many civic center designs," he noted, "have been adopted by American cities, but this Group Plan of Cleveland is the only one so far which has been . . . carried out." Two buildings had been completed, he noted, a third one begun, and a fourth one ready to be started in the near future. "Nowhere else has such actual progress in civic improvement been made, and Cleveland should be proud of the energy and enterprise she has shown in this movement. She should also be proud," he noted finally, looking back on his own long planning career, "that her leadership

Cleveland Civic Center, looking north toward lake. Author.

in civic improvement has had a great influence on other places; on the men in them who are striving to awaken in their own towns the same fine spirit your people have manifested during the many years you have steadily been pushing forward the Group Plan of Cleveland."[24]

A contemporary English critic, writing in the *Town Planning Review*, voiced many of the same sentiments. The new Cleveland concept in civic center planning, he argued, was important because it was "one of the first to be projected . . . certainly the finest in design, and . . . the furthest advanced toward completion." The progressive journalist and architecture critic, Herbert Croly, reviewing the plan in the *Architectural Record*, also agreed that the plan for Cleveland was already a success. "There is no other city in the country," he wrote, "where the local aspiration toward cleanliness, comeliness, and wholesomeness of municipal life has received abler and more varied expression. . . ."[25]

One of the cities that Cleveland influenced lay clear across the American continent on a peninsula of the Pacific Coast, a city that Burnham, like most of its visitors, found charming, challenging, and unique. San Francisco was the next city to gain Burnham's services as a planner; in

Cleveland Federal Building and Library. Author.

creating the San Francisco Plan, he drew heavily on his recent experiences in Cleveland. Yet, while the modest Cleveland effort met with relative success, the ambitious schemes for San Francisco met—for the most part—with tragedy and defeat.

To a certain extent in Cleveland and in his later plans for San Francisco and Chicago, Burnham worked both for, and at cross-purposes with, any truly "progressive" movement in American life and architecture. While basically a supporter of capitalistic individualism, he also saw the need—perhaps in the interest of conserving that system—for greater social collectivization and cooperative sacrifice among individual citizens. Long-range, large-scale planning would, he realized, proscribe certain rights and prerogatives of the individual citizen. He believed, however, that in the United States of the early twentieth century, rampant individualism had gone too far and that the system's inherent atomism was slowly destroying itself. He realized that there was in the United States what a later observer would call "an excess of democracy." And to meet that problem, at least in an architectural and environmental sense, he urged a greater combination of central planning and voluntary individual cooperation.

If indeed such ends and means can be labeled Progressive, according to the lights of the day, and identified with other parallel currents in American society, the actual finish and form that Burnham's projects often assumed were, by contrast, derivative and reactionary. His energetic fight for changing, building, grouping, and restructuring the face of America's urban landscape, assumed the dimensions of a real reform movement or at least of an important architectural arm of that movement. His resorts, however, to antique academic formulas as the recommended style of the "New Metropolis" were self-defeating and contradictory.

While the spatial groupings, circulation solutions, and landscaping suggestions of the Cleveland Group Plan contained elements of functional and aesthetic merit, both for the present and future, the planners retreated in their actual architectural proposals to the warmth and safety of the neoclassical womb. And taking the path of least resistance, following the lead of the acknowledged experts, the otherwise progressive city officials and the Cleveland public followed them into the comfortable and less demanding orbits of the tried and the familiar. Eschewing the inventiveness and the originality of the modern architecture of their own generation—of the Chicago School and the Prairie School, for example—the commissioners and the citizens of twentieth-century Cleveland opted for the ambience of L'Enfant's Washington, of the World's Columbian Exposition, and of numerous, earlier Old World references. And to a great extent, that tension of adventure and retreat, that dichotomy so evident in the Cleveland Group Plan, symbolized much of the Progressive Movement itself. In the Cleveland plan, the duality of the Chicago Fair's influence was once again confirmed.

IX
The Promise of Urban Planning
The San Francisco Plan of 1905

At my feet lay a great city. Miles of broad streets, shaded by trees and lined with fine buildings . . . stretched in every direction. Every quarter contained large open squares filled with trees, along which statues glistened and fountains flashed in the late-afternoon sun. Public buildings of a colossal size and architectural grandeur . . . raised their stately piles on every side. . . .

EDWARD BELLAMY
Looking Backward

THE WORD "PROMISE" seems to have delighted the journalist Herbert Croly, for he used it often in his writings. Long celebrated for his reform treatise, *The Promise of American Life* and for the influence of his thought on Theodore Roosevelt and other reformers, Croly preceded his years on the national scene with a longer yet lesser known career as an architecture critic. In early 1906, he wrote an essay for the *Architectural Record* on Daniel Burnham as city planner and on his recently published plan for, as Croly called it, "The Promised City of San Francisco."[1]

Burnham's plan, Croly wrote, "should be of peculiar interest, not only to architects and to the residents of the Pacific Coast, but to all Americans whose patriotism contains any infusion of national aesthetic aspiration. . . . Such a plan was demanded by two conditions—first by the unique opportunity which the site affords, and second, by the execrable manner in which, up to the present time, this site has been mutilated."[2]

Long before 1906, however, concerned and observant San Franciscans

174

had expressed the same sentiments, attributing the "mutilation" that Croly described to the familiar forces of individual greed, aggressive commercialism and social inertia. Few, of course, ever denied that the city of approximately 350,000 was economically prosperous and that it indicated signs of even greater prosperity. Fewer still failed to acknowledge the buoyant, exuberant and often bawdy ambience that gave to San Francisco the reputation of a wide-open, fun-loving city. Such moral permissiveness, however, had also permeated City Hall and the greater part of the 1890s had witnessed a series of bribery and extortion scandals.[3]

The few and sporadic attempts at reform were generally unsuccessful until the administration of the progressive aristocrat, James D. Phelan. Under Phelan's leadership from 1897 to 1901, San Francisco enjoyed generally honest, efficient, and economical government. The mayor obtained a liberalization of San Francisco's charter that granted the city the right to purchase and operate all "public" utilities. Pending such acquisition, the charter placed new restrictions on the granting of franchises to private owners. But in 1901, Phelan found himself caught in the middle of a bitter war between the forces of labor and capital. As much opposed to big labor as he was to big business and to what he sensed as essentially autocratic tendencies in both, Phelan's moderate, political liberalism forced him to make an unpopular decision. In the bloody San Francisco strike of 1901, he used police to break up picket line violence, thereby incurring the enmity of the unions. Equally alienated from the opposing forces of management, he realized the futility of seeking re-election himself, and his party's candidate lost the mayor's chair to a heterogeneous political coalition shrewdly manipulated by boss Abe Ruef. Under the banner of the Union Labor Party, Phelan's mayoral successor, hand-picked by Ruef, was the handsome, adroit, former leader of the local musicians' union, Eugene E. Schmitz, whose surface charm and convincing bravado covered for years his talents for graft.[4]

Forced by the Schmitz-Ruef victory into at least temporary retirement, James D. Phelan and the cast-out reform forces determined that their energies and resources should be rechanneled into some continuing, though unofficial program for the city's improvement. Like most progressive leaders, Phelan's group, for the most part, was composed of well-bred, well-educated, respected, upper-middle-class business or professional men who, if not actually wealthy, were usually "well-fixed."

They strongly resented their political impotence and desperately needed to compete and "keep up" with the newly victorious amalgam of suspect labor leaders and bribe-paying businessmen. And while nursing their wounds and working for re-election, they found a cause that suited their talents: the crusade for a new city plan.[5]

Phelan and his ousted colleagues were not alone, however, in calling attention to San Francisco's cultural and architectural problems. Editors, educators, and civic-minded businessmen were already sounding alarms, attacking their city's smugness and complacency. It was especially fashionable among most San Franciscans to jest condescendingly about their city's superiority to Los Angeles to the effect that the southern city was little more than a desert outpost. The natural setting, the excellent harbor, and the urbane social climate of the northern city seemed to assure most San Franciscans that they need never fear any competition from the South. But more critical northern Californians replied that such a view was dangerously outdated. Allan Pollok, manager of the St. Francis Hotel, insisted, for example, that "San Francisco has been asleep while Southern California which offers nothing like the inducements we have within our grasp to lay before visitors, has taken possession of the tourists and the wealthy people from the East who come to California looking for homes. Los Angeles has gone far ahead of us in that direction."[6]

Pollok reminded his fellow citizens that, despite its superb location, San Francisco was sadly lacking in man-made cultural amenities. Its civic and commercial architecture left much to be desired. In comparison to Los Angeles, he argued, San Franciscans lacked the sense of community and civic pride that was essential for motivating improvement. In Los Angeles, the "citizens have worked together . . . and the result is apparent even to the casual observer: for the tourists make it their stopping place for the winter, while many of them . . . make it their home. San Francisco sees them passing by her doors." Business and civic leaders should join forces for concerted action. There was, he asserted, "no denying the fact that we are lacking in many of the essentials which no really great metropolis can afford to be without and that the times are propitious for those of our capitalists who are possessed of civic pride to give substantial support to all undertakings that conduce to agreeableness of life in this community." San Francisco, he believed, should and could become for Americans "what Paris is to Europeans—the great city of pleasure." Numerous other citizens echoed Pollok's calls for reform.[7]

Phelan, in particular, encouraged and articulated the growing civic sentiment, calling for a city plan "before it is too late . . . prepared by a competent person or commission, as has been done recently for the city of Washington, D.C., and for Cleveland, Ohio. . . ." Such a plan, he argued, must "show what old streets should be widened or new ones made; where public buildings should be located; where new roads should be laid out . . . and once having a plan, we can build with confidence." In calling for a "competent person or commission" to renovate San Francisco in the manner of the recent plans for Washington and Cleveland, he was obviously alluding to the possibilities of acquiring the services of Daniel Burnham.[8]

Burnham and Phelan had met each other briefly during Burnham's previous business and social visits to San Francisco. Willis Polk, Burnham's junior colleague, in charge of the firm's San Francisco office, had served as the go-between, discussing the possibility of a San Francisco plan with both men as early as the fall of 1903. On October 27, for example, Burnham wrote to Polk regretting that on his last visit he "did not see Mr. Phelan, as making the plan for San Francisco would be the most delightful occupation possible." More encouraging correspondence followed and in contemplating the possibilities, Burnham became increasingly excited. "As I said before," he wrote again to Polk, "I could not undertake such a thing unless given a completely free hand. It would have to be a labor of love or I could not touch it and therefore I would not wish to take even a retainer." He would ask only for expenses, but expenses, he felt, would have to include a research trip abroad.[9]

He was certain, he wrote to Polk, that a "study of the old hill-towns that run down to the sea is essential. This may not seem to the inexperienced man to be a necessity," he argued, but the Washington project had convinced him that without such a study, the work there "would have suffered severely. We learned what to avoid and what to do." Similarly, he believed that "the San Francisco designers should see the towns all around the Mediterranean. Your city wants the best," he told Polk, "but the human brain is not comprehensive enough to evolve it without seeing the important things men have already done for similar locations. You know how meager are the available documents and also

that no document is of much value when compared to the thing itself.
There are thirty towns on the western slope of the Anti-Lebanons north
of Beirut. Do you suppose one could fail to find among them things he
ought to know if he is to make suggestions for San Francisco?" Though
he returned to Europe several times in the next few years, Burnham did
not actually make the recommended trip before composing the San
Francisco Plan. He did not have to; he had already seen the places he had
suggested and they had moved him greatly. It was obvious in the fall of
1903 that Burnham wanted desperately to do a San Francisco plan. Perhaps he sensed that his prospective patrons already knew he had the
experience he himself had proposed was necessary and that this knowledge would strengthen their inclinations to engage him.[10]

In San Francisco, Phelan and his associates were likewise becoming
more excited and encouraged, and on January 4, 1904, they invited a
group of leading San Franciscans sympathetic to their cause to meet
later in the month at the Merchants' Exchange "to formally discuss a
plan for the improvement of San Francisco." Editor Fremont Older of
the *San Francisco Bulletin* hailed his friend Phelan and the movement's
other sponsors. "The committee," he noted, "seems to mean business,
and men who mean business can do wonders in a short while. These
men are accustomed to producing results. They have what is called
executive ability; that is, the faculty of doing things while others are
talking about doing them. It is time for every public spirited citizen to
come forward."[11]

At the Merchants' Exchange meeting on January 15, the select group
of "public-spirited citizens" organized themselves as the "Association
for the Improvement and Adornment of San Francisco" and, not surprisingly, elected Phelan their president. Discussion of previously recommended areas of improvement continued and Phelan summarized the
content of Burnham's proposals in his recent letter to Polk. Phelan then
appointed an executive steering committee that included such citizens
as the hosteler Alan Pollok. From approximately twenty original participants the association's founders agreed to broaden their base to include
all genuinely interested citizens, and within a year, membership exceeded four hundred. The widely publicized goals of the association
were "to promote in every practical way the beautifying of the streets,
public buildings, parks, squares, and places of San Francisco, to bring
to the attention of the officials and people of the city the best methods
for instituting artistic municipal betterment; to stimulate the sentiment

of civic pride in the improvement and care of private property; to suggest quasi-public enterprises and, in short, to make San Francisco a more agreeable city in which to live."[12]

By late April, the association agreed to Phelan's suggestion that they extend a formal invitation to Daniel Burnham, and on May 1 the architect arrived in San Francisco, accompanied by his wife, to survey and discuss the possibilities. "All up early to see entrance to mountains," his diary read for the last day of the train trip, "all in snow until Dutch Gulch, then burst of summer and wonderful, flowery, blossoming California. Everything at its best." For two delightful weeks, Burnham explored in great detail an area with which he was already more than familiar, talking, dining, and socializing with personal friends and with civic and association officials. He swam and fished in the ocean at Carmel and he particularly enjoyed the exciting novelty of touring the area "in automobiles." On May 4, the association honored him with a lavish dinner and on May 6, he spoke to a large gathering of representatives of civic groups, including the California Club, the Merchants' Club, and the Outdoor Art League. After listening to suggestions and soliciting advice from the collective membership, Burnham addressed the two hundred citizens in the confident and optimistic metaphors of Progressive nationalism. "No such intelligence," he told his audience, "was ever before found among seventy million people as exists in the United States, and the education which obtains can only result in the great improvement of cities which is now going on. We have our foot on a stairway leading to a place which no other people have ever reached." He was pleased to note that the suggestions offered him "showed that the citizens have intelligence and advanced ideas."[13]

The civic response to Burnham was as warm as Burnham's own response had been to San Francisco. Fremont Older's *Bulletin* was the most enthusiastic newspaper, but even the conservative *Chronicle* gave guarded approval. The plans Burnham outlined were grand indeed, "but alas," the *Chronicle* warned, "it is not the plans which present difficulties, but the execution. . . . As one looks at the beautiful eminences once so easily available for public purposes and adornment, there comes a deep feeling of regret that at the birth of San Francisco there was present no Washington to foresee its future and no L'Enfant to lay down the lines of its growth. To that, however, at once succeeds the reflection that if all this could have been far more easily arranged for a half century ago than now, that which is necessary is far easier of ac-

complishment now than it will be half a century hence. And this reflection should be the father of the swift determination to do the duty
of this generation."[14]

After nine weeks of orientation and discussion, Burnham returned to
Chicago to examine other civic and architectural projects on his calendar and to discuss the San Francisco project with his able new planning
assistant, Edward Bennett. In advance of his next San Francisco visit,
Burnham also requested special working facilities. In a letter to Willis
Polk, he described his need to be up and away from the city's congestion, and "to camp up on Twin Peaks." "Could use a big double tent
or build a room in which Bennett might winter," he noted. "Being up
there we can constantly see the city and everything else and this will be
of great value to us. Who owns the ground? Can we get permission?
Could we have a barrel of water, a stove, wood, etc., up there and inci-
dently a Chinese servant to cook and do things? This scheme might
seem visionary," he admitted to Polk, "but you can realize the value of
it to me." He did not "want to work on the San Francisco scheme in a
down town office," but instead "must be where the influence about
me shall stimulate Golden Gate Thoughts." He was certain that "the
Twin Peaks would best suit, because from that location I can see clear
around the compass—the Lake Merced Country, the sea, the Presidio,
the town, the Bay and the mountains beyond." Before the age of aerial
photography, Burnham sought a panoramic perspective by simply requi-
sitioning the highest mountain.[15]

As in most other things, he got what he asked for. In late September
he arrived with Bennett to begin work. Edward Bennett was a young
English architect, and a recent graduate of the Ecole des Beaux Arts,
whom Burnham had met and "taken to" instantly. Later, indeed, in describing Bennett, he also succinctly described himself. Bennett had, he
said "a deep and reverend spirit"; he was "a poet with his feet on the
earth." Work continued unbroken for weeks and included the usual
touring, surveying, thinking, discussing, photographing, sketching, drafting, and writing. In the autumn of 1904, leaving Bennett in charge,
Burnham sailed for the Philippines, at the request of the American
government, to prepare city plans for Manila and Baguio. Returning in
the spring of 1905, he rejoined the work in progress, commuting and
communicating between Twin Peaks and his Chicago office. By July
he could write that "the plan is nearly completed and will be published

in a few months. . . . Nothing has been omitted which ideal conditions seem to demand."[16]

On September 15, 1905, he submitted the report to the Improvement Association stressing in his cover letter the contributions of Bennett. "San Francisco deserves and in years to come will surely receive the best and broadest treatment," he wrote. "The endeavor on my part has been to find the logical lines on which this treatment must necessarily develop, and to record them. If I have been successful in this attempt, the Association may rest assured that this report will make its own way as years go on—and that it will be a document of increasing value to the community. The scope of the report covers work," he continued, "to be done during the next fifty years. It is evident that this work will go forward gradually from time to time." The most pressing improvement to be made, he noted, was the building of an outer boulevard skirting the waterfront. Once that was done, he believed, the whole civic line would be affected. And perhaps, he admitted, "it is quite possible that I am too conservative regarding the length of time necessary for the carrying out of the whole plan. The movement in the direction of extensive public improvements is accelerating," he concluded, "and the demands of the people are everywhere broadening, and it may well be that what seems a stupendous undertaking will not be regarded so a little later on." Far too optimistic in his faith for the plan's "inevitable" success, Burnham's largeness of vision and faith in the future again led him to "make no little plans."[17]

The scope of the plan was general, Burnham wrote in an introductory statement. "It is not the province of a report of this kind to indicate the exact details very closely." He also knew that "all the work indicated can or ought [not] to be carried out at once or even in the near future. A plan beautiful and comprehensive enough for San Francisco," he said, "can only be executed by degrees, as the growth of the community demands and as its financial ability allows. The plan is so devised that the execution of each part will contribute to the final result" that would "combine convenience and beauty in the greatest possible degree." He believed that "a scheme of parks, streets, and public grounds for a city, in order to be at once comprehensive and practical, should take into account the public purse of today and embrace those things that can be immediately carried into effect, but should in no wise limit itself to these. It should be designed not only for the present but for all time to come. While prudence," he acknowledged, "holds up a warning finger, we must not forget what San Francisco has become in fifty years and what it is still further destined to become. Population and wealth are rapidly increasing," he argued, "culture is advancing. The city looks toward a sure future wherein it will possess in inhabitants and money many times what it has now. It follows that we must not found the scheme on what the city is, so much as on what it is to be. We must remember that a meager plan will fall short of perfect achievement, while a great one will yield large results, even if it is never fully realized."[18]

Again, in the San Francisco Plan, Burnham exemplified trenchantly the opposing, yet complementary sides of his nature—the romantic dreamer and the pragmatic realist, qualities that likewise characterized many of his urban Progressive peers. "The first step in civic improvement," he urged, for example, "should be towards ideal streets, faultless in equipment and immaculately clean. Until this is taken, monuments and statues are out of place; men and events can be much more effectually commemorated by street improvements." He became more poetic, however, when suggesting the treatment and the possible uses of those streets. The outer boulevard, he proposed, should be "beautifully treated. There should be enough space to allow a foot or two of earth for planting. It will then be an ideal place for a ride or a walk, the passer-by looking down on the shipping below, and when he tires of watching the activities and listening to the voices of the men engaged in the work of the port, he may note the changing aspects of the sea and study the effects of sunshine and shadow on islands and mountains seen through the masts of the ships. This treatment will lend delightful variety to a drive on the boulevard, and will add a special charm to the life of the city."[19]

Though Burnham insisted that the plan was general and would contain a minimum of detail, its 184 pages included sufficient elaboration to illustrate the general points. Of all discerning professional critics, Herbert Croly not only wrote the most favorable review, but provided as well the best short summary of the plan's essential features. His critique epitomized the reaction to Burnham's planning ideas by Americans who considered themselves progressive in such matters. Croly first lamented, as Burnham had done, the generally irrevocable factor of the existing gridiron street plan, unimaginative and inconvenient even in the flattest of cities but totally inappropriate for much of the hilly San Francisco topography. Total alteration of the right-angled layout would, however, be virtually impossible, and Croly approved of Burnham's compromise proposal to encircle the city with the grand outer boulevard, to which all other major streets would lead. In addition to the boulevard, there would be a number of new diagonal streets, which would facilitate circulation and unite the older and the newer sections of the city. In an era when the automobile was still a little-known rarity, Burnham also issued far-sighted calls for one-way traffic on the smaller, more congested streets.[20]

The new San Francisco, Croly noted, would be grouped around a civic center of cultural and governmental buildings situated at the important intersection of Market Street and Van Ness Avenue. Business was obviously pushing out in that direction, "and in selecting this location for the core of his new city, Mr. Burnham has effected a useful union between his ideal plan and the actual business expansion of the city." From that civic center plaza would radiate the most important avenues, which would, periodically, widen into traffic circles and spawn more subsidiary radiating streets. A broad thoroughfare, the so-called Panhandle, would connect Golden Gate Park with the central plaza and then proceed eastward through the plaza to the bay. The Panhandle would, in effect, constitute an oblique cross axis to the main artery of Market Street, the two streets meeting at the proposed civic center.[21]

Croly admired the logic of the scheme and believed that "everybody who knows the city will understand that it constitutes an ingenious and complete means of connecting by broad thoroughfares its several main divisions." One arm of Market Street would aim for Twin Peaks and the great new sections beyond. Another would lead in the opposite direction to the shops and banks of the financial district. The Panhandle, on the other hand, would "run from the Plaza to the one park of which San Francisco can be proud at present, and its continuation beyond the Square will give direct means of communication to a busy manufacturing district." Bisecting the two obtuse angles that Market and the Panhandle would form on the north and south, Van Ness Avenue would then lead north to "what is at present the most desirable residential quarter," and south to the railway station, at which point all the trains coming from the south would enter the city. "Thus the residence, the financial, the shopping and the manufacturing regions," he noted, "are tied together with broad, convenient and imposing thoroughfares, while at the same time the most beautiful parks and undefiled hills are made much more accessible than they are at present."[22]

Croly particularly approved of Burnham's ambitious plans for the city's park system. "The steep hills," he wrote admiringly, "on and around which so much of San Francisco is and must be built, and commanding as they do magnificent views of the noble bay and fine country sides to the south, afford on their crowns and slopes, opportunities for parks, which in themselves would repay a journey across the continent." Such opportunities he lamented, had, "so far been largely neglected, Golden Gate Park being the only important exception. Even Telegraph Hill, which is so steep that nobody but very poor people will live on its slopes, and around which so many racy historical memories gather—even Telegraph Hill has been left in a squalid, disheveled and almost useless condition." He was pleased that the Burnham plan proposed to restore and recover such mutilated areas.[23]

It also seemed logical that, instead of the irrationally straight, steep, and right-angled streets, the new plan called for "level contour roadways around the sides of the hills . . . accented at places of interest by

Bird's-eye perspective of San Francisco from Twin Peaks showing the proposed changes. *Report of a Plan for San Francisco.*

Proposed treatment of Telegraph Hill, San Francisco. *Report of a Plan for San Francisco.*

terraces and approached gradually from the abutting streets. The top of Telegraph Hill is to be made into a park, especially designed, in order to give some kind of foreground to the views of the shipping and bay to be seen therefrom, and the lines of approach are to be completely reformed." Pacific Heights and Russian Hill would be reached by circular parkways with appropriate variants of the same treatment for Lone Mountain, Buena Vista Park Hill, Potrero Heights, Bernal Heights, Sutro Heights, and the hills south of Islais Creek. Croly rejoiced that the Presidio would become a great landscaped park, as a monument to the United States Army. "But the Twin Peaks and the Lake of Merced beyond," he believed, "are to be made the occasion of the largest and probably the most beautiful park of all . . . and by the time San Francisco has a population of several millions, it may well be the most convenient spot for the great popular festivities . . . for public fetes and entertainment on a very considerable scale, so that this park will contribute more than any other single feature of the city to the fulfillment of San Francisco's obvious opportunity to become a great pleasure resort."[24]

In reviewing so briefly the plan's major features, Croly failed, under-standably, to note a number of its interesting but less obvious aspects. Though Burnham had remarked, rather vaguely, that the city's residen-tial areas should "develop as necessity demands," they should neverthe-less "be studied in anticipation for the right size of block, size of street and general disposition, preservation of viewpoints, park areas, etc., in order that once settled into place the best districts may be valuable to all and initial errors will not have to be rectified at great cost." He then proposed one of the plan's more interesting and significant sociological

Plan of proposed San Francisco Civic Center. *Report of a Plan for San Francisco.*

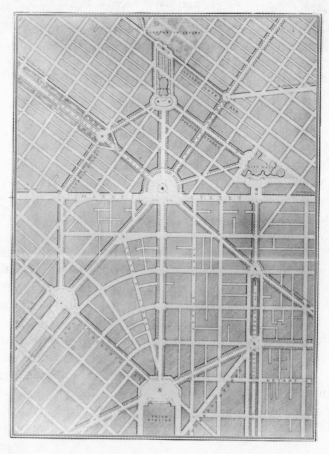

Bird's-eye view of San Francisco from the bay. *Report of a Plan for San Francisco.*

ideas arguing modestly that "a great charm might be lent to certain quarters, particularly the less expensive and flatter sections of the city by the elimination of some of the streets in the monotonous system of blocks and the substitution of a chain of park-like squares, formed in a measure by the unused or misused backyard areas. The isolated square of the Old World," Burnham noted, "unless maintained by wealthy residents, is a quiet, almost desolate spot, seldom feeling the throb of life. The chain is suggested to obviate this, and induce a current of life to flow agreeably from end to end to the exclusion of unnecessary vehicles, thus leaving the main traffic to the intermediate streets." In that way, he argued, the "Park chains would become public avenues of beautiful planting, in which one could walk with great comfort, and where children could play, free from the danger of traffic. Such a system," Burnham concluded, "would provide well for children who seldom know any life except that upon the streets of the city and would be the natural approach or connecting link between the larger parks and play grounds." Furthermore, he added, with unconscious irony, the cordons of parks would be especially significant in case of a future general con-

flagration. Suggestions for such urban land reform, however, have generally made little headway against the dominant American impulses toward privacy and individualism—needs usually satisfied only by cutting
up potentially useful communal areas into smaller, protected, isolated
plots.[25]

It was also understandable that Croly and his contemporaries might
also pass over one of Burnham's "minor" observations that would loom
much larger later in the century. On the question of air pollution, Burnham admitted that San Francisco was better favored than many large
cities. It was indeed rather "happily placed in regard to its smoke-
producing section" since for the most part the factories were to the south
of the point where the prevailing westerly winds would blow across the
city. "The building of factories should therefore be discouraged on the
north side." Because there were occasional southern winds, "it would
be advisable to place these concerns whose smoke is particularly dis-
agreeable or injurious as far to the south as possible." Burnham also
made brief recommendations for the location and treatment of schools,
churches, hospitals, cemeteries, jails, "the almshouse," future water
reservoirs and especially subways. "Rapid underground traffic," he insisted, "solves the problem of moving large crowds from one center
to another in a manner that no surface system can accomplish. . . ."
Subways, he argued, should be constructed beneath all the major diagonal streets, especially Market Street, the city's most important thoroughfare. Indeed, despite its numerous Baroque extravagances and its
frequently grandiose spatial effects, the San Francisco Plan dealt with a
number of real and important urban problems. Especially in its park
and circulation proposals, it was more than merely an abstract design.[26]

With the San Francisco report, Burnham reached a new maturity as a
theoretician and practitioner of the new art of "planning." The Chicago
World's Fair, after all, had been only a temporary construct. The Washington Plan of 1902, while more lasting and comprehensive, had drawn
heavily on L'Enfant's older but neglected ideas. The Cleveland Group
Plan had dealt with new problems but had confined itself largely to the
relatively narrow focus of the downtown civic center. The plan for San
Francisco, on the other hand, covered the whole county and a large
portion of the peninsula. While touching on numerous and varied problems, Burnham's chief concern in San Francisco was the opening and
modernization of the city's rigid and cumbersome gridiron street arrangement. Indeed, in proposing both the cutting of new streets and

the widening of old ones, his most obvious reference was Baron Haussmann's replanning and rebuilding of Paris for Emperor Louis Napoleon in the 1850s and 1860s. Burnham was also aware of the contemporary mid-century restructuring of Vienna, especially the development of
the circular Ringstrasse, constructed on the former site of the old medieval city wall. Possibly the Ringstrasse inspired his proposal of the
shoreline drive to encircle San Francisco. Le Nôtre's work at Versailles
and the ancient and modern Roman precedents were always important
references. But, in terms of opening an older congested city—as opposed
to creating a new city altogether—the Haussmann example was paramount. By 1900, Burnham had become an avid reader and had collected
an impressive professional library. He was, no doubt, familiar with
Haussmann's *Reports* and *Memoires* and, most important, he had seen
the work first hand. His assistant, Edward Bennett, had studied in Paris
and, through personal observation, had also imbibed the Frenchman's
planning message. The results were evident in the San Francisco and
Manila plans. They would become even more manifest in Chicago.[27]

On the evening of September 27, 1905, to mark the formal acceptance
of the plan, the members of the Association for the Improvement and
Adornment of San Francisco and leading city officials held a grand banquet at the St. Francis Hotel. At the end of the dinner, they drank a
standing toast to the health of Daniel Burnham. William Greer Harrison, vice president of the San Francisco association, read Burnham's
cover letter accompanying the report. Two days later, the association
secretary, Thomas M'Caleb, wrote Burnham that the "plan has met
with both expert and popular success in this community. All classes are
pledged to see that its principal features are carried out as soon as possible." Even Mayor Schmitz seemed genuinely enthusiastic, a fact
which took on added significance when, to the liberals' chagrin, he won
re-election in the fall mayoralty race. To generate enthusiasm and support for the project, the city promptly appropriated money to have the
plan printed and distributed widely. Burnham was particularly concerned that the printing be perfect in every detail.[28]

While the report was being printed, Burnham continued, as he had
done with the Cleveland plan, to think and to talk about areas that the
plan, by definition, was *not* to cover, and to pipe-dream with Bennett
about the possible improvement of the entire Bay Area. He was especially attracted to the idea of a splendid treatment of the Pacific Coast,
southward of San Francisco, a project that evoked in his mind work

comparable in beauty to that of one of his favorite painters, the English proto-impressionist, J. M. W. Turner. "What you say about Half-Moon Bay is very seductive to me," he wrote to Bennett. "I should like nothing quite so well as to deal with that problem. . . . Won't they make for me 25 or 30 photographs? The shore itself and the approach to it from inland is the thing I would like to know all about. There has long been in my mind a dream of a water-side improvement such as was never perhaps carried out except by Turner in his visions of ancient towns by the sea. No where on earth is the ocean availed of by men as it should be. Perhaps we can set the pace and inoculate the men of the Pacific coast with the right ideas."[29]

Burnham knew of course that such grandly ambitious schemes would have to wait until after the fulfillment of the more immediate plans embodied in his report. Little did he realize that very soon, even the plan's most modest proposals would seem remote and untenable, that within a few months, his and the city's pleasantest dreams would die in the face of spectacular nightmare. Early in 1906, Daniel and Margaret Burnham sailed for Europe. On the morning of April 18, the earthquake struck. Fire destroyed all of the original drawings and models and most of the copies of the newly printed plan.[30]

The San Francisco fire and earthquake constituted one of the greatest calamities ever to strike an American city. Over five hundred people died in the disaster and four square miles became little more than ruins and rubble. The many forms of medical, economic, and psychological relief arranged for the victims and refugees were strong and immediate. Burnham himself sent $2000 to his friend Joseph Worcester to be used for relief cases as he saw fit "during the harder times to come." He was still in Europe when the disaster occurred and he promptly booked passage for immediate return to survey the scene.[31]

While lamenting the calamity and personal tragedy, a number of leading San Franciscans, especially James Phelan, saw the catastrophe as a natural stepping-stone to the implementation of the Burnham plan— as indeed the time when the plan's major features could be effected most logically, economically, and conveniently. Others argued that the situation's pressing contingencies called for precisely the opposite kind of rebuilding. What the city needed, they asserted, was quick, emergency reconstruction, anything, in fact, to revive the city's business and economic life, not the grand, ambitious, and inevitably slower building and planning for the distant future that Burnham had recommended.[32]

Much of the public in California and elsewhere awaited and reacted to Burnham's return as though he were some sort of special oracle who could help to resolve the San Francisco tragedy and suggest the correct and appropriate answers for meeting the problems that it posed. The day after his arrival home, he noted in his diary that the papers were "full of interviews with me regarding the San Francisco disaster." In those interviews and in private letters, Burnham expressed his great concern and continued interest in the city but doubted that he would "be employed in the rebuilding of San Francisco except as to such pieces of work as may come to our firm." He was "going out there, it is true . . . but I expect," he said, "to get through with this in a very few days. . . ."[33]

Before and after he revisited the city, however, Burnham urged that the city enact stringent fire and building codes as Chicago had done in the central business district after its fire of 1871. Something had to be done in San Francisco to prevent more of the dangerously flammable, rickety, and gerrybuilt structures that were already being built throughout the burned area. His own steel-framed skyscrapers from the 1890s had withstood the quake and fire reasonably well. He wrote to Mayor Schmitz that "a study of the direct effects of the earthquake . . . should be made at an early date, because any reliable theory of rebuilding must rest upon the facts developed by the inquiry. Outside capitalists, he believed, would be "disinclined to furnish money for San Francisco buildings unless strictly enforced municipal laws shall make conflagrations, and the shaking down of walls and partitions practically impossible in the future. No building of any sort should be erected from this time on that shall involve the use of wood or other combustible material. A proper fireproof ordinance," he realized, "will cause some hardship, but, if enforced, will place San Francisco upon a footing superior to that of any other city in the world, and the mere fact that the new city is to be strictly fireproof will go far toward restoring the confidence of moneyed men and corporations."[34]

When Burnham returned to San Francisco, Phelan, the San Francisco association, and even Ruef and Mayor Schmitz greeted him with high expectations. Working with the mayor's reconstruction advisory committee, the Committee of Forty, as it was called, Burnham surveyed the burned-out city and selected those parts of the original plan that seemed most relevant to current needs and possibilities. Chief among these was a plan for widening old streets and building new ones, some parts of the work to begin immediately, others to take place over a period of the next five years. The association members were optimistic that the accomplishment of such proposals would also lead to the ultimate and total unfolding of the entire Burnham plan. Still largely under the control of Boss Abe Ruef, the city's Board of Supervisors approved the modified proposals, and Burnham returned to Chicago elated and confident. He had personally gone before the board and pleaded diplomatically, though with some exaggeration, that the new report "had nothing to do with the proposed beautification of the city but was designed simply to give quick and easy communication and to relieve the congestion of the downtown district."[35]

After he left, however, the promoters of the plan realized how much they missed and needed his forceful and persuasive personality, and in July of 1906, Senator Newlands sounded him out on the chances of his moving to San Francisco to be the first head of a permanent commission in charge of the promotion of the plan and the supervision of the city's reconstruction. Though Newlands made reference to the Cleveland commission, he told Burnham that his proposed commission for San Francisco would go beyond that one in scope. In Cleveland, after Burnham's commission actually submitted the plan, it served chiefly as an artistic advisory committee. In San Francisco, such a body would have had far broader and longer-lasting powers. Burnham, Newlands suggested, should give at least one year of his "undivided time to questions of rehabilitation, including in this not only public works, but the work of organizing the different interests and occupations on an intelligent basis of cooperation." After the initial period in which he would give his "undivided attention," Burnham would serve in an advisory capacity to the permanent planning commission.[36]

Burham appreciated Newlands' proposal but he declined the offer for several reasons. Chiefly, it conflicted with his other planning and architectural obligations, especially the long-awaited, recently awakened movement for a great Chicago plan. Burnham also knew that he was no longer a young or a completely well man, and that he had to concentrate and conserve his energies for the tasks already before him. "I wish to God," he wrote Willis Polk at the same time, "that I were young as you are and able to stay just there in San Francisco and let my fancies loose upon the town." Had he been able to accept the offer, he intimated, he would indeed have preferred to be "in charge" and would have tried to reconcile the conflicting forces. He admitted that he was skeptical that a series of committees could accomplish the task. "The soul of real things does not hatch under committees," he wrote. "You cannot rehabilitate by artificial means. The growth of a great city rests on commerce, and commerce never builds on a shaky foundation. Confidence must always be at the base of it." He regretted therefore that Newlands and his San Francisco association cohorts were willing to allow so many wooden and flammable temporary buildings to be built. "Temporary" buildings, he felt, often had a way of becoming all too permanent.[37]

On August 8, however, several days after he had answered Senator Newlands' unofficial enquiry, he received a formal and equally insistent offer from Mayor Schmitz. "The Municipality and the citizens of San Francisco are very desirous," Schmitz wrote, "of having adopted as much as possible of the plans prepared by you. . . . With that in view we feel that the author of those plans should be the one to lay the foundation and to direct the work." Schmitz made the request "not only on behalf of the municipality but also on behalf of the thousands of public spirited citizens who are interested in the rebuilding of San Francisco who feel that you are the man to direct its reconstruction." Schmitz acknowledged that he was aware of Burnham's declination to Newlands, but hoped very much that Burnham would reconsider. They would make him "an officer of the municipality" and would be "willing to make any reasonable concessions." Schmitz concluded his offer affirmatively and confidently and indeed very much in the Burnham manner: ". . . We want you, we are determined to have you, and we expect you not to refuse this offer," he wrote, "but to accept it under such restrictions as you may think necessary to suggest."[38]

Burnham regretted that he had to say no to such solicitation but it was "not possible to accept," he replied to Schmitz, because of the fact that failing health and "obligations already assumed and which cannot be transferred make such a course impossible. You will understand without my saying so that there is no question of money involved in the decision. It is made entirely on the ground that I cannot undertake the work at any price."[39]

Without Burnham's presence to call the plays, direct the work, and cajole opposing forces, even the revisions of the San Francisco Plan began to fall on evil days. After a long and complex struggle, further complicated by continuing municipal scandal, the economic arguments of rapid reconstructionists quite simply overcame the association advocates for the slower and more permanent adherence to the Burnham plan.

Indeed, in a system that depended so largely on the institution of free enterprise for emergency relief in the wake of disaster, it was not surprising that the same forces would govern the manner of rebuilding and recovery. Whether or not Burnham, himself, could have altered the trend would never, of course, be known. Reminiscent of the fate of Wren's London Plan, following the fire of 1666, the San Francisco Plan was virtually ignored. Only later and much more slowly, and even then only in a fragmented and emasculated form, did any of Burnham's ideas make their way onto the San Francisco landscape. One such fragment—the circular drive and stepped terraces—appeared in the ultimate treatment of a portion of Telegraph Hill. Some of the spirit of his urban circulation proposals also reached fulfillment in the later development of the subway and cross-town freeway systems, but his aesthetic dreams were less well represented in the ultimate design for the moribund civic center.[40]

Perhaps the drabness of that Beaux Arts civic complex, designed in the late teens by John Galen Howard and others, is the source of the feeling among many latter-day San Franciscans that the city has indeed fared better without the Burnham plan. Had the city been "Burnhamized," they argue, the "Victorian" atmosphere, so increasingly refreshing as the century wears on, might never have survived. Would not Burnham, they ask, have changed the city's character, as the world knows and loves it? The answer is both yes and no and involves a number of tantalizing ifs and might-have-beens.[41]

In addition to the superb geography, it is argued, much of the city's magic emanates from the warmth and variety of its neighborhood life and that neighborhood insularity has come about partially as a result of the incommodious circulation system, a system or lack of system that has preserved the pockets that Burnham's grand thoroughfares would have punctured. The proposed outer drive, however, completely rimming the entire peninsula, would have shared the heavier vehicular traffic load and accordingly would have helped preserve the pedestrian-oriented interior areas.

Another argument against the unrealized plan is more purely architectural and suggests that Burnham's changes would have destroyed the distinctive San Francisco "look." But that contention fails to acknowledge the paradoxical fact that it was the fire and the rebuilding, not the absence of the plan, that assured the preservation of that atmosphere in the first place—the fire and the subsequently exigent reconstruction that created, in effect, an "instant" late-Victorian city. The area that was re-

built after 1906—the area that forms the world's image of San Francisco
—was one of the last large urban areas in the world to be built so uniformly in nineteenth-century styles that were already passing elsewhere.
In San Francisco, a stylistic mood was rescued from a natural obso-
lescence and piecemeal attrition and was suddenly born anew at the last
possible moment of its life cycle. Had the fire not occurred and had
Burnham's original plan been slowly developed, it is likely that San
Francisco would have demolished and replaced its old Victorian buildings in the same random fashion typical of most other cities. Because
they were built anew, however, in the period following the fire, when
their stylistic cousins elsewhere were fading and decaying, such buildings would survive and live on into a different and fast-changing era,
which would place high value on their textured patina and exuberance.
Even if Burnham's altered plans had been adopted after the fire, it is
not likely that his neoclassical recommendations would have gone beyond
the major public structures. And even there, it is unlikely that his stylistic
preferences would have survived beyond the 1920s. In addition, within
the inherent stylistic limitations, they would have possessed a happier
aesthetic and environmental character than the present set of rather
static civic center compositions. George Post's contemporary Capitol
Square in Madison, Wisconsin, for example, for which Burnham served
as a one-man selection jury, reflects a more interesting and successful
neoclassical achievement and suggests the possibilities unrealized in the
San Francisco group. Still, ironically, it was the fire that preserved the
architectural character of the great city on the bay. Burnham's plan
would have enlarged the park system, protected the shoreline, and would,
no doubt, have improved San Francisco's physical efficiency, but it would
not, in itself, either before or after the fire, have greatly altered its late
Victorian architectural ambience.

   Despite speculations on what might have happened, however, the fact
is that the earthquake and fire did occur and that the Burnham plan
was not adopted. However much Burnham himself must have regretted
its natural and human adversaries, he must also have known, in his own
terminology, that his planning achievement was not a "little" one. It had
drawn on his past accomplishments and would stimulate future ones.
Even though destined to remain the most famous ghost of the City
Beautiful Movement, it constituted both for him and others, a significant and influential reference point. Burnham's regrets, in fact, over the
problems of the plan were mingled with excitement over the prospects

for his other projects: especially the Philippines and his own great city of Chicago. They were also tempered by his own essential optimism for San Francisco. "If that city," Croly had written in 1906, "becomes adequate to its opportunities, if it ever fulfills the extraordinary promise of its existing condition, it will be because its leading citizens understand what the opportunity is, and do not shrink from the sacrifices which its fulfillment demands." If that occurred, San Francisco would "become one of the most precious national monuments of the American people."[42] But Burnham had said that all along. His devotion exemplified the city's hold upon its admirers—pragmatists and visionaries like Burnham himself—who would continually seek to realize its "promise."

X

The Imperial Façade

The Philippine Plans of 1905

They that dig foundations deep,
Fit for realms to rise upon,
Little honour do they reap
Of their generation,
Any more than mountains gain
Stature till we reach the plain. . . .

RUDYARD KIPLING
"The Pro-Consuls"

AFTER COMPLETING his initial survey and general outline for the San Francisco Plan, Burnham sailed for the Philippines in mid-October 1904. He had won the commission to make plans for the colonial cities through an interesting combination of social, personal, and professional circumstances. Chiefly, he owed his selection for the exotic mission to his increasingly impressive architectural reputation and to his long friendship with a young and ambitious Massachusetts Brahmin, W. Cameron Forbes.

Forbes was a well-bred, well-educated scion of one of New England's most distinguished families. His maternal grandfather was Ralph Waldo Emerson. His paternal forebears were successful merchants and bequeathed to Cameron both considerable wealth and continuing responsibilities in managing the family's holdings. A keen sense of family identity, however, did not keep young Forbes from seeking challenges beyond the comfortable orbits of Massachusetts society and commerce. His uncle, Malcolm Forbes, had long been a friend of Burnham's, and it was through that relationship that Cameron and Burnham met.[1]

Burnham recognized early Cameron Forbes' promise and sympathized

with his restlessness. It was Cameron's special desire to represent the
U.S. government abroad. In 1902, therefore, when Forbes applied for a
government job in Panama, Burnham wrote to President Theodore
Roosevelt that there was "no one in the country better fitted to be
United States Canal Commissioner." Forbes failed to get the Panama
job but he recognized Burnham's help and interest and acknowledged
his appreciation by presenting to Burnham a recent biography of his
grandfather Emerson. "I am reading it," Burnham replied enthusiastically, "and am half way through the first volume. What a wonderful
man he was! Everything he did interests me."[2]

Burnham and others continued to extoll Forbes' qualifications to the
President, and early in 1904, Roosevelt appointed Forbes a commissioner to the Philippines. "I have to do largely with the development
and improvement of the Islands," Forbes wrote to Burnham, "all corporations, railroads, transportation, etc. being in my hands, besides the
Police which are now entrusted to the maintenance of the peace of the
Archipelago. I am quite as well pleased with this as I should be with
the Canal," he wrote, "and think it is a field for the application of energy such as seldom comes to a young man. . . . I want to thank you
for the interest you have taken in my affairs and the help which you have
given me which I feel had a great deal to do with my securing this appointment." The Philippine mission, Burnham replied enthusiastically,
"is constructive in a higher sense than is that at Panama, and you will
be responsible and independent in your work. Now young Cameron! We
shall see what you are made of."[3]

Before Forbes left for the Orient he began the search for an architect
who would follow him to the Philippines to prepare appropriate plans.
The secretary of war, William Howard Taft, whose department was in
charge of colonies, had originally suggested that he engage a "landscape
architect" and Forbes' thought rather naturally turned to Frederick Law
Olmsted, Jr., but Olmstead was, for various reasons, unable to accept
Forbes' offer. As Forbes continued his search, however, it seemed illogi-
cal to restrict himself to a landscape architect and he broadened his net
to include building architects as well. For unexplained reasons it had
somehow not occurred to him that Burnham might be interested and
on April 1, he wrote to his and Burnham's friend Charles McKim: "It is
one of the projects of the Philippine government to build a new city
5000 feet above the sea, which will be to the Philippines much what
Simla is to India. It is part of the plan for me to get some landscape

architect to go out and try to lay out a new city, and in addition to make some plans for the development of Manila. I have been trying very hard to get F. L. Olmsted to go, but he feels that he cannot, and does not know who to recommend. Can you suggest anyone? Perhaps you would like a little trip to the Philippines yourself! If so I am starting about the middle of June and should be proud of your company."[4]

On the same day, he also wrote to Burnham soliciting his suggestions and thanking him again for his help and good wishes. "I feel with you," he wrote, "that this is my chance to prove myself if I ever am to have one and shall go at it with the idea of doing the best I can." He repeated the architectural requirements he had mentioned to McKim. "I have tried to get Olmsted to go," he wrote, "but he finds his work too exacting, and though I am still urging him he has practically declined. I wish you would let me know who you suggest to undertake this." He did not mention to Burnham that he had made an informal offer to McKim and he was pleasantly surprised when Burnham intimated that he, himself, might like the job. He was also, no doubt, a bit embarrassed that he had not considered Burnham earlier. "Believe I may be able to arrange for just the right architect," he wired Secretary Taft. "Please communicate with me before closing with anybody." He then arranged for Taft to meet and interview Burnham, and Taft was quickly convinced that Burnham was right for the job.[5]

In early May, however, Forbes discovered that he not only had his first choice Burnham, eager for the job, but his second choice as well. "I received a letter from Mr. Burnham in San Francisco," he wrote to Secretary Taft, "that he could not go to the Philippines until the autumn but that if the thing could be postponed until then he would like to know it and would probably arrange to go out. I also had a letter from Mr. McKim," he added, perplexedly, "in which he said that if it could be delayed, he too might like to come out. This looks like an embarrassment of riches." Yet, though he had actually approached McKim first, he regretted now that he had not asked Burnham and he confided to Taft that "Personally I prefer Burnham . . . as he has the business ability to get things done and provides from his organization the artistic ability of the special kind wanted. . . . Please let me know . . . if you think it is wise to wait for Burnham." Taft's earlier interview had convinced him that they should "wait until Autumn for Burnham; he is too good a man to lose." Forbes then made the formal offer, and Burnham accepted.[6]

Burnham undertook the new assignment in much the same spirit Forbes undertook his. As patrician and moderately liberal Republicans, both men identified with many of the reform currents that were changing American life. They believed, however, that there were limits to the speed with which change might safely occur. They also accepted as a *fait accompli* the existence of an American empire, whatever ambivalence they may have felt about the way the new territories had been acquired. While believing ultimately in "the Philippines for the Filipinos," they accepted the position that, for the time being, the Filipinos needed a period of tutelage in which the more "advanced" Americans could help effect a "progressive civilization" by instruction and example. Despite the opposition of the anti-imperialists, Burnham and Forbes represented a school of thought that argued that "the United States, having overthrown the Spanish government . . . was under obligation to see that the government established in its place would represent all and do injustice to none." Both men had friends and acquaintances in the anti-imperialist camp, but they never waivered in their conviction that a period of trusteeship was essential for ultimate Philippine self-rule. As advocates, likewise, of "progressive" planning for American cities, it seemed natural and proper that those progressive urban programs should be implemented in American areas overseas.[7]

Burnham's commitment, however, to such long-range goals "for the Filipinos" did not exclude a more immediate consideration of American national needs and conveniences. As a reader and admirer of Rudyard Kipling, Burnham was no stranger to the rationale of the "White Man's Burden." In describing the Philippine work, he also stressed the need for "adapting the city of Manila to the changed conditions brought about by the influx of Americans, who are," he believed, "used to better conditions of living than had prevailed in those islands." Ultimately, indeed, he studied the problems and prepared his plans in the light of both idealistic and pragmatic goals.[8]

When McKim learned that Burnham wanted and was being considered for the Philippines job he put aside his own tentative wishes to do the work and wrote congratulatory greetings to both Burnham and Secretary Taft. The encouragement from his close friend cheered Burnham greatly. "I have no doubt," he wrote McKim, "but that your letter to Secretary Taft will strengthen me in his mind as an artist and a man of good taste, although he has been cordial beyond my desserts already. I have not failed to notice that whenever you come in contact with any of my friends, they seem afterward to have an accession of faith in me. It is a fine thing in this world to have someone strengthen your hands behind your back as you do for me." He also appreciated McKim's professional advice on the Philippine project. "I shall be disappointed," he wrote, "in any large undertaking of mine, if I did not get your word sooner or later."[9]

Pierce Anderson, one of Burnham's designers, went to the Philippines as his assistant. Leaving Bennett behind to complete the details of the San Francisco Plan, Burnham sailed on October 13, 1904, accompanied by his wife, his youngest daughter, Margaret, and his close Chicago friend Edward Ayer. While crossing the Pacific, Burnham had time to ponder one of Forbes' earlier descriptions of the situation in the Philippines. First there must be a plan for the physical redevelopment of Manila, a centuries-old city with some 220,000 people. Then, according to Forbes, there were "several thousand acres of land which Secretary Taft compares to the Adirondacks in general effect, situated 5000 feet above the level of the sea and 145 miles from Manila by railroad. . . . It is proposed to move the government up there during the summer months putting up buildings for them, hospitals for the Army and for the Navy and perhaps for civil use, and to allow Government employees the privilege of taking a lot of land and building on it . . . and they are very anxious to have this laid out on beautiful lines."[10]

The Burnhams enjoyed the Pacific voyage. On October 19, they stopped briefly in Hawaii and on October 30, they debarked in Yokahama, Japan. On the following day, they took the train to Tokyo, then "rickshawed around wonderful walls covered with pine trees and dined at the American minister's." They spent all of November touring Japan and Burnham continued to record his amazement and delight: "Party rickshawed all day," he wrote, in several typical diary entries, "lunched at Mano Park Restaurant on border of Lotus Lake. . . . All went to a review of the Japanese troops (8000 men in line) by Mikado and Crown Prince. . . . Party at hotel in Nikko; went to see the Temples and waterfalls . . . went to lawn party for Sir Charles and Lady MacDonald, who are the British Legation people. . . . Went to large garden party of Marquis 'Someone' . . . then to Mikado's garden party where we saw him and his family. . . ." Katayama, the imperial architect took them "to the Imperial Gardens after lunching with us." In Kyoto they visited Katsura Palace and "saw Geisha dancing . . . and in the evening saw the great Japanese wrestling matches." Their Japanese vacation ended on November 27 when Mrs. Burnham and Margaret departed from Yokahama to await Burnham in Hawaii. He and Pierce Anderson started southward to the Philippines.[11]

They stayed in the Philippines for approximately six weeks, talking with government officials, inspecting and surveying the pertinent sites, working with maps and "on the ground," and enjoying besides considerable socializing and sightseeing. Burnham's travel diary preserved not only his itinerary but glimpses as well of American colonial life in the tropics. His study and inspection tours were accompanied by considerable pomp and fanfare. As a visiting dignitary, he was received and entertained with all available turn-of-the-century colonial civility. Province officials arranged lavish "fiestas." Native servants attended his every need. After studying the Manila area, it was necessary to venture north to the future site of Baguio, and Burnham, Anderson, and Forbes spent the Christmas week in the mountains of Luzon. There they faced more primitive conditions and accommodations, as the rugged terrain demanded occasional travel by foot and by horseback. Even there, however, due chiefly to Commissioner Forbes, the amenities were not lacking, and Burnham relished the trip immensely. Though the foot hikes and horseback riding occasionally fatigued the aging Burnham, the spectacular scenery and the area's architectural possibilities impressed and sustained him.[12]

On January 16, he and Anderson left the Philippines and sailed for Hong Kong. The two days of rest on the China Sea were pleasantly therapeutic and Burnham reflected on both the recent and the distant past. "On board Fremont in the China Sea," he recorded on January 18, "out of sight of land; weather beautiful, water entirely smooth; evening air grew cooler and we enjoyed it; . . . not a ship in sight all day." He was also struck by the recollection that this was the "fiftieth anniversary of the arrival of Edwin Burnham, wife, and five children in Chicago, where they arrived on the 18th of January, 1855, at the old dock of the Michigan Central Railroad, at the foot of Lake Street; Daniel H. Burnham then eight years and four months old."[13]

On January 19, they sailed into the "magnificent harbor of Hong Kong; scene was most interesting; went ashore in launch, found a Chinese guide, then went up on mountain by rail and chair and . . . then to the ship on a sampan." On January 20, his reflective mood continued and he wrote in his diary that "This was my wedding day." As they sailed for Japan, he and Anderson worked on the Baguio Plan and then spent another week sight-seeing in Japan. On February 3, they embarked, aboard the "Siberia," for Hawaii, with "about 60 passengers, among others about a dozen young Russian officers paroled from Port Arthur, which fell a month ago." They arrived in San Francisco on February 19.[14]

After returning to Chicago, Burnham wrote to Charles Moore that "the dive into the Orient has been like a dream. The lands, the people, and their customs are all very strange and of absorbing interest. It surprises me to find how much this trip has modified my views, not only regarding the extreme East, but regarding ourselves and our European precedents. It will take time to get a true perspective of it all in my mind." Through the spring and summer of 1905, Burnham worked both with Anderson on the Philippine plans and with Edward Bennett on the plan for San Francisco. "We design to produce a condition," he wrote to a friend, "which shall make Manila what the Spaniards used to call it—'The Pearl of the Orient.' "[15]

Despite the generally "imperial" manner of his and of all City Beautiful planning, the Manila Plan was remarkable in its simplicity and its cognizance of Philippine conditions and traditions. Concise and straightforward, its technical recommendations for streets, parks, railroads, and public buildings echoed many of Burnham's increasingly familiar proposals for Washington, Cleveland, and San Francisco. Yet, its qualifying details took proper note of the tropical climate and the mañana ambience of the Spanish-Philippine tradition. New public buildings for cultural and governmental institutions would be grouped into a large civic center, near the bay, south of the old walled inner city. The siting and arrangement of such buildings would be formal, but the actual architectural recommendations called for treatments less severe and monumental than had seemed appropriate in Europe and America.[16]

The need for more open and convenient transportation routes in the existing areas of gridiron street arrangement again prompted Burnham to recommend superimposed diagonal arteries, radiating from the civic core to all the outlying sections. Such an arrangement, he suggested, would be "entirely fitting for both practical and sentimental reasons; practical because the center of governmental activity should be readily accessible from all sides; sentimental because every section of the Capital City should look with deference toward the symbol of the Nation's power. . . ." In most situations, he contended, "the planning of a town should be carried out [so] that a person may pass from any given point to any

Burnham's general plan of Manila (1905) with important public buildings erected between 1906 and 1914 indicated in black. *Architectural Record.*

other point along a reasonably direct line." New and future streets would conform as much as possible to the natural contours of the land. While allowing prime space along the river and the seashore for the use of private clubs and the building of a luxury hotel, Burnham also made democratic concessions, reserving even larger land areas for the public. Indeed, the Manila Plan included much that was reminiscent of Burnham's other work and involved solutions to urban problems that he deemed appropriate to cities everywhere. And like most other examples of City Beautiful planning, the Manila Plan focused on the improvement of public facilities, ignoring and bypassing as outside its purview, such crucial social needs as public and low-rent housing facilities.[17]

The uniqueness of the Manila report resulted largely from Burnham's concern for the special character of Manila itself. "Most of the existing buildings," he noted, "were erected in Spanish times and are of a distinctly Spanish type. They were for the most part built of wood with projecting second stories. . . . The roof which still further overhangs the buildings was commonly covered with beautiful dull red tile, and the effect of the whole is unusually pleasing. . . . The old Spanish churches and the old Spanish government buildings are especially interesting and in view of their beauty and practical suitability to local conditions could be profitably taken as examples of future structures." In the older sections, "the general effect of the existing well-shaded, narrow streets," he thought, was "picturesque and should be maintained."[18]

He prefaced his recommendations for the treatment of the waterfront with attention to "protracted periods of intense heat during which all exertion is accomplished at excessive cost of physical strength." Recognizing, of course, that while the "climate conditions are unchangeable, means for mitigating their effects are fortunately within reach. Besides the possibility of abundant foliage and fountains of water," he observed, "Manila possesses the greatest resources for recreation and refreshments in its river and its ocean bay. Whatever portions of either have been given up to private use should be reclaimed where possible, and such portions as are still under public control should be developed and forever maintained for the use and enjoyment of the people." He recommended fountains as in Rome and Washington for Manila as aesthetic and psychological relief from the long summer heat. "If the use of parks as an architectural accessory has long been common," he suggested, "it has remained for the modern city with its immense and congested population to show the necessity of them as breathing places for the people. These parks are oftenest of two types—playfields of moderate sizes in the heart of the city and large sylvan stretches located in the outskirts where more ample areas permit the laying out of beautiful walks and drives in the midst of a romantic landscape."[19]

One remnant of old Manila that Burnham believed should not be preserved was the ancient moat surrounding the *Intramuros*, or inner city. Now stagnant and hazardous to health, Burnham urged that the moat be drained and filled, much as the Habsburgs had done in Vienna, and planted with trees and grass to provide a useful and pleasant circular park. Less drastic modifications, however, should be made in the old city walls. "Certain of the old walls surrounding the *Intramuros*," he wrote, "have been in existence since the sixteenth century. Viewed as one of the few remaining examples of a medieval fortified town, they possess singular historical and archeological interest while their imposing appearance gives them a monumental value. The objections to their presence is based on alleged obstructions of traffic and ventilation. As obstacles to the free circulation of air, their moderate height as compared to that of adjacent buildings seems to make them comparatively unobjectionable."

With regard to their disadvantages as obstacles to traffic, their method of construction would allow the "piercing of an occasional gateway without destroying their effect. . . ."[20]

Another feature of the Manila landscape that Burnham saw as promising was the neglected system of canals. "The narrow canals or *esteros* ramifying throughout Manila, with their almost stagnant water and their unsanitary mud banks, would appear at first sight to be undesirable adjuncts of the city. Yet for transportation purposes they are of the utmost value, and in spite of the serious problems involved in properly widening, bridging, and maintaining them, they should be preserved . . . their availability to the poorest boatman making them peculiarly valuable." The *estero*, he believed, could indeed be "not only an economical

Proposed treatment of central Manila, as planned by Burnham and detailed by Parsons. *Center:* Mall and Luneta; *lower right:* club buildings; *lower left:* hotel; *left center:* projected park surrounding old walled city. *Architectural Record.*

Air view of central Manila in the early 1920s. *Lower right:* residential section; *upper left:* Mall, hotel, and club buildings; *upper right:* government buildings. National Archives, Washington, D.C.

vehicle for the transaction of public business; it can become as in Venice, an element of beauty."[21]

While recognizing the city's peculiar qualities and making recommendations for their preservation, Burnham could not totally refrain from European allusions as he closed his Manila report. "On the point of rapid growth," he wrote, "yet still small in area, possessing the bay of Naples, the winding river of Paris, and the canals of Venice, Manila has before it an opportunity unique in the history of modern times, the opportunity to create a unified city equal to the greatest of the Western World with the unparalleled and priceless addition of a tropical setting."[22]

The proposed summer capital of Baguio, on the other hand, though less "tropical" than Manila, was no less exotic. Situated to the north in the rugged mountains of Luzon, the seasonal government and resort town, Burnham believed, must combine efficiency with a deference to the scenic and romantic setting. "The Baguio meadow," he reported, "is about one half mile wide by three-fourths of a mile long, and is roughly

Air view of central Manila in the early 1920s. *Lower left:* Parsons' Manila Hotel (1912); *lower right:* Mall and public gardens; *upper center:* park surrounding old walled city. National Archives, Washington, D.C.

eliptical in shape." Within the larger setting of very high mountains the town was immediately "surrounded on all sides by low hills attaining an elevation of 100 or 200 feet above it. At two points, on the north and south, the encircling ridges sink nearly to the level of the central plain; the southern opening admits the new Benguet Road" from Manila "and the northern opening gives exit to a small stream which rises in the valley and makes its way toward the north. The essential conditions are, therefore, an enclosed hollow dominated by low hills and connecting ridges." The central problem was "finding the best location within this area for the principle elements of the town, namely, business, municipal buildings, and National Government buildings."[23]

Burnham assumed that level ground was the most convenient for transaction of business, and that the business district should occupy "the level floor of the meadow and the gentler slopes of the ridge to the

Northwest. The municipal buildings, while demanding close contact with the business quarter, should yet be given a location and a set of approaches of unmistakable dignity." The government buildings also, "while needing to be reasonably accessible from the business quarter, should be located and so treated in their approaches and surroundings as to make clear their pre-eminence over all other buildings of the city." From neighboring elevations, therefore, the two principle groups, municipal and national, would "face one another from opposite ends of the valley."[24]

Except for the straight main axis running northeast and southwest between the municipal and governmental centers and the secondary axis running northwest to the business section, the roads and streets of Baguio would be of a necessarily irregular nature following the contours of the mountainous terrain. Recreational and residential building areas would adjoin and radiate from the three main areas of the town when and wherever practically and aesthetically appropriate. The plan of Baguio was a rustic and miniature version, Burnham later wrote, of the "plan made by L'Enfant for the City of Washington, in that it provides for such buildings as may be needed for governmental offices, for the

Burnham's plan for Baguio, as modified and executed by Parsons, major axes at center left and upper right. Courtesy Chicago Art Institute.

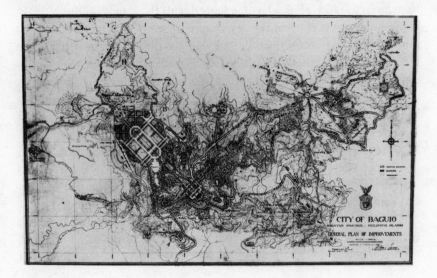

service of the city itself, and for the healthfulness, convenience and recreation of the people; and all these functions are so arranged as to make a unified and orderly city." Like the longer and more detailed Manila Plan, Burnham considered the Baguio report "frankly preliminary in character," and hoped merely that it might "seem to suggest the general lines along which the new municipality may grow into a composition of convenience and beauty." Indeed Burnham's closing sentence of the longer Manila Plan contained his sentiments and his hopes for Baguio as well. "In keeping pace with the national development," he wrote, "and in working persistently and consciously toward an organic plan in which the visible orderly grouping of its parts one to another will secure their mutual support and enchantment, Manila may rightly hope to become the adequate expression of the destiny of the Filipino people as well as an enduring witness to the efficient services of America in the Philippine Islands."[25]

Burnham again charged no professional fees, accepting only reimbursement for expenses directly connected with the Philippine work. His assistant, Anderson, received a salary, as had Bennett in San Francisco, but Burnham believed that his personal philanthropy would allow him more freedom and give more weight to his proposals. In accepting the reports, on behalf of the government, Secretary Taft thanked Burnham for his "very great generosity and self-sacrifice." It was, Taft wrote, "one of those rare instances of devotion to the public interest of which I wish we could see more. I wish to give personal testimony to the comfort you have given to those of us who are charged with the responsibility of making improvements . . . in the certainty that we . . . can make no mistake in following your direction and lead for the next fifty years." The *Inland Architect* echoed Taft's praise. Burnham's work in the Philippines, it believed, would establish a plan that would "in the years to come, develop civilizing influences side by side with commercial advancement. It is too soon to speak biographically of Mr. Burnham's work in these directions," it suggested, "but the country has in him a combination of rare gifts, the development of which will be best appreciated in another generation."[26]

With his submission of the reports to Taft, Burnham ended his official connections with the project. Yet he subsequently assumed almost full responsibility for selecting a permanent architect to move to the islands and begin the job of carrying out his plans. He also maintained, through his friend Cameron Forbes, a lifelong interest in the progress of the Philippine work. He was especially delighted when his protégé Forbes was later appointed governor-general.

Burnham began interviewing prospective architects as soon as he returned home, but when he wrote to Forbes in August 1905, he confessed that he had not yet found the man. Several promising prospects had "entertained the idea," he wrote, "but it is the old question of patriotic duty as against money interests." Finally, however, he found his man in William E. Parsons, a graduate of Yale and the vaunted French Ecole des Beaux Arts. Parsons' quiet creativity, his apparent fund of practical wisdom, and his Beaux Arts credentials impressed Burnham and ultimately the young architect succumbed to Burnham's persuasion. Convincing Parsons to execute the Philippine work was indeed one of Burnham's most fortunate accomplishments.[27]

Working closely with Cameron Forbes, the young American architect Parsons spent eight full years in the islands designing buildings, executing and detailing Burnham's larger plans, and using Burnham's Manila and Baguio reports as instructive models for his own city plans of Cebu and Zamboanga. Following the advice in Burnham's report to learn from the better Spanish and Philippine examples, Parsons in general designed buildings of warmth, efficiency, and engaging simplicity. Utilizing the vocabulary of indigenous Spanish-Philippine architecture, Parsons' buildings usually had plain, broad surfaces of solid pastel colors and were usually topped by handsome tile roofs. His most dominant architectural elements, both functionally and aesthetically, were the broad, deep archways and the shaded porches and covered loggias that connected the cool interiors of his spacious buildings with the light and heat of the tropical climate. Suggestive of the more famous contemporaneous work of Irving Gill and his California followers, Parsons' best designs combined a successful mixture and abstraction of Spanish, Oriental, and modern "industrial" building to forge a new architecture appropriate for a tropical climate. Whereas Gill abstracted and drew from Spanish-American examples, Parsons independently drew inspiration from similar features in the Spanish-Philippine tradition. Especially in his designs for the Philippine General Hospital, the Manila Hotel, the Army-Navy Club, the Normal School, and the Y.M.C.A. in Manila, and in his plans for schools and public structures throughout the provinces and barrios, Parsons produced buildings of an architectural quality that rivaled the best modern work in Europe and the United States. Drawing from both Spanish examples and the elegant simplicity of the rural Philippine

Parsons' Philippine General Hospital, Manila, 1910, showing the court-yards and interior open-air corridors connecting the wards. Bureau of Insular Affairs.

The colonnaded, open-air corridors of Parsons' Philippine General Hospital. Bureau of Insular Affairs.

Parsons' Army-Navy Club, Manila, ca. 1910. Author.

vernacular, the American buildings would continue to serve as models for Philippine building both before and after the Second World War.[28]

Perhaps Burnham's and Parsons' combined architectural success stemmed partially from their over-all images of the Philippine adventure. Perhaps the Philippines suggested to both of them an exotic ambience that called for a lighter and less formal treatment than Burnham deemed fitting for American mainland cities. By generally avoiding, at least in the earlier buildings, the grandiose Beaux Arts neoclassicism that marred Burnham's other plans, Parsons helped ensure, in the early years at least, that the City Beautiful Movement would realize its greatest architectural success not on American but on foreign, colonial soil.

Unhampered, under the colonial circumstances, by cumbersome democratic processes, unharassed for the most part by local opposition, as had been the case in San Francisco, the building of Baguio and the re-development of Manila proceeded as quickly and surely as Burnham could ever have hoped for. There were temporary setbacks, of course, and various elements of the Burnham plans never materialized, but on the whole progress was clear and continuous. Forbes kept Burnham posted for the rest of his life on the progress of his plans both in spirit and detail. "Please remember," he wrote in a typical letter, "that the Burnham plan is sacred and is being strictly adhered to."[29]

As Burnham had become increasingly involved with the Philippines, he found himself defending more vigorously his and his country's colonial efforts. "I was in Springfield, Massachusetts," he wrote to Forbes on June 9, 1905, "at luncheon with the members of the Board of Trade and met your friend Sam Bowles of the *Republican*. I said some very emphatic things across the table and Mr. Bowles said he was very much surprised at what I had to say. I asked him if he was an anti and he said he was, whereupon I laid myself out . . . at least so far as the Governor Wright and the Commissioner from Massachusetts Forbes are concerned. I don't think Mr. Bowles got much comfort out of the conversation." Burnham's support prompted Forbes to write him that he only wished "we had a few more champions like you gathered around."[30]

Indeed, as the years passed and added their countless demands on his thoughts, Burnham continued to ponder the Philippines and the mean-

Parsons' provincial government building, ca. 1912, Capiz. *Architectural Record.*

Typical Parsons provincial Philippine school building, ca. 1912. *Architectural Record.*

ing of what he deemed to be a different kind of empire. His firm, his family, and a plan for his home city would from then on consume his active attention, but a letter of 1906 to Forbes expressed a recurring life-long sentiment: "My mind turns longingly to the Orient," he wrote, "and I would like to be there again. . . ."[31]

Though an integral part of a dubious American imperial adventure and rationalized always in the staunchest of imperialist rhetoric, the architectural phase of the American mission to the Philippines wrought better than even its mentors knew. While inevitably inhibited, as with much physical planning, by subsequently inadequate or conservative social and economic policies, the Burnham plans for Philippine urban development ultimately helped to improve and reorder the national landscape. Despite their autocratic origins and their initial deference, especially in the new city of Baguio, to elitist and special colonial American interests, their general functional and aesthetic improvements would continue to serve the Filipinos well. Though the cities were heavily damaged during World War II, the general outlines of Burnham's innovations survived that conflict as a partial basis for postwar Philippine urban development.[32]

Concurrent with such development, however, the Philippine cities continued to experience both new and old urban problems and to suffer and decay like most of the world's cities. Burnham's work, like most other planning, did not solve any problems for all time or all problems at any time. But his plans were a new beginning and they did make a difference. As a creature of time and a consciously time-bound figure of history, Burnham could hardly have asked for more.

XI
Promoter and Benefactor

The Architect as Philanthropist

I appeal for an ideal thing, for the establishment of a beauty that shall be ever present to do its pure and noble work among us forever. . . .

DANIEL BURNHAM

1903

For HIS WASHINGTON, San Francisco, and Philippine plans Burnham charged no professional fees. Together with his long-range plans for Chicago, those huge planning enterprises were his greatest philanthropic undertakings. Freely donating time, energy, and talent, which would have yielded handsome monetary sums if devoted to private pursuits, Burnham offered his skills in exchange for other kinds of rewards. Already possessing a comfortable fortune, he gave himself to philanthropic endeavors that allowed him personally to enlarge himself and expand his influence. He also believed that if he charged no fee his clients would have to give him a freer hand in the expression of his ideas than they might have done had they been paying for his services. Since the plans were, in essence, a gift, the recipients, he felt, would accept them more quickly and easily. If and when his ideas were theoretically accepted, he knew that their implementation would be enormously expensive.

Such philanthropy also helped to advertise his name and to make his other professional services more remunerative and more in demand. Burnham was certainly fully aware of the material and psychological rewards that accompanied philanthropy. Yet, despite that usual mixture of motives, his reforming zeal was remarkably pure and sincere. Fused complexly like all human behavior with defensive strains of egotism and

217

self-interest, Burnham's gifts of time and talent exemplified for the most part his basically altruistic nature. Giving in a way that few other architects did and in a way that few other philanthropists could, Burnham was indeed unusual in the history of both architecture and philanthropy.

There were three institutions that claimed his greatest loyalties: the American Academy in Rome, which symbolized for him, in part, the cultural legacy of America's European antecedents; Harvard University, from which he held an honorary degree, but to which in his youth he had failed to gain admission; and the Chicago Symphony Orchestra, an acknowledgment not only of his own lifelong love of music, but of the city that remained at the center of his life and thought. While subscribing to countless other enterprises, these three institutions best exemplified his philanthropic interests.

Like many other contemporary developments, the American Academy in Rome was an outgrowth of the World's Columbian Exposition of 1893. Originally conceived by Charles McKim, the idea for an academy appealed to other members of the exposition fraternity, especially Francis Millet, Augustus St. Gaudens, and Daniel Burnham. McKim remained throughout the leading figure in the institution's development, but Burnham emerged as perhaps his chief lieutenant and one of the movement's better fund-raisers and promoters.

It seemed essential to men like McKim and Burnham that there be established in Rome itself a base for the study of classical and neoclassical architecture. The "Roman look" had become quite visible and fashionable in American architecture and city planning, certainly, in part, the result of the Chicago Fair. But its qualities had also permeated painting and sculpture and, in fact, had left a mark on almost every area of artistic design. To perpetuate and solidify this trend, to provide a depth and substance often lacking in the proliferation of amateurish Roman imitations, to get at the source, to commune on the spot with the Roman legacy, young American architects, McKim and Burnham argued, needed a school in Rome to facilitate the strengthening and broadening of their architectural education. After a period of general training in American schools and practical experience in architectural offices, the best candidates would compete for awards and the best of the best would be selected. The results, it was assumed, would be amply illustrated in each student's work and artistic achievement upon his return to America.

"The most fitting situation for an academy of Fine Arts" the exposition painter Edwin Blashfield contended, should "be in the place where

the best existing examples for study can be made most acceptable to the
student. If you add a background sympathetic to the consideration of
the greatest art, you have an ideal environment. Rome unites these conditions as does no other city. She unites them within her own walls and
again, better than any other town, she fulfills the further and important
condition of being central, a pivot upon which a relatively short radius
of travel may sweep Athens, Cairo, Constantinople, Paris, London, Madrid, putting at the service of the student the Greek fountainhead of art,
the Roman development of Greek methods, the Byzantine Evolution,
its succession in Oriental and Occidental art, the medieval and contemporaneous art of France, the collections of Vienna, Munich, Dresden,
London, Madrid."[1]

The student attending the American Academy, Blashfield believed,
should not be an inexperienced neophyte. "First he should know the
spelling and grammar of art. . . . Next he should have seen enough of
modern art and its tendencies to safeguard him from such conservatism
as could harden into archaism and quench the vital spark in his artistic
temperament, as should convince him in fact that he must bring something with him to Rome, there to grow in strength, and that he is not to
find his all there. He is not," he argued significantly, "to steal the sacred
fire from the altar of antiquity, but is rather to comfort and feed at it
that particular spark which is his individual allotment by inheritance
after it has passed down the centuries and through generations of tem-
peraments of his own people." The work of Burnham and McKim
would not always have escaped Blashfield's castigation of conservative
historicism, but the artist and architects were in at least theoretical
agreement.[2]

Most of the leading American architects for at least a generation had
attended the French Ecole des Beaux Arts in Paris and many had, in
fact, imbibed their neoclassicism there. They saw that establishment
French architects had never completely forgotten the Roman legacy and
they noted the prominence and influence of the French Academy in
Rome, established by Colbert in the time of Louis XIV. They failed to
realize that academic French art, both in Paris and Rome, was losing its
primacy to other modes and sources of inspiration, less formal and less
restricting incubators of influence—from the southern French country-
side to the streets of Montmartre. Still, it was the French Academy,
housed in the sumptuous Villa Medici, that became for the American
classicists the model and inspiration in founding their own school.[3]

Though begun by architects for the training of architects under the name of the American School of Architecture in Rome, the school broadened its scope in 1897 to include painters and sculptors. In that same year, it was incorporated under a charter from the state of New York, as the American Academy of Fine Arts in Rome. In 1901, the American secretary of state permitted the United States ambassador in Rome to become an ex officio trustee of the academy and "to secure for it all the privileges and exemptions that are accorded like institutions of other countries by the Italian government." In February 1905, the United States Congress passed a bill of incorporation supplanting the original New York charter, in order that the school "might have the moral and legal support of the United States."[4]

The path to success was neither straight nor easy, however. In its first ten years, the greatest problem was funding, and it was in that area that Burnham furnished his strongest support. The school, Charles McKim hoped, would be "national in character, endowed, and maintained through the public spirit of individuals." He and Richard Hunt attempted to tap that "spirit" in the East. Burnham was put in charge of the West. In his initial campaign Burnham raised approximately $2000, primarily in the form of individual $100 contributions from such business acquaintances as John J. Glessner, Martin A. Ryerson, and George M. Pullman. Especially enthusiastic about the American Academy's possibilities was the novelist Edith Wharton, who started a movement of influential women to raise more funds for the Roman school. Initial funds went to pay for rent, director's salary, and operating expenses. Individual students were sponsored by universities who took money from their foreign traveling scholarships on the condition that their own students abroad spend the majority of their time in Rome under the tutelage of the academy's director. Such an arrangement assured the institution of qualified students in its beginning years until money could be raised for a permanent scholarship endowment of its own.[5]

The success of the school as both an architectural studio and an expanded school for painting and sculpture encouraged the sponsors by the turn of the century to seek even larger subscriptions. Henry Walters, a Baltimore art patron, lent the money to purchase the handsome Villa Mirafiore as the academy's home. Later he canceled the debt and, in effect, gave it as a gift. The goal of McKim and Burnham was to acquire an endowment of at least $1,000,000, to be made up chiefly of major donations of $100,000 or more. The persons or institutions contributing that amount would be entitled to the rank of founder. Smaller donations might be pooled and given in the name of a local institution. The financier J. P. Morgan led the way to become the first founder. Henry Walters of Baltimore and James Stillman of New York followed his lead. Harvard alumnus Henry W. Higginson contributed the necessary amount on behalf of his alma mater. St. Gaudens gave Burnham all the credit for winning over Henry Frick of Pittsburgh, a client of long standing; but they had less luck with the millionaires of Chicago.[6]

Burnham's aim was to raise $100,000 to be pooled and presented on behalf of the University of Chicago. His canvass included both residents and expatriates, anyone in fact with the most remote Chicago connections. In this spirit, he even importuned the infamous and erratic tycoon Charles T. Yerkes, then residing in London, far removed from his shadowy American past. In writing to Yerkes, Burnham appealed to his sense of patriotism, subtly challenged his position in the business and social world, and flattered his yearning for artistic and cultural involvement. Similar in some aspects to all of his solicitations, the letter nicely summarized Burnham's conception of the Roman Academy. "At the close of the World's Fair in Chicago," he began, "a few of the artists . . . conceived the idea of putting American art on an equal footing with France. As you know, for two hundred years, France has maintained a national school of fine arts in Rome which is located in the superb old Villa Medici. To this school are sent the ablest young Frenchmen, who have fought for the honor and defeated all comers for years. They stay four years and when they return they are feted by the government and are like the old Greek winners of an Olympic. It is entirely due to this high training," he asserted, "of her very best, star men that France gained and absolutely maintained her supremacy in Architecture, Painting, and Sculpture."[7]

Burnham reviewed for Yerkes the brief record of the American Academy: "The men who in 1895 organized our American Academy in Rome maintained it themselves for many years, until, indeed, its great value met with national recognition. In January of this year, Congress passed a bill of incorporation making the Academy national in the broadest sense. The President, who had enthusiastically supported the measure, promptly signed it as soon as it was passed. A congratulatory dinner was thereupon given in Washington, at which the President was the principal guest and speaker. Mrs. Roosevelt and her guests occupied the gallery." After setting the stage of social grandeur and prestige, he then told Yerkes: "Most of your distinguished business acquaintances were present, including the principle bankers, railroad and university presidents and ecclesiastics in the country, also several of the cabinet: Hay, Root, and Taft; many senators and representatives." By this time, presumably, Yerkes would be crying to get in, but Burnham had not finished. "It was," he continued, "probably the most important dinner ever given in the United States. . . ." He then listed the names of the men and the institutions that had given $100,000 and become founders and described that position of honor in graphic detail. "The names of the founders of this great national school," he wrote, "will be recorded in the villa in Rome, and there can be no higher distinction for a family than the association of its head with this source of inspiration. In Florence, the name of Medici is as high today as it was four hundred years ago and in Genoa, the Doria name is the same, and this is principally so, because the two families were the patrons of the fine arts."[8]

He then exaggerated the campaign's success by noting that "while our million dollars may be said to be in sight it seems to me that we should have a fund of two hundred thousand dollars in addition for library and equipment." He hoped, of course, that Yerkes would become a founder or at least contribute substantially to the Chicago endowment. In making the final pitch, Burnham implied, without saying so, that Yerkes might purchase back considerable legitimacy and respectability by contributing to so noble a venture. "This is an ideal cause," he affirmed, "and one in which a man will gain just distinction of a high order. Your connection with the academy would give you a delightful status in the most select art and government circles in Rome, Paris, London, and the United States." He then flattered Yerkes' financial position by an implicit comparison to his own. "I should like," he lamented, "to be able to take this opportunity for myself and my family." He concluded by noting that "your interest in art has always been very great and this makes me think that you will grasp the importance of the Academy." He then alluded to his only real personal connection with Yerkes, as he closed his letter: "I often think of you and your strong support of me in the World's Fair, when I needed it."[9]

Believing strongly in everything he had said, Burnham must have also wondered if the tone of the letter seemed fully right, and he sent it to St. Gaudens for criticism. "If you approve it," he told the sculptor, "put it in the mail. He may do it, who knows! But it is doubtful." The letter delighted St. Gaudens, and he replied to Burnham that "if Yerkes re-

sists your letter to him which I received just now and will mail to him
tonight, it will show that the rocks of New England are feather beds in
comparison to the stoniness of his heart." Despite the passion of Burnham's letter, however, Yerkes declined the invitation, due to other commitments, and perhaps, in part, to the "stoniness of his heart."[10]

Burnham had no better luck with other prospective founders, but he
did raise a number of smaller contributions from the Chicago area. He
himself contributed $10,000, and the journalist Victor Lawson pledged
$5000. Other donors included Marshall Field and the Cyrus McCormick
family, but the sum was short of the $100,000 needed to make the uni-
versity a founder. He wrote his friend James D. Phelan that he was
having a hard time in the Midwest because the Art Institute, the University of Chicago, and Northwestern University were "hitting the same
people for big money at the same time."[11]

He hoped, however, that Phelan and Willis Polk might do better in
California and raise enough money to establish the University at Berkeley as one of the American Academy's founders. The Californians were,
in fact, making progress toward that goal when the San Francisco earthquake and fire occurred in 1906. At that time, despite his concern for the
academy, Burnham insisted that the California money be returned to
each of its donors in view of the more urgent demands at home. With
the $100,000 commitment from Frick, however, and numerous smaller
pledges from other sources, Burnham's share in the academy's fund
raising helped to achieve the ultimate goal. "How much the Academy
owes to you for the great interest you have taken and for all that you
have done cannot be measured just yet," McKim wrote, but "the record
will show the middle west and far west to your credit."[12]

The academy's fortunes increased and prospered and Burnham maintained a lifelong interest in its activities. A letter to Frank Millet of
1910, for example, indicated his concern for the academy's character and
atmosphere. It was, and would for years continue to be, an all-male institution, and Burnham believed strongly that the students should be allowed to behave informally as men and as artists. They should have privacy and freedom, he thought. The academy was not a camp or a
dormitory. In discussing the appointment of a new director, Burnham
objected to Millet's suggestion "that his wife has knowledge of Roman
society and skill in playing the game." "Dear Frank," he complained,
"this is the very thing you *don't* want. We have had mistresses in the
Academy of Rome and what has come of it? . . . Imagine a woman

presiding in the Villa Medici! Would any French artist stand it? There should be no woman in the Mirafiore. The students there are not boys. They do not need 'the influence and refinements of a home,' and they do need entire freedom to work each according to his own nature, following his own moods. Any restriction put on him will vex and interfere, and any set social formality about him frets his life. No woman can live there without making a nest for herself in the Villa. . . . 'My boys,' and 'What I hope for my boys.' These phrases are quoted by me. The dear ladies I met in the Roman Academy used them. They brooded over the School!!"[13]

"The Academy needs a master and not a presiding lady," he wrote, summing up his views on the institution's program, "and the master should be an architect, one who knows the laws and can constantly hold the work to them; leaving all students full freedom of artistic feeling and individual expression, but making sure so far as he is able to that the thoughts of his students' brains and the work of their hands shall be sane—one whose sole heart is in this work. It is a great opportunity for the right fellow. He should not look upon it as a temporary employment but must go into it with the hope and intention of making it his life work. He should have bodily and mental vigor. . . . To send home three men annually who shall become a true leaven in America seems to me to be our object. The Academy should not be a benevolent institution, but a seminary furnishing all the people of this country the right sort of influence. This we need constantly in order to keep our progress in the right direction. To me," he concluded, "the individual designs of buildings our Roman scholars may make are not so important as the spirit they will introduce and keep alive among us."[14]

When Burnham wrote McKim of the plans of the Chicago Architectural Club to award a Roman academy scholarship, McKim advised him significantly to require that all design competition submissions be "classic in character. If you do not insist upon this you will be likely to get all kinds of Yahoo and Hottentot creations which prevail in the East and still occasionally crop out in the West in spite of the send-off you gave the world in 1893." And yet, as a later critic of McKim's statement would note, "the Yahoos and Hottentots would exist, Academy or not, and their vigor would breed a style capable of giving form to modern institutions."[15]

The movement to establish the American Academy in Rome was in fact the epitome of Burnham's classical leanings. His love of pomp, ceremony, and architectural magnitude made his interest in Rome and things Roman quite natural if not inevitable. "The Julius Caesar bust is something I desire greatly," he wrote, characteristically, to academy director George Breck in 1909, as he thanked him for acquiring and shipping it to him.[16]

America in Rome was, in Burnham's frame of reference, the direct opposite of America in the Philippines. He and his countrymen had gone to the Philippines in the spirit of benevolent conquest, with the mission of "civilizing" the backward Filipinos. They went to Rome in another kind of quest, as humble and deferential seekers and communicants, to be educated and further "civilized" by an older and presumably superior culture. They conceived of their Roman endeavor as a return to the Source for inspiration and refreshment. Their critics saw it only as a retreat to an antique womb.

As a benefactor and supporter of Harvard University, Burnham's efforts were less far-reaching and dramatic. His gifts to Harvard were donations of time and counsel—advice and opinions concerning the university's programs in art and architecture. Requested by and for the Board of Overseers, Burnham's visits to Harvard and his various resulting reports had intensely personal implications. His efforts for Harvard as an older man compensated in part for his failure to matriculate there as a student and gave in a sense legitimacy to his tenuous university connection. His Harvard involvement perhaps also represented an atavistic gesture to his own New England ancestry and to the ancient generations of Harvard-oriented forebears. As a holder of a Harvard honorary degree, Burnham was entitled to all the powers and privileges of a graduate including the right to serve on committees. Charles Francis Adams, therefore, as chairman of the Standing Committee on Reports and Resolutions, a committee on committees, appointed him in October 1904 to the Committee on Fine Arts and Architecture. The chairman of the committee was the noted professor of humanities Charles Eliot Norton. The duties of the members were to inspect and report on the arts and architecture curricula, the Fogg Museum, and the architectural development of the campus. It was the latter problem that most concerned Norton, Burnham, and fellow committeeman Frank Millet and the one to which the committee gave its prompt attention in early 1905.[17]

The committee's report revealed its disgust with the tradition of picturesque eclecticism that permeated Harvard and much of the western world in the second half of the nineteenth century. Such deliberate

Victorian "irregularity" offended, of course, their neoclassical biases, but more concretely it offended their sense of unity in design. Authored chiefly by Burnham and Millet, the report of 1905 noted that "Fifty years ago, Harvard College possessed buildings of simple construction and unpretentious character, built of similar material, of the same style and color and so located with reference to one another as to present the appearance of a well-ordered group. Harvard College now possesses many buildings of expensive construction but of unrelated architecture and so related with reference to one another as to give an impression of incongruity. Lack of reciprocal arrangement," it noted, "coupled with absence of uniform style, color, and scale has produced this condition. Each of the buildings erected in recent years has seemed to assert itself and clash with its neighbor, so that in spite of the architectural excellence of certain of them individually considered, the total effect is disorderly."[18]

The committee believed that "the unfortunate results of this condition are obvious. That the college viewed as a national institution should present an exterior out of harmony with its high function is unfitting; that the college, viewed in its more intimate relation, should leave in the minds of its graduates a memory of inharmonious surroundings is more regrettable; yet, even these drawbacks," it asserted, "are small compared with the positive disorderly and lasting influence exerted by such surroundings in the undergraduate mind in its most formative period." In emphasizing the importance of the psychological factor, the committee asked: "If order and system are requisite in intellectual work, are they not equally so in those material conditions amidst which the work is done? It should be borne in mind that while only certain of the students enter deeply enough into the intellectual life of the university to reap the full benefit of its training, yet all of them by the mere fact of their residence in Cambridge, are subjected to the insistent teaching of material environment. The one pervasive influence, in short, that is common to the lives of all Harvard men is that of the outward aspect of the university."[19]

The committee then reminded the overseers of the contemporary movements in area planning that were sweeping the country both on college campuses and, on a larger scale, in American cities. Harvard, it urged, must adopt a comprehensive plan if its future architectural development was to improve upon its past. Adams later reported that the committee's indictment had had a strong effect upon the overseers and, though immediate effects were hard to perceive, the committee persisted in its recommendations and a campus plan was slowly evolved to guide the university's later architectural development.[20]

Burnham served on the Committee on Fine Arts and Architecture the rest of his life and enjoyed his associations with his adopted university. His ideas on the problems and improvement of the Harvard campus mirrored his preoccupation with "uniformity" in his other planning endeavors. Whatever influence his ideas and his presence may ultimately have had upon the development of Harvard, however, the Harvard connection was unquestionably important and comforting to him in the prime and waning years of his life.

Of all the causes to which Burnham gave his time, money, and entrepreneurial talents, those that centered in Chicago always claimed his greatest interest and devotion. For the last decade of his life he was a trustee of, and contributor to, the Chicago Art Institute. He was greatly interested in the institute's expansion program and he delighted in its major acquisitions of important objects. He loved to wander through the great galleries of the institute and remained actively interested in its welfare and its programs all of his life. He also contributed to the Field Museum and, near the end of his life, he supported the launching of Harriet Monroe's *Poetry*, the magazine which later became famous for its sponsorship and publication of such promising, new writers as Carl Sandburg, Ezra Pound, T. S. Eliot, and Robert Frost.[21]

Yet, of all Chicago cultural institutions, the one that claimed Burnham's most ardent support was the Chicago Symphony Orchestra. He favored the orchestra over the institute primarily because it needed his services and his help more urgently. While the institute had an older history and already rested on a comfortable endowment, the symphony's financial health was considerably more shaky and uncertain. Burnham loved music. He often spoke of the subtle connections between architecture and music—the musical values of architecture and the architectonic qualities of music. His favorite composer was Beethoven and he owned a cast of the famous Beethoven life mask. His tastes, however, were versatile and varied. He liked Bach and the older masters and also such "moderns" as Richard Strauss. His musical interests led to friendships with the great Chicago conductors Theodore Thomas and Frederick Stock, and those associations in turn naturally deepened and enriched his appreciation of music. He was an active supporter of the Chicago symphony from the year of its founding in 1891. In 1895, he was elected to the Board of Directors of the Orchestral Association and from 1899 to 1912, he served as its vice-president.[22]

Without endowment and with the traditionally heavy orchestral operating expenses, the symphony crept by from year to year with Burnham and other private benefactors being forced to make up the deficits. The deficits were never less than $15,000, and each year Burnham had to launch another campaign for funds. "I, myself, have given $250.00 a year for many years," he wrote to one prospective contributer, "and . . . expect to do it as long as I live unless we can have a regular fund."[23]

One of the orchestra's greatest needs was for a new symphonic hall, designed specifically for its use and reserved exclusively for its own performances and practice sessions. Since its founding in 1891, it had played in Adler and Sullivan's huge and sumptuous auditorium, but the symphony concerts never filled it and the sparsely scattered audiences did nothing for the orchestra's or its patrons' morale. For the good of the orchestra and to attract more patrons, the Board of Directors knew that a new orchestral hall was necessary. To build the hall and provide the necessary endowment for operating expenses, Burnham and the other trustees launched a massive fund-raising drive in 1903 that ultimately ensured the orchestra's lasting financial success. It also placed Burnham in the familiar role of promoter and solicitor.[24]

"The facts are," he wrote his friend Edward Ayer, "that we have gone our length. This year the deficit will be $20,000, and it will be met and paid by ten of the trustees because they are unwilling to humiliate themselves by begging any longer as they have been accustomed to do every year. We now want to set the orchestra on its feet and have done with it," he wrote. "Unless this can be done, the greatest artistic institution we or anyone else in the world possesses, must be given up. Do the very best you can, old man. . . . Everyone will have to strain himself, I suppose, but we musn't lose, must we?"[25]

All of Burnham's letters contained much the same message, but as much as possible, each request was tailored to the personality and character of the recipient. "I am asked to write you on behalf of the Chicago orchestra," a typical letter read. "I do this willingly because I believe in it from the bottom of my heart. I do not take up the commercial question except so far as to convince myself that a model music hall built and owned by the orchestral association, will enable them to carry on their work without any floating debt and without again appealing to the people to pay for a deficit. . . ."[26]

"We have enough public libraries, universities, hospitals, and art museums," he asserted. "We also have an orchestra which stands without an equal. It has taken many years of hard work to bring it to its present efficiency and it has cost a little short of a million dollars to meet the annual deficits since it was first organized. The time never comes when a thing of ideal beauty in art can be wholly supported by entrance fees. That which is precious must always be paid for by the self-sacrifices of time and money." He admitted, however, that "we have come to the end of the tether on the basis of paying the annual deficits by begging for the money and we must either raise a fund once and for all to house and maintain the orchestra or we must give it up." In an era when he was urging that the city promote a plan of improvement and beautification, he was sure that it also needed "a house exactly fitted for the work in which may be heard the greatest things in music that men have ever dreamed and in which these things may be heard to the best advantage, so that we Chicagoans, although we do not have about us those beauties which appeal to the eye, may yet rest confident that our ears shall hear the supreme works that men are capable of. I appeal for an ideal thing," he wrote, "for the establishment of a beauty that shall be ever present to do its pure and noble work among us forever, and I profoundly believe that music has more influence over men's hearts than anything else in art."[27]

"Will you double your subscription?" he wrote to another subscriber who had already given $10,000. "We are now putting the last reserves into the fight and we must all go in like old-fashioned gentlemen, shoulder to shoulder. I raised mine to $25,000," he acknowledged, "which is a big chunk of my fortune." By the end of 1903, donations were pouring in, large and small, and Burnham was becoming optimistic. He had always felt a bit apologetic for Chicago vis-à-vis the culture of New York and New England and while whistling loudly to men outside the area, he continued to indulge himself in a kind of regional inferiority complex. "It seems to me," he wrote to his fellow trustee Norman Ream, "that what you told me two years ago about the growth and advancement of this city is near at hand. We are the ugly duckling still, perhaps, but the change is not far off, and your prophecies will surely be fulfilled." Owing largely to Burnham's efforts, the Orchestral Association, by 1904, had nearly reached its initial goal of $750,000, and the building of Orchestra Hall was nearing completion. Designed and built by his own architectural firm, Burnham remitted the usual architect's fee which would have totaled some $15,000.[28]

The greatest tragedy of the triumphant accomplishment was that Theodore Thomas lived to conduct only five performances in the new building he had waited for so long. After his death from pneumonia in early 1905, Burnham insisted that the hall be named in his honor. The loss of Thomas was a severe blow to Burnham and was mitigated only by his developing friendship for Thomas' successor, Frederick Stock. Stock came often to Burnham's house in Evanston, sometimes for dinner and to spend the night; at other times to Burnham's parlor to speak to the "Women's Orchestra Study Club." In the later years of his life, Burnham would often invite soloists and ensembles from the larger symphony to come to Evanston and perform at his numerous social functions. He attended the symphony almost every week he was in Chicago. He never regretted the time and money he gave to the orchestra. He knew that it more than repaid his efforts.[29]

In addition to his larger philanthropic enterprises, Burnham also contributed time and money to many local Chicago causes and to numerous dependent friends and relatives. "I have contributed a large amount of money to the hospital on the Ridge," he wrote in a typical answer to a request, "so that I am not in shape to do as much as I would like for your hospital, but I find I can squeeze out one hundred dollars which I send with much pleasure." He contributed $1000 to the Chicago Y.M.C.A. but asked that his gift be anonymous and listed simply as "from a friend of the cause." Sometimes he turned down a request from an institution. "I thank you for the opportunity of subscribing to your church fund," he wrote a minister in Evanston. "In looking over my records, I find that there is due me from the church, for professional services $629.20. This, with interest makes the total about $1,000.00. I have already given as much as I can afford toward the support of this church."[30]

Burnham was especially kind to his less affluent brothers and sisters and nieces and nephews. In 1901, he wrote to his brother Lewis who had just gotten a job after being unemployed for some time: Alice, Lewis' wife, had $100.00 for October, Burnham wrote, "after this I shall send no more to her, as I understand your $150.00 per month will cover all expenses. I am always glad to do anything," he assured him, "but I presume you prefer to have me stop sending checks now that you have a good salary, yourself." On another occasion when Lewis was again out of work, Burnham took him in to a supervisory position in his own firm. Burnham felt especially responsible for older relatives and friends. "Uncle William will come out home," he informed his wife. "Then we can talk the case over and provide for him, as it is our happiness to do for those we should take care of."[31]

He presented handsome gifts to his nieces and nephews on wedding days or other special occasions. He was especially pleased, for example, to put $1000 in a trust fund upon the birth of his nephew and name-sake, Daniel Burnham Woodyatt. He was also willing to help his relatives out in times of special need. When a niece, Bertha Layton, received a gratuity from him and responded that she would pay it back later, Burnham wrote her that she must "not misunderstand. It is a pleasant privilege to help the starters of our family. We all need the friendly hand and we elders find it part of our happiness. So forget the little matter and remember that you and Sherman owe me nothing." Toward the end of his life, he decided to divide some money among his relatives rather than include them in his will, which he devoted to his wife and children. He presented each share as a part of "what I am doing for my brothers and sisters and their children. I am doing this while I live rather than by will after my death because I think it is the wisest and best way and because I think the funds in each case are needed now by those I am giving them to." In the age before Social Security benefits, Burnham took responsibility for a wide circle of dependent and semi-dependent relatives.[32]

He also contributed to the support over the years of a growing number of friends and acquaintances. He financed a large portion of the architectural education of John W. Root, Jr., the son of his deceased partner. When his close friend George Lord faced serious business reverses and went into bankruptcy, he contributed large sums to help him recover. Regarding the Lords, he also told Margaret that they must both be "watchful and see where help can be judiciously applied from time to time." Eda Lord later wrote them that it was "stimulating and helpful to be remembered as you two . . . have remembered me all these years. Such constancy is rare and I realize it more fully as the years pass. You both have great natures and so you can love your friends greatly. I am blessed indeed to be counted one of them." When Winnie Oliver, a former nurse for the Burnham children, invested small sums in stock with which Burnham was familiar, he wrote her that he understood that there were "some extraordinary expenses for the Realto Company to pay at this time, so that they may not pay the next dividend for three months. I know you are in need of some money so I enclose herewith a check for fifty dollars. With love from all." In 1907 he wrote to his friend Charles Deering about a former neighbor and mutual friend. "You probably know the predicament that Katherine Wyman is in with her family and no means," he wrote. "I am going to make a contribution to take things along." He encouraged Deering to do the same, and when the recipient thanked him and promised to repay him, he wrote her that "the sum was a gift, not a loan. You yourself have many times stood by when your sympathy for others called on you to help. We all must help in his or her time."[33]

Burnham had an enigmatic relationship with Louis Sullivan. After 1905, Sullivan's finances and psychological stability went from bad to worse, and Burnham made cryptic diary references to Sullivan's calls at his office. On August 25, 1911, he noted that Sullivan had agreed "to send me his painting by Ricci," but Burnham did not say whether or not he was paying for the painting. On the same day Sullivan presented Burnham with a set of the handsomely detailed original drawings of his noted St. Paul's Methodist Church in Cedar Rapids, Iowa, with the seemingly warm inscription, "To Daniel H. Burnham, with the best wishes of his friend Louis H. Sullivan." On November 13, 1911, Burnham noted again in his diary that "Louis Sullivan called to get more money of DHB."[34]

Burnham's smaller benefactions, like his larger philanthropies, were not all monetary, however. Often they were simple acts of kindness that helped to make life better for someone else. "My very dear friend George Wells . . . ," he wrote to another friend Norman Ream, "has been having sciatica and has suffered constant pain since February. It seems as though it would never end. I remember your troubles of the same sort many years ago, and it would be a great comfort to Wells to know that the pain *does* come to an end, and that the thing *does* run its course, and I hope that you may be able to say from your own experience something to encourage him. The thing has been going so long it has worn away his courage, and if you can give him a bit of your memory as to how long the pain lasted in your case, we can use this to help our man hold on. He is one of the finest men I know, and I am naturally anxious to put out a hand, and I believe it will make him feel better to know that all he needs is a little more patience to carry him through."[35]

As a result of such kindnesses, Burnham gained a wide reputation among his friends as a helpful and sympathetic counsellor and confidant. And in such a capacity, he received a range of visitors from the critical Sullivan to an aspiring young nephew of Cameron Forbes. Forbes had written to his nephew that he believed Burnham had "one of the greatest and most comprehensive minds that I have ever run across. . . . I have talked with him about your plans, and he is taking an intense interest and believes that you are capable of great things. I have asked him if he will talk over with you your plans and possibly suggest a course, and he says he will." Chicago would not "be far for you to go, and yet however far it was, even if you had to go to Chicago for five minutes' talk with him, it would be worth your while."[36]

A philanthropist and benefactor, both in usual and unusual ways, Burnham's giving was selfish, as all giving is selfish, in the sense that it brought him genuine pleasure and well-being. He had worked hard to acquire his modest fortune and his professional advisory abilities. But unlike many others who have done the same, he never found giving difficult.

XII
The Private Life of a Public Man

*Burnham was a singular and complex character; the only novel
I ever longed to write would have attempted to present him as
its hero.*

HARRIET MONROE
A Poet's Life

By THE MID-1890s, Daniel Burnham had become a celebrity.
Though already well-known in Chicago and in architectural circles,
Burnham's part in the Columbian Exposition and in its numerous social
and cultural off-shoots had made his name and face familiar to more and
more people. Burnham liked the pace and the excitement of this public
life, but he also relished personal self-indulgence and the development of
private interests. Burnham's tastes, interests, and commitments in private, however, reflected and echoed his public behavior. There seemed
remarkably little dichotomy or contradiction between his public and private roles. His thought and behavior in those less-guarded moments illuminated the public man. They also reflected currents in the larger
society.

Burnham had always been concerned about his health and physical
appearance. Standing well over six feet tall, he was especially noted for
his erect posture and carriage, a feature that added, no doubt, to his reputation for "pomposity." He had a deep resonant voice and a gracious
"cavalier" manner. He was a fastidious dresser and ordered many of his
suits from the best London tailors. Paul Starrett, a draftsman in his firm,
described him as "one of the handsomest men I ever saw. He had a
beautifully molded head, a great crown of dark brown hair that curved
low over his broad forehead, a thick reddish-mustache above his powerful jaw, a quick, direct glance out of his deep-blue eyes. He had a mag-
netic personality. That, combined with his magnificent physique, was a

Burnham portrait by Anders Zorn, 1899. Courtesy Chicago Art Institute.

big factor in his success. It was easy to see how he got commissions. His very bearing and looks were half the battle. He had only to assert the most commonplace thing and it sounded important and convincing."[1]

He liked to exercise and was almost evangelical in his zeal to have others keep themselves in shape. He had installed a small gym in the corner of his firm's drafting room and he urged his employees to join him in using it. He had been a good fencer in his younger days and never hesitated to take the foils and educate his draftsmen by example. Like many vigorous men, however, Burnham loved to smoke, eat, and drink. He purchased expensive cigars by the thousand, and recorded in his diary that on one evening his servants "bottled a cask (52 gals.) of California wine." Not surprisingly, his gourmet predilections led to an expanded waistline, and the added weight offended both his vanity and his concern for staying healthy. His beloved golf game was apparently not strenuous enough for his reducing program and in 1905 he hired a "trainer" to come periodically to his home and lead him in various body conditioning exercises. He paid the gymnast Charles Carver $1000 to lead him through two hundred exercise sessions, and, because of this patronage, received a cut rate for similar exercises for his son Daniel, Jr. The workout usually consisted of calisthenics and jogging, followed by a cold shower. He recommended Carver to his equally dapper and vainglorious friend, Charles Wacker, and to another acquaintance, Charles Deering, he wrote that Carver "desires to add you to his list of victims and I take pleasure in saying that he had done me a lot of good. His work with me makes life quite different." He confessed to his client, the banker James B. Forgan, that the "benefit to me physically is much greater than I had supposed could be obtained at my age." Like one of his heroes, Theodore Roosevelt, Burnham also subscribed to the imperatives of the "strenuous life."[2]

Burnham resolved periodically to watch his diet and, while never completely eschewing the pleasures of the table, did consume what he considered the most refreshing and nutritious foods and waters. To cure his aches, he followed various remedies. "Everyman at our age has pains in his back," he wrote his friend, the painter William Keith. "Don't let the doctors scare you. They always do if you listen to them. About four years ago one of them told me I was going down grade very rapidly. He honestly meant what he said, but in spite of that, he was a liar. I never was in better condition. It is a mighty good thing though to drink French Vichy or some water similar to it. Take a good big tumbler of it every

Burnham and McKim, rear seat, on Wisconsin hunting trip. Courtesy Houghton Mifflin Company.

morning with your breakfast. I do this every day. Never omit it." He also informed Fred Coleman, his chauffeur, butler, and personal factotum, in a note, that he was "sending for some more Idan-Ha water. As soon as it comes, please put a bottle on the table every morning and be sure that Mrs. Burnham gets one half of it in her cup. Would like to consider this a fixed order, and not to be changed without speaking to me about it." Also, he instructed, "use the prunes every morning. Try to get them up in as tasty and as attractive shape as possible."[3]

He was constantly concerned with the health of his friends. In 1905, for example, Charles McKim seemed ill and on the verge of a nervous and physical collapse. Burnham was certain that McKim needed to get away from his sedentary and demanding New York routine, and ar-

ranged for a therapeutic hunting trip to the woods of northern Wisconsin. On October 6, Burnham, McKim, and McKim's personal physician left Chicago by train for Cable, Wisconsin, met a local guide and
woodsman who provided them with dogs, and then ventured farther
inland by wagon to "Crescent Camp," where they fished and hunted for
a week. Despite his avowed and generally fulfilled goal of communing
with nature, Burnham could not refrain from providing certain amenities in the most regal fashion. Prior to embarking, he had written to the
local Wisconsin station master informing him that he was sending from
Chicago "among other things, a barrel of oysters. Please put them on
ice." Organized meticulously by Burnham, the planner, the trip was a
therapeutic and gastronomic success. "Our whole party, including servants, being nine men," he wrote Charles Moore, "has been in the woods
ten days." McKim, he believed, was in better health and spirits. "We
have slept in an open tent with a log fire at the end, having for beds the
boughs of the balsam tress covered with mattresses. We have breathed
the northern frosty, night air of October with great benefit to ourselves."[4]

Burnham's rich and indulgent tastes competed with his health and
physical fitness programs. He made graphic diary notations of his various
ailments, including bowel problems. He also learned in 1909 that he had
incipient diabetes, which, in the days before the use of insulin, affected
his entire system and the degree and rapidity of his recovery from other
diseases. Particularly troublesome for the rest of his life was a recurring
foot infection, prevented from ever healing completely by the diabetes.
To combat the problem, he hired his nephew Rollin Woodyatt to be his
personal physician, and launched his new diabetic health program as
vigorously and systematically as he did everything else. He missed rich
food but took an almost aesthetic delight in the particulars of his new
diet. In 1909, he wrote Albert Wells that he was, for the moment, free
from sugar and that he ate no bread of any kind except flat cakes made
from almonds. They were very good, he reported clinically, "and have
brought about for me a soft, easy, and regular stool, a more satisfactory
state of body than I can remember for some years." He was also pleased
that his doctor had allowed him to "drink a half pint of claret regularly" as "a part of the regular diet."[5]

Burnham loved gadgets and exalted in the wonders of technology—
from the smallest shaving razors to the largest, finest automobiles. He
bought the new Gillette safety razors in gross, to distribute as gifts to

friends, and made diary notes of everyone he knew who had bought an automobile. "Glad to hear you have an automobile," he wrote his son-in-law, Albert Wells, in 1901, "and hope it is not of the blowing-up kind. I think the automobile is better than the horse for a good many reasons."[6]

In June 1903, on the train from New York to Chicago he met his old acquaintance Samuel Insull and noted that upon arrival they had taken "the latter's automobile for Evanston," and "knocked over a man in Edgewater." About that time he bought a car for himself, but its rattles and malfunctions disturbed him, and he decided to turn it in and temporarily rent one. He had received several citations for minor traffic violations and was now ready to pay for automotive convenience without legal responsibility. He approached the Locomobile Company of America as though he were discussing a new horse and carriage. "I take pleasure in making the following proposition," he wrote: "To hire of you a first class 22 horse-power, covered car to be kept in perfect condition by you at your own expense, stable, clean and sweet blankets, gasoline, oil, waste, and repairs; also a first class chauffeur satisfactory to me. You to be exclusively responsible for breach of police laws and results of accidents to the car or to other vehicles or persons. The car to be ready and at my disposal night and day and to be used by us and our guests merely as passengers." For such elegant service he agreed to pay $500 a month for three months. The expense was apparently well worth the convenience, prestige, and freedom from fear of arrest.[7]

By 1906, however, he had purchased two more cars, "one larger and the other a run about." They seemed constantly in need of repair and in 1907 he again resorted to renting a car and chauffeur "to be at my service day and night. . . . The man to be neat and well groomed, cheerful, and obliging. You to furnish everything of every sort these four days and to charge me $35 per day."[8]

Once while attending a banquet in Detroit for the dedication of one of his buildings, Burnham sat next to the young manufacturer Henry Ford and listened appreciatively to Ford's talk of providing a car for the masses. While favoring, indeed, a car of moderate cost within reach of more people, Burnham, himself, could not resist the more elaborate models. His own role as designer, furthermore, demanded that he devise a distinctive and personalized auto body to be custom made and fitted to a standard Locomobile chassis. It epitomized the demanding and "conspicuous" consumer in Burnham's make-up. The "Burnham mo-

bile" was to be built, he meticulously instructed the Limousine Carriage
Manufacturing Company, "with a round corner similar to the design on
the corner of the vehicle shown in your little red covered booklet. Body
to be built so that there shall be at least 49 inches on top of the rear
cushion, thus making it very comfortable for three people. Body to be
made with two drop seats, folding down flush back of driver's seat; with
wide side doors (easy to get in and out). Top to be built stiff enough to
carry small trunks without springing. Door hinges and locks to be extra
strong. Body to be trimmed in either morocco, cloth, or leather, which
I will determine later, and to include satin head-lining; also to be fitted
with an electric roof light and cigar lighter, with proper wiring for same,
and to have ash receiver and ventilator in cross partition. Megaphone
Speaking Apparatus, silk cord package carrier on the roof; fitted with
toilet cases, card cases, and bundle carrier. Entire job to be tight all
around (a perfect fit with no squeak). Painting and varnishing to be
strictly first class, very dark blue color, no natural wood. Glass frames
cloth covered. Outside front seat to be properly protected with no. 1
Pantosote curtains with celluloid lights in same. Glass front to be standard Limousine Construction, hinged to turn up into the roof. A set of
patent leather wind guard doors for the front seat is to be included.
Price for the complete body fitted to the Chassis, Fifteen hundred
($1,500.00) Dollars; terms twenty per cent with order, balance net cash
on delivery. You are to re-paint and refinish the chassis, including hood
and fenders, at the time body is put on, so that the car will look new
when finished. . . ."[9]

Though a lover and connoisseur of trains and railroads, and a skeptical
admirer of the dangerous new "flying machines," it was the automobile
that came as an answer to a combination of Burnham's needs and demands. Despite its expense and its breakdowns, collisions, and encounters with the law, it stood in Burnham's mind for luxury, speed, convenience, prestige, technological modernity, and sheer unrationalized fun.

Burnham was unabashedly concerned with material and physical
things. But his private life also included an intense personal involvement
with intellectual and aesthetic matters. His son Daniel, Jr., remembered
"the never ending effort on his part for adding to his fund of knowledge
on subjects related to the fine arts," and "the many interesting books
that he owned and which received his constant study during what in the
lives of other men would be called their hours of recreation. I look back
with very happy memory," he recalled, "to a business trip that I took

with father to California in 1908. On this trip we took ten volumes of Gibbons' *Rome* with us, and never in my life have I been compelled before or since, to be mentally alert as I was then, reading aloud to him the early history of the Catholic Church. I can remember on a great many occasions," he continued, "when we were reading aloud in front of the den fire at home on winter evenings, when we would run across some subject on which he was not familiar, he would compel me to get out the *Encyclopedia Britannica* and look up the point in question for him."[10]

Burnham's correspondence was full of book orders, ranging from *The Life of Hideoshi*, the Japanese general and ruler, to Perelles' *Views of the Chateaux* and including other titles such as the *Life of Voltaire*, Repton's treatise on landscape architecture, and a ten-volume set of the Stratford Town Shakespeare. He loved the tales and poems of Kipling and the novels of Dumas. Kipling's "The Proconsuls" was a particular favorite. He also subscribed to a sheaf of journals, ranging from the popular *Collier's* and *American Magazine* to the esoteric *Magazine of Christian Art*. He was an avid newspaper reader and a clipper of favorite pieces. And like most Americans of his day, he smiled appreciatively at the wisdom of "Mr. Dooley."[11]

His cultural interests were always wide—his first love was the symphony but he enjoyed the theater, opera, and ballet as well. He often took his family to summer plays and concerts at Ravinia, near Chicago. In New York, in particular, he seldom missed an opportunity to attend the opera with the late-arriving cavalier of the Metropolitan, Stanford White. He enjoyed the standard favorites, including Bizet and Verdi, and he also admired the Wagnerian music dramas. He took special note of the grand comedy, *Die Meistersinger*, perhaps because he so identified with the warmth and largeness of its protagonist, Hans Sachs.[12]

He kept abreast of contemporary developments in painting and sculpture, but his greatest love not surprisingly, was reserved for Old Masters. "Yes, Tintoretto is a pretty good painter," he wrote to a friend. "You remember that Ruskin makes him one of the two greatest landscape painters, the other being Turner. I presume he meant to refer to Tintoretto's backgrounds. There is no other painter equal to him in his own realm. I always like the name, too. It seems to fit him so well." Before leaving for Europe in 1906, he wrote Willis Polk that he planned to spend most of his time in Tuscany. "I find," he said, that "the thing I need most is a better knowledge of the Italian wall painting masters, and I am going to give all the time possible to their work." At the same time, he wrote the painter Jules Guerin that, indeed, "a couple of months seems a very short time to devote to this work, but I hope it will help me toward a better appreciation of works of art."[13]

There was no mention in his journals or letters of the avant-garde Picasso or Matisse or even of the older Impressionists and Expressionists whose works lined the galleries of the Chicago Art Institute. He did, however, admire the art nouveau paintings of his friend Guerin and later commissioned him to illustrate the sumptuous printing of his *Plan of Chicago*. He also liked the pre-Raphaelite and Impressionist work of John La Farge, and commissioned him to assist in the decoration of several of his own projects. His private collection of paintings consisted chiefly of the work of pre-Impressionist friends, William Keith, Francis Millet, and Laurence Earl, all competent, respectable, eclectic, and somewhat old-fashioned American "Victorian" romantics. The most distinguished painting in his own collection was quite probably his own portrait by the contemporary Swedish Impressionist Anders Zorn.[14]

Burnham's tastes in sculpture, as in painting, harked back to the World's Columbian Exposition and to the sculptors who had worked there, including Karl Bitter, Daniel Chester French, and his old Chicago colleague Lorado Taft. His greatest loyalty in that regard, however, was reserved for his intimate friend Augustus St. Gaudens. Like so much Victorian art that Burnham admired, St. Gaudens' pieces were substantively romantic and technically realistic. The finest piece of sculpture, perhaps the finest work of art that Burnham owned, was a female head given him by St. Gaudens, a variant of the head from the sculptor's celebrated Adams memorial in Washington's Rock Creek Cemetery. He kept the head on his library mantel, and he visited the larger memorial whenever he was in Washington.[15]

Burnham would maintain that he had never had "anything to do with politics" and his later public involvement with politicians was indeed for the most part limited to cultural and artistic affairs. As a private citizen Burnham was a staunch Republican. He had a pleasant acquaintanceship with Presidents McKinley and Theodore Roosevelt and a closer friendship with President Taft. He was intimate with numerous Cabinet members from McKinley's treasury secretary Gage to Roosevelt's navy secretary Paul Baker. Both were Chicago men and Burnham had known them for many years. He considered himself a Progressive Republican, strongly opposed to old line leaders like Speaker Joseph Cannon of Illinois. He especially admired Theodore Roosevelt, more as a man and a personality perhaps than as a politician. He had first met Roosevelt at the Columbian Exposition and had seen him frequently while working on the Washington Plan in 1901 and 1902. The friendship, however, remained essentially personal. In 1904, for example, Burnham wrote to the President and reminded him that "when you were governor, you wrote a word or two on the fly leaf of one of the hunting books which I have. It would be a great favor to me if you will do the same on this one." There was much indeed in Burnham's swagger, vigor, and pontifical adroitness that strongly resembled Roosevelt; in physical ruggedness, in manner, and in personal style both men shared obvious similarities. Burnham's frequent use, in fact, of such words and expressions as "bully!" and "strenuous" might well have come from Roosevelt's influence.[16]

Though he never ran for office after the abortive, youthful attempt in Nevada, Burnham gave moderate financial and moral support to the local activities of the Republican party. Immediately before the 1908 Republican convention in Chicago, he wrote to his friend Fred Upham, Chairman of the National Republican Convention, that a "young man named Rolf called on me this morning for an advertisement in the Republican convention magazine. I never advertise directly or indirectly, any more than a family physician or a family lawyer. I recognize, however, that we will all have to do something toward the good cause this year, and personally I shall be ready when the time comes." He also reminded Upham that several "friends will be staying with me at convention time. Can you let me have some good seats? It will be a great accommodation and very much appreciated."[17]

Burnham's political philosophy was in most instances, near the middle of the road. He believed in the idea of free enterprise capitalism, shorn of its excesses and grosser injustices by progressive governmental controls, and he worked on the assumption that with proper regulation, reform, and receptiveness to change, the economic system could coexist compatibly with political democracy. The most succinct statement of his personal political views came in 1905 when he entered into a brief controversy with the liberal Massachusetts journalist Samuel Bowles. Bowles was a fervent anti-imperialist and the friendly argument began one evening at a dinner party when Bowles objected to Burnham's defense of America's mission in the Philippines. The discussion then turned to broader ideological questions and continued in several letters later exchanged between the two men.

"I began life," Burnham admitted to Bowles, "very much inclined toward world-wide free trade and communism, but experience has brought wiser counsel. Both are logical, human nature being eliminated, but neither is possible until the majority of men are unselfish. No doubt," he remarked, "a trial of Communism will be made from time to time as has happened more than once." He cited the example of Brook Farm, in which his parents and their friends had been greatly interested. But from his point of view, such communal experiments never achieved their goals in a truly sustained way. However significant they may have seemed as symbols or models, it was more important, he argued, to work out society's problems in the larger society itself. "Each for all is good when you love your neighbor as yourself," he reasoned, "but is hard on you when you do not."[18]

"Are a majority of men unselfish?" he asked. "If not, then try to control their passions. Curb the trusts, tax incomes, increasing the rate as the incomes increase. Do anything necessary to protect society by law. Enforce law. But do not attempt to make the social fabric rest upon a mirage, a vision that shows something afar off, but which in reality is still far below our horizon. Character, which is self-control, is not yet fundamental enough," he believed, "to stand the dead level strain of a commune, wherein all initiative for the sake of wealth or distinction or for any other human desire is done away with."[19]

While favoring a degree of government intervention, he still held reservations about its right to ultimate power over the individual. "Let the government govern, but not possess," he wrote to Bowles. "It can more surely handle men if it stands aloof and above them. Do not let the government in any degree vie with man in his activities for others or himself, but let it control his activities to lines of sanity for him and his neighbors." He feared public ownership and the growing bureaucracy, he wrote to Bowles. "To create a government machine is surely to invite the use of it. All politicians favor movements tending to create more public officials, but private citizens ought to be vigilant in the direction of cutting down the number of public officials." Burnham's political philosophy embodied, for the most part, an enlightened conservatism, a willingness to change and reform a system so as to ensure the preservation of its ostensibly "better" features, the features in fact that favored "individualism."[20]

Burnham's middle position in the political spectrum of his time was further illuminated in two other situations. Though not quite a believer in the possibilities of "free trade," he was in favor of reciprocal tariff agreements. Each morning he read the "Washington Letter" of the columnist William E. Curtis, and he wrote to his friend Curtis in 1902 that "the one for Reciprocity pleases me extremely. It places the history of the matter clearly before us. I wonder why the Democrats don't take up reciprocity and make a campaign on it. They could knock the Republican Party out on it, and you had better be careful how you suggest such things. Reciprocity is sure to become the great element in all dealings between civilized nations."[21]

He also responded favorably to the philosophy of United States Steel mogul, Judge Elbert Gary. On October 15, 1909, Burnham was flattered to be invited to attend a testimonial dinner given in Gary's honor by J. Pierpont Morgan and other capitalists associated with the steel industry. Gary's remarks at the dinner iterated the axioms of moderation, stability, propriety, sobriety, goodwill, and fair play, the business philosophy, in short, that characterized the "new managers" and the "new" industrial leadership. Gone, Gary said, were the cut-throat days of the "survival of the fittest" credo, a philosophy which rationalized too often the oppression of the poorer and the weaker by the richer and the stronger. Cooperation among industrialists and businessmen with an interest in service as fully as in profits, should be the keystone or the new philosophy of business. While anticipating the "service" platitudes of the incipient postwar "service" clubs, Gary's philosophy of yielding to win and modifying and mollifying to conserve basic interests complemented indeed the very similar ideas of Daniel Burnham. Burnham was delighted, he wrote in 1909, to have been at the dinner and to have heard Judge Gary's paper which had, he believed, "produced a profound effect throughout the country." Most other "progressive," wealthy Republicans would probably have agreed.[22]

Burnham's letter on the benefits of trade reciprocity was, however, something of a rarity. Most of his letters on specific issues dealt with essentially nonideological matters. He was a dedicated conservationist and was always alert to problems of environmental pollution. In 1907, for example, he wrote to Senator Shelby Cullom, protesting the action taken by the House Committee on Agriculture to abolish the Bureau of Biological Survey. "I strongly recommend," he wrote, "the retention of this bureau because of the good work it is doing for the preservation of wild birds and game." In 1910, he petitioned various congressmen asking them to support the creation of Glacier National Park.[23]

While on the national level Burnham took the role of the somewhat passive Republican Progressive, on the local and personal level he was less politically reserved. He did not hesitate, for example, to push the claims of his son-in-law George T. Kelly, who was seeking the superior judgeship in Cook County. He also wrote to his friend, the journalist, Victor Lawson, "as a matter of duty, to call your attention to the candidacy of young Hollett for the State Legislature. He is the sort we ought to have all the time, a man of real character and ability, and I hope you will support him strongly. He should have us all at his back. Such men are rare in political life." He wrote to a number of leaders in the state legislature urging them to support such things as larger appropriations for the graduate school of the University of Illinois. "The university is doing important work in our state," he asserted, "and everything possible should be done to enable it to work to the best advantage. Any appropriation which will enable it to strengthen the work already undertaken and to take up new branches should be supported."[24]

Burnham also made it a point to maintain good relations with local Chicago politicians, including the colorful alderman from the notorious First Ward, John "Bathhouse" Coughlin. Burnham's son Daniel, Jr., later recalled that "Bathhouse John was an old friend and great admirer of my father, and he had a lot of charm, as all successful politicians must have. When I came on the stage," the younger Burnham admitted, "he extended this friendship to me and for many years he helped me out with political favors. . . . Among his string of race horses, he had one named "Dan Burnham," for my father, and another named "Wacker Drive." I put a bet one day at Arlington Park on "Dan Burnham" and watched the nag finish last."[25]

Burnham suggested at least part of his formula for influencing people and gaining personal favors in a letter to his friend Laurence Earl. Earl wanted desperately to get his son an appointment to the naval academy just as Burnham had done for his son Hubert. Earl had family connections in Chicago, but, at the time, he lived elsewhere. He saw little chance of his son's getting the appointment from his district of residence and quoted to Burnham a suggestion from a mutual acquaintance as to how the appointment might be maneuvered clandestinely through Chicago connections. Burnham did not like the sound of the suggestion and wrote to Earl that he was "astonished that Mr. Wernz would give you any such advice. I would never for a moment think of doing such a thing and would much rather my son should fail in life than to obtain any favor except in the old straight-forward manner. . . . The way to do is to bring your friends to bear good and strong on the man you want to influence and find somebody who has weight with him if you possibly can. . . . If Ray should be appointed from here, it would have to be because of your really belonging to Chicago and he would probably have to come here and stay for three months, but it is better to get him appointed right from his own part of the world if possible. You may remember," he warned his friend, "that I told you that Mr. Wernz was an expert in his own direction and I also hinted pretty strongly to you, which you seem to have forgotten, that he was not a man whose principles I cared particularly for."[26]

He explained to Earl, however, that there were also other possibilities. The appointment for his son Hubert, for example, had come "through President McKinley . . . because the President believed in the boy from the bottom of his heart. . . . I have your boy in mind," Burnham wrote later, "and hope I may be able to put an 'egg' somewhere that will do him good. The President has several appointments vacant every year under the law. He reserves these for sons of naval people according to custom. But, Roosevelt is a generous hearted fellow and believes in manhood. If you could see him yourself with some strong letter of recommendation, and take the boy along so that the President could get his eye on him, there might be a chance of his taking one of his quick likings which could result favorably to Ray." Burnham believed strongly in approaching politicians and indeed all people, "in the old straight-forward manner." His reputation both for honesty and for influence suggested that such tactics brought him reasonable success.[27]

Part of such success, both in business and in private life, also came from Burnham's carefully cultivated position in Chicago society. He was a member of numerous clubs including the Chicago Club, the Union League Club, and the Glenview Country Club, all of which were primarily social and conceived chiefly for dining and recreation. He also belonged to the Chicago Commercial Club, an exclusive organization of the leaders in the business community, which met approximately once a month for elaborate banquets and speeches by eminent figures on local and national topics. The Chicago Literary Club and the literary Little Room also had strong social overtones, though Burnham's participation in their activities was apparently minimal. The Chicago Architectural Club and Cliff Dwellers Club were social and professional clubs for men affiliated with the arts and architecture. Burnham was a founder of the Cliff Dwellers and enjoyed its club and dining room atop the roof of Orchestra Hall.

The Chicago Commercial Club had no formal clubhouse or meeting place, usually holding its banquets in the Chicago Auditorium. It had, however, a strong sense of in-group solidarity and Burnham was concerned that its members should be men of only the "better sort." On one occasion, for example, he recommended for membership, "Mr. Arthur Orr, capitalist," a man who was, Burnham thought, "a great success financially, but no more so than is deserved on account of his fine character and qualities of head and heart as a gentleman."[28]

Burnham reserved perhaps his greatest social loyalties for the Chicago Club and the Republican-oriented Union League Club. It was to them that he took his most distinguished visitors: the inventor Thomas Edison, the critic Bernard Berenson or an occasional President of the United States. He took a great interest in the clubs' activities and the details of their operations. He had long admired the clubhouses in New York, and in 1903, he stated, or overstated, his belief that the building of a new Union League clubhouse was "the most important thing we have to do in Chicago today. . . . It will be a turning point in our history if we get it going and will do more to do away with our reputation than anything we can do." Still apologizing reluctantly for Chicago's social inferiority, he asked a fellow member "to urge it early and late" and hoped "that we can get the building very soon. It is one of those things that failing to do will set us back for a generation and will make us the laughing stock from New York to San Francisco."[29]

When Burnham went to the Orient in 1904, he asked John Clark, the president of the Chicago Club, to "give me a letter identifying me as a club man," as an entree to Western society in the Far East. After Paul Morton became a member of Roosevelt's Cabinet in 1904, Burnham and other friends of Morton's wished to present him with an appropriately inscribed trophy and memento. In making the arrangements Burnham wrote the jeweler in charge that the "Hon. Paul Morton, Secretary of the Navy, has been accustomed to lunch at the Chicago Club for many years at the so-called 'Round Table,' and his friends, about twenty-four in number, desire to make him a present recalling the pleasant life they have had together for so many years when lunching at the same board." Despite such obvious clubbiness and elitism, however, Burnham seemed shocked and a bit hurt when a minor city official re-

marked disdainfully "that the club and Burnham were a lot of aristocrats." Like affluent and socially prominent Americans of other eras,
Burnham wished both to eat and to have his cake. Imbued with an honest concern for the needs and cares of others, he still indulged without
apology in the life style of a leisure class. While he wanted the amenities of the European elite he did not, however, want such pleasures to
threaten his legitimacy as an American. Remembering his Puritan and
his Revolutionary American ancestry, and educated to appreciate their
ideological legacies, he wanted to live the aristocratic life—but without
the odious labels that his country had taught him were "un-American."[30]

Burnham enjoyed the festive and expansive side of Chicago high society. In 1902, for example, he was a member of the Chicago Committee
for the Reception and Entertainment of his Royal Highness Prince
Henry of Prussia. On March 2, 1903, he recorded in his diary that he
went in the morning "to receive President Roosevelt," rode in the subsequent procession and dined with him in the evening. The diary also
included notations of society balls and numerous receptions such as
"Mrs. Henry D. Lloyd's reception in the Fine Arts Bldg." and "James
Deering's ball at auditorium which lasted until 4 AM Sat. morning."
Once when Margaret was visiting their daughter Ethel, Burnham wrote
and insisted that she arrange to return home for a dinner party two
weeks hence at the home of the steel maker, Charles Schwab. "It is his
sixty-seventh birthday," Burnham wrote, "and I want to make amends
for my many failures to go there on invitations." Periodically the Burnhams held massive and sumptuous entertainments at their home in
Evanston, on their anniversaries, for example, or on the occasion of
their daughters' debuts and marriages. Usually, however, the gatherings
at Evanston took on a smaller and more intimate and informal character.[31]

As oriented, indeed, as Burnham was to the ways and to the importance of formal society, his greatest satisfactions ultimately came from
less formal relationships with his close friends, his neighbors, and his
family. Burnham loved to be with those closest to him and when he
could not see them, he wrote to them faithfully. Like most of his peers
in that pre-Freudian era of flowery and unabashed sentimentality, he
was seldom inhibited in his expressions of affection for his related or unrelated male and female intimates. To an old Chicago friend, John
Whittaker, he wrote in an idiom characteristic of his less formal moods.
"I cannot tell you," he began, "how delighted I was to see your old fist

Burnham home in Evanston. *Architectural Record.*

Burnham's study. *Center:* Zorn portrait; *right:* photograph of St. Gaudens' Marian Adams sculpture; *left:* cast of head from the Adams sculpture. *Architectural Record.*

A Fourth of July celebration on the Burnham lawn, ca. 1900. Courtesy Houghton Mifflin Company.

again on paper. It was very good of you to write me, and as you know only too well you are never long out of my thoughts. I do not forget the kind old days and the happy hours I spent with you; I would like to have them all over again. . . . Will you tell the Madame that we think of her and talk of her often and say to her for me, as one of my friends told me on his death bed, 'You are mighty-well liked.' I hope you will come here and play golf with me. Let me know when you will do it and we will try to break camp and go into the wilderness together. . . ."[32]

Many of Burnham's professional "downtown" friendships had, over the years, merged into personal and family relationships. Still others had emanated from the Dempster Street neighborhood in Evanston itself. The businessman, Charles Dawes, later the nation's vice-president, lived nearby. The Dawes and the Burnham families exchanged frequent visits and the two men often met and conversed on the ritualistic commuter train ride to the Loop. Once when some guest of the Burnhams had inconvenienced a neighbor, William Brown, by parking in his garage, Burnham wrote a formal apology insisting that "if there is anything I dislike it is imposing upon a friend, especially when he is the closest one I have." When the family chauffeur ran over another neighbor's dog, Burnham seemed sincerely grieved. "The death of the little dog last Saturday has caused us much sorrow," he wrote. "Mrs. Burnham and I deeply regret this, the first unpleasantness with a neighbor that has ever happened to us. We sympathize with you and your little daughter and wish there were some reparation we might make. . . . It was difficult for me to say to you on Saturday all that I felt."[33]

The Burnham house was constantly full of neighbors and Chicago friends: the musicians Theodore Thomas and Frederick Stock, the poet Harriet Monroe, the novelist Henry Fuller, all of whom would come to dinner and sometimes stay overnight. Certain friends, such as George and Eda Lord, would occasionally bring their easels and paint with Burnham. Others would play cards or listen to music. There was always a casual, neighborly ambience about the spacious house. Christmas Day, the Fourth of July, and most Sundays were reserved for the children, the neighbors, and close family friends and relatives. "Lunch for ourselves and all our neighbors on our lawn," read a typical Independence Day diary notation, "Ball game and all the young men out on lawn in fancy dress. In afternoon, tea on the terrace and in evening the young men played a burlesque of Uncle Tom's Cabin out on the lawn."[34]

The closer friends from out of town also had an open invitation to stay in Evanston whenever they came through Chicago: McKim, Keith, White, Moore, St. Gaudens, Millet, Forbes, the Olmsteds, Polk, and numerous others. Occasionally, notables in the intellectual and cultural world, who were not among the Burnham intimates—President Charles W. Eliot of Harvard, for example, and Paderewski, the pianist—accepted their overnight hospitality. For the most part, however, the Evanston life was reserved for the more intimate circle.[35]

While his relatives, neighbors, and closest friends counted heavily with Burnham, his strongest loyalties, interests, and attachments were with his immediate family. Apparently there was never any serious erosion in his marriage, Margaret continuing through the years to hold his love and admiration. Like her husband, she was handsome, stylish, and personally engaging. Into their later years Burnham delighted in her good looks, her wit, and social poise. Her freshness and "animation" pleased him greatly and he spoke admiringly of those qualities to his friends until the end of his life. Though Margaret did not have his own degree of intellectual curiosity, she had a good aesthetic sense and he appreciated her opinion in matters of taste. He frequently asked her for advice in personal and in professional matters and she influenced him in numerous small and subtle ways. A typical diary entry noted "Mrs. B. reading aloud in re: English landscape gardening in the evening after

Margaret Sherman Burnham, ca. 1890. Courtesy Houghton Mifflin Company.

dinner." Likely as not, however, the reading was a command performance, at the direction of her husband.[36]

Though before their marriage, Burnham had indeed led a "convivial"
bachelor's life, Margaret, apparently, after their marriage, held his complete sexual attention and fulfilled his needs for intimate female companionship. "I wish for you," he wrote from Europe in 1901, "not now
and then, but every minute. You are the heart of my life. . . . Home in
Evanston fills my longing. . . ." On January 19, 1911, when they were
forced to be apart on their wedding anniversary, Burnham wired her:
"All well and send love to you, my dearest wife. Proud to belong to you
after thirty-five years of married life with you." Margaret Burnham was
also an attentive mother and provided the traditional nineteenth-century
counterpoise to Burnham's role at the stern and demanding father. She
differed occasionally with his rigorous disciplinary standards, but, especially in the raising of their sons, she reluctantly deferred to his decisions
on their treatment.[37]

Burnham loved his children intensely and longed for their happiness
but this included plans for their worldly success. Over the years, he had
arrived at definite notions about success and about the ways to achieve
and secure it. He had experienced enough failure in his own early life
to make him think he knew its causes and its consequences and to make
him vow that neither he nor his children would ever again drift in its
dark direction. His self-awareness assured him, of course, that in the
long run he had "succeeded," but memories of his lack of formal education and the "right beginning" haunted him constantly and he felt
always, though he could not define it, that he had somehow "missed" a
great deal. Given his abundant drive, his vision, and his efficient executive sense, he might indeed have gained from college more knowledge,
more discipline, and more confidence in developing his own artistic
originality. Perhaps, on the other hand, the academic influence would
have quenched his expressiveness even more in that early period than it
did later in the long and difficult years of self-education. In any case,
he determined that his children would not "waste" their youths in idle
wandering and dreaming. They should work and strive in the older tradition of their Puritan ancestors and as he himself had finally done
just before it was too late.

His current affluence and social position both helped and hindered
his ambitious plans for their development. It provided them a comfortable and culturally stimulating home environment. It furnished the

necessities, and when advisable, the luxuries of life. It assured their being able to afford the finest schools. But it also encouraged, he knew full well, the attendant evils of softness, complacency, and a tendency to drift. The ultimate financial security and comfort of his own boyhood had encouraged, he thought, many of the latter qualities in himself. His own even greater wealth must not have the same effect on his children. He determined that his children would have wealth's advantages without its disadvantages, that they would use it for the things money could buy but would not allow it to hamper their acquisition of the things it could not buy. They must work and behave, and conserve by choice, as children of parents with lesser means did by necessity.

Most of Burnham's motives in raising his children were sincere and altruistic efforts to help them succeed and live happy and useful lives. In part, however, his handling of his children revealed his obvious human need to relive and restructure his own life through them. In varying degrees and in various ways, Burnham's children were indeed a success. In same cases, they succeeded because of his lovingly motivated discipline; in other cases, perhaps, they succeeded despite it or in reaction to it. Sometimes indeed his strictures so infuriated them that they determined to succeed just to "show him." Ultimately, however, they seemed to appreciate the guidance, the advantages, and the love he gave them and returned his favors with the affection and companionship of youth. The father-child relationships revealed much about the senior Burnham.

Burnham allowed his wife considerable freedom in the raising of their daughters but with the mutual understanding that the girls would develop within the strictest "lady-like" limits. Ethel, born in 1876, was the oldest of the five children and was always something of her father's favorite. Margaret, or "Peg," the fourth child, was born in 1884. Both girls went to fashionable "finishing" schools and took the grand European tour. Ethel later attended Smith College and Peg went to Miss White's School in Paris. Both made formal social debuts and both had elegant society weddings. Until their debuts and marriages, however, Burnham felt they should live as modestly and circumspectly as possible. In 1903, for example, Burnham instructed Peg's chaperone for her forthcoming tour of Europe: "I do not want her to have anything that is at all conspicuous in the way of dress, either in color or form. I want her to keep in the most exact lady-like limit." Such caution was prompted by Burnham's fear that Peg was perhaps a bit too spirited, a bit "too fond of the boys," and a bit too flamboyant, if left to her natural tastes and inclinations.[38]

Any early worries about his daughters' flaunting of proprieties, however, was countered by their choice of husbands. In 1900, Ethel married Albert Wells, the distinguished scion of a prominent Massachusetts family. Six years later, Margaret married the attorney George Kelly, an Irish Catholic Wisconsinite. Burnham approved of both marriages and developed great affection for his two sons-in-law. Both men had "proven" themselves before entering the family and Burnham took pleasure in their accomplishments. As with his grandchildren later, he could enjoy and appreciate them without the sense of direct responsibility he felt for his own sons.

The eldest son John was the child that Burnham least understood and least appreciated in the earlier years. John was quieter and more reserved than his father or his other brothers, and Burnham seemed to have had less rapport with him initially than with the other children. In the familiar quadrangle of family life, moreover, before the birth of the three later children, Burnham tended to favor Ethel, and Margaret tended to side with John. But a letter to Margaret, when she was out of town, revealed Burnham's basic concern for both of his oldest children. John, he believed, needed closer supervision in his high school studies. "I am going to hear him recite each and every lesson this winter," he wrote, "and give up everything to do my whole duty by him. I feel that the next nine months are his critical ones and I propose to sacrifice myself in order to do the utmost I can for him. I don't really think it will be a sacrifice," he then admitted, "but on the contrary a great pleasure. . . . We have carried Ethel through to her college life safely, and she will be a finely trained woman. We must do the same with John, standing by him till he catches on for himself." John's scholarship improved and he later attended Princeton University, but he returned to Chicago in 1902 without fixed goals or professional aims. Long impatient with what he considered his son's indolent dilatoriness and lack of independence, Burnham finally informed John one night after supper that the time had come for him to make his own way. If he hung around home, dependent on his father, he would, Burnham believed, never find himself. He must start at the bottom and "prove his mettle," finding his own chances and devising his own solutions. There was no better time, Burnham told the young man, than that very moment, and Burnham sent him out "with $10 in his pocket." Margaret thought the banishment was far too abrupt, but Daniel was convinced it was exactly what John needed.[39]

After working for a time, quite unhappily, in the coal business, John later took a job with the Santa Fe Railroad. In late 1903, he returned to Chicago and with a younger broker named Albert Butler founded what became a successful brokerage house. Burnham seemed pleased with his son's new success but he was always more reluctant to express this to John than he was to others. He still continued to underestimate his son and was pleasantly shocked when a friend suggested in 1911 that of all the young men in Chicago business, John Burnham was indeed one of the most promising figures. Though the earlier banishment had strained their relationship, Burnham warmed considerably in later years in his respect and his feeling for his oldest son. John, meanwhile, feeling affluent enough by 1905 to propose to his childhood sweetheart, became engaged to young Catherine Wheeler, a neighborhood child of old family friends. Burnham liked Catherine as he did all of his in-laws and wrote in a jaunty diary notation that he had "called at Spaulding's with John and helped him select an engagement ring for Catherine." Ultimately John returned something of his father's respect and affection, but he never forgot the youthful estrangement. Later, he admitted that his father had been partially right and that he had probably profited from the forced independence. His relationship with his father was marked, however, by a certain reserve that reflected the earlier sting.[40]

Hubert, the second son, achieved a closer relationship with his father than did his older brother John. Yet John and Hubert were also close, and when Hubert felt the inevitable paternal wrath, John was there to sympathize and advise. Born in 1882, and prepared at the Chicago Manual Training School and at Phillips Academy, Andover, Hubert was, unlike his brothers, an eager and a disciplined student. In 1901, he received an appointment to Annapolis where he also compiled a distinguished record. Burnham was sure, he wrote to a friend, that "Hubert will do his duty and be an honor to the service." On August 25, 1901, his diary notation seemed especially melancholy: "went into Chicago with son Hubert," it read, "who was taking himself off to his naval school in Annapolis. It was a sad parting for us all, as he will not be again under our control but that of his country's government." After Hubert had entered the naval academy, Burnham wrote him that he had received word that he was "doing first class work. You can imagine how pleased we are my dear son." The next year, he wrote rather wistfully that

"Everybody is well here, but we are lonesome, those of us who are left."[41]

Despite Hubert's scholarly and intellectual acumen, however, his personal habits were not outside the range of paternal criticism and advice. Hubert was a spendthrift, Burnham feared, and possibly at times enjoyed too thoroughly the youthful pleasures of the bottle. "Don't have a debt of even a penny and don't take a drink of any sort," he warned him before a forthcoming cruise. "If you should give me a good report for a month, you would just about double up my happiness." But he wanted periodic progress reports: "You have not written me since you got back from the cruise," he chided, "as to whether or not you have any indebtedness. You know what I told you about the exact truth in such matters. This is the sort of bravery that is more important than physical bravery. Physical bravery without moral bravery is not of much importance."[42]

After graduating from Annapolis and serving briefly on active naval duty, Hubert decided, rather abruptly, and with his father's encouragement, to resign his commission and to study architecture. In 1906, to his father's delight, he went to Paris to attend the Ecole des Beaux Arts. Burnham must have relished his own vicarious involvement through his son. The senior Burnham had always loved Paris and was full of suggestions, both solemn and carefree, for keeping Hubert fully occupied. The American ambassador Robert McCormick had helped in facilitating Hubert's appointment to the Ecole and Burnham wrote that he wanted him "to go as soon as you possibly can and make a formal call on McCormick. Do this in the most elegant manner you can because the McCormicks are very formal people. . . . He is a highly valued friend of mine and has been since we were young men."[43]

By 1907, Hubert had grown restless and wanted to return to Chicago and actively begin his new trade. He had gained a great deal from his years in Paris and the chief loss, he felt, in stopping his studies would be the failure to attain the "first class" degree. His quandary prompted a significant and revealing letter from his father: "I am in receipt of your good letter," the senior Burnham wrote, "regarding the length of your stay in Paris. I do not know how much of prestige you might miss because of not reaching the 'first class.' This is not so important, however, as really acquiring what you need of knowledge and skill. I do not often mistake the shadow for the substance! In this whole matter, there has been enough said, and it is for you to judge and act as to you is plainly wise." He advised him, however, not to act on his desires alone, "but on a balanced judgment, remembering that your way of settling things now will be your way of settling things always. If you are impatient in important actions now you will always be. If you can really acquire what you need between now and Christmas," he wrote, "then the only question left open regards the value of prestige. Give this a full consideration." Implying then that the world he would live and work in, might regard the degree with great importance, he closed by lamenting: "We must take human nature as it is, not as we should have it."[44]

After weighing alternatives, however, Hubert decided to return to America. Part of his reason no doubt was to hasten his marriage to a Washington belle named Vivian Cameron, whom he had met in his days at Annapolis. After two years of practical work in his father's Chicago office, however, Hubert decided to finish his degree and he returned with Vivian to Paris and the Ecole. Burnham continued to write him as before. He wished, as always, that they would "be a little more business like" and when touring in Europe would keep their families informed of their whereabouts. Yet, for the most part, the letters to Hubert showed Burnham as unabashedly affectionate: "We think and talk of you constantly," he wrote in 1911. "You are very close and dear, both of you, though three or four thousand miles away. I like the way you are working and the quality of it. I am sure you are doing just what we wanted and hoped for."[45]

If Hubert seemed to Burnham the most perfect of his children, Daniel, Jr., was of all the children, most like Burnham himself; and the senior Burnham knew it. As the baby of the family, he was admittedly spoiled by his doting and mellowed father, who allowed him liberties denied to his older brothers. Born in 1886, Dan was the only Burnham child to spend all of his boyhood in Evanston. By the time he was ready to go away to school, his father realized that in raising his youngest son he had violated many aspects of his own child-rearing canon. Dan had acquired, he felt, too many of the dreamy, "wild," and undisciplined qualities that he himself had had as a youth. Though fearing he had waited too long in doing so, he determined therefore to help Dan reform himself. He wrote to several friends asking advice on a school for his son "where there are no girls and where he can have special attention. He is a fine youngster, but needs someone to hold him to work until he is older." He was determined that Dan should ultimately go to Harvard and decided finally that Middlesex Preparatory School in Concord, Massachusetts, was the ideal answer for all of Dan's needs.[46]

Burnham and Daniel, Jr., ca. 1894. Courtesy Houghton Mifflin Company.

Burnham's letters to Dan at Middlesex and to his headmaster, Frederick Winsor, revealed a great deal about the senior Burnham. They illuminated further his formulas for success, and his own ideas, however conservative, for beating the woes and pitfalls of adolescence. "I want him to have the extra tutoring and care," he wrote to Winsor in 1901, "that may be necessary to hold him good and hard during this vague time of his life. He is noble and loyal, and his thoughts are sane and I am sure he will be a useful man . . . if he can be trained into concentrating." Young Dan received an adequate allowance and Burnham insisted "that he be held strictly to this without any variation. He should keep his accounts in a book and this I regard as . . . more important for him than for most boys." Burnham admitted to Winsor that "this sounds rather stern, but it is not intended to be. I feel that the greatest good I can do for my dear son is to help him to self-control." It was school policy that all students should attend a church on the weekend and Burnham was "willing that Dan shall choose for himself regarding the Church he attends, but after having made the choice, I would like him to stick to it and not change about from one place to another." Discouraging educational experimentation for the sake of concentration, Burnham wanted him "to keep steadily in the course he takes whatever it may be, because there is a family tendency to get tired of doing the same thing very long."[47]

By 1903, Dan's progress had fluctuated many times. Burnham acknowledged Winsor's criticisms of "his want of early training." He regretted that Dan's work was uneven and that his conduct was sometimes disrupting. "My estimate of him is as follows," he wrote. "He has a powerful mind. He has high imagination and much will power and ideals rather high . . . [but] with his ambition and idealism go the qualities of a dreamer and consequently he does not concentrate himself, so that instead of doing effective work, he allows himself to wander over wide fields of beautiful thought. This should not be allowed to go on. Can you suggest a cure?" Rather than simply encouraging his good qualities and allowing things to take their course, Burnham was convinced that he needed discipline above all else. He was also concerned that Dan's pursuit of women was too intense and advanced for his tender age. "He has a moral and intellectual sluggishness," he wrote, "which needs very radical treatment. If it were a question of his physical state, one would put him to hard exercise under conditions that would be dead sure to bring out the best in him. I realize that his case is outside of that usually found among boys and it seems to me a little unfair to ask that the school burden itself with the usual treatment needed in this case." In addition moreover, to advising the headmaster, Burnham discussed the same matters with Dan.[48]

At Middlesex, Dan was surprisingly receptive to much of his father's criticism and recorded feelings of genuine guilt that he was unable to live up to his father's expectations. He seemed to be convinced, in fact, that there were opposite and conflicting sides of his nature, one dark and evil; the other brighter, more promising, and reflective of his father's image. In cultivating the "good" side, he took on his father's qualities, in style and rhetoric as well as substance. While aimed, therefore, at eradicating "faults" in his son that he saw as reflections of his own earlier self, the senior Burnham's reform program had the palpable and ironic effect of further curtailing his son's individualism. Substituting

perhaps for an atavistic "wildness" a learned canon of Burnham morality, Dan tended, both deliberately and subconsciously, to emulate his
father more than any of the other children did.[49]

Like his father, Daniel, Jr., began, at Middlesex, to keep a diary of his
daily activities and, with few interruptions, he kept it up all his life.
One of the most significant items in his school-boy diary was a group of
maxims on the fly leaf taken from Franklin's *Poor Richard's Almanac*.
Whether or not he put them there at his father's suggestion, they reflected strongly the elder Burnham's sentiments and ever-present influence. "Deny self for self's sake," the maxims began. "Would you live
with ease, do what you ought, and not what you please." "Be slow in
choosing a friend. Be slower in changing." "To be humble to superiors is
duty, equal courtesy to inferiors nobleness." "He that cannot command,
cannot obey." "Do not do that which you wouldn't have proven."[50]

The notations in Dan's diary of 1904 were more introspective than
those either in his father's diaries or in the future journals of his own
later years. They revealed a sensitive and charming young man of sixteen
who, though obviously rambunctious, was probably more mature and
sensible than his father realized. In any case, the mark of D. H. Burnham, Sr., was everywhere apparent. When, for example, a friend decided to leave school and return to Evanston, Dan admitted that "I did
want to go back with him, but I guess that I am getting more here than
I would get at home in the line I kneed [sic] at present. I know if I was
at home, I wouldn't do my work properly and that now is what I ought
to put first above everything else. . . ." His melancholy mood continued
through another day when "Mr. Taylor said that I showed a lack of
intelligent work and that I was highly developed in some ways and not
in others. I feel tonight that I would like to get away from here and
forget the place, but I am going to stay and prove to them I am some
good." One notation above all others characterized his similarities with
his father. It had to do with both art and human nature. "Today I went
in with Jack Coolidge," he wrote, "to see the Whistler paintings at Cop-
ley Square. It certainly is about the finest collection of painting that I
have ever seen and some of his water colors and cloud effects are really
wonderful. . . . After this, we went over to Jack's for lunch, and I had
the pleasure of hearing his father talk on the paintings. He looks like a
man who would be great if he only had *push!*"[51]

The next order of business in Burnham's program for Dan was to get
him into Harvard. It was a traumatic period for both father and son. It

vividly reminded the elder Burnham of the same time in his own life when he had followed his own New England preparation with dismal and disappointing failure in the Harvard entrance examinations. Fearing that Dan had not prepared adequately at Middlesex, Burnham hired private tutors for a year before the examinations. When the time came and it appeared that Dan's performance was very much on the borderline, Burnham wrote an importunate and somewhat pathetic letter to the Harvard authorities. "I have just seen Mr. Malcolm Ewen," he wrote, "who has just tutored my son Dan for the past year. Before going to the examinations which occurred last week, Mr. Ewen told me that Dan was thoroughly prepared. I told him that he should go to Cambridge with Dan because I knew that Dan would have stage fright and that he would not do himself credit in examinations. I knew this would happen, because at his age I suffered in the same manner. I went to Harvard for examinations myself . . . with two men not as well prepared as I; both passed easily, and I flunked, having sat through two or three examinations without being able to write a word."[52]

He was obviously worried that Dan's performance would not be adequate either. "Mr. Ewen says, and I believe," he continued, "that Dan is well prepared, and I hope you will convince yourselves of it, for the youngster is really of a very powerful make-up. He needs to know that he is a winner, and, as soon as he does, he will show his real quality, as I have been able to do. It is the keenest regret of my life that someone did not follow me up at Cambridge . . . and let the authorities know what I could do. Mr. Ewen thinks Dan has passed but that he will be conditioned. If this be so, I am satisfied and believe that once in, my son will do well, but if there is any question," he pleaded, "cannot I see you before the final decision? Mr. Ewen says Dan knows algebra better than any man he knows, but he fears he did not do himself credit in it."[53]

Dan did receive a conditional pass, and Burnham was delighted. But the first Harvard term before the first exams was another period of tormented trial—for both father and son. "Yes, the price is very large," Burnham wrote to Dan, "but I cannot, while yet you are a minor and in my charge, allow you to score a failure no matter what the cost. Everything now depends on your devotion." He then reiterated and enumerated the familiar Franklinian maxims for success and exhorted Dan to "keep this letter and show it to me when next we meet. *Remember, until examination* you are not to go to Southbridge; you are not to take any meals in Boston and only go there if absolutely necessary to see your doctor. You are not to go to any shows of any sort, or make any social calls. *Remember:* For six weeks you are to devote every moment to hard work getting up early and going to bed early; always on the tick of the clock. Eat lightly; don't gorge and fill yourself up full. Do not eat any sweets; do not eat bread. Do not eat potatoes, sugar, or candy in any form. Are you man enough to follow these instructions six weeks?" he asked. "You must not gamble or bet. This is a point of honor between us. . . . Letters received today from Hubert and dated in Paris," he closed, "say that he is in the best studio and that his patron assures him that he will be able to regularly enter the school in December. Now Dan I want you to see how soon you will be fit to join him. If you do first rate work in Harvard, you may possibly enter the Ecole des Beaux Arts about two years from now and thus get the benefit of being one year in the Latin Quarter while Hubert is still there."[54]

Dan never matriculated at the Paris Ecole but he did enjoy two years at Harvard. In recalling later his Middlesex and Harvard days, Dan acknowledged that he and his father even shared the same heroes. "British historians might perhaps be inclined to call our class 'Edwardians,' " he wrote. "But I do not agree. The moving spirit of our day was Teddy Roosevelt. It was he who made most of the news which we absorbed. . . ." Concluding finally in 1907 that he was anything but a scholar, Dan and Burnham agreed that after two years at Harvard, he should return to Chicago, and begin a practical apprenticeship with the family firm. His years at Harvard, however, had served him well, introducing him to the arts and architecture and to the abundant life he would continue to cultivate. Between his freshman and sophomore years, he and his parents met Hubert in France and made a grand tour of French and English architectural monuments. They concentrated especially on Gothic cathedrals and had a pleasant and instructive family holiday.[55]

Young Catherine Wheeler, who lived nearby and who would ultimately marry Daniel's oldest son, John, recalled years later her image of the senior Burnham both before and after his children grew up. In their younger days on nice Sunday mornings he would take them all—his own and his neighbors' children—for long exploratory hikes and excursions. They would either trek into the ever-changing woods or along the shore of the nearby lake. She recalled the image of a huge Pied Piper followed by a line of diminutive, admiring children. Later, when the children had left and returned and Catherine, herself, had entered the family, she

The Burnham family, ca. 1910. *Left to right, seated:* Margaret, Daniel, Sr.,
Ethel, holding son George; *standing:* Daniel, Jr., John, Margaret, and Hubert. Courtesy Cherie Burnham Morris.

recalled the continuing Sunday gatherings of the clan. After breakfast,
Burnham would conduct, as before, the informal and highly personal
religious services in the library, reading passages from Swedenborg, and
discussing the mysteries and wonders of life. Naps or swims or outdoor
treks would follow the mid-day lunch. In the evenings after the buffet
dinners, they would gather around him on the terrace in summer; in the
library in winter. He would hold forth for a time, regaling them with
stories, and then abruptly would demand to play bridge or whist. He
was a terrible card player, she recalled with amusement, but never a
timid or defensive one.[56]

By 1910, Burnham's family life included the pleasure of grandchildren. "The open season for babies has come," he wrote to Hubert and
Vivian in Paris. "Margaret has another girl; one . . . is crawling around
on our veranda and when this is not happening the Woodyatt, Kelly, and

J. Burnham . . . youngsters fill in the time. That veranda was needed. Also the cork floor. The latter deadens the sound of feet of the nurses and their charges, and it also allows of softer bumps. Margaret is well as can be and so are the others."[57]

His own happiness, however, did not allow him to forget the less fortunate lives of others. He thought particularly of Dora Root, the widow of his beloved early partner. He recalled those early days when he and John had dreamed of the future that he was now experiencing so abundantly. He admired the way Dora Root had discharged her responsibilities, and he wrote to her periodically to tell her so. Her letters to him were equally appreciative. They also expressed, however, the poignant regrets of a woman who wished for more than she had gotten out of life—a life that compared to his and Margaret's seemed tired, empty and unfulfilled. "It means much to me that you think I have done well all these years," she wrote. "I have such grave doubts about myself whenever I stop to think about the subject, that a word of encouragement from one who has so wonderfully sounded out his life, gives me a new impetus. If absorbing myself before the coming generation, and humbly passing on the torch, is the whole duty of women, I believe I have earned a word of praise."[58]

Perhaps, however, she also envied the freedom and accomplishments

The woods at the Burnham home. Courtesy Houghton Mifflin Company.

of her sister Harriet Monroe, and she admitted to Burnham that she wondered "if a little self-development would not have been worth while. These young people rather take it out of us. If John had lived, all would have been different. Under the stimulus of his exhilarating life, I would have been his wife as well as the mother of his children. And it would have been interesting! As for you Dan—John certainly [would have been] . . . proud of you—we all are that. Those who know you best, the proudest of all. You have been big and great and fine and your influence is felt all over the land. Could a man desire more? Your family is all about you. They adore you and are following after you! It is really beautiful. I love to think of you and Margaret, the children, and the babies and the terrace. Everything just as it should be. . . ."[59]

So it seemed to Dora Root. So it may well have seemed to Burnham —despite the ancient problems of living in the world and of raising one's children to live in it too.

XIII
The Architecture of Capitalism

D. H. Burnham and Company
1891–1912 ·

During this period there was well under way the formation of mergers, combinations and trusts in the industrial world. The only architect in Chicago to catch the significance of this movement was Daniel Burnham, for in its tendency toward bigness, organization, delegation and intense commercialism, he sensed the reciprocal workings of his own mind.

LOUIS SULLIVAN
The Autobiography of An Idea

DESPITE THE DEMANDS of his numerous other commitments, Burnham continued over the years to run one of the world's largest architectural firms. In 1891, with Root's death, and with his own time committed mostly to the fair, Burnham left a young lieutenant, Dwight Perkins, in charge of the downtown office. From 1891 through 1893, Burnham maintained only minimal connections with the firm. Acquisition of new commissions necessarily declined and the office staff concentrated on completing work in progress.[1]

After the fair, Burnham restructured his force, drawing additional men from his exposition staff. Charles B. Atwood, who assumed Root's duties as the fair's design consultant, also took on Root's duties as chief designer in the firm. In addition to Atwood, the architect Ernest Graham, and the engineer Edward Shankland returned with Burnham from Jackson Park to the Loop. With Atwood's death in 1896 and Shankland's resignation in 1898, Graham became the sole junior partner. The firm's legal structure then remained unchanged until Hubert and Daniel, Jr., entered as junior associates in 1910.[2]

In 1908, however, "as a means of relieving somewhat Mr. Burnham's onerous responsibility," the two partners reorganized the office, putting Graham in general control of the subordinate departments of design, working plans, and superintendence. In direct charge of each department they placed Pierce Anderson, Edward Probst, and H. J. White, respectively, each of whom had entered the firm in the late 1890s as assistants in their specialties. Continuing many of the practices he had initiated as the chief administrator in the partnership with Root, Burnham indeed borrowed heavily from the business and organizational principles of his capitalistic friends and clients. Even more than in the later days with Root, the firm which evolved as D. H. Burnham and Company moved further away from the old "atelier" organization and closer to the huge corporate hierarchy that so characterized big business. At its peak in 1912, there were "not fewer than 180 men on the payroll." After 1900, the firm established a small suboffice in New York under the authority of Ernest Graham and another in San Francisco directed by Willis Polk. Both offices were established to strengthen the firm's name and reputation on the East and West coasts and for the convenience of the increasing number of clients in those two areas.[3]

Despite the extensive delegation of work, Burnham continued to keep in touch with the details of each activity. He also held the work force to specific standards. "I note the following men are not quite as prompt as they should be," he wrote to Probst in an office memorandum. "This is getting to be a serious matter, and you must be strict in every case. Please so notify each. These men must not continue to come in late. Please set an example by being absolutely on time." While demanding punctuality and efficiency, however, Burnham was a generous and humane, if essentially paternalistic, employer. His pay scale was considered good for the time and the working conditions pleasant. "Our force works 44 hours per week," he informed an inquiring journalist, "closing at four o'clock p.m. Saturdays. . . . Our vacation periods are limited to two weeks each year for each individual. We have no fixed rule for allowances for illness, but are controlled by the necessities for each individual case. We observe the following holidays: New Year's Day, Washington's Birthday (½ day), Decoration Day, Fourth of July, Labor Day, Thanksgiving Day and Christmas."[4]

Individual problems and illnesses commanded Burnham's sympathy and personal attention. "As I told you yesterday," he wrote to one draftsman, "I am very sorry that you are sick, but do not let it worry you.

Everything will be right when you come around. You are bound to win; you have lots of friends who are glad to press your fortunes to the utmost. Take it easy until you are perfectly well and do not be anxious, you have the world before you." Periodically, Burnham and Margaret entertained the office force in Evanston. On one Sunday afternoon, Burnham noted that they "began a lawn reception for the employees of the office, their sweethearts and wives, lasting until 7 P.M. Music on terrace and in house."[5]

Burnham was especially proud of his designing force, headed after 1900 by Pierce Anderson, a graduate of the Ecole des Beaux Arts. There were always several other graduates of the Ecole on the staff, including Edward Bennett, the Paris schoolmate of Anderson's who assisted Burnham with the San Francisco and Chicago plans. As it had been in the days of the partnership with Root, the drafting room of the Burnham firm was considered to be a valuable and prestigious beginning for young, ambitious architects. The list of successful professionals who passed through the firm on the way to independent careers was long. In addition to Bennett, who moved on to city planning, it included, among others, the noted school and residential architects: Dwight Perkins, Thomas E. Tallmadge, and William E. Drummond.[6]

There was, however, one designer whom Burnham could not recruit, one whose talent he admired and coveted who could not be bought for any price or prize. Burnham had known young Frank Lloyd Wright professionally through Louis Sullivan and personally through their mutual friend, Edward C. Waller. The Wallers lived across the street from Wright's elegantly prophetic Winslow House and one evening, in the mid-1890s, they arranged for a meeting of Wright and Burnham—the setting for Burnham's famous offer to Wright. "Sitting there, handsome, jovial, splendidly convincing was 'Uncle Dan,'" Wright recalled. "To be brief, he would take care of my wife and children if I would go to Paris—four years of the Beaux Arts. Then Rome—two years. Expenses all paid. A job with him when I got back. It was more than merely generous. It was splendid. But I was frightened. I sat embarrassed not knowing what to say."[7]

Wright thanked "Uncle Dan" for the astonishing offer but protested that it was simply too late. "I am spoiled already," he replied. "I've been too close to Mr. Sullivan. He has helped . . . spoil me for the Beaux Arts. . . ." But Burnham had not finished: "You are loyal to Sullivan, I see Frank, and that is right," he said. "I admire Sullivan when it comes to decoration. Essentially he is a great decorator. His ornament charms me, but his architecture? I can't see that. The Fair, Frank, is going to have a great influence in our country. The American people have seen the classics on a grand scale for the first time. You've seen the success of the Fair and it should mean something to you too. We should take advantage of the Fair." Wright pondered Burnham's offer and considered its fabulous material dimensions, but to Waller's and Burnham's stunned incredulity, he declined the offer to join Burnham's empire. Had Burnham known Wright better, he would have understood that his vast creativity demanded a lonely, personal freedom, that the man who could ultimately not even work for Sullivan could certainly not adjust to the organizational rigors of the world's largest architectural firm, a firm now committed largely to the classical revival. For Daniel Burnham, the Wright refusal was a rare and significant defeat. For most everyone else, there was magic in the Burnham touch.[8]

The varied new projects that were always on the drawing boards and the pleasant ambience of the drafting and reception rooms made the offices of the Burnham firm a natural and lively mecca for the casual visits of downtown friends or the more formal calls of distinguished visitors and clients. A small kitchen and pantry adjoined Burnham's library. Food and drink were always available and would usually appear at appropriate times on the long library conference tables. The fields of interests of visitors varied enormously, including the Cincinnati craftsman William Taylor, the maker of Rookwood Pottery; the art critic Bernard Berenson; and the British ambassador to the United States, the Honorable James Bryce. The governor of Mississippi, James K. Vardaman, called to discuss with Burnham his state's proposed memorial to the Confederate president, Jefferson Davis. Though Mississippi ultimately commissioned another architect for the job, Burnham so impressed Vardaman with his gracious business hospitality that the Governor sent him the unusual present of a large sack of Mississippi corn meal! Burnham, though amused, thanked Vardaman warmly.[9]

In 1906, Burnham moved from his commodious office in the Rookery Building on La Salle Street, which he had built and then occupied since his early days with Root, to the top of another of his products, the new Railway Exchange Building. Even larger and more elegant than the suite on La Salle Street, the new office had the additional advantage of overlooking Michigan Avenue, Grant Park, and the Lake. It seemed to friends and relatives to be a natural observation deck for viewing pa-

Burnham's office at the Railway Exchange, Chicago. Courtesy Houghton Mifflin Company.

rades, regattas, and the activities of Grand Park. Of special interest in 1911, for example, was the national exhibit and demonstration of the spectacular new "flying machines," and Burnham recorded having "lots of people" in the office for several days to witness the marvels of the aeroplane pilots.[10]

For the most part, however, Burnham and his staff stuck to their primary business of designing buildings. Between 1891 and 1912, they produced the plans for over two hundred executed structures. Whereas Burnham and Root had covered a wide spectrum of building types including houses, churches, small businesses, and skyscrapers, the work of D. H. Burnham and Company inclined even more toward the large tall commercial office building. The firm did build smaller structures, of course, both residential and public, but its trademark was the skyscraper in its various forms.

Stylistically, the buildings of D. H. Burnham and Company fell into three major groupings. First, there were skyscrapers and commercial buildings in the idiom and tradition of Burnham and Root, buildings that fitted residually under the historical rubric of the Chicago School, buildings usually designed to the specifications of particular clients, who insisted on structures of the older Chicago style. Second were the buildings in the White City tradition, structures of classical or Beaux Arts Renaissance motifs. Such edifices included libraries, museums, banks, railway stations, and government buildings. The third and perhaps the largest category featured buildings that were a combination of the first and second types, tall commercial structures that eschewed the aesthetic characteristics of the Chicago School and draped the basic Chicago frame with heavier, more traditional façades.

Most of Burnham's clients were businessmen who sensed in Burnham the makings of an artistic ally. Burnham approached such business clients in a variety of social and personal settings, but ultimately he dealt with them as businessmen on businessmen's terms. Burnham was an artist in businessman's vestments, an artist, indeed, with whom the capitalists could communicate and identify. The final decision on the form of particular buildings grew out of a complex development of site, client, and building-use analysis. After the formalities of preliminary negotiations, Burnham would study the client's needs and aspirations and make tentative suggestions with rough on-the-spot sketches. He would then relay his ideas to Atwood, Anderson, or one of the other designers and later would present his client with more tangible proposals. After more give and take and amalgamation of ideas, the client and Burnham, or one of the associates, would finally come to general decisions on style, design, arrangement, and costs. The work would then return to the drawing boards for detailed analysis and final drafting. Clients' preferences and suggestions figured largely in all of Burnham's work, but he also knew they expected to get ideas from him. While deferring as much as possible to their individual choices, he was never hesitant in urging a particular course when convinced it was the best. Yet, because he deferred as much as he did, there was a complex and eclectic variety in Burnham's work that was not characteristic of the smaller Sullivan *oeuvre*. Indeed, because he so often refused to honor clients' wishes, Sullivan's architecture remained more consistently original. But, in the process, he, no doubt, lost numerous clients who had ideas of their own.

The single skyscraper of D. H. Burnham and Company that most clearly reflected the legacy of the Chicago School was the famous Reliance Building of 1894. In 1890, Burnham and Root received a commission to plan and supervise alterations on an older five-story building on the southwest corner of State and Washington streets. Leases for the upper floors would not expire until May 1, 1894, but the owner of

Reliance Building, Chicago, 1894, before removal of cornice. Courtesy Chicago Art Institute.

Reliance Building in the mid-1960s. Author.

Railway Exchange, Chicago, 1903. Author.

the property wanted work to begin immediately on the vacant first floor. Since a tall office building was planned for the site after the lease expirations, Burnham and Root decided to place jacks under the four existing floors, later to be demolished, and to construct the new first floor on a foundation capable of carrying the future fourteen-story building. Yet, by the time the leases on the upper floors had expired, Root was dead and Atwood was the firm's chief designer. Whatever tentative plans Burnham and Root may have made for the completion of the upper floors, Burnham and Atwood in 1893 conceived new plans of a brilliant and highly prophetic import. Carrying the possibilities of the steel skeleton frame several steps beyond that of any existing structure, Burnham and Atwood produced a breathtaking glass tower of fourteen stories. Obviously resting on the Chicago steel frame, the building's façade was a tightly stretched skin of glass and terra cotta that confined and articulated the crisp and shallow bays. Over two-thirds of the street-front wall surface was glass—a radical and prophetic ratio that heralded the glass architecture of the twentieth century.[11]

The crispness and structural clarity of the Chicago aesthetic returned from time to time throughout the buildings of Burnham and Company but never so strikingly as in the Reliance. Two fine structures, for example, rose in Chicago in the Heyworth Building (1903) and the Railway Exchange Building (1905) in Chicago. The First National Bank in Cincinnati, completed in 1903, also echoed many of the school's familiar trademarks, as did the Fleming Building in Des Moines, of 1909, the Alworth Building in Duluth, of 1910, and the First National Bank Building in Hutchinson, Kansas, of 1911. After the Heyworth and Railway Exchange buildings of 1903, however, only two of Burnham's Chicago buildings truly followed the canon of the Chicago School—the Chicago Business College of 1910 and the strikingly austere Butler Brothers Warehouse, completed in 1913. All of those structures were buildings of quality, expressing, at least in their framing and façades, values that identified them with the great Chicago output of earlier years. Their problem, however, was that their identity was precisely with the great buildings of the 1880s rather than an outgrowth of that tradition. The Reliance was indeed such an outgrowth, as was Louis Sullivan's Schlesinger and Mayer Store at the turn of the century. As successfully, in fact, as the Heyworth, the Railway Exchange, and the Chicago Business College may have fulfilled the criteria of the early Chicago School, they seemed to antedate, rather than follow, the pinnacle achievement of the

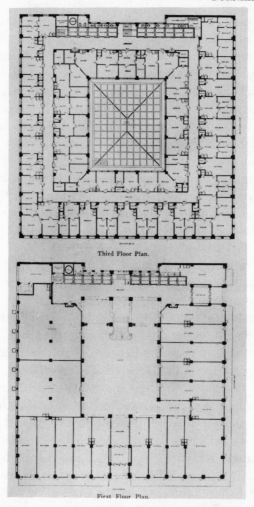

Railway Exchange, plan. *Architectural Record.*

Reliance Building. In addition merely to echoing the tradition of the 1880s, the finer buildings of Burnham's later years also had serious internal contradictions. The outside design and the internal arrangement, for example, of the Railway Exchange contributed to one of Burnham's best and most solid creations, but the formal, neoclassical, interior detailing was disturbingly cacophonous and stylistically inappropriate.[*12]

* For a more detailed discussion of the problems involved in interpreting the Reliance Building, see footnote 12, p. 427.

In sharp contrast to the buildings designed in the aesthetic purity of the early Chicago School and to Burnham's own latent and lingering allegiance to its principles, was the side of his output that instead mirrored the recent Chicago World's Fair. Catalyzing the incipient classical revival that had gained new life in the 1880s, the Exposition of 1893 had convinced Burnham and many of his future clients that architectural dignity, formality, and monumentality were synonymous with classical motifs. For the most part, the fair had actually reflected Renais-

Heyworth Building, Chicago, 1903. *Architectural Record.*

Alworth Building, Duluth, Minnesota, 1910. *Architectural Record.*

First National Bank, Hutchinson, Kansas, 1911. *Architectural Record.*

sance and Baroque variations on Greece and Rome, but unbothered by archaeological distinctions, the viewers became certain that they wanted buildings of similar moment for their real-life banks and libraries. Burnham was all too happy to oblige. With the death of Root he had virtually lost his aesthetic gyroscope, and he felt less secure in the Chicago idiom that was basically Root's and Sullivan's. In attempting also to compensate for his lack of academic training, he had searched for a "style" that he could learn on his own and that had ample references on which he could rely. The obvious answer lay in the classic Greek orders and their Roman and Renaissance variations.

Despite the limitations of Burnham's stylistic vocabulary, however, the interior of even his most "classical" buildings seemed generally well planned and "functional" according to the needs of his clients. A sympathetic contemporary critic, A. N. Rebori, perceived such qualities, for example, in the neoclassical Illinois Trust and Savings Bank, completed in 1897 at the corner of Jackson and LaSalle streets. Part of the structure's effect, he wrote, was "due to the impressiveness of a two-story monumental building occupying one of the choicest corners in the business heart of Chicago. It is an essay in classic architecture achieved by

Butler Brothers Warehouse, Chicago, 1913. *Architectural Record*.

Illinois Trust and Savings Bank, Chicago, 1896-97. *Architectural Record*.

the application of a simple and well-proportioned Corinthian order.
. . . The delicately framed window openings, which are in themselves
in perfect scale, and the carefully studied detail of the entire granite
exterior present a masterly adaptation of academic architecture." The
inside of the building, Rebori believed, was "no less interesting than the
outside, for every department is carefully studied and the architectural
treatment was determined by the construction and uses of the place.
. . . For the general disposition of the plan there was no fixed precedent,
and the forms resulting from this distinction have the welcome effect of
unsought novelty."[13]

Other neoclassical buildings followed. The Simmons Memorial Library, built in 1899, in Kenosha, Wisconsin, was a domed neo-Roman
structure employing elements of the Ionic order. Cincinnati's Schmidlapp Memorial Library, of 1905, took the form of a Doric-ordered Greek
temple. While completing the plans for the Cincinnati building Burnham wrote the donor, his friend Jake Schmidlapp, that it was his "ambition to make this library for you one of my best efforts"; and the
building remained always one of Burnham's favorites. The St. Louis
County Court House, of 1909, in Duluth, Minnesota, and the Rock

Schmidlapp Memorial Library, Cincinnati, Ohio, 1905. *Architectural Record.*

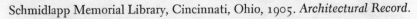

Claridge Hotel, New York, 1910. Courtesy Douglas Leigh, Inc.

Island Savings Bank of Rock Island, Illinois, of 1911, were typical, un-
distinguished examples of Burnham's classical eclecticism. Chicago's Orchestra Hall, of 1905, was acoustically superb but esthetically rear-guard,
at least in its neo-Georgian Michigan Avenue façade. New York's Claridge Hotel, of 1910, was an esthetically unimaginative but functionally
competent essay in a classically inspired mode of the French Baroque.[14]
    Designed and built over a period of years, the mammoth "Roman"
Field Museum of Natural History was not completed until 1920, eight
years after Burnham's death. His part, however, in the early planning
stages, especially in matters of decorative detail, left an interesting
insight into his value system and to at least part of his sense of the

meaning of American history. The four major decorative features of the new museum, he proposed, should be colossal statues of Christopher Columbus, George Washington, Abraham Lincoln, and Marshall Field. Such figures would, he wrote to a friend, "cover the history we desire to refer to: That of the discoverer of America, that of the Founder of America, that of the Liberator of America, and finally, as typical of Peace and Prosperity, that of the Merchant and the Manufacturer whose beneficence naturally follows and completes the work for which the first three laid the foundation." That the Marshall Field type represented the culmination and embodiment of the dreams and work of the Founding Fathers was an unconsciously ironic and hyperbolic commentary on a contemporary historical controversy, centering on the work of historian Charles Beard. But Burnham was on more solid ground when he saw Field as the symbol of the nation's prosperity.[15]

The greatest product, however, of Burnham's protracted classicism was undoubtedly the Union Railroad Station for Washington, D.C., started in 1903 and completed in 1907. Designed as an integral part of the new plan for Washington, Union Station would not only accommodate the train lines of railroad magnate Alexander Cassatt, who had

Union Station, Washington, D.C., 1903-7. Author.

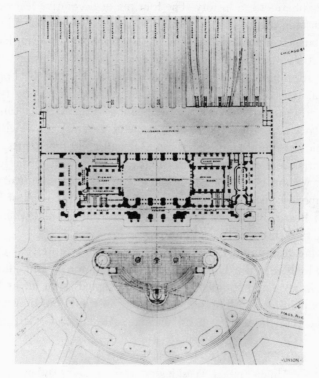

Union Station, plan. *Architectural Record.*

agreed to give up his old position on the Mall, but would also be the
Washington depot for all the other railroad lines linking Washington
with the farthest parts of the country in one true Union Station. Conceived by Burnham and recognized by others as a fitting "vestibule to
the nation's capital," the station was one of the largest projects Burnham's firm ever handled. As such, it raised considerable problems, especially in Burnham's relations with the building's contractors, Ralph
and Theodore Starrett. Burnham frequently had abrasive dealings with
his buildings' contractors because he liked to think of himself as the
over-all supervisor. Consequently, he often entered areas that the builders considered their private domain. Though his interference often
caused friction, his dominating aggressiveness frequently seemed necessary to move a job along to meet commitments and deadlines.

"I think it is advisable that you should know personally from me," he wrote to Starrett, "that the Washington job is not going right. It needs the exclusive attention of the very strongest man in your connection. When we recommended your company to Mr. Cassatt, you told me that you yourself would attend to this job. I now request that either you or Ralph give this thing exclusive attention and that you do it at once. There is great dissatisfaction, which is hurting your company, and in my judgment no one except a master can lift this job out of the rut. It will not avail your reputation to explain afterwards that legally you are not to blame for delay. What the heads of great corporations look for in a man," he asserted significantly, "is success under difficulties, and nothing goes with a worse grace than constant explanations of failures. This is a very big man's job. It cannot be handled by anyone except the boss. It needs and must have you or Ralph, or both, not merely for a month or two, but until it is done."[16]

The Starretts did give the job their personal attention and the pace of construction quickened. Ultimately, the completed station admirably handled all of its railroad traffic and constituted Burnham's most successful essay in the classical mode. Omitting the usual high-arched train

Union Station, waiting room. *Architectural Record.*

shed at the rear, the building contained two primary elements, the central train or midway concourse, leading on to the open train platforms, and the elaborate main waiting room or passenger concourse at the front. Rising high above the arched entrance porch, the vast, barrel vault of the main waiting room ceiling was explicitly expressed as the building's dominant exterior feature. The station fronted on to a magnificent plaza leading southward to the Capitol and featured central inscriptions composed by Charles Eliot, president of Harvard, decorative sculpture by Louis St. Gaudens, the brother of Burnham's friend Augustus, and a central fountain sculpture by Lorado Taft. Far fresher in conception than Burnham's adjacent post office building, the Union Station ranked with New York's Pennsylvania Station and Grand Central Station as perhaps the leading examples of what a later historian would ambivalently label "Burnham Baroque."[17]

While continuing, on the one hand, to design great skyscrapers that were basically in the old Chicago mode and, on the other hand, to cultivate for ceremonial structures, the multi-faced legacy of traditional classicism, the most numerous and characteristic offerings from the Burnham firm represented a blending of those two extremes. Most buildings, indeed, that Burnham produced in the years that followed the fair and Root's death, were neither futuristic glass towers like the Reliance Building nor neo-Roman temples like the Field Museum. They were multi-storied office buildings for tough-minded capitalists who possessed no more than average aesthetic gifts, men who wanted both the functional modernity of Chicago construction and the modish effects and trappings of the classical vogue. Burnham was able and willing to supply them with both.

As in the larger corpus of Burnham's work, his "middle genre" of "classicized" skyscrapers also ran the spectrum of relative excellence to meretricious excess. Many of the better middle buildings, especially in the earlier years, compared favorably with the leaner, purer examples of the Chicago tradition. In linear clarity, for example, the Fisher Building of 1896 resembled the great Reliance Building of two years earlier, but it differed from the relatively chaste Reliance in its greater and more obvious use of neo-Gothic ornamentation. The Merchants Loan and Trust Company of 1900 was similar in style and excellence to the later Railway Exchange, except for minor classical detailing on the upper façade and a considerably heavier treatment of the interior. The same applied to the McCreary Store in Pittsburgh and the First National

Fuller (Flatiron) Building, New York, 1903. Author.

Bank of Chicago, both completed in 1903. The triangular Flatiron
Building, built in New York in 1901, was, because of its shape and location, one of Burnham's most elegant skyscrapers. For years acclaimed
as the world's tallest building, the crisp, slender Flatiron, towering over
Broadway, was marred only by an overly busy surface ornamentation.
On the other side of the middle group of Burnham's classicized skyscrapers were buildings that Thorstein Veblen would have joyfully included in his most pejorative categories. Dripping with excessive classical ornamentation were such structures as the People's Gas Company

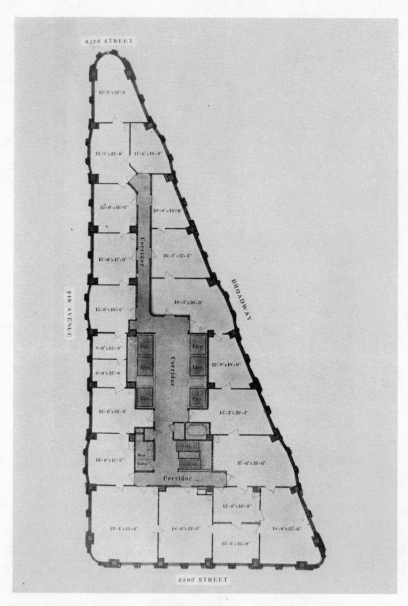

Flatiron Building, plan. *Architectural Record.*

Michigan Avenue, Chicago, between Jackson and Adams, showing three buildings by D. H. Burnham and Company. *Left to right:* the Railway Exchange, Orchestra Hall; *far right:* the People's Gas Building (1910). The building to the right of Orchestra Hall is the Pullman Building, designed by S. S. Beman. Library of Congress.

Building in Chicago (1910), and the Conway Building, and Continental and Commercial National Bank Building, both completed in Chicago only in 1914.

The most typical buildings of the large middle group, however, usually avoided either the excellences or the gross excesses of the group's two extremes. They numbered in the dozens and spread across the country and included such structures as the Ellicott Square Building, in Buffalo (1892); the Land Title Building, in Philadelphia (1897); the Continental Trust Building, in Baltimore (1900); the Frick Building and the Oliver Building, in Pittsburgh (1901 and 1908); the Edison Building, in Chicago (1905); the Scanlan Building, in Houston (1909); and a New York skyscraper of 1912 known by its address at Eighty Maiden Lane. Most of the famous new department stores for which Burnham became the acknowledged authority—Field's, Gimbel's, Wanamaker's, Filene's, and Selfridge's (London)— also fell within the aesthetically neutral middle category. Difficult to classify because of its three

Continental and Commercial National Bank, Chicago, 1912-1914. *Architectural Record.*

separate divisions of heterogeneous styling, Burnham's Pittsburgh Union Station (1898-1902) was a favorite of contemporary and later generations. The starkly functional and efficient single-span train shed at the rear of the complex was largely hidden from public exposure by a tall central office tower, similar in detail to the typical Burnham skyscraper, but the eye-catching trademark of the entire composition was the sumptuous carriage entrance concourse attached to the front of the central office section.

Only volumes could detail the complex stories of the structural make-up, the aesthetic properties, and the client-architect relationships that went into the building of each of Burnham's skyscrapers. Spare illustrations must suffice.

The Chicago First National Bank, for example, completed in 1903, characterized the fusion of styles and values that were embodied in the typical Burnham and Company skyscraper. Commissioned by Burnham's friend, bank president James B. Forgan, the building was designed with special assistance from his San Francisco associate, Willis Polk. The building's proposed height, however, conflicted with a recent city ordinance requiring special permits for buildings above a certain height and prompted Burnham to petition various members of the Board of Aldermen. To Edward Cullerton, for example, he wrote that it would be a great favor "if you will take up the matter of a permit for the First National Bank of Chicago and support it. We are just entering upon a very prosperous time in Chicago," he wrote in his best booster rhetoric, "Everything looks bright in the future provided the people who are

Union Station, Pittsburgh, 1902. *Architectural Record.*

First National Bank, Chicago, 1903. *Architectural Record.*

ready and willing to spend large sums of money for important improvements are not hampered by unnecessary restrictions. A large number of
tall buildings in Chicago," he wrote, "have gone up 16 stories and very
much higher. In justice, others should be allowed to build as high. This
will in no way interfere with the appearance of the town, but will bring
about a regularity which will make things impressive." It would, in fact,
"add to our status as a great metropolis the more of these buildings there
are." He then closed the request with his characteristic personal touch.
"I have always found you," he said to Cullerton, "a man ready to see
and forward the interests of the community in which we have both been
brought up, and I trust you will give this thing your full and hearty

Main stairway, First National Bank, Chicago. *Architectural Record*.

Main banking room, First National Bank, Chicago. *Architectural Record*.

President's Room, First National Bank, Chicago. *Architectural Record*.

support." Convinced by Burnham's assertions that the eighteen-story building was both safe and necessary, the aldermen approved the permit.[18]

As with several of Burnham's other skyscrapers, the completion of the First National Bank occasioned a detailed description and review in a special supplement to the *Inland Architect and News Record*. The journal's commendation was consistent with most contemporary reactions to his work. It spoke to all of Burnham's biases. "A massive structure of steel and granite looming skyward over 200 feet and covering a large ground area in the heart of Chicago's commercial center," it began. "This is the new home of the First National Bank, the great financial institution of the West. It is a marvel of what may be termed

American architecture. It combines beauty with utility, strength of foundation and superstructure with power of expression of a great mass in simple lines and magnificent proportions, broken only by horizontal courses essential in the composition." While later critics would find the bank building overly heavy, the anonymous contemporary writer thought it gave "the impression of beauty and grace. Like a single glistening shaft, its fine proportions hold the interest and command the admiration. The human mind worships grandeur and this is one of the secrets of the power of the old masters over all generations. They were right in principle and practiced the truth. Masters of today will be equally honored if they but hold to the truth." Burnham must have glowed in agreement.[19]

"To even the average man on the street not architecturally informed," the flowery review continued, "who has not traveled abroad and lingered in the old Italian cities, the exterior of this great building suggests that its interior contains a bank of something more than ordinary extent and he would be disappointed if anything of lesser scale or of proportions unworthy of its exterior were found therein. How much more than this is suggested to the imagination of the traveled and trained architect by this great exterior. . . . Its designer once said," he continued, referring to Burnham directly, "that in architecture, the biggest thing was the best thing to do—and here he did it nobly—inside and out. . . . One enters the building with the exterior in his mind, prepared to find just what is there. The three wide entrances invite one from the side walk into the hall of the building . . . here the grand Italian staircase seems to greet and to invite one to the bank above. . . . There is a nobility in the conception; a palatial air about that hall and grand stair-case which reminds the traveled and educated architectural mind of the palaces of Naples, of the great Roman and Florentine palaces. The steps, the balustrade, the paneled walls, the coffered ceiling, the great chandelier, the grilles, the design of the marble floor are all in scale and harmony and thoroughly Italian in the best sense, and almost Roman in dignity."[20]

"White marble was the material in which the designer chose to express himself," the reviewer pointed out in rhetoric that echoed the building's own qualities. "With this, the floor contrasts finely; its inlays of Sienna, Verde antique, Numidian marbles in panels, lozenges, discs, and bands, in the white ground. Turning and looking down the stairway or upward at the exquisitely paneled ceiling in white and gold, or through the arched opening toward the street, the vaulted gray and gold ceiling of the president's room showing in the view, or gazing at the corner arches and stairs to the directors' rooms on the third story, one is well satisfied, and turns back to enter the portals of the great banking room, prepared and expectant. No one could enter here without being much impressed by its vastness, its magnificent scale and proportion. . . ."[21]

The writer then described the elegant details of each room of the bank and complimented its numerous technical and commercial features. They combined, he thought, "the most approved requirements of a great banking house with those of a first class modern office building. Architecturally the building outranks most of its class. It is a dignified expression upon broad lines of progress in art, combined with a high appreciation of architectural propriety in detail and marks an era of architectural growth in the adaptation of the laws of art to the modern business structure."[22]

Most of Burnham's communications with Forgan and with the various artists and contractors over details of the design and general building problems were transmitted in personal conversations, either face to face or over the telephone. Few records, therefore, survived of the day-to-day, month-to-month progress of that or of any other local Chicago projects. On out-of-town jobs, however, Burnham wrote frequently and attentively to all persons concerned with each enterprise. His involvement with Henry Frick, for example, and the building of his Pittsburgh skyscraper, illustrated Burnham's minute concern with the large and small details of the operation. Built contemporaneously with the First National Bank Building, the Frick structure was ultimately less successful in total effect. It evoked no praise as extravagant as the bank reviewer's, though it raised in Burnham the usual high expectations.

He wrote to Frick that he wanted to build the "perfect building" and requested permission to hire the finest artists to assist in the decoration. He selected the painter John La Farge to design and execute a central stained glass window. To create the building's major piece of lobby sculpture, he commissioned J. P. Proctor, a protégé of St. Gaudens. La Farge's window, Burnham thought, "should be a golden color, light as possible, having the effect of an old Greek coin." In reviewing the designer's initial sketches, for a glass that featured a female figure, he gave the artist detailed suggestions for implementation. "The figure itself," he wrote, "should have the effect of tallness and of stateliness. It

Frick Building, 1901 (*right*), and Frick Annex, 1905 (*left*), Pittsburgh. *Architectural Record.*

should therefore be longer in the legs. It is too familiar and human as it is. . . . The beautiful arrangement of the hair melting away into the clouds of the background appeals to me strongly and I accept it; but the drapery is not wind-blown. It falls naturally as in a calm. I feel the inconsistency of this when compared with the movement in the hair and if possible, I should still like to see the effect of the drapery blown back to correspond with the backward flow of the hair. The face," he concluded, "is very beautiful, but it is very human. Cannot you impart a

Stained-glass window by John La Farge, Frick Building. *Architectural Record*.

more goddess like cast of countenance? I hope you will be patient with me for I have the success of this piece of work very closely at heart."[23]

He made a similarly detailed criticism of Proctor's marble lion. "My impression now," he wrote after seeing the initial model, "is that the lion is a little small in scale, and that the first drawing made by you would be better. . . . The handling and conception of the thing," he felt, "is very splendid. It has real power in it and I like the technique very much. I think we are going to get a great thing out of it."[24]

Burnham valued his own rapport with Proctor and La Farge, but when Frick later asked to see the work in progress for himself, Burnham feared that his characteristic candor might intimidate the artists. "When you see them, don't let anyone criticize," he cautioned Frick, "the things are just in that sensitive condition that may throw the men off unless they feel that we are pleased. These things are so very good, I fear to have either of the artists attempt to change. When once a man of this rank attempts to suit a layman, he nearly always loses the vision he has in his own mind. If you see anything you desire to have altered, let me know and I will try to effect the change. . . ."[25]

Burnham had more serious problems with the contractors and the building materials. It was necessary, for example, he wrote a foreman, to replace the granite cornice with one made of "heavy copper—to act as a gutter and carry the water back, not allowing it to drip on people's heads on the street." It was also essential, he believed, because "the frost in the long run may get between the granite and burst out." With the general contractors, the Fuller Company, Burnham encountered the same frustrations he had known with the Starrett Company on Union Station. "As you know," he wrote the company's president, "it is Mr. Frick's habit to go thoroughly into the details of his affairs and any inadvertences . . . would naturally come to his notice." Frick had complained not only of their shoddy workmanship, Burnham noted, but of their slowness and reluctance to finish on time. To remedy the various problems, Burnham made specific demands. "We have Frick's letter signed by himself," he wrote, stating that the work was "very unsatisfactory. Think it your duty to this large job on which you are earning so great a sum to respond to our request. . . ." In desperation Burnham dispatched the tough-minded Ernest Graham to go to Pittsburgh and supervise the job himself. In doing so, he assured Frick that Graham "is better than myself in pushing the job and I am sure his presence there will give you utmost satisfaction." Total satisfaction, it seemed, was for Henry Frick a rare commodity, however. After Graham had left Pittsburgh and returned to New York, Burnham wrote him reluctantly that he must return immediately to conciliate Frick, who had "written another foolish letter about the mechanical plant."[26]

In addition, moreover, to his chronic complaints, Frick was also slow in fulfilling his own financial obligations. "The bill for $40,000 is on account and not a final one," Burnham wrote the steel tycoon late in 1902. "In paying this, you hold back enough to cover all future services you may require. But of course you know without my saying so that we will always be at your call in any case, as we are at the call of all our clients. This job," Burnham admitted, "has been an exceedingly difficult

Marshall Field Retail Store, Chicago, 1902. *Architectural Record.*

one for us, far exceeding in its urgent and consistent demands on us anything we have undertaken before. The result," however, Burnham was certain, "is the most beautiful and practical building in the world, a monument not surpassed in any time or place. We feel very proud of it and I know you do. The amount we now ask is justly due and has been earned. The sum has been counted on by us and we have committed ourselves in an undertaking in which we urgently need it. Not being capitalists, we are much concerned not to have any question arise regarding our fees, and I hope you will send us a cheque . . . realizing that we need our money very much now." Burnham was pleased to have Frick's business, but at times he wondered if it was worth the costs.[27]

Burnham especially enjoyed his work for the great merchants—Marshall Field, the Gimbel brothers, John Wanamaker, and Edward Filene. His plans for their stores were much alike and had qualities in common with his better office buildings of the later period. There were similarities, for example, between the façades of each of them and that of the archetypal First National Bank in Chicago. Massive, solid, impressive—and ponderous—the Field and Wanamaker buildings especially echoed in surface details an enlarged version of both the Roman and Renaissance palazzo traditions.

In building his stores for both New York and Philadelphia, Burnham had some of the same problems with Wanamaker that he had had with Frick. There were constant minor complaints and requests for revisions. The merchant was also slow in paying his bills on schedule. Daniel, Jr., recalled that "there came a stage near the completion" of the Philadelphia store "when he had owed us over a year" in the amount of several hundred thousand dollars. The firm needed the money so badly that "my father, after many requests for payment, finally in desperation, took the matter up with the celebrated lawyer, Mr. John G. Johnson," who promptly arranged payment. When Burnham asked Johnson about his own fees, Johnson replied surprisingly that there would be no bill since he was also Wanamaker's attorney and "it had been a pleasure for him to have the opportunity to lecture the old gentleman and to try to persuade him it was good business practice to be more prompt in his payments."[28]

When completed, the Wanamaker store covered "an entire block," Burnham wrote proudly to a friend, "which measures 500 feet by 250 feet, in the center of the city. There are three stories below the sidewalk and twelve stories above. Each one of the latter is high enough to allow of a division into two stories at some future time, when extra room for the business is demanded. When this is done, the building will be twenty-four stories high from the attic to the sidewalk level. The exterior is of very beautiful granite, the Italian Renaissance style being employed in the design. The building as a whole, both inside and outside, is the most monumental commercial structure ever erected anywhere in the world. Its total cost has exceeded Ten Million Dollars."[29]

Though the building reached completion sometime earlier, Wanamaker wanted to hold the dedication ceremonies on December 30, 1911, to commemorate his fiftieth year in business. As the building's architect, Burnham would of course have a prominent part in the ceremonies, and he decided to make the most of the occasion. He invited some fifty prominent Chicagoans from business, government, the professions, and the arts to go to Philadelphia as his guests. For the grand procession, he chartered a private train, each man having a separate compartment. His invitation announcing the event noted that "the President of the United States will make the opening dedicatory address and the ceremony will be one of unusual interest and great significance." Burnham made no pretense of modesty as he closed the invitation: "As this great work is the most notable of its kind that has ever been undertaken by man," he wrote, "and as it has been done by us here in Chicago, it would be a matter of great pride and satisfaction to Mr. Wanamaker and to us if you and other gentlemen of this city would accompany me to Phila-delphia and be present at the ceremony." The President's participation in so high a celebration of American commercial entrepreneurship em-phasized with pungent clarity the nation's commitments to the capi-talist spirit. It was not certain, however, at the actual dedication, whether Wanamaker, Taft, or Burnham would be the most exalted personage.[30]

Burnham's train arrived in Philadelphia early on the morning of the thirtieth and his entourage went immediately to inspect the new store.

Wanamaker's Store, Philadelphia, 1909. *Architectural Record*.

Interior, Wanamaker's Store, Philadelphia. *Architectural Record.*

Following that, Daniel, Jr., recalled, Wanamaker "gave a breakfast in the vast new dining room for approximately 350 guests, assembled from all parts of the country. . . . At the speaker's table were many notables including Wm. H. Taft, President of the United States, who made a dramatic entrance up the main aisle to the music of a brass band . . . accompanied by several generals and admirals in full dress uniforms." Dan recalled that "President Taft spoke briefly and was followed by several other notables. When Mr. Wanamaker made the principal speech, he told about how he had built up his business over fifty years and how proud he was at the completion of his vast new building. He complimented my father and said he was a great and most distinguished architect. When it was my father's turn to speak, he graciously thanked Mr.

Wanamaker and concluded by saying—which brought down the house
—'I doubt if I am as great an architect as Mr. Wanamaker has said I
am; but if I have become a good architect, it has been because of the
education I have received at the expense of my clients.'" After returning
to Chicago, Burnham wrote to his friend Theodore Ely that "the ceremony was a fine thing, except old John talked too much—but then, it
was his day."[31]

The façade of the department store for Edward Filene, the great Boston merchant and philanthropist, was less successful aesthetically than
the Field and Wanamaker stores, but the building's functional and technical attributes were equally advanced. Noting Burnham's reputation
and successes as a department store architect, Filene commissioned him
to spare no expense in creating an efficient and attractive store. His announcement of Burnham's selection for so choice a commission, however, brought hostile criticism from R. Clipston Sturgis and several
other Boston architects who felt that Filene should have given the job
to a local firm.[32]

Filene's response was an able answer to such provincial criticism and
an eloquent tribute to Burnham's reputation. "Several of your correspondents," he wrote the *Boston Herald* in September 1911, "have criticized the bestowal of important commissions on outside architects, and
since the firm of which I am a member has been mentioned among the
list of offenders, your readers might be interested in our reasons for making Mr. Daniel H. Burnham of Chicago the architect of our building."
He then described at length Burnham's buildings and achievements and
the numerous honors accorded him for his work. "In keeping with the
times," he then asserted, "his firm has come to specialize among other
things in the architecture of great retail establishments. A part of his organization is exclusively engaged in this work. . . . The modern retail
establishment is a very complicated machine for distributing merchandise, and the problems of construction and equipment involved are
quite as important as purely architectural considerations."[33]

"It seems to me no reflection on Boston architects," Filene continued,
"that the foremost specialist . . . in department store architecture
should come from Chicago, but it should be a reflection on us if we
did not try to have the best for our business that was obtainable. I believe this decision will be agreeable to the great body of Boston architects. In painting, the best artists have never been in favor of keeping
out foreign works by import duties. No one wants the art museum re-

Filene's Store, Boston, 1912. Author.

stricted to work by Boston artists. The bringing of notable foreign art
only results in helping American artists. So it is with architecture. Any
other view is provincial and unworthy. Boston artists enter freely into
the architectural opportunities of other cities. . . . Doubtless no one
heard of complaints here when other cities demanded our Richardson,
nor now in regard to the many buildings our Boston architects are building in other cities." Though a great believer in local loyalties, Burnham
would have agreed even more warmly with Filene's defense of architectural laissez faire.[34]

Though Burnham increasingly concentrated on larger buildings, he occasionally produced charming residences and smaller structures. The pleasantly "modern" design of some of his small and simple buildings for the Chicago park system elicited frequent praise from local citizens and out-of-town critics. Though his residencies for the businessman Stanley Field and the steel-maker Charles Schwab, for the most part, were ponderous essays in traditional genres, the Washington house for his old Philippines friend General Henry Corbin showed definite elements of the contemporary Prairie styles of his friends George Maher and William Drummond. Indeed, Burnham admired much of the residential work of Chicago's younger modern architects. He was delighted, for example, to accompany Maher on a tour of his Prairie houses. He obviously admired Frank Lloyd Wright and had once described Wright's epochal Winslow House as "a gentleman's house from grade to coping." Only occasionally, however, did he succumb to the pleas of a friend or a regular client and indulge himself in the smaller idiom that he actually enjoyed. The rustic stone and shingle-style bungalow for his friend James Parmelee in New Jersey, for example, gave him special satisfaction. "I will be very glad indeed," he wrote to Parmelee, "to go into the matter of bungalows with you. They are things I am very fond

Sherman Park Buildings, Chicago, 1903. *Architectural Record.*

Corbin House, Washington, D.C., 1907. *Architectural Record.*

of, and I would like to spend the rest of my life making them. I want to know something about the stone around there, and no doubt we can get up a scheme that will be delightful in every way."[35]

Such jobs were exceptions, however. Early in the century, he had written to a friend that he had decided "to have a dozen good jobs a year, or more. I am organized to do this number and do them well. I refuse all minor things, including dwellings. One dwelling will give more hard work and more actual worrying than any one work I have." He was sure he had "not a quarter as many jobs as Carrère and Hastings or McKim, Mead, and White, and yet, I am sure that my work receives more of my undivided thought than theirs per job." By 1906, he could make the statement that he did "not care to take a job that will not amount to at least one hundred thousand dollars."[36]*

Despite the fact that he often refused commissions, however, he also desired and solicited jobs that he did not receive. He sought but did not get, for example, the commissions for the new St. Paul's Cathedral in Pittsburgh, the Frick Mansion and the City National Bank in New York, the train station in San Francisco, a resort hotel in Havana, and the renovations and additions to the Military Academy at West Point.

* See Appendix A for comparative building costs, 1870–1970.

Composite of Burnham's Buildings from a drawing by Willis Polk. Courtesy Chicago Art Institute.

Such instances were rare, however. For the most part, Burnham felt satisfied with his firm's achievements. "Modern commercial buildings," he wrote to a prominent editor, "are all constructed on the principles worked out in my office during the last fifteen years." And despite his immodesty, he was partially right.[37]

However much he gloried in his fame, in his buildings, or in his sense of personal accomplishment, he was equally proud of the important human contacts that his business helped to bring him. His clients and associates were indeed "the strongest people in the country," and in all his many "outside" projects, he valued and depended on their friendship and support. Acknowledging a letter that had praised a recent building, Burnham wrote Stanford White that he was "the best fellow in the world. I am deeply pleased with your letter. Praise from you is more than I ever hoped to deserve. The world is a brighter place because of your thoughtfulness in sending me your approval. I shall hold my head higher because of it." To a similar letter of appreciation from a client, Jake Schmidlapp, Burnham replied that Ernest Graham had "just showed me your letter . . . and I want to tell you how deeply we both feel the constant kindnesses you pour on us. It makes a man realize that life *just as it is* is sweet and mighty worthwhile."[38]

Of all Burnham's vast architectural projects, the one that consumed him most was the plan for the improvement of Chicago. Far more important than his miniature White City was the darker and larger city that lay beyond. Far more compelling than his schemes for the Rookery, or the Railway Exchange, was the dream that transcended individual buildings—a dream that made the pragmatic architect a visionary planner of his city's growth. Though he obviously never minimized material considerations, the architect of capitalists could also work in the Chicago Plan for the larger majority that never commissioned buildings.

XIV
Beyond the White City

The Chicago Plan of 1909

> He met half-way the universal expectation that the spirit of the
> White City was but just transferred to the body of the great
> Black City close at hand, over which it was to hover as an en-
> lightenment—through which it might permeate as an inform-
> ing force.
>   "Good!" he thought; "there's no place where it's needed
> more or where it might do more good."
>
> HENRY BLAKE FULLER
With the Procession

In 1913, the writer Hamlin Garland described in one of the prominent
architectural journals an informal gathering of writers and artists that
had taken place some ten years earlier in the country near Chicago,
where "Daniel Burnham, the great builder, detailed for us his plan for
a new and beautiful Chicago. As he talked on quietly, easily," Garland
remembered, "describing his vision of a great front park, harbors and
lagoons, indicating here and there on a roughly drawn map, the civic
centers and the great architectural plazas . . . I, for one, came to think
of him with surprise as a poet, a dreamer, one who was dwelling in the
far future, and I am quite sure the other men shared to some degree
my feeling. 'It is all too fine, too splendid to come in our day,' was my
own thought."[1]

Other Chicagoans shared Garland's doubts. Yet although they were
skeptical, they were willing to be convinced. They knew of Burnham's
reputation for pragmatic realism as well as for visionary idealism. It was
not the man they doubted anymore. The man had proved himself. Completion of the fair by 1893, for example, had seemed to many an insuper-

able obstacle, but Burnham had pushed it to completion and to what most contemporaries considered astounding success. But compared to the vastness and complexity of his proposed plan for Chicago, the make-believe city now seemed tame indeed. The toughest challenge of Burnham's career, in fact, would be to convince his fellow Chicagoans that the dream was viable and that it could very well be begun in their own time.

Burnham's thoughts on Chicago urban reform had been formed much earlier, of course, than the "dreamy" discourse Garland remembered from 1903. Perhaps they had begun to take shape unconsciously when he returned to Chicago as a young man in 1870, or when he started an independent architectural firm in 1873 after the great fire called for vast rebuilding in the city. Certainly his part in creating the White City stimulated his thoughts on the possibilities of urban planning in general and of Chicago planning in particular. Despite the numerous and increasing interests and responsibilities that settled upon him following the fair, from that time on, at least, a plan for Chicago was never far from his mind.

Although its park system was larger and better than those in some other American cities, thanks to the earlier landscaping of Horace Cleveland and Frederick Law Olmsted, nineteenth-century Chicago had its own share of problems, including political corruption, vast areas of slums and poverty, and a physical ugliness and inefficiency, born of rapid, unguided, and haphazard growth. These problems seldom escaped the scorn of visitors. The growing awareness of such conditions in the 1890s, however, stimulated Chicago's civic awakening and built a determination among Chicagoans to correct the city's social, political, and physical problems. In 1894, for example, the Civic Federation began its attempts to clean the political stables. In the following year, Jane Addams issued her *Hull House Maps and Papers* on lower-class social and working conditions and continued to arouse consciousness and disturb consciences with the work of her social laboratory on Halsted Street. The world's fair, on the other hand, under Burnham's leadership, had signaled the beginning of a different kind of civic reform.[2]

While Americans pondered the broader implications of the fair, Burnham and Atwood took what was perhaps the first specific step in the Chicago Plan movement. Study and contemplation had convinced them that Chicago should preserve the Fair site and the shoreline north of it as a permanent park, a park that would connect the exposition grounds with the business district in the center of the city. Shortly after the fair was over they even drafted some tentative plans. "On the election of Mayor George B. Swift, an old school-boy companion of mine," Burnham wrote in his diary in 1896, "I urged that [an] ordinance looking forward to the improvement be adopted at once." Swift and several city commissioners "looked over the plans, [and] were enthusiastic" and began making arrangements with the Illinois Central Railroad, whose tracks bordered much of the desired and unused shoreline. "This night, July 27th," Burnham recorded enthusiastically, "an ordinance prepared here in this office passed the council, giving the lake front to the South Park [Board] . . . a great public work, which will be memorable if finished according to our designs as now seems probable."[3]

The scheme for the South Shore Drive and park formed the nucleus of the later Chicago Plan. Burnham spent much of the remainder of 1896 pondering and revising his and Atwood's initial sketches and discussing his ideas with influential citizens. One of the more important citizens was James W. Ellsworth, a leading patron of the exposition and of Chicago development in general. In his plans for the South Shore Drive, in fact, Burnham had, since 1894, received more encouragement from Ellsworth than from perhaps any other citizen. It was in 1896 at a dinner in Ellsworth's home that Burnham first presented his revised park sketches and ideas. The guests, particularly the tycoons Philip D. Armour, Marshall Field, and George Pullman, caught the planner's enthusiasm. On November 24, 1896, over lunch in his office, Burnham continued the discussion with Ellsworth, Field, Norman Ream, and Owen Aldis. In December, he prepared a more formal paper, which he read in separate appearances before the Chicago Literary Club, the Evanston Back Lot Club, and the Chicago Art Institute. He continued to host luncheon meetings for leading civic leaders and to speak more formally to various civic groups.[4]

After testing his ideas before a number of such smaller gatherings, he moved on to larger and more powerful audiences. On March 27, 1897, he presented his paper to the Chicago Commercial Club, the city's oldest, wealthiest, and most prestigious business organization. One week later, on April 3, he gave practically the same address to the younger Merchants' Club, the junior and allegedly more progressive counterpart to the older organization. In both appearances, he appealed to the civic, economic, and humanitarian impulses of his listeners, selling and promoting his ideas with the vigor and enthusiasm that had now become his trademark. His suggestions and proposals formed the core of the later plan and included proposals to widen streets and enlarge the city's park system. He gave special emphasis to the improvement and enrichment of the lakeshore.[5]

In the defense of his proposals, he argued the intrinsic value of art and beauty for all people in all kinds of environments. "When a citizen is made to feel the beauty of nature, when he is lifted up by her to any degree above the usual life of his thoughts and feelings, the state of which he is a part is benefited thereby," he began. Aesthetic renewal would "add a new and beneficent element to individual lives in the city," especially to the great masses who could not enjoy such pleasures from private resources, whose financial conditions precluded extensive traveling and necessitated their dependence upon the city for recreation and cultural enrichment. If a plan of urban renewal were to be carried out, he asserted, Chicagoans would be taking "a long step toward cementing together the heterogeneous elements of our population, and towards assimilating the million and a half of people who are here now but who were not here some fifteen years ago." Accepting the apparent inevitability of a fluid but palpable class system, Burnham believed that citizens in the lower economic echelons ought to be guaranteed a number of natural and architectural civic amenities.[6]

Burnham reminded the businessmen that aesthetic and environmental reform could have stupendous benefits for Chicago's commercial and financial growth as well. There were no contradictions, he maintained, between beauty, efficiency, and material prosperity in other great cities of the world. On the contrary, he noted, contemporary Paris was an example of such mutually beneficial interaction. "You all know that there is a tendency among our well-to-do people to spend much time and money elsewhere and that this tendency has been rapidly growing in late years. We have been running away to Cairo, Athens, the Riviera, Paris, and Vienna, because life at home is not so pleasant as in these fashionable centres." No one had ever estimated the amount of money "made here in Chicago and expended elsewhere." he said. "but the sum must be a large one. What would be the effect upon our retail business at home if this money were circulated here?"[7]

While never discounting the value and pleasure of travel, Burnham maintained that part of the reason the wealthy left Chicago and visitors avoided it was that the city itself was unattractive. "Does any one grown rich in the mines, the forests, or the plains of our country come here to live, or even to linger for the sake of pleasure? Does he not pass through our city," Burnham asked, "remaining only as long as he is compelled to, so that we get the benefit neither of his money nor of his presence among us? What would be the effect upon our prosperity if the town were so delightful that most of them who grow independent financially in the Mississippi Valley, or west of it, were to come to Chicago to live? Should we not without delay do something competent to beautify and make our city attractive for ourselves, and . . . these desirable visitors?" If Chicago were to take such action, Burnham asserted, the world would see "another transformation as occurred in '93 at Jackson Park, only this time the result will be far more beautiful, and, better still, it will be permanent. . . . Beauty has always paid better than any other commodity and always will."[8]

What kinds of prosperity should Chicago foster and maintain, Burnham asked rhetorically. "Not that for rich people solely or principally," he argued, "for they can take care of themselves and wander where they will in the pursuit of happiness; but the prosperity of those who must have employment in order to live. Do not these latter depend upon the circulation among them of plenty of ready money, and can this be brought about without the presence of large numbers of well-to-do people?" In proposing reforms, it seemed to Burnham, "evident at the outset that to attain a satisfactory result, we should aim at nothing less than a supreme improvement, that no half-way measure will do; that if we must lead, we must not be niggardly in what we undertake for Chicago." After such characteristically vigorous optimism, however, he ended his exhortation on a lower key. "It is not claimed," he maintained, that in its present form "this plan is the best that can be devised, or that it covers all that should be done. It is not even put forward with any urgency for its adoption in whole or in part, but merely as a sketch, showing that an improvement of great magnificence is possible and entirely practicable."[9]

The clubs received the speech with interest, but Burnham realized that many more such efforts on his part would be necessary before a general enthusiasm would emerge to stimulate concerted action. As he continued to expand and refine his ideas, he also realized that he would have to increase the sense of "urgency" he had initially played down. His own city would be slower to act than other municipalities across the country and would fully heed Burnham's exhortations only after his work in other cities had embarrassed and raised Chicago's competitive

Burnham's water color of the South Shore Drive. Courtesy Houghton Mifflin Company.

spirit. Yet, while becoming increasingly prominent on the national front, Burnham continued both formally and informally to expound his plans for Chicago. Wherever possible, at business meetings downtown and at social gatherings in Evanston, he urged the leaders of Chicago to work with him toward promoting a plan for the city's physical renewal. Little else happened, however; the dinner and club meetings in 1896 and 1897 were the last large show of interest in the project for several years. When interest did revive at the beginning of the century, it was painfully slow and reserved.[10]

In January 1901, the Commercial Club invited Burnham to become a member and in that same year, the club president, Franklin McVeagh, suggested that the club take up the city improvement project it had discussed earlier. Burnham, of course, was happy to pull out his sketches and start talking again. In 1902, he wrote enthusiastically to Charles Moore that "the Washington work has started up anew the interest here in beautifying this city on the lines of my old work five years ago." By 1903, however, nothing tangible had resulted from the discussions and a younger group of businessmen from the Merchants' Club decided to take up the project. The chief instigators of the move were Walter Wilson, the club president, Charles D. Norton, its secretary, and a recently elected member, Frederic Delano. Delano remembered that he "had been impressed with the fact that the club was running out of live subjects, and, as it seemed to me, was somewhat prone to take up critical, 'pin-pricking' methods, rather than doing something constructive. I talked with Norton and suggested that we ought to undertake some big piece of work that would really leave its imprint in the city, and I suggested the general plan or scheme for the future development of Chicago." Norton liked the idea and both men "thought that if we could get Burnham to take hold of it, we could do a fine piece of work."[11]

They then enlisted the support of club president Wilson and several days later paid a visit to Burnham. Burnham told them that he "liked the idea very much, but was afraid he could hardly undertake it for the Merchants' Club, in view of the fact that the Commercial Club . . . had made some beginnings in this direction, and he referred to a meeting," as Delano recalled it, "at which he unfolded to the Commercial Club the plan for a lagoon and parkway between Grant Park and Jackson Park. Although I tried to make Burnham see that the idea we had in mind was very much more comprehensive and far-reaching, he did not feel that it would be justice to the Commercial Club to let the Merchants' Club run away with this idea. We therefore decided to drop the plan for the present. However, the more I thought about it, the more I was impressed with the possibilities of the thing, and I think the same was true of Charlie Norton."[12]

While talking to, and waiting on, the Commercial Club, Burnham continued his interest and support of the existing municipal agencies that were making slow but real progress in improving the city. To his friend Henry Foreman, president of the South Park Board, he wrote in 1903, praising his plan "regarding an outer line of parks and parkways. I have read it with deep interest. It is inspiring to know that an officer of your high position has taken up such a scheme and is pressing it forward in such an able manner." Burnham was also pleased that his firm had the contract for designing most of the South Park system's recreational buildings. "In view of our aim," he wrote to Foreman in 1904, "to bring about results of the highest order, by means as nearly approaching the conditions of nature as possible, I recommend the adoption of a scheme providing an open air Natatorium in the Public Parks, thus making the sport seasonable. I think the moral effect will be thus obtained by the most striking and simplest means. I further recommend," he concluded, in the spirit of the strenuous life, "the addition of ample showers and a cold plunge for winter use."[13]

The same year he wrote a long and buoyant description of the developing park system to Richard Watson Gilder, editor of *Century Magazine*. The South Park Board had just purchased land for fourteen new parks and playgrounds in the poorer districts of the South Side and the West Side, the tracts ranging from ten to two hundred acres. The Olmsteds were in charge of landscaping and were beautifully complementing his own firm's work on the buildings. Each park would have some sort of gymnasium, "social halls for the men and women and young people of the neighborhood . . . swimming pools under cover . . . wading pools for children, running tracks for men and boys . . . extensive space for open field sports" and "shaded drives and walks for waterways." It was the purpose of all concerned, Burnham told Gilder, "to make these parks as beautiful as possible, and we have had untold joy in working out the schemes." He was also delighted with the social effects the new parks were clearly having on the people. One small park, for example, was just "nearing completion and the police say it has changed the young people in the neighborhood so much that certain crimes have all but disappeared." Burnham was indeed no "all or nothing" man. While pushing and waiting for the larger and more visionary developments, he was happy to work for tangible, smaller gains within the spirit of his larger dreams.[14]

In 1906, however, since nothing tangible had come from the Commercial Club discussions, Norton and Delano of the Merchants' Club "again took hold of the matter and conferred with Burnham. At that time," Delano recalled, "we found that Burnham was a good deal more disposed to go ahead. He said it was evident to him that the Commercial Club would never take hold of the matter, that younger men must do it, etc., etc. Thereupon Charlie Norton took the leading part in the work and I served as secretary of the Plan Committee." On September 21, 1906, Burnham noted the important meeting with Norton and Delano. "I agreed to take charge of a new planning for Chicago," he wrote, "with the understanding that I am to have an entirely free hand in the choice of my associates and assistants."[15]

Burnham and the club members immediately began to form a committee and to organize their vast new project. As the club's new president, Charles Norton also became chairman of the Chicago Plan Committee. Charles Wacker served as vice-chairman, David Forgan as treasurer. Other committee members included Edward Butler, Frederick Delano, and Walter Wilson. A "sum of $20,000 will be sufficient," Burn-

ham thought optimistically, "to pay for everything except the printing
and editing of the report. This money will be needed at the rate of
$1500.00 to $1700.00 per month" to pay for supplies and assistant's
salaries. As the director of the project, Burnham donated his services
free of charge. Meetings of the committee began at once, and on October 13, 1906, Burnham spoke at a dinner of the entire club membership.
It seemed appropriate, he advised before hand, to invite to the dinner
several outside guests, including city officials and Illinois congressmen.
"The presence of the national officials," Burnham wrote to Norton,
"will help the Washington as well as the Chicago work and the occasion
is sure to bring about a realization of the seriousness of the people's purpose to do away with disorder and to substitute civic beauty and convenience." At the time, however, few Chicagoans were aware of the
negotiations that would so greatly affect their city's subsequent development. Two other local phenomena reigned foremost in the public mind.
Both the Cubs and the White Sox had won their respective baseball
league penants in 1906, and the city looked forward to an intra-urban
world series. Far more important, in the long run, Upton Sinclair's
novel, *The Jungle*, had just been published, focusing local and national
attention on the city's industrial, labor, and sanitation problems.[16]

Yet, after years of long and frustrating delays, Burnham and the
Merchants' Club had finally begun to act. The possibilities looked good
—so good in fact that the older and less aggressive Commercial Club began to regret its earlier dalliance and present exclusion. Most of its members, now, in fact, wished to have a part in the huge planning project;
and because they wanted inclusion so badly, they arranged a compromise with the men of the Merchants' Club. Several factors were involved. The Commercial Club had indeed considered the project earlier
and longer than had the Merchants' Club. Burnham was a member of
the older group and though he had ultimately committed himself to the
Merchants' Club, he felt loyalty to his own men and wished to see them
included. A nucleus of Commercial Club members had not lost interest
in the project, nor given up hope that their club would take it on. Interested members from both clubs had in fact for several years carried on
an informal dialogue about the project among themselves.[17]

There were also social and economic factors that must have played an
equally important part in the ultimate collaboration. The venerable
Commercial Club had the reputation of being the more conservative of
the two groups in regard to selection of members; and indeed its rolls

included an older, wealthier, and more socially elite group of men. The Merchants' Club for the most part included younger, less wealthy, beginning men with a slightly more liberal reputation than their Commercial Club seniors. There were obviously men in the Merchants' Club who might never have received invitations to join the Commercial Club. Yet the younger group also included men that the older club would have liked to have.

Though by tradition members belonged exclusively to one or the other of the two organizations, much of the membership could have indeed been interchangeable. Both clubs were composed of members and friends of the Chicago business community. Both sought the common goal of improving Chicago's economic, civic, and cultural life. The Commercial Club was wealthy, however, and it was obvious that before the new plan was finished, a great deal more money would be needed than the junior club could furnish. Rather than continue to compete, therefore, with less than maximum effect on such giant projects as the Chicago Plan, the clubs decided in late 1906 to merge their memberships and work together as one body. "Business Men's Clubs Merge to Boom City," the newspaper headlines read, "Plan of Uniting the Merchants and Commercial Organizations follows Decision to Further Chicago's Interests."[18]

Because they had started the planning project, it was agreed that Norton, Wacker, Delano, and the other officers of the Merchants Club would continue to serve as the ruling officers of both the planning committee and of the larger new organization. In exchange, however, it was agreed that the new group's title would be "The Commercial Club," in deference to the age and reputation of the venerable older body. By 1907, the expanded Commercial Club was ready to go forward with its work on the Chicago Plan. The long dormant seeds that Burnham had planted and cultivated so assiduously were now, at last, beginning to take root.

Burnham spent practically all of 1907 and 1908 in Chicago working on the plan. Again, his assistant was Edward Bennett, who directed a staff of draftsmen and artists in the workroom penthouse atop the Railway Exchange. Norton, Wacker, Delano, and Wilson, now the officers of the enlarged Commercial Club, continued to hold the chief positions on the general plan committee. The special subcommittees included equally prominent club members and citizens. Chaired by the merchant Edward B. Butler, for example, the Committee on the Lake Front in-

Chicago Plan Committee of the Commercial Club, 1909. Courtesy Chicago
Art Institute.

cluded such prominent Chicagoans as Charles G. Dawes, John V. Far-
well, Victor Lawson, and Harold McCormick. The capitalist Clyde M.
Carr served as chairman of the Committee on Streets and Boulevards,
supported by members James L. Houghteling, Fredrick Upham, and
Charles Wacker. The banker Joy Morton headed the Committee on
Railway Terminals, which included Franklin MacVeagh, Cyrus McCormick, Martin Ryerson, John G. Shedd, and Albert Sprague. Montgomery Ward president Charles H. Thorne directed the Committee on
Interurban Roadways while Charles G. Dawes, Charles L. Hutchinson,
and Walter Wilson made up the Finance Committee. Most of the men
were friends of Burnham's. Many of them had been his clients. Between
April 1907, when the committees were appointed, and the end of February 1908, Secretary Delano's records indicated that "no less than ninety-
two regular and largely attended Committee meetings have been held.
In addition there have been at least two hundred conferences with vari-

ous public officials, including the Governor, the Mayor, the Park Boards and many others."[19]

It was in such meetings that Chicago aristocrats mingled agreeably with such earthy politicians as "Bathhouse" John Coughlin. The support, moreover, that Coughlin and others like him gave to the plan, demonstrated forcefully that it was something more than a rich man's project. In one meeting for example, when someone speculated on the millions of dollars it would ultimately take to implement the plan, Coughlin made an impromptu but impassioned speech. After alluding to the sums that other cities had raised and to the projects they had begun, he announced that if Chicago could not produce the necessary funds, it was "a city of pikers and deserved to take a back seat."[20]

To carry on their deliberations, however, the planners and committeemen needed information about Chicago, and Burnham and his staff took responsibility for obtaining it. Hundreds of requests for information and professional advice left Burnham's office in 1907 and 1908. To the Chicago Historical Society, he wrote for information and authentication of data concerning the city's early history. From the American Civic Association, he requested maps, plans, descriptions and information on over twenty major American cities. He asked Huntington Wilson, an assistant secretary of state, to furnish the same types of information for over a dozen foreign cities. "In work of this nature," he wrote to Wilson, "the experience of other cities is invaluable as a guide. . . ." He especially wanted to obtain detailed studies of "pre- and post-Haussmann Paris. We fear that it may be somewhat difficult to gain all we require," he wrote, "unless the French authorities be officially urged to give it and unless further, our American officials in Paris shall persevere in the matter. Therefore, if it be not inconsistent with the customs of your office in such matters, we respectfully ask you to give us your most valuable and essential assistance."[21]

He was equally interested in the smaller details of Chicago's economic, social, and cultural life, especially in such matters as transportation, health, and educational needs. His request for statistics from nine leading shipping companies was typical of the countless number of inquiries that he made: "In making a study of the City Plan of Chicago," he wrote, "it will be necessary to use data which I believe you can give me. I therefore request you to do me the great favor of sending me the following: the height: average, minimum and maximum, of vertical dimension above water line, required for free passage under bridges of:

mass, carrying lights, derricks used for cargo, and the funnels of your steamships." From the harbor master at the Lake Street Bridge, he wished to know "the average and maximum number of times per day the bridges individually are opened. Also the proportion of large steamers to small craft passing through." He requested similarly detailed statistics from rail and streetcar lines.[22]

To his son Hubert, studying in France, he wrote for legal information regarding the heights of buildings in Paris. He also asked Hubert to search in Paris for detailed photographs of the waterfront treatments of some thirty European cities, which he and Bennett needed "in studying the lake and river shores of Chicago." He also wrote a number of letters like this one to his nephew, the physician Rollin Woodyatt: "In my report on a Plan for Chicago," he stated, "I want to define as exactly as possible the sphere of influence of Chicago." He was sure that "we can be helped in forming an opinion on this question by some information regarding the territory surrounding Chicago from which patients come to the Chicago hospitals or in which their influence may be said to be the dominant one." He made similar requests concerning the backgrounds of students at Northwestern University and the University of Chicago.[23]

In addition to securing specific information by mail, however, Burnham and Chairman Norton thought it would also be helpful to bring in "interesting and influential persons to look over and express their idea of the plan" as it was being formulated in the committees and on the boards. Burnham was used to a stream of visitors to his own office anyway, and he welcomed the chance to invite interested laymen up to see the sketches and give their opinions. After examining the plan atop Chicago's highest building, they might then make comparisons with the sprawling, unfinished city below. To many, the contrast was too striking to comprehend. To others, the plans seemed eminently workable.[24]

On December 4, 1907, the celebrated social worker, Jane Addams, came to lunch as Burnham's guest, to see the plans and discuss the city's problems. Though in his 1897 speech, Burnham had speculated on the possibilities of elegant residences along the south shore, he had changed his mind over the years and by 1907 had determined that the shore should remain open and available to all the people. Addams strongly approved the notion and encouraged the development of lakeshore and other parks for the public benefit of the poorer, immigrant groups. She left no record of her reactions to other aspects of the plan; Edward Bennett recorded only her enthusiasm for the lakefront proposals.[25]

In March 1907, Frank Lloyd Wright came to call, and in May of the same year Louis Sullivan was Burnham's guest at lunch. Sullivan left no record of his impressions of the plan, but Wright once referred to it in surprisingly complimentary terms. In speaking years later to a London audience, Wright shocked his listeners by insisting that Chicago was the world's most beautiful city. When asked to justify his claim, he argued "first of all because it has a generous park system, the greatest on earth. You may drive nearly all day without going away from the boulevard and park system. . . . Another reason is that, thanks to . . . Dan Burnham, Chicago seems to be the only great city in our States to have discovered its own waterfront. Moreover, to a greater extent than any other city, it has a life of its own." No tribute could have pleased Burnham more.[26]

Other visitors in the mid-planning stage included the pianist-statesman Paderewski, who showed, Bennett remembered, "the keenest interest in the plan." When a visiting railroad official expressed skepticism at the magnitude of the plan, Burnham merely "showed him Paris and convinced him that such things had been done in the past by cities of smaller prospects than Chicago." The younger Olmsted and the architect Thomas Tallmadge expressed their approval and offered suggestions. Larger groups came as well. When the skeptical and contentious members of the Harbor Commission came to call, Bennett recalled Burnham's splendid performance, and noted that in defending the plan "he was in fine form."[27]

Commercial Club members often brought their visiting business associates to see the work. One such meeting particularly impressed Burnham. "I was met by one of the very powerful men of Chicago this morning," he wrote to his Washington friend Charles Moore. "He came with Mr. Speyer, the New York banker, to look over the plan. He told me without prompting him that Mr. Speyer was very deeply impressed and that he finally said, 'How does it happen that you men of Chicago can get together and do such things? We cannot in New York, nor can the men of any other city!' With this as a text," Burnham continued, the Chicago man had talked to him very much in the same terms that he had recently talked to Moore. "He even used my exact expression," Burnham wrote, "namely, 'the Chicago Spirit is a precious thing. The Community should realize what it means.' "[28]

By 1908, the plan was going well, but much work remained in both written descriptions and graphic illustrations. On January 17, Bennett recorded that "Mr. Burnham worked at his report until past midnight and then decided to sleep in his office." On January 25, 1908, Burnham and Bennett took examples of the completed work to a Commercial Club dinner where Burnham spoke and showed lantern slides of the plan's progress. The club received the plans warmly and passed a motion "approving the general direction of the work." On February 28, the general committee invited the members to visit the drafting rooms, but unfortunately Burnham was not there to greet them. His diabetes was worse and the recurring foot infection had again necessitated surgery. After visiting him in the hospital, Bennett noted in his diary that Burnham "was as usual—serene. We talked of Swedenborg or rather I listened to him discourse on the subject and came away strengthened in purpose." After another visit several days later, he noted that Burnham seemed better. "We talked of the plan," he wrote, "but more of the philosophy of life—and his belief in the infinite possibilities of material expression of the spiritual."[29]

By late spring Burnham was back at work in both of his downtown offices. His draft of the report needed editing and polishing; Moore

Proposed Chicago waterfront and interior developments painted by Jules Guerin. *Plan of Chicago.*

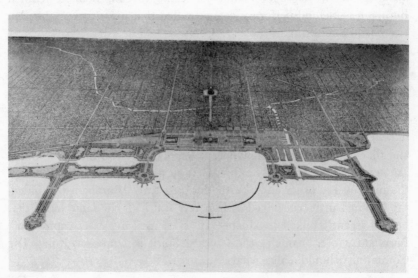

would take it through that final editing as the artists and draftsmen completed the illustrations. By late 1908, it was ready for the printer, and, by the early summer of the following year, it was finally ready for distribution. It appeared with deliberate symbolic intent on July 4, 1909. "The Chicago Plan is out, and has caused a sensation," Burnham wrote to Ernest Graham on July 8. "The drawings are beautifully displayed in the Art Institute." Later in the month, he wrote to Moore that the plan seemed "successful even beyond our hopes."[30]

Sumptuously printed by the Lakeside Press, *The Plan of Chicago*, was a beautiful and elegant book. The drawings and watercolors by Jules Guerin and the black and white sketches by Jules Janin nicely complemented Bennett's maps and Burnham's text, as edited by Moore. Fortunately, however, its scope and significance even transcended its aesthetic success. "Chicago in common with other great cities," Burnham's introduction began, "realizes that the time has come to bring order out of chaos incident to rapid growth, and especially to the influx of people of many nationalities without common traditions or habits of life. . . . The real test of the plan will be found in its application," he continued, "if the plan is really good it will commend itself to the progressive spirit of the times, and . . . will be carried out. It should be understood, however, that such radical changes as are proposed herein cannot possibly be realized immediately. Indeed the aim has been to anticipate the needs of the future as well as to provide for the necessities of the present."[31]

In introducing the essential features of his ideas, Burnham made it clear that "the plan frankly takes into consideration the fact that the American city, and Chicago pre-eminently, is a center of industry and traffic. Therefore attention is given to the betterment of commercial facilities; to methods of transportation for persons and for goods; to removing the obstacles which prevent or obstruct circulation; and to the increase of convenience. It is realized, also, that good workmanship requires a great degree of comfort on the part of the workers in their homes and their surroundings, and ample opportunity for that rest and recreation without which all work becomes drudgery." In addition to those considerations, "the city has a dignity to be maintained; and good order is essential to material advancement. Consequently, the plan provides for impressive groupings of public buildings and reciprocal relations among such groups."[32]

He reminded his readers that "during the second half of the nineteenth century the population of Chicago increased from thirty thousand to two millions of people. Today all conditions point to continued gains. The days of chance and uncertainty are past. The days of doubtful ventures are gone and the hazards of new fortunes. The elements which make for the greatness of the city are known to be permanent; and men realize that the time has now come to build confidently on foundations already laid." The lines that followed those observations were perhaps the most thoughtful and sensitive in the whole report. "The growth of the city," he wrote, "has been so rapid that it has been impossible to plan for the economical disposition of the great influx of people, surging like a human tide to spread itself wherever opportunity for profitable labor offered place. Thoughtful people are appalled at the results of progress; at the waste in time, strength, and money which congestion in city streets begets; at the toll of lives taken by disease when sanitary precautions are neglected; and at the frequent outbreaks against law and order which result from narrow and pleasureless lives. So that while the keynote of the nineteenth century was expansion, we of the

Regional Plan of the larger Chicago area, dotted lines showing proposed connecting links in existing circulation system. *Plan of Chicago.*

General map of Chicago showing proposed network of streets, parks, and waterways. *Plan of Chicago.*

twentieth century find that our dominant idea is conservation."[33]

By "conservation," however, he did not mean conservatism, and in so defining himself, he posed the kinds of questions that have always concerned the greatest planners. "The people of Chicago," he believed, "have ceased to be impressed by rapid growth or the great size of the city. What they insist asking now is: How are we living? Are we in reality prosperous? Is the city a convenient place for business? Is it a good labor market in the sense that labor is sufficiently comfortable to be efficient and content? Will the coming generation be able to stand the nervous strain of city life? When a competence has been accumulated, must we

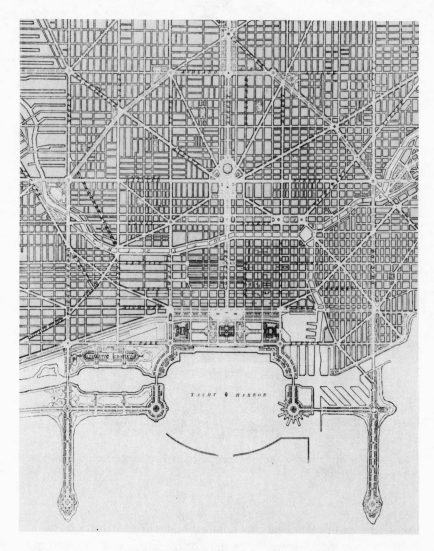

Plan of Chicago harbor and Civic Center development. *Plan of Chicago*.

go elsewhere to enjoy the fruits of independence? If the city does not become better as it becomes bigger, shall not the defect be remedied?" Those were the questions, he believed, that the most alert and vigorous citizens were asking, especially the younger "men and women of ambition and self-reliance who are lured [from the country] by the great prizes which in a democracy are open to the competition of all."[34]

Such words could, of course, have been interpreted as cynical statements of intentions to keep laborers "contented" and docile, whatever their condition, for the sole benefit of the exploiting classes. Yet, however appropriate such an interpretation might seem to later generations as an over-all turn-of-the-century description of the American capitalist system, it had in Burnham's case, at least, no such cynical or subtly repressive connotations. It illustrated again Burnham's "conservatively liberal" acceptance, for the time, of a graded but mobile class system and a determination on his part to ameliorate and improve the lot of the poorer classes. Indeed "within the system" that slowly allowed for organic change, Burnham addressed himself in the Chicago Plan to improving—more quickly—the quality of urban life for all Chicagoans.

In studying the details of the plan, it was obvious to all who saw it that Burnham's conception of a new Chicago had progressed far beyond his early idea in 1894 of a waterfront development between Grant Park and Jackson Park. It had become not only a plan for the City Beautiful but for the City Practical as well. It was indeed the first of the great "master" or regional plans later to become prominent throughout America in the twentieth century. The plan called for the redevelopment of the whole Chicago area within a sixty-mile radius of the city's center, including an elaborate system of outer parks and radial and concentric boulevards; an aesthetic and useful lakefront park system twenty miles long along Lake Michigan; an increase in the number and quality of interior parks; a grouping and relocation of railroad tracks and terminals; the straightening of the Chicago River for more efficient water and riverside transportation; myriad changes in the width, construction, function, and general appearance of individual streets, both grid and radial; a monumental civic center at the intersection of Halsted and Congress streets designed to mark the city's future center of gravity; and an efficient inner harbor development, enclosed by windbreaking causeways stretching a mile out into the lake. The plan enlarged, cleared, and improved the central passageway between north and south sides through the Loop while bringing the West Side into a closer and more convenient relationship with the rest. It established a system then unsurpassed in America of connecting the city's center with its outlying suburbs and of linking the suburbs one with another.[35]

The plan was drenched with Burnham's mystical, Swedenborgian rhetoric and with his sometimes paradoxical effort to tap both the vibrant and peculiar "spirit of Chicago" and the older, classical European spirit of things eternal. "It is in the grouping of buildings united by a common purpose—whether administrative, educational, or commercial —that one must find an adequate method of treatment," he wrote, "or again in far-stretching lines of lagoons, inviting the multitudes to seek recreation along the endless miles of water front; or in broad avenues where the vista seemingly terminated with a tower by day, or in the converging lines of lights by night, in each case the mind recognizing that there is still space beyond. Always there must be the feeling of those broad surfaces of water reflecting the clouds of Heaven; always the sense of breadth and freedom which are the very spirit of the prairies."[36]

Throughout the report, Burnham returned to his major themes of commercial and individual convenience and enrichment. Though he insisted that both considerations applied interchangeably to all aspects of the plan, he tended in his own mind to identify the waterfront with luxury, tourism, and commercial attraction and the therapeutic inland neighborhood parks with the needs and pleasures of the people. Despite his commitment to himself and to Jane Addams that the waterfront should be designed to draw out the working classes, Burnham's ultimate recommendations alluded more strongly to another image, a return, in effect, to some of his original propositions of the 1890s. "Imagine this supremely beautiful parkway," he wrote, "with its frequent stretches of fields, playgrounds, avenues, and groves, extending along the shore in closest touch with the life of the city throughout the whole waterfront. What will it do for us in health and happiness? After it is finished, will the people of means be so ready to run away and spend their money in other cities? Where else can they find such delightful conditions as at home? We should no longer lose so much of the cream of our earnings now spent in other lands. When this parkway shall be created our people will stay here, and others will come to dwell among us—the people who now spend time and large amounts of money in Paris, in Vienna, and on the Riviera. It will turn back the stream of profits which have to such a large degree gone away from us, and everyone living here will feel the result of this change, for between prosperity and bad times there is often but a small percentage, and the community that can keep its earnings at home prospers."[37]

As important as the lakefront, he argued, were the cultivation of neighborhood parks and nearby forest preserves for recreation and communion with nature. "Fifty years ago," he wrote, "before population had become dense in certain parts of the city, people could live without parks; but we of today cannot. We now regard the promotion of robust health of body and mind as necessary public duties, in order that the individual may be benefited, and that the community at large may possess a higher average degree of good citizenship. And after all has been said," he added, significantly, "good citizenship is the prime object of good city planning." Criticized in later years for his typical Progressive overreliance on the efficacy of parks and for his failure in the plan to come to terms with the problems of slum and ghetto housing, Burnham acknowledged in the plan's early stages that parks were only a partial solution to the problem of the slums. Leaving indeed the vexing housing problem to other hands and later generations, he alluded to it significantly in what was perhaps the most radical statement in the report: "Chicago has not yet reached the point," he believed, "where it will be necessary for the municipality to provide at its own expense, as does the city of London, for the rehousing of people forced out of congested quarters, but unless the matter shall be taken in hand at once, such a course will be required in common justice to men and women so degraded by long life in the slums that they have lost all power of caring for themselves."[38]

Burnham's recommendations for railroad consolidation epitomized his numerous proposals for solving traffic, circulation, transportation, and communications problems. The question was not so much one of growth, but one of conservation and regulation, he believed. "Chicago has been made largely by the railroads," he wrote, "and its future prosperity is dependent upon them. In the past, however, it has been the increase in the number of roads reaching this city which has built up its commerce; but now, with twenty-two trunk lines entering Chicago from every possible direction, and with connections extending to all portions of the country, the question of numbers has ceased to be the important one. The present problem is to handle the traffic of the railroads with dispatch and at the lowest cost. The city is too large for each railroad to attempt to maintain a separate system unrelated to that of any other except the physical connection of the tracks. The time has come to develop one common system for the handling of freight—a traffic clearing house. The whole perplexing and intensely intricate subject requires not only the careful study of men expert in such matters, but also a spirit of mutual forebearance and conciliation among railroad managers for the sake of promoting the general good. . . ." In calling for new union passenger stations and collective cooperation on the shipping of freight, Burnham believed that "the conclusion is inevitable. Either nearly everyone of the great railroads must increase and improve both its main line and such of its freight houses and yards as are now located in the part of the city, or they must cease to bring all freight into the congested business center. Separate roads operating separate and independent rights of way to the separate and independent freight houses cannot do the work."[39]

He also admonished the railroad companies to improve the appearance and convenience of their physical plants. Throughout the report he stressed the psychological importance of the architectural environment. Many of Chicago's stations, he contended, were simply "not pleasant. They should be bright, cheery, and inviting in a high degree. More study, not more money, is needed for this work. Let the architectural schools and societies take up this topic; it demands artistic imagination as well as skill. Let the man who undertakes this problem think of the hundreds or even thousands of people who must habitually use the given station, and let him do his utmost to bring into being for these people something that shall be a joy to them. A delightful station conduces to cheerfulness as a man goes to work and as he comes home, while a shabby or neglected station produces the opposite effect."[40]

The plan was, of course, not without its unexplained contradictions. One in particular has disturbed later generations. Much in the manner of Haussmann's Paris, most of the plan's drawings and renderings seemed to call for neo-Baroque buildings of almost identical height and cornice line—evoking an image of almost totalitarian order—especially toward the proposed civic center on the less developed West Side. How could Burnham, later critics have asked, ignore the jagged and spectacular skyline of the Chicago Loop that his and others' celebrated skyscrapers had made possible? Burnham, himself, must have never fully resolved the contradiction. One thing critics have failed to notice, however, is that especially near the lake, the "uniform" buildings were very tall indeed, reaching as high as approximately twenty stories. Apparently Burnham

Jules Guerin's painting of the proposed Chicago Civic Center. *Plan of Chicago.*

foresaw that height as the ultimate aesthetic maximum limitation and assumed that all future buildings could rise precisely that high and no higher. Economic losses would presumably prohibit their building lower. It is chilling, however, to speculate that Burnham might have favored the eventual destruction and replacement of the older, lower, and slimmer masterpieces of the Chicago School for blocks of such gigantic monoliths. His sanctioning of the destruction of his own epochal Montauk, for the archetypal D. H. Burnham building of the First National Bank indicated that he might have approved such a course, both for economic and aesthetic reasons.

Despite, however, the technical and aesthetic limitations that became more obvious with changing needs and tastes, much of the plan was indeed extremely far-sighted. Published in the same year that Henry Ford produced his first Model T, it proposed, for example, the first double-decked boulevard, one level for commercial, the other for regular traffic, which came to seem more remarkable as automobile traffic increased.

Leonardo da Vinci had proposed such an innovation for Milan four centuries before, but nowhere before Chicago's Wacker Drive had it been executed so effectively.[41]

Both the planners and the Commercial Club realized "that from time to time supplementary reports will be necessary to emphasize one feature or another which may come prominently before the public for adoption. At the same time, it is confidently believed that this presentation of the entire subject accomplishes the task which has been recognized from the outset, namely . . . to make the careful study of the physical conditions of Chicago as they now exist . . . to discover how these conditions may be improved" and "to record such conclusions in the shape of drawings and texts which shall become a guide for the future development of Chicago."[42]

"People flock to those cities where conditions are good, where means of recreation abound, and where there are attractions for the senses and the intellect," Burnham wrote in summarizing his plan. "Persons of wealth and refinement seek such cities as their abiding places; and those who have accumulated wealth in a city bent on improvement remain there. Moreover," he asserted, "there is no stronger appeal made to the American citizen of today than comes from the call of one's native or

Old South Water Street and river front before the implementation of the Chicago plan's recommended improvements, ca. 1910. *Plan of Chicago.*

Wacker Drive and Chicago River front development, mid-1960s. Courtesy
Chicago Association of Industry and Commerce.

adopted city to enter upon the service of creating better surroundings
not only for one's self, but for all those who must of necessity earn their
bread from the sweat of their brows. Nor is the call of posterity to be
denied. To love and render service to one's city, to have a part in its advancement, to seek to better its conditions, and promote its highest interests—these are both the duty and the privilege of the patriot of
peace."[43]

The local and national response to the plan was overwhelmingly favorable. One friend, John Alvord, especially admired "the breadth of the
ideas and the magnificence of the conception. . . . It is given to some
of us," he wrote to Burnham, "to plod along with the more material,
every day wants of life, and we can only pause to appreciate the fact that
there are men in the community who have time, thought, interest, and
genius enough to look forward to the larger needs of the community. It
will always be of intense interest to me to follow in every way possible
the working out of this great project, and I trust that in some small way
I may be able to help it along."[44]

Chicago River front treatment with bridges as recommended in the plan, 1963. Walter Krutz. Courtesy Chicago Historical Society.

Another friend, Theodore Ely, wrote a more personal letter. "The beautiful book came yesterday and gave me an evening of great enjoyment," he wrote. "It is too great a work to discuss in a note, but I do want to say one thing, and that is that I am glad *you* did it. I can appreciate the many hours of thought that you have given to this problem. It shows it. And now from far and near I see and hear the most complimentary words spoken and written. The prophet is the biggest man, after all, and you are one, for you look into the future of the living conditions of humanity. You have given your great experience and talent to the solution of the undertaking and so deserve all praise. . . ."[45]

Having taken the lead in initiating and producing the Chicago Plan, Burnham felt that others should take responsibility for its long and complex implementation. The ultimate success and efficacy of the plan, demanded, he felt, that he not be the one to advocate his own proposals. In November 1909, after officially receiving the plan as a gift to the city from the Commercial Club, Mayor Fred Busse appointed a 328-member planning commission to give advice on and oversee future Chicago de-

velopment along the guidelines of Burnham's proposals. Much in the
same manner in which Burnham had earlier inspired Chicago's leaders
to accept the plan, the commission began to inspire and to solicit the
support of the people of Chicago. Under the energetic leadership of its
chairman, Charles H. Wacker, the wealthy brewery heir, and its managing director, Walter D. Moody, the commission carried on an unprecedented campaign to arouse public interest. Through numerous
pamphlets, a two-reel motion picture, a slide lecture series, and various
other promotion devices, the Chicago Plan idea entered the home and
the market place. The Chicago School Board agreed to use an elemen-
tary version of Burnham's report as an eighth-grade civics textbook. Ministers and rabbis throughout the city agreed to preach sermons in their

Proposed treatment of upper Michigan Avenue, Chicago. *Plan of Chicago.*

Upper Michigan Avenue, Chicago, before implementation of the plan, ca.
1918. Courtesy Chicago Historical Society.

churches and synagogues incorporating the idea championed in the
plan.[46]

The most important years of the plan's realization occurred in the
two decades between its publication in 1909 and the beginning of the
Depression in 1929. Although elements of the scheme would continue
to unfold throughout the century, the most significant projects took
form in the 1920s. In the teens and twenties alone, costs of execution exceeded $300,000,000. Typical of the developments in that important pe-
riod were such crucial projects as the early and precedent-setting widening of Twelfth Street, later renamed Roosevelt Road; the broadening
and enrichment of upper Michigan Avenue above Randolph Street and
north of the river; the building of Wacker Drive and the various river-
front facilities and accoutrements; and perhaps, most important, the
land-fill development of Grant Park and the long lake shoreline to the
north and south. Created on new land east of the old Illinois Central
tracks, the vast lakeshore area from Grant to Jackson Park served both

recreation and circulation functions and was named Burnham Park in honor of its patron.[47]

Though facing inevitable alterations over the long span of its enactment, Burnham's Chicago Plan formed the basic outlines of the city's development and expansion in the twentieth century. For various, and generally defensible reasons, the grandiose civic center proposed for the nexus of Halstead and Congress streets never came to fruition, although a central traffic interchange and an even greater building complex would later occupy the same area in the form of a Chicago campus for the University of Illinois. The successfully realized parts of the plan centered, for the most part, on Burnham's recommendations for the shoreline, the

Upper Michigan Avenue, Chicago, 1933. Courtesy Chicago Historical Society.

Unimproved Grant Park site, Chicago, ca. 1920. Courtesy Chicago Art Institute.

Grant Park and harbor development. *Center:* Buckingham Fountain, Chicago, late 1960s. Author.

parks, the river, and the street and circulation systems. Broad enough to allow room for growth and flexibility, yet detailed enough to provide specific direction, the plan became something of a model effort, influencing the plans for numerous other cities, both in America and abroad. The plan was especially admired in Germany, where it even came to the attention of the emperor. "The German Kaiser is ambitious to make his capital the finest city in the world," wrote William E. Curtis, the Berlin correspondent of the *Chicago Record-Herald*, "and seizes every suggestion and every opportunity to promote its grandeur and perfection. Last summer he was thoroughly stirred up by the plans for the improvement and beautification of Chicago which were prepared by Daniel H. Burnham" and "has appointed a commission to prepare a similar plan for the city of Berlin based upon a future population of ten millions in the year 2000. In his enthusiastic and impulsive way, the Kaiser declared several times that the Burnham plans were the most perfect and satisfactory

South end of Grant Park and north end of Burnham Park, Chicago, 1947, with *left to right*: Shedd Aquarium, Adler Planetarium, Field Museum, yachting harbor, and Soldier's Field. Howard Wolf, courtesy Chicago Historical Society.

Grant Park, looking north from the Field Museum, mid-1960s. Author.

that he had ever seen, and expressed a profound regret that his capital is so solidly built up and lacks the lake frontage of Chicago so that they cannot be applied more closely in the improvements he contemplates."[48]

Though he deliberately left its execution to others, Burnham watched the plan's development with the greatest interest for the rest of his life. And occasionally, he felt it necessary and appropriate to re-enter the arena to argue and explain. Once, for example, when he felt that Park Commissioner Henry Foreman was bowing to private interests and compromising on the plan's proposals for the treatment of Michigan Avenue, Burnham reminded him that "it is not our Chicago manners to let objections like this stand in the way of a broad noble improvement. If you do this, it will be a precedent for all that is to follow and we shall have people following this bad example—and excusing themselves on the score of it, every time. Do break away from this shallow anchorage, my dear Henry, and go out to sea."[49]

While he must have known that stormier days of both victory and retreat would lie ahead for his plan, for his city, and for those who followed him in advocating their success, Burnham took pleasure in the

Chicago camaraderie that the struggle had inspired and in the obvious victories that were already won. "Here my fellows are in aggressive civic work," he wrote Cameron Forbes in 1911, "and several of the important parts of the Chicago Plan are at the verge of accomplishment. A lot of our fellows who have been in the campaign for four years are now more aggressive than ever; these men never let up; their story should be written and published as an example for all other towns." And late in the same year, he answered congratulations from his old friend Owen Aldis. "Of course, we *do* do things because there is a spirit always working at very high pressure, a spirit that does not exact leisure. I am perhaps a little quicker to run and open the valve than the others," he replied to Aldis' praise of his talents. "That is about it—a door opener—but how proud we should be of such a crowd! Was there ever another like it? It goes on and on and one can see no abatement of enthusiasm or of endeavor from decade to decade. It is LIFE to be of it."[50]

From the warnings of his doctors and his own strong premonitions, Burnham must have known that his work on the Chicago Plan would be his last major effort. It must have pleased him to realize that, like himself, it was big, and followed supremely his credo to "make no little plans."

Central Chicago and lake front, mid-1960s. Courtesy Chicago Association of Industry and Commerce.

XV
Uncle Dan

. . . If you asked people in the know, [ca. 1912] . . . to tell
you who had done the most for current American architecture,
they would probably say that Sullivan had made some imagi-
native proposals and designed beautiful details, that Wright had
built some interesting houses in the Middle West, that Cram's
Gothic churches were excellent, that Cass Gilbert had mastered
the skyscraper and Paul Cret the problem of a government
building, but that if you were looking for giants you had better
first go to New York and seek out the elegant taste and the
highly developed talent of Charles Follen McKim and his
partner Stanford White; they might go further and tell you
that the heart of the whole enterprise lay in Chicago in the
resourceful and indomitable planner, the real Titan, the emperor of architecture, "Uncle Dan" Burnham.

                    JOHN BURCHARD AND ALBERT BUSH-BROWN
    The Architecture of America, A Social and Cultural History

BACK IN 1905, a reporter asked Burnham to comment on the rumor
that he was considering retirement. Burnham scoffed as he pointed to
his numerous unfinished projects and commitments. He remarked, however, that if the reporter were to come back in another ten years he
might get a different response. Yet, in just about half that time, Burnham had arranged his affairs to make semi-retirement possible. Having
completed the Chicago Plan, he determined now, finally, he would have
to reduce the rapid pace of his life. His health was getting worse and
his doctors had intimated that, despite his best intentions, even Daniel
Burnham could not live forever. He refused new planning and promotion projects and attempted to stay out of the public eye. In the fall of
1909, for example, he discouraged a journalist who proposed to write an
illustrated biography. "Please don't," he told him. "You are a young

man and I am an old one. Wait until I have gone, and then do what you like. . . ." As for now, he added, "I have had enough mention and am content 'to sit on the veranda and smoke my cigar in peace,' as Uncle Remus says."[1]

Burnham must have known that as much as he enjoyed a peaceful smoke on the veranda, he would not be able or willing to sit still for long. He would always remain interested in the implementation of his city plans, the execution of his firm's buildings, and the welfare of numerous philanthropic projects. Still, he resolved after 1909 that there would be a change of pace and of tone to his activities. He would leave to others the initiation of new projects while he would assume a more sedentary, advisory role.

He had declined planning offers long before 1909, of course, but the earlier refusals were due chiefly to an already-packed and overcrowded schedule. As early as 1905, for example, he refused an offer from Springfield, Massachusetts, but in doing so gave his customary encouragement and best wishes. "Your movement," he wrote, "is entitled to the support and sympathy of everyone and you should have all I could give were I free. The desire shown so strongly in many cities is one of the most encouraging expressions of the . . . American mind toward good order." He also voiced regrets at being unable to accept a similar offer from Oakland, California, that came on the heels of his completion of the San Francisco Plan. "The possibility of planning for Oakland allures as nothing else could," he wrote. "I am aware that this is the opportunity to do the sort of work I dearly love. . . . It is a little glimpse of paradise you offer but I must turn my face away from it." The commission for an Oakland Plan was subsequently entrusted to Charles Mulford Robinson, a talented contemporary of Burnham, who likewise worked in the City Beautiful genre. In addition to the Oakland offer, Burnham felt constrained for various reasons to decline other commissions, between 1906 and 1912, from dozens of other cities, large and small, including Fort Worth, Atlantic City, St. Louis, Minneapolis, Duluth, Portland, South Bend, Detroit, Montreal, Nashville, Memphis, Newark, and Brooklyn. The list of refusals extended to many smaller communities as well, including Grand Rapids, Michigan; Elmira, New York; Trenton, New Jersey; Erie, Pennsylvania; Tampa, Florida; Amherst College; and the University of Illinois at Champaign.[2]

After 1911 he even refused to write articles on city planning. "I cannot do the article for you," he wrote in 1912 to an editor friend, Joseph

Millet, "and no assistant can do it for me. I have struck my last city planning lick now and evermore, time without end, amen! Would do it for you if for anyone, you old guitar-playing . . . cuss, but I'll bedurned if I spend any more time on this sort of thing." He then alluded to a rumor that he was to do more planning in the Far East. It was rumored, he wrote playfully, that the Chinese "want me to lay out a capital over there, but I can't think of it, although it would be fun, especially if they would regard me as an official and let me wear a cap with a glass ball on top, and keep me manicured with long curly fingernails."[3]

While refusing to work on such cities as Detroit and Brooklyn, he did, however, agree to go in an advisory capacity and discuss the cities' needs and problems with officials and interested citizens. "The planning for Brooklyn allures me," he wrote in 1912, "although I cannot take part in it. It should comprehend all Long Island." He was also happy to talk with his friend and client Edward Filene about the merchant's movement for a city plan for Boston. In many cases, after refusing offers, he recommended that his assistant Edward Bennett be considered, and Bennett, in fact, ultimately received commissions from Duluth, Portland, and Minneapolis. Bennett naturally reflected Burnham's influence and led the group of Burnham's followers who comprised the City Beautiful Movement. "Mr. Burnham came up and spent several hours," Bennett recorded in 1910, "going over the . . . problems of Portland and Minneapolis. His great vision and grasp of the situation are always an inspiration!"[4]

Numerous institutions and individuals continued to seek his advice and recommendations on various architectural projects. At the request of Columbia president, Nicholas Murray Butler, for example, he submitted a list of twenty possible candidates for a soon-to-be endowed chair of architecture at the university. Some of Burnham's advice, however, was unsolicited, such as that which he gave in 1911 to the city of Madison, Wisconsin. Five years earlier, the state of Wisconsin had retained Burnham to serve as a one-man jury to select the winning design for a new state capitol. Burnham chose the design of George B. Post of New York and maintained an interest in Madison's development even as the elegant state house neared completion. One development near the university campus aroused his concern and disapproval. "I have seen the design published in your paper," he wrote the editor Richard Lloyd-Jones, "for a monumental entrance to Camp Randall. There does not seem to be any proper reason for a triumphal arch on this ground, no matter how well it might be designed. A triumphal arch is never used by able architects unless the axis on which it is to stand is one of great dignity. The mere sentiment connected with an arch is not in itself sufficient reason to warrant its use, unless (as is not the case here) a great roadway of high importance runs to and through it; but were the axis of a dignity to excuse the use of a great arch, this design is in itself unsatisfactory. Were it executed, I feel that the State of Wisconsin might throw itself open to the severest sort of criticism." Much to Burnham's chagrin, Wisconsin ignored his advice and built the arch. Usually his recommendations, both voluntary and solicited, received more sympathetic treatment.[5]

He also continued more strongly than ever his lifelong practice of praising and commending new architecture, painting, and sculpture that caught his fancy. He wrote Cass Gilbert, for example, praising his "most noble" Woolworth Building. He had not, on the other hand, always liked the work of his friend Lorado Taft, but in 1911, Taft's new sculpture of the Indian Chief Black Hawk evoked from Burnham the warmest commendations. Since the "Black Hawk" unveiling, he wrote to Taft, he had returned again and again to look at it. "I am going again tomorrow," he admitted. "Each day I have had it in mind to hunt you up and tell you what a deep impression the statue made on me. It is the best thing of its sort done in any day." He appreciated especially "the superb simplicity of the thing and the mystery. I congratulate you from the bottom of my heart."[6]

Culminating Burnham's long career as a spokesman and adviser for the arts, architecture, and urban planning, were two honors conferred on him in 1910. One was the invitation from the Royal Institute of British Architects to speak at the great Town Planning Conference in London. The other was his appointment by President Taft to become the first chairman of the newly established national Commission on the Fine Arts. He could not have been more pleased. He had been recognized by his native country and by the nation of his ancestors.

He and Margaret left for Europe in the early fall of 1910, having shipped ahead the drawings and models of the Chicago Plan that would be installed as a major exhibit of the conference. Before the conference began, they stopped in Paris, and in Germany they attended the Passion Play at Oberammergau, performed for one season at the beginning of each decade. In 1910, before the village had become a tourist attraction, visitors stayed in the homes of actors and villagers. It was characteristic of Burnham that he arranged for his party to stay in the home of the actor who played the part of Jesus Christ![7]

In London, Burnham titled his address to the conference "A City of the Future Under a Democratic Government," and in it, he reiterated many of the ideas espoused in his earlier plans. The speech particularly echoed themes from his recently published *Chicago Plan*. He identified planning with progressivism and declared that rich public facilities were a right of the democratic masses. "You know well," he insisted, "that the deep interest taken in the subject throughout the world marks, not a passing fancy, but a definite step in the development of man. . . ." In a capitalistic democracy like the United States, he believed, "all men are their masters within the law," but "only a few are able by individual ability and effort to live in delightful surroundings; the rest have to take things as they come; and yet, all crave such surroundings, no matter how much they despair of obtaining them."[8]

But, he asked, "will not the people of a continuing democracy awaken sometime to the fact that they can possess as a community what they cannot as individuals, and will they not then demand delightfulness as a part of life and get it? You may think," he acknowledged, "that any realization of this sort will be a long time coming, but remember that the growth of public improvement has been very rapid during the last few years, so rapid, in fact, that one hardly dares to set a limit to what may be done in a single decade. . . . We do things that would have made our forebears think us magicians, because we are equipped with scientific knowledge and experience which they did not possess. The men of 1850 knew much, but those of 1910 know enough more to make their work seem marvelous in contrast, and we may be sure that the men of 1960 will regard us as we do our predecessors." And yet, he believed, "it is not merely in the number of facts or sorts of knowledge that progress lies: it is still more in the geometric ratio of sophistication, in the geometric widening of the sphere of knowledge, which every year is taking in a larger percentage of people as time goes on. And remember that knowledge brings desire and desire brings action."[9]

Burnham then addressed himself to a number of the "material topics" recently covered in the Chicago Plan, including especially his recommendations for ideal park, street, and transportation systems. He also discussed more fully than he ever had before the ominous question of air pollution. "The air of the city of the future will be pure," he asserted optimistically, "its pollution in our time is due to dust, smoke, and gasses from manufacturing plants. Smoke will disappear when fuel is properly consumed, and this must be soon because we are not using much more than half of the heat units of coal—an extravagance which has begun to be very serious. Up to our time, strict economy in the use of natural resources has not been practiced, but it must be henceforth," he warned, "unless we are immoral enough to impair conditions in which our children are to live. . . . The obvious way to economize in the use of coal is to burn it at the mines and to transmit power, light, and heat by wire, which is entirely practicable and already in use over long distance. There may be other means of transmission," he thought, "besides electrical ones; the intelligent men of tomorrow may find them."[10]

He then went on to illustrate, with specific examples, how waste materials could be rechanneled and utilized so as not to contaminate the atmosphere and weaken the health of the citizens. If he viewed the automobile too optimistically and failed to perceive the future dangers caused by automotive exhaust, he was, nevertheless, far ahead of his time in his general concern about pollution, its causes, and its cure. "The use of horses in a great city is near its end," he argued, ironically, "because motor vehicles are becoming very cheap and will soon be more economical, and with the passing of the custom of using horses will end a plague of barbarism which we still live in. When this change comes, a real step in civilization will have been taken. With no smoke, no gases, no litter of horses, your air and streets will be clean and pure. This means, does it not, that the health and spirits of men will be better? . . . and the people living in sweeter conditions should be better citizens, should they not? Thus you see that clean air is an affair of state."[11]

Returning to his familiar theme of big and little plans, he concluded that "the question always arises when a given town is under consideration whether it would be wisest to limit suggestions to present available means, or on the other hand, to work out and diagram whatever a sane imagination suggests. If the first be made your limit," he believed, "your work will be tame and ineffectual and will not arouse that enthusiasm without which nothing worthwhile is ever accomplished; it is doubtful, indeed, if even the meagre things proposed will be carried into effect. Such is humanity!" He did not mean, of course, "that the obvious and commonplace are to be neglected, far from it, but to realize them one should seek for more."[12]

The enthusiasm and the atmosphere of the conference was exactly to Burnham's taste. In responding to a toast at the final banquet, he sug-

gested, with his usual hyperbole, that "when we come to leave our work
to our surrogate, or speak to our sons perhaps for the last time, many of
us will say, 'The proudest moment of my life was in London at the
Town Planning Conference of the Royal Institute of British Architects.' " Yet, while impressive and important, both in his and in others'
minds, the conference was not equal in honor and responsibility to his
appointment by President Taft in the same year as chairman of the national Commission on the Fine Arts.[13]

Burnham received notice of the appointment in June 1910. In accepting the position, he addressed his old friend Charles D. Norton, the
personal secretary of President Taft. "Please convey to the President,"
he wrote Norton, "my deep appreciation of the honor he has conferred
on me, an honor which rounds out my life in a manner unhoped for,
and which seems to me in my profession as the Chief Justiceship must
seem to a lawyer." Despite his intentions to pull away from new responsibilities, he could not resist the opportunities that the position promised. He knew that it would be more than honorary and that it would
demand hard work, but it seemed somehow well worth the effort. Besides, it was nōt a totally new enterprise after all; it had definite connections with his earlier Washington work and the Plan of 1902. Burnham
had continued to take an interest in the progress and problems of all his
city plans, but, perhaps because it was the first and because it involved
the seat of the national government, he had maintained an even greater
and longer interest in Washington. Second only to his loyalty to Chicago, Washington had remained almost constantly on his mind.[14]

Following the presentation of the plan in 1902, the Burnham commission had ceased officially to exist. The Roosevelt administration had
continued, however, to consult the members on artistic matters and on
various building projects that seemed to threaten the spirit of the plan.
The commission members, themselves, especially Burnham, McKim,
and Moore, also watched the capital's architectural development on
their own and frequently called to the President's attention what they
considered incipient violations of the plan. In several such instances,
Roosevelt intervened personally and prevented the violation from oc-
curring. In 1904, for example, at the request of the commissioners, he
ordered that the new Agriculture Building be located farther south than
planned so as to preserve the width of the future grand Mall. Without
legal status and formal organizational structure, however, the unofficial
board of "artistic advisers" slowly withered away. House Speaker Joseph

Cannon continued to oppose both the plan and its advocates. President Roosevelt generally supported the spirit of the plan, but felt presumably that he could protect it adequately with the power of his office and personality and with unofficial advice from expert consultants. His successor, President Taft, on the other hand, recognized the arguments for a permanent, official advisory body, and in 1910, despite Cannon's protests, sought and received congressional approval for a Fine Arts Commission.[15]

Besides Burnham, Olmsted, and Moore from the original 1902 commission, Taft appointed the sculptor Daniel Chester French, the painter Francis Millet, and the architects Thomas Hastings and Cass Gilbert to the commission. "I am overjoyed to find you are on it," Burnham wrote to Moore. "It does feel like old times revivified and made better. As we now set the game so will the future be. You know what this means; it is not the details but the real spirit we must make first and ever keep to the fore." To Millet, he also rejoiced that "we are again in the saddle together."[16]

Preliminary administrative questions included the exact and proper name for the commission, a problem not resolved in the congressional act. Burnham admitted that for aesthetic reasons he preferred the "American Commission of Fine Arts," but feared that the restricted use of the word "American" might offend the Latin American nations to the south. "We are taking pains in this matter," Burnham wrote the President's secretary, "because a proper title always carries proper authority, and we want to start right." The official title consequently became "The Commission of Fine Arts of the United States of America."[17]

The duties of the commission included consideration and criticism of the architectural aspects of all major building projects of the Federal Government. Though originally understood as applying only to the District of Columbia, the President ruled that, upon request, the commission should also advise on the design of major federal construction projects throughout the country. Such duties demanded both time and energy and Burnham commuted constantly between Chicago and Washington.[18]

Of all the issues that concerned the commission during the years of Burnham's chairmanship, the one that became the most significant historically was that involving the nature and location of a memorial to Abraham Lincoln. Talk and debate over a fitting tribute to the martyred President had been in the air for most of the half-century following his death. In the Washington Plan of 1902, however, Burnham's commission had recommended a definite site at the extreme western end of the central Mall axis on the Potomac River. To contrast with the height of the central Washington Monument and to complement the massive Capitol building at the eastern end, the commission had recommended an impressive but simple building of a basically horizontal orientation. The Fine Arts Commission reiterated that recommendation.[19]

By 1910, moreover, Congress had appointed from its own ranks a special Lincoln Memorial Commission which included, among others, the implacable Joseph Cannon! Cannon's hostility, however, to the Fine Arts Commission was balanced by President Taft's position of friendliness as chairman of the congressional group. In 1911, therefore, Taft surprised no one when he asked Burnham's commission for detailed commentary and specific recommendations on the several major suggestions for the proposed memorial's form and treatment.[20]

Such proposals came from a variety of sources for various types of monuments and memorials. Some favored a location between the Capitol and Union Station or at various points outside the city. Others liked the idea of a "Lincoln Highway" from Washington to Gettysburg. The commission squelched one suggestion of a monument in Arlington on the grounds that a tribute to Lincoln should not rightly be placed in the territory of the old Confederacy. While attempting to deal fairly with each of the major possibilities, it was no secret that the Fine Arts Commission favored adherence to the older proposal of the Potomac site, as espoused in the Report of 1902. In marshaling their arguments, the commissioners were pleased to quote the sentiment of Lincoln's friend, John Hay. "As I understand it," Hay had said to Charles McKim, "the place of honor is on the main axis of the plan. Lincoln of all Americans next to Washington deserves the place of honor. . . . His monument should stand alone, remote from the common habitations of man, apart from the business and turmoil of the city—isolated, distinguished, and serene. Of all the sites, this one near the Potomac is most suited to the purpose."[21]

Cannon, it seemed, favored any location that the commissioners disapproved, and reiterated his determination to keep the memorial from "that God-damned swamp." Champ Clark, of Missouri, another commission member, continued to favor a portrait sculpture. "If I had my way," Clark stated to Burnham, "I would build just a statue, and it should be bigger than the Collosus of Rhodes." Burnham acknowledged to Millet that he "didn't even say a word to this" and hoped "the sneer of pity in my mind did not appear in my face. When an ignorant man says, 'I don't claim to know *much* about architecture, but I do know what I like and don't need anyone to tell me,' he is hopeless and trying to tell *him* anything would be much like trying to show a blind man pictures."[22]

Despite the opposition of Cannon, however, a majority of the Lincoln commission voted to accept the recommendation for the Potomac site. They then asked the Fine Arts commissioners to recommend an architect. Henry Bacon of New York was promptly proposed. When Bacon went to Washington to appear before the committee, it was feared that Cannon might continue to create trouble and Burnham made sure that the Speaker was aware of the fact that Bacon was an Illinois native. "I am very glad," Burnham wrote Bacon later, that "your Washington meeting went off so well and that you got near Uncle Joe. He is a clansman and an Illinois Boy counts with him and this is a legitimate help when you have already won the job largely on your own merits."[23]

Bacon got the job and designed the Lincoln Memorial, built on the site and in the general manner proposed and confirmed by Burnham through the years. Daniel Chester French sculpted the great central statue of Lincoln. When it was finally dedicated in 1922, someone asked the ancient Cannon what he thought of the finished memorial and his admission seemed to vindicate Burnham's long and bitter struggle. "I have been in many fights," Cannon replied, "some I have lost—many I have won—it may have been better if I had lost more. I am pleased I lost the one against the Lincoln Memorial." The placing of the memorial on the recommended site also assured the completion and the integrity of the Mall as Burnham and L'Enfant had both envisioned it. Winning the fight for the memorial and the Mall also vindicated the early work of the Fine Arts Commission and indeed helped to "round out" a major part of Burnham's life.[24]

The only serious professional problem that clouded his years of arduous "retirement" was Burnham's unfortunate conflict with the American Institute of Architects. Always a critical though proud and loyal member, Burnham had served over the years on committees and projects and had, of course, been twice elected president. His chief concern in 1911 was with the recently published revision of the institutes' by-laws, particularly the requirement that A.I.A. members refrain from architectural competitions unless the prospective commissioning client made public the rules and guidelines governing the competition. The A.I.A.'s motive was undoubtedly to promote fairness in award procedures, but Burnham felt that the safeguards had gone too far. Often, he felt, they prevented his and others' firms from acquiring legitimate contracts.

In a letter to institute president Allen K. Pond, an old Chicago colleague, Burnham explained the reasons for his concern. "Last summer," he wrote, "a competition was called for by a Board of Directors for a very large important building; they were entirely unwilling to lay their proposed code of competition before the American Institute of Architects; they refused believing that no one had the right to dictate to them how they should do their private business; their Executive Committee visited my office and requested me to go into the competition. The code, as they proposed it," Burnham noted, "was perfectly satisfactory in every respect, and no one could find fault with it, and yet, because I am a member of the . . . Institute . . . and bound by its rules . . . I was compelled to tell them I could not compete."[25]

He then acknowledged that "a new case has come up which is of such vital importance as to make it impossible for me to refuse to go into the competition, and yet the owners take the same ground as did those mentioned above—they will not allow the American Institute of Architects to dictate to them in any way, shape, or manner. Now, this being the case, I am compelled to refuse to compete—as I did last summer—or else to resign from the Institute, because I am not in the habit of attempting to carry water on both shoulders." Burnham, therefore, reluctantly offered his resignation, to take effect immediately. "I would not do this," he assured Pond, "if I felt that the Institute is right in the position it takes, but from my point of view, it is strictly trades unionism to say to members that they may not take employment, except under agreements which have been submitted to you and have your approval. I very much regret," he concluded, "leaving the Institute to which I have belonged nearly all of my professional life, and of which I have twice been president."[26]

Upon his resignation, he entered the proscribed competition with a clear conscience and with the assurance that the matter was settled. It was not as settled as he thought, however. While many members regretted his resignation as a personal loss to the institute, several officers, including Pond, resented his action as a threat and rebuff to professional policy. They therefore ignored his letter of resignation and, forgetting his lifelong contributions to the profession, proceeded to insult Burnham and to challenge his integrity. Late in January 1912, R. Clipston Sturgis, chairman of the A.I.A. Judiciary Committee, informed Burnham matter-of-factly that in entering the competition, he had violated the A.I.A. constitution and would have to "stand trial" for his transgressions. The notice hurt and angered Burnham, and he replied to Sturgis, "as you are well aware, I resigned before entering the competition and have not been a member since that time." He wrote a similar letter to President Pond, rebuking him for never acting on his resignation and for insulting him so odiously and tastelessly. The affair hurt Burnham deeply, but he had no cause to regret his action.[27]

For the most part, however, 1911 and 1912 were pleasant years for Burnham. His business had never been better and he liked the way his junior associates were running things. He kept commuting to Washington on commission business and continued encouraging the Chicago work. Always an avid correspondent, he wrote more and more personal letters to his relatives and friends, and in all of them there crept a greater note of nostalgic wistfulness. Long possessed with a poignant sense of wonder at the mysteries of the world and of life and death, Burnham became more reflective and philosophical as the years passed. He began to think and write more about his parents and about his early childhood in New York and Chicago. "If I could," he wrote to his old friend Theodore Ely, "I would like to meet you . . . in September, late, and go to see my birthplace where I have not been since 1855."[28]

He was also concerned about his brother Lewis, to whom he had earlier given a job as a construction supervisor. "I have been thinking about you much of my time lately," he wrote Lewis in late 1911, "and more especially during the last two weeks. We are now all well past sixty, the last of us—Clara—having passed that mark last June and it is time that those of us who can do so should begin to get a little peace on earth, if this is ever to come at all. In my case I am looking forward to more freedom from care and to give my dear wife what comfort she can get out of me for the future. I think this should be your way of looking at your case." Since Burnham had already divided a part of his fortune among his less wealthy relatives and had arranged that Lewis should receive a regular stipend after retirement, Burnham insisted that Lewis stop work on his next birthday and live on the income from his trust fund. "I cannot tell you when I may be able to see you," he concluded, "but I will when I can, and it may be soon. You know well how I love you and yours and desire your happiness."[29]

In addition to a concern for his relatives, Burnham also felt strongly attached to his numerous nonrelated beneficiaries, and he took an almost fatherly interest in John Root, Jr., whose French education he was helping to finance. The restaurant design that Root had sent him was very good, he thought. "No wonder it received a mention. You should get mentions every time . . . and will no doubt. Are you arranging to travel during the next year and a half?" he asked. "I hope so; it is very necessary. You should see everything in Italy, France, and Spain and closely analyze all the principal things: the mass and the details. This is as important as the school work, furnishing the supplement that gives vitality to scholarship, and at the same time forming a storehouse for the imagination to play on later. Why not arrange to give the time to this work everyday you can snaffle from the school? . . . I wish I could do what I recommend" he concluded, "and be with you, fancy free, color box in hand, with a crust of bread and the glory of youth, a glory that passes away too soon. Now is your chance, my son, it will never return."[30]

Though certainly no longer young and with considerably more than a crust of bread, Burnham and Margaret sailed again for Europe with their usual gusto in the spring of 1912. Their daughter and son-in-law, Ethel and Albert Wells, accompanied them. It was Burnham's seventh visit to Europe. All looked forward eagerly to meeting Root and Hubert and Vivian in Paris. Burnham's chronic foot infection was causing him considerable pain, but after a few days at sea, he felt better. He discovered to his pleasant surprise that Charles Thorne, his old Chicago friend, was aboard and the Thornes, Wellses, and Burnhams settled down to enjoy a pleasant voyage together.[31]

Realizing that their vessel, the *Olympic*, would soon be passing near her sister ship, the *Titanic*, Burnham suddenly decided on April 14 to cable a greeting to Frank Millet, returning to Washington after several months in Italy attending to Roman academy business. The wireless operator reported that he was unable to send the message, however, and when Burnham pressed him for an explanation, the operator told him that the previous night the *Titanic* had crashed into an iceberg. The *Olympic* was, in fact, already headed for the scene to serve as a rescue vessel, but another ship turned out to be closer and the *Olympic* was ordered to proceed on course. The list of survivors numbered mostly women and children. Most of the men, including Millet, had stayed

Burnham on his last trip to Europe, 1912, with Margaret and their daughter and son-in-law, Ethel and Albert Wells. Courtesy Houghton Mifflin Company.

aboard conducting rescue operations, and had perished when the ship had suddenly submerged. Recording his grief at the news of the catastrophe, Burnham wrote in his diary that "Frank Millet, whom I loved was aboard her . . . thus cutting off my connection with one of the best fellows of the Fair." Indeed, despite their close connections over the years on various other artistic enterprises, it was their connection at the Chicago Fair of twenty years before that still seemed to Burnham the most significant. He had always considered the fair the turning point of his life. With the earlier passing of Olmsted, McKim, and St. Gaudens, and now the death of Frank Millet, the exposition fraternity was thinning out. Burnham felt the loneliness keenly.[32]

Though the tour proceeded as planned and the Burnhams delighted in both Europe and the reunion with Hubert, the loss of Millet and the *Titanic* tragedy cast an ominous pall upon the whole adventure. After landing at Cherbourg, they saw Mont St. Michel and then went south to sunnier Nîmes and Arles. From southern France they crossed to Italy and revisited their favorite places. After memorable days in Pisa, Florence, and Milan, they headed north. Geneva, Basle, and all of Switzerland seemed to Burnham more beautiful than ever. "The view from the ridge above Biel," he wrote on May 22, "is the finest in Europe; from this spot, 6300 feet above the sea, every Swiss mountain can be seen."[33]

It was his last recorded paean to the beauty of the world. He died a week later in Heidelberg, Germany, going quietly from a big and strenuous earthly life to the misty Swedenborgian afterworld. As the immediate cause of his death, the physicians diagnosed colitis, complicated by food poisoning and by worsening diabetes. He had felt much worse after reaching Heidelberg, and on May 29, with very little warning, he went into a coma. Without regaining consciousness, he died on June 1, 1912, three months before his sixty-sixth birthday. Though indeed longer than average life expectancy for men of his time, Daniel Burnham's life seemed somehow abnormally short for a man of his power and intensity. Burnham's body was cremated and the ashes returned with the family to Chicago for burial.[34]

The nature and the quantity of the responses befitted him. President Taft made a public statement both as Chief Executive and personal friend. Architects, public officials, Chicago neighbors, and unknown admirers issued tributes and came together in mourning. Most of the eulogies summarized his accomplishments in architecture, planning, philanthropy, and cultural leadership. All of them extolled his virtues as a man. The most fittingly flamboyant gesture came from Frederick Stock and the Chicago Symphony. Receiving the news of his death just before a concert, Stock ended the program with an interpolated tribute. Dramatic, but appropriate as for few other men, Stock led his and Burnham's orchestra in the Funeral March from Wagner's *Götterdämmerung*.[35]

Burnham's brother-in-law, the Swedenborgian John Goddard, delivered the eulogy at the interment on the small island in the lagoon in Graceland Cemetery, and noted the qualities so long associated with Burnham's name: "his straight-forward business principles, his integrity, his faithfulness in all the relations of life—as husband and parent and citizen and friend; his large view of life, embracing the whole . . . world. . . ."[36]

The grave of Daniel and Margaret Burnham on the Wooded Island in Graceland Cemetery, Chicago. Author.

WANT PARK NAMED TO HONOR BURNHAM

South Park Commissioners Asked at Memorial Meeting to Perpetuate Memory of Architect Who Made Chicago Beautiful.

Glowing tributes were paid the memory of the late Daniel Hudson Burnham yesterday by the Chicago plan commission in special session at the Hotel La Salle. Resolutions were unanimously adopted requesting the South Park commissioners to give the name "Burnham park" to the proposed park extending from Grant to Jackson park.

The meeting was held as a memorial to the great architect and all business was suspended. The story of how Burnham threw his heart and soul into the work of making Chicago beautiful, and how he sacrificed to further this end, was told both in letters from absent members and by those present. His work was characterized as immortal, a monument which will stand forever to its author's memory.

Letter From Mayor Heard.

Mayor Carter H. Harrison was unable to attend the meeting. A letter from him which told of the debt which the city owes to Burnham was read by Frank I. Bennett, vice chairman of the commission, acting in the absence of Chairman Charles H. Wacker, who sailed yesterday for Europe. Mayor Harrison dwelled upon Burnham's plans for making the city beautiful.

Walter D. Moody read a letter from Fred A. Delano, in which he likewise asked that Burnham's memory be honored by the naming of the park after him.

Commercial Club President Speaks.

"As one associated with Burnham and his work, I would like to say a word in appreciation of his unselfishness," said Clyde M. Carr, president of the Commercial club. "He not only gave to the people of this city days, weeks and months of his valuable time in planning for the civic beauty of Chicago but he gave over his offices. He refused to accept any remuneration for his services; instead he donated large sums of money for the publication of the Chicago plan book. I express the admiration, love and affection which every man associated with him could not help but feel."

Wireless Message Sent Wacker.

The following message was sent by wireless to Charles H. Wacker, aboard the Kron Princess Wilhelm, en route for Europe:

"The Chicago plan commission, in session today, send you their heartiest greetings and wish you a most pleasant journey and safe return. Your suggestion, Burnham park, adopted.   "JOHN M. EWING."

The committee named by the acting chairman to present the resolution to the South Park commission asking for the naming of "Burnham park," consists of John W. Scott, Edward A. Bancroft and Clyde M. Carr.

DANIEL H. BURNHAM, FAMOUS ARCHITECT, DIES IN GERMANY

Builder of Great Chicago World's Fair Fair Succumbs to Blood Poisoning

HIS FAMILY WITH HIM

Master Designer Created "City Beautiful" and Many Other Noted Structures

SOME OF D. H. BURNHAM'S ACHIEVEMENTS

The World's Columbian expositions.
Plan for beautifying lake front.
Union station, Washington, D. C.
Masonic temple.
The Monadnock building.
The Woman's temple.
The Montauk.
The Rialto.
The Rookery.
Plan for city beautiful.
Proposed new Union depot.
Peoples' Gas building.
Railway Exchange.
Insurance Exchange.
New Field museum.
New city of Manila.

Daniel H. Burnham, world-famous architect and creator of the Chicago "city beautiful," died today in Heidelberg, Germany. Death overtook the noted Chicagoan while he was motoring in Europe with his wife and other members of the family.

The announcement of his sudden end, which shocked his thousands of friends in Chicago and Evanston, where he lived, came in a cablegram to his son, Daniel H. Burnham, Jr., from Albert Wells, his brother-in-law. The cause was not stated, but Mr. Burnham's secretary attributed his death to a return of an attack of blood poisoning of several years' standing.

Chief of construction of the Columbian exposition in Chicago in 1903; designer of some of the greatest office buildings in the world, and originator of ideas for the cities beautiful, Mr. Burnham earned for himself a reputation that extended all over the world.

Planned Long Auto Tour

When he departed for Europe on April 20 last, he was accompanied by his wife, Mrs. Margaret Burnham, his son, Hubert, and his daughter and son-in-law, Mr. and Mrs. Albert Wells. They had planned an extended automobile tour of the continent, including historic places throughout Italy, France and Germany, returning to America about July 1.

In connection with the trip, Mr. Burnham had planned to study new ideas in architecture. It was his custom to go to Europe every year for this purpose.

The Burnhams had toured France from Cherbourg and had just entered on their trip through Germany when Mr. Burnham was stricken. He was 64 years old and when he left Chicago appeared to be in the best of health.

The death of the architect removes from public life the greatest inventive mind in architecture the country has known. During the years since fame, honor and fortune came to him, following the wonderful works displayed at the Columbia exposition, Mr. Burnham had been one of the busiest and hardest-worked men in his profession in the world.

Of late years thousands of demands had been made upon him for his services, most of which, on account of pressing work, he had been compelled to refuse.

His most recent work was on the Columbus memorial monument, which, it is planned will be dedicated in Washington on June 8, and for which he designed the pedestal and setting.

Known All Over the World

Through his long professional career, Mr. Burnham gained a reputation which spread from the narrow confines of the Chicago of 1871, until he became known in all the capitals of Europe, and even in the orient. Again and again he was called from his office on East Jackson boulevard, to consult with the royal architects of England, France and Germany.

America and Europe long regarded him as the leading authority on municipal buildings, and he had been sought as the designer of more buildings than any architect of his century.

Originated "Chicago Beautiful"

The plan to beautify Chicago's lake front originated with Mr. Burnham shortly after the world's fair. For years he had dreamed of the time when the city should redeem the lake front and make Chicago the most beautiful city in the world.

Other architects had made suggestions, but it remained for the master mind of Mr. Burnham to conceive a scheme which would be at the same time, beautiful, practical, and which would not involve great loss to the millions invested in lake front business.

The design submitted by Mr. Burnham for the improvement of the lake front was drawn on a large scale and was displayed at the Hotel Metropole in 1896. It later was shown at the Merchants' club, and attracted the widest attention throughout the city. Such men as Marshall Field, George M. Pullman and P. D. Armour were loud in their praise of the plan. From that time until the present, Chicago has clung to Mr. Burnham's ideas.

Cities All Over U. S. Call Him

The news of his plan for the city beautiful spread throughout the country and his services at once were demanded by cities from Boston to San Francisco. Washington had spent thousands of dollars in seeking a plan for beautifications, but nothing satisfactory had been developed.

Mr. Burnham was called into consultation, and with the other leading architects of the country, drew up the plan under which the city now is making improvements. When completed they will make Washington the most beautiful capitol city in the world.

Pittsburg Dispatch
June 2, 1912

Death Takes Greatest Of Architects

D. H. Burnham Dies at Heidelburg, Germany, While on Auto Tour

FAME INTERNATIONAL

Designed Largest and Best Buildings in Pittsburg, New York and Chicago

[*Special Telegram to The Dispatch.*]

CHICAGO, June 1.—A private dispatch was received here today saying that D. H. Burnham, architect of the World's Fair in Chicago in 1893, died today in Heidelberg, Germany. Mr. Burnham was making an automobile tour of France, Germany and Italy.

He had an international reputation and had designed buildings in many of the largest cities besides laying out plans for beautifying different cities.

Mrs. Burnham and a son and daughter accompanied him to Europe.

In Chicago Burnham was the architect for the Masonic Temple and a dozen large bank buildings. He designed the buildings at the World's Fair here. He also designed the $5,000,000 Gas Corporation Building here.

Helped Rebuild San Francisco

Burnham was the chief architect at San Francisco during the rebuilding of the city following the earthquake, and his plans for reconstructing the business district were carried out by the city. Notable among his buildings there is the Chronicle Building.

Eighty buildings in the heart of New York City's financial district were designed by Burnham. He was the architect for the John Wanamaker store buildings in New York and Philadelphia.

Burnham served on the fine arts commission appointed by the Government to supervise the reconstruction of many Federal buildings in Washington.

Built Pittsburg Buildings

Architect Burnham designed some of the largest buildings in Pittsburg. He had comparatively few acquaintances here, but was much liked by those who knew him. The Pittsburger who was probably best acquainted with him was D. B. Kinch, manager of the Frick Building and Frick Annex, for both of which Mr. Burnham was the architect. Mr. Kinch speaks of him as a man of wonderful personal magnetism and lovable character, although very modest and retiring.

Among the Pittsburg buildings designed by Mr. Burnham, in addition to the two Frick buildings, was the Highland Building, also owned by H. C. Frick; the Union Station of the Pennsylvania Systems, the Oliver Building and the First National Bank Building. The work on these structures was carried on under the supervision of Mr. Burnham's assistants, and he visited Pittsburg very rarely during their construction.

Pittsburg Index   June 8

A Successful "Failure."

Forty-six years ago four young men from the New Church School in Waltham applied for admission to Harvard. Daniel H. Burnham was the only one who failed. Then he applied to Yale and failed in his examination there. A week ago Mr. Burnham died in Germany, the acknowledged leading architect of the world. Harvard, Yale and other great universities had conferred degrees upon him.

Dozens of the world's greatest buildings remain as monuments to the architectural skill of Mr. Burnham. He was largely instrumental in developing the modern sky-scraper. Railroad companies called upon him to design their mammoth stations, and governments asked his assistance in planning great buildings. Municipalities requested his advice in city planning. Mr. Burnham is said to have delighted most in the services he rendered the public through assisting in city planning. He was a semi-public servant who was always ready to serve in beautifying cities and buildings.

Friends of Mr. Burnham declare that his failure to pass examinations for entrance to Harvard and Yale stimulated new ambitions. There is frequently more danger in success than adversity. Probably the world was the gainer by Mr. Burnham's failure to pass Yale and Harvard examinations.

Pittsburg Banner   June 6

Death of a Great Architect.

Daniel Hudson Burnham, an American architect of international reputation, died in Heidelberg, Germany, on last Saturday. He was born in Henderson, N. Y., in 1846. He moved to Chicago with his parents in 1856, and made that city his home for the rest of his life. He took up the study of architecture, and in 1872 founded the firm of Burnham & Root, which, with its continuation under the name of D. H. Burnham & Co., has designed some of the best known buildings in the country. Mr. Burnham was chief architect and director of works in planning the Chicago Exposition, in 1893, which was probably the climax of his achievements. He was chairman of the commission which has been considering a plan for the beautifying of Cleveland. He was appointed by the government to plan the reconstruction of Manila and Baguio, in the Philippines. He also planned the reconstruction of the cities of Chicago and San Francisco. Mr. Burnham went to Brooklyn last fall and took part in the organization of the city plan movement. When the permanent Brooklyn Committee on City Plan was organized his services were engaged. Mr. Burnham was chairman of the National Commission of Fine Arts. He was a fellow of the American Institute of Architects and president of that body in 1894. Yale, Harvard, Northwestern University and the University of Illinois gave him honorary degrees.

Providence, Rhode Island, Journal   June 3

A Great Architect.

Daniel H. Burnham of Chicago, whose death abroad was reported yesterday, was perhaps best known in connection with the World's Fair in his own city; but he has left more lasting monuments in many magnificent buildings throughout the country and in his unrivalled work in city planning. President Taft's tribute to him is not overdrawn or undeserved. Our largest New England universities recognized his excellent public service by conferring upon him honorary degrees, although unfortunately he did little work in this part of the country. He earned a rank among the foremost architects of America, and is to be classed with Richardson, McKim and Carrère, none of whom gave of his time and skill more liberally in the public interest.

Knoxville, Tennessee, Sentinel   June 4

DEATH OF DANIEL H. BURNHAM.

Few men in our country could have been spared so illy as Daniel H. Burnham, whose sudden death at Heidelberg, Germany, is announced. Mr. Burnham was 64 years of age but he was thought to be in perfect health. He was as active as most men of forty and was engaged in work of great value to the American people. He was a member of the fine arts' commission of Washington, which is planning and directing the improvements of the national capital, the location and style of new government buildings, the creation of the Mall and the location and design of the Lincoln Memorial. His mind conceived much of the great Chicago improvement plan, which is to cost $500,000,000 in execution. He was the

Newspaper headlines upon Burnham's death, 1912. Courtesy Chicago Art Institute.

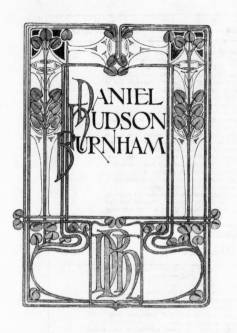

DANIEL HUDSON BURNHAM

At a regular meeting
of
THE COMMERCIAL
CLUB OF CHICAGO
held on
December fourteenth, nineteen hundred twelve, the
following resolution was
adopted by a unanimous
and rising vote:

IN THE DEATH OF DANIEL HUDSON BURNHAM, THE COMMERCIAL CLUB has lost one of its most distinguished members and his Club associates, a valued and loyal friend. FOR more than thirty years Mr. Burnham was a leader in all movements toward a better Chicago. But his genius was too great to be limited to the confines of any one city. He belonged to the nation and ever will rank among our great Americans.

DANIEL BURNHAM was a man of vision. He saw things in a large way, leaving details to others. TO him came the vision of a city of white palaces, and it is largely due to his genius that Chicago is today renowned for creating the most artistic of the World's Expositions. It was his instinct for harmony and his gift of leadership which brought about so ardent a spirit of co-operation that the designs of the many architects were made to blend into one sublime and harmonious whole. AT great personal sacrifice, he gave up his private practice during three years of Fair building. He thus made possible the opening of the gates on the appointed day in spite of difficulties that would have disheartened another man. HE was a leader in the movement for town planning. His genius gave inspiration to plans for many cities. Finally, he was the creator of the Commercial Club Plan of Chicago, which is destined to become an everlasting monument to his memory. To this Plan he devoted three years of his time, and, what is known to but few members of the Club, he personally contributed a considerable portion of the cost of its creation. DANIEL BURNHAM'S dream of a great white city became a splendid reality. His more glorious vision of a beautiful Chicago will yet be realized, and each step taken toward carrying out the Plan will be an added tribute to the memory of this great man.

Edward B. Butler

William L. Brown

Edward F. Rippeus

Committee

Clyde M. Carr

President

Walter B. Smith

Secretary

Commercial Club Memorial upon Burnham's death in 1912. Similar memorials came from the Chicago Art Institute and the National Commission on the Fine Arts. Courtesy Chicago Art Institute.

Epilogue

No Little Plans

THE TONES and emotions of the funeral eulogies continued through the 1910s to heighten and solidify Burnham's posthumous reputation. And, in 1921, with the publication of Moore's affectionate portrait, that consensus wafted into the 1920s. Burnham continued to be praised and revered, especially for the largeness of his vision and his plans.

But, in the mid-1920s, the tone began to change, spurred on by the catalyst of Sullivan's attack. Borrowing a metaphor from Thomas Dixon's *The Clansman*, Sullivan described Burnham's influence as a "small white cloud" that slowly grew and covered all—as Dixon earlier, and with different connotations, had identified the white cloud with the Ku Klux Klan. By the late twenties and early thirties, as Sullivan's writings became more widely known, as "modern" architecture regained its vigor, as Wright recovered from his temporary doldrums, and as European modernism broadcast its message, the world of architecture increasingly lost patience with the derivative neoclassicism of the Burnham era.

Burnham's own gravitation toward the neoclassical orbit, and his subsequent leadership and promotion of its program, had had, of course, personal as well as social dimensions. After Root's death in the early 1890s and the resulting loss of his human stylistic gyroscope, Burnham had turned to the authority of the book, to the canon and vocabulary of academic classicism. He had no longer felt secure in the Chicago idiom that was basically Root's and Sullivan's. But what had begun for Burnham as a personal defense reaction, had quickly become, with the impetus of the Chicago Fair, a spirited and aggressive architectural crusade. The fair had indeed been "classical" for expedient as well as for aesthetic reasons; yet its and Burnham's resulting popularity had strongly reinforced his neoclassical leanings. Later in the twentieth century, however, that popularity waned.

Other developments in the thirties raised additional doubts of the Burnham achievement, not only of its already questionable stylistic canon, but of other hitherto sacrosanct qualities—Burnham's compulsion toward "uniformity" and his willingness to think big. Sullivan had already labeled it "megalomania." For as the fascist regimes of Germany and Italy planned public spaces of unprecedented proportions and reared architectural monuments of super-human scale, the world took another look at the question of "bigness." What kind of bigness? Bigness for what? Grandiose parade grounds engulfing the individual? Burnham, himself, had encouraged such magnitude, perhaps more than he realized, though under other circumstances in a different time and place.

Recent critics and historians have attempted to redress the long, fashionable practice of attacking the Burnham School—the neoclassicist architects and City Beautiful planners—a revisionist movement, no doubt overdue. Yet, in seeking to do justice to those complicated figures, we can still not avoid assessing their weaknesses—significant weaknesses that affected our times. For the lapse into derivative historicism was, then as always, a reflection, in part, of a spiritual and intellectual indolence, a lack of creative vision and courage. It involved, in some ways, a failure of nerve, just as, in other ways, it suggested the opposite: for in its frequently swollen grandeur and magnitude, in the megalomania of its vast proportions, it represented, indeed, an excrescence of nerve, a compensating thrust of indulgent bravado. And so, from a distance of over half a century, it is easy to see dark qualities in Burnham, qualities largely unknown to himself.

It is less easy, however, to see and to remember that in still many ways, he was as great as he knew himself to be, as important as his contemporaries believed. Innovations soon become familiar and comfortable, taken for granted, and easily forgotten. And, because this book has stressed those achievements, they need be only briefly reiterated here. In four different areas, above all others, Burnham made original and distinguished contributions: first, in the development of the skyscraper form, in the perfection of tall, office building "systems," especially in matters of layout and internal arrangement; second, in the creation of the large, modern architectural office, a "system," again, of hierarchical departments of specialists working together, a system that reached its contemporary apogee in such generally distinguished firms as Skidmore, Owings, and Merrill and its less happy nadir in countless building empires across the land; third, in his early encouragement of the "comprehensive" planning concept, the "master" plan embracing entire urban and geographical regions, a concept that evolved from his early planning fragments to its fullest approximation in the Chicago Plan, an idea allied with the larger Progressive Movement, a concept again with a very mixed legacy, but one that still owes much of its genesis to his work; and, fourth, his achievements as a cultural enterpreneur, an architectural philanthropist, who organized and encouraged, in a capitalist democracy, the public as well as the private arts, who promoted, in a large and magnanimous way, the more accessible public institutions to replace or to complement the less accessible private ones. Burnham's own description of himself was, finally, a modest one: "I am perhaps a little quicker to run and open the valve," he had said. "That is about it—a door opener. . . ." He failed to note that the doors he opened were often jammed before he encountered them and that those who entered them, though often finer specialists than himself, might never have entered at all without his help. He declined to mention the energy released by his opening of the doors and the new and abundant areas beyond, which the door-openings illuminated.

In all of those ways, he equalled or surpassed Sullivan, his erstwhile antagonist in life and in death. Still, in sheer design genius, in artistic prescience and originality, Sullivan reigned supreme. How different their qualities and yet, how valuable both of them have been. A shame, we think, fleetingly, that we cannot graft the one's qualities onto the other. Yet, all history is poignant because it is over. We cannot move backward to recast and rearrange, to protect lost innocence, to save our earlier selves. The Sullivans and Burnhams of our history have been distinct and different voices, separate and unmergeable. As students of history, we accept that and continue trying to understand them both—while knowing, here and now, that as citizens and architects, there is always the need and the possibility of synthesis.

Appendix A

A Chronological List of the Buildings of
Burnham and Root and D. H. Burnham and Company

This list basically updates, enlarges, and wherever possible, corrects the building lists in Appendixes C, D, and E of Charles Moore's *Daniel H. Burnham, Architect, Planner of Cities*. The data in Moore's lists have been re-evaluated and reorganized by comparison with numerous primary and secondary sources, especially contemporary newspapers and architectural periodicals. This does not mean, unfortunately, that the data in the new lists are necessarily complete or perfect, and persons wishing to suggest further emendations are urged to contact the author via the publisher. An imperfect updating, it was felt, was preferable to none at all. A catalogue raisonné is badly needed of the buildings of the two Burnham firms. Only then can all such data be substantially confirmed. In the lists below, the legal distinction between the names "D. H. Burnham" (as the firm was officially named, 1891-94) and "D. H. Burnham and Company" (as it was named from 1894 to 1912) has been ignored, and for reasons of clarity, "D. H. Burnham and Company" has been used throughout. For the same reason, buildings completed through 1891 have been assigned to "Burnham & Root" since *most* of the buildings were in fact designed and begun before Root's death in January 1891. Root, of course, had a major part in designing several buildings that were not completed until 1892 such as the Masonic Temple, the Woman's Temple, and the Monadnock Building. The buildings in all cases are listed chronologically by completion date. Major buildings whose construction stretched over several years are discussed in the text.

Burnham and Root

DATE	NAME	LOCATION
1873	C. Mason House	Chicago
1874	John B. Sherman House	Chicago
	H. L. Story House	Hinsdale, Illinois
	Washington Heights Female Academy	Washington Heights, Illinois
1875	George E. Adams House	Chicago
	Henry D. Lloyd House	Chicago
	Mrs. Catherine Price House	Chicago
	Stockyard Exchange Office	Chicago Stockyards
1876	Don A. Solyer House	Valparaiso, Indiana
	F. F. Spencer House	Chicago
1877	A. H. Burley House	Chicago
	O. W. Clapp House	Chicago
	W. C. Eagan House	Chicago
	Edward Engle House	Chicago
1878	Isaac Eldredge House	Chicago
	Mary A. Roset House	Chicago
	Joseph Sears House	Chicago
	General Phillip Sheridan House	Chicago
1879	W. T. Baker House	Chicago
	Eugene Fisk House	Chicago
	A. Hayden House	Chicago
	Fred Newell House	Kenosha, Wisconsin
	E. H. Stickney House	Chicago
	J. M. Walker House	Chicago
	E. J. Warner House	Lake Forest, Illinois
	Hugh R. Wilson House	Evanston, Illinois
1880	Fallon School	Chicago
	Geoffrey Bessy Factory	Chicago
	M. M. Farr House	St. Louis
	Stephen Gale House	Chicago
	Julia Porter House	Chicago
	Norman B. Ream House #1	Chicago
	St. Gabriel's Convent	Chicago
	S. A. Smalley House	Chicago
	South Park Bridge	Chicago
	John Whittaker House	St. Louis
1881	C. C. Baker House	Chicago
	Jonathan W. Brooks, Jr., House	Chicago
	Augustus Byram House	Chicago
	Arthur J. Caton House	Chicago
	W. F. Cobb House	Chicago
	Thomas Dent House	Chicago
	S. E. Eagan House	Chicago
	Sarah O. Eagan House	Chicago

DATE	NAME	LOCATION
	Grannis Building (rebuilt in 1885–86 as Illinois National Bank Building)	Chicago
	Charles A. Gregg House	Chicago
	Tappen Halsey House	Chicago
	Marvin Hewitt House	Chicago
	Henry H. Shufeldts House	Chicago
	Byron L. Smith House	Chicago
1882	Owen F. Aldis House	Chicago
	John B. Alling House	Chicago
	Frederick Ayer Store	Chicago
	Arthur Bingham House	Chicago
	John C. Black House	Chicago
	James Charnley House	Chicago
	Chicago Provision & Grain Stock Board Office	Chicago
	W. B. Farr House	St. Louis
	C. B. Farwell House	Chicago
	John V. Farwell House	Chicago
	C. M. Fullerton Apartments	Chicago
	Maj. H. A. Huntington House	Chicago
	W. C. Kelley Barn	Chicago
	Palmer V. Kellogg House	Chicago
	H. M. Kinsley House	Chicago
	A. J. Kirkwood House	Chicago
	George A. Marsh House	Chicago
	J. A. Mason House	Chicago
	Montauk Building	Chicago
	J. Robertson House	Chicago
	Smith, Burdette & Company	Chicago
	C. B. Souther House	Cedar Rapids, Iowa
	W. D. Walker Houses (5)	Chicago
	J. H. Wrenn House	Chicago
1883	George D. Baldwin House	Chicago
	Miss Annie Barnette House	Chicago
	A. E. Bornique Dance Academy	Chicago
	James W. Brooks House	Chicago
	Brunswick Hotel	Chicago
	Thomas R. Burch House	Chicago
	A. C. Burnham House	Champaign, Illinois
	Calumet Club House	Chicago
	Chicago, Burlington & Quincy R.R. General Office Building	Chicago
	Chicago, Burlington & Quincy R.R. Library and Station	Creston, Iowa
	Chicago, Burlington & Quincy R.R. Station	Galesburg, Illinois
	H. A. Christy House	Chicago
	Charles W. Clingman House	Chicago

DATE	NAME	LOCATION
	Garfield Park Casino	Chicago
	Guaymas Hotel	Guaymas, Mexico
	George V. Hankin House	Chicago
	Z. S. Hilbrook Houses (5)	Evanston, Illinois
	Sidney A. Kent House	Chicago
	H. M. Kinsley Barn	Chicago
	W. R. Linn House	Chicago
	George S. Lord House	Evanston, Illinois
	Matthews & Cornwell Houses (2)	Chicago
	Frank C. Osborne House	Chicago
	G. W. Smith House	Evanston, Illinois
	A. A. Sprague House	Chicago
	Robert Strahorn House (#1)	Chicago
	Clara W. Woodyatt House	Evanston, Illinois
	A. McD. Young House	Milwaukee
1884	Atchison, Topeka & Santa Fe General Office Building	Topeka, Kansas
	Mrs. I. Atkinson House	Chicago
	S. T. Byrne House	Chicago
	Calumet Building	Chicago
	J. W. Carpenter Apartments	Chicago
	Chicago, Burlington & Quincy R.R. Station	Des Moines, Iowa
	Counselman Building	Chicago
	John Davis House	Chicago
	Joseph Frank House	Chicago
	Forty-Third Street School	Chicago
	Loomis Building	Chicago
	John McCully House	Chicago
	A. Mackay House	Chicago
	George E. Marshall House	Chicago
	George W. Spofford House	Chicago
	Robert Strahorn & F. R. Baker House (duplex)	Chicago
	C. C. Thompson House	Chicago
	Henry D. Warner House	Chicago
	Washington Park Skating Rink	Chicago
	Col. Waterman Houses (4)	Chicago
	G. H. Wheeler House	Chicago
1885	Chicago, Burlington & Quincy R.R. Station	Mendota, Illinois
	C. C. Collins Houses (3)	Chicago
	Mrs. M. F. Crosby House	Chicago
	A. Crossman House	Chicago
	George P. A. Healey House	Chicago
	Insurance Exchange	Chicago
	M. C. Jones House	Chicago
	Kansas City, Clinton & Springfield R.R. Station	Clinton, Missouri

DATE	NAME	LOCATION
	Kenosha Court House & Jail	Kenosha, Wisconsin
	John H. Leidigh House	Chicago
	Thomas Lord House	Evanston, Illinois
	Montezuma Hotel	Las Vegas, New Mexico
	J. H. Pearson House	Chicago
	Norman B. Ream Warehouse	Chicago
	Sherman Factory	Chicago
	Sixty-First Street School	Chicago
	Mrs. E. E. Springer Apartments	Chicago
	A. L. Thomas House	Chicago
	Traders Building	Chicago
	Union Bank Building	Chicago
	O. D. Wetherill House	Chicago
	Violet K. Whittaker House	Bar Harbor, Maine
1886	Armour Memorial	Chicago
	Edward E. Ayer House	Chicago
	Mrs. A. Baldwin House	Chicago
	Edward A. Burdette House	Chicago
	Commerce Building	Chicago
	DuPont Warehouse	Chicago
	Gun Club House	Henry, Illinois
	William E. Hale House	Chicago
	G. V. Hankin Apartments	Chicago
	David K. Hill House	Chicago
	Illinois National Bank Building (rebuilt after fire—formerly known as Grannis Building)	Chicago
	McCormick Offices & Warehouse	Chicago
	L. K. Merrill House	Chicago
	Lewis B. Mitchell House	Chicago
	Frederick K. Morrill House	Chicago
	Rialto Building	Chicago
	L. P. Smith Store	Chicago
	Reverend Henry P. Willard House	Chicago
	J. H. Winterbotham House	Chicago
1887	Art Institute of Chicago (original building)	Chicago
	Ayer Monument	Howard Illinois
	Buena Park R.R. Station	Chicago
	Julien M. Case House	Marquette, Michigan
	Chicago, Burlington & Quincy R.R. Station	Kewannee, Illinois
	Chicago, Burlington & Quincy R.R. Station	Lawndale, Illinois
	Church of the Covenant	Chicago
	Charles Counselman House	Chicago
	Davidson & Sons Theatre & Offices	Milwaukee

DATE	NAME	LOCATION
	Davidson & Sons Warehouse #1	Milwaukee
	Dime Savings Bank	Peoria, Illinois
	Charles M. Hill House	Chicago
	Kansas City, Fort Scott & Gulf R.R. Station	Fort Scott, Kansas
	Lawrence Maxwell, Jr. House	Cincinnati
	Dr. J. S. Mitchell House	Chicago
	C. W. Needham House	Chicago
	J. W. Nolan House	Chicago
	Henry J. Peet House	Chicago
	Phoenix Building	Chicago
	Philip Raeber House	Chicago
	Norman B. Ream House #2	Chicago
	St. Gabriel's Church	Chicago
	St. Louis Hotel	Duluth, Minnesota
	Lot P. Smith House	Chicago
	M. C. Stearns House	Chicago
	Robert Strahorn House	Kenwood, Illinois
	Ed Sturtevant House	Chicago
	Thomas Templeton House	Chicago
	United States Bank	Topeka, Kansas
	United States Building Company	Atchison, Kansas
	Hugh R. Wilson House	Evanston, Illinois
	Y.M.C.A. Building	Kansas City, Missouri
1888	American Bank Building	Kansas City, Missouri
	Argyle Apartments	Chicago
	Board of Trade Building	Kansas City, Missouri
	Chamber of Commerce Building	Peoria, Illinois
	Davidson & Sons Warehouse #2	Milwaukee
	First National Bank	Peru, Indiana
	W. H. Frost House	Los Angeles
	Dr. Charles G. Fuller House	Evanston, Illinois
	Grand Avenue Station	Kansas City, Missouri
	Haven School	Evanston, Illinois
	Haymarket Monument (base)	Chicago
	J. J. Hoch House	Chicago
	James L. Houghteling Houses (4)	Chicago
	Kansas City, Fort Scott & Memorial R.R. Station	Cherokee, Kansas
	Kansas City, Mobile & Birmingham R.R. Station	Aberdeen, Mississippi
	Lake View Presbyterian Church	Chicago
	James L. Lombard House	Kansas City, Missouri
	John McCarthy Apartments	Chicago
	Max A. Meyer House	Chicago
	Midland Hotel	Kansas City, Missouri
	J. C. Pennoyer House	Chicago
	Pickwick Apartments	Chicago

DATE	NAME	LOCATION
	William Pretyman House	Chicago
	The Rookery	Chicago
	William Scarritt House	Kansas City, Missouri
	J. R. True Store	Chicago
	Volney C. Turner House	Chicago
	Union Station	Chicago
	Union Stockyards & Trust Company Bank	Chicago Stockyards
	Union Stockyards & Trust Company Office	Chicago Stockyards
	R. S. Wheeler House	Chicago
	Wilson House	Pekin, Illinois
1889	Chemical Bank Building	Chicago
	Chicago, Burlington & Quincy R.R. Station	Ottumwa, Iowa
	John Davis Houses (2)	Chicago
	Amanda F. Farlin House	Chicago
	Graham School	Chicago
	P. J. Kasper House	Evanston, Illinois
	Lincoln Park Sanitarium	Chicago
	Marion Hotel	Indianapolis, Indiana
	Arthur Orr Apartments	Evanston, Illinois
	T. P. Randall House	Chicago
	George Scott House	Lakeside, Illinois
	I. N. W. Sherman House	Chicago
	Mrs. E. E. Springer House	Chicago
	Union Stockyards & Trust Company Office	Chicago
	Unity Street School	Chicago
	Edward H. Valentine House	Chicago
1890	Mrs. George Adams House	Chicago
	A. L. Bell House	Chicago
	G. W. Brandt House	Chicago
	William Brown House	Evanston, Illinois
	Chronicle Building	San Francisco
	A. H. Dainty House	Chicago
	Reginald de Koven House	Chicago
	J. Gelert Studio	Chicago
	William Hale Observatory	Chicago
	James J. Hoyt House	Kenosha, Wisconsin
	William G. Metzger Mill	Chicago
	Pacific National Bank Building	Tacoma, Washington
	O. W. Potter House	Chicago
	Rand-McNally Building	Chicago
	Society for Savings Bank Building	Cleveland
	Edward H. Valentine House	Chicago
1891	Central Market	Chicago
	Chicago Daily News Building	Chicago
	Fidelity Trust Building	Tacoma, Washington

DATE	NAME	LOCATION
	First Regiment Armory	Chicago
	William J. Goudy House	Chicago
	Great Northern Hotel	Chicago
	Herald Building	Chicago
	Mills Building	San Francisco
	John B. Sherman Monument	Chicago
	Science Hall, Beloit College	Beloit, Wisconsin

D. H. Burnham and Company

DATE	NAME	LOCATION
1892	George Adams House	Chicago
	Ashland Block	Chicago
	William L. Brown & H. P. Post House	Evanston, Illinois
	Chicago, Burlington & Quincy R.R. Station	Burlington, Iowa
	Cuyahoga Building	Cleveland
	Dexter Park Horse Exchange	Chicago
	Ellicott Square Building	Buffalo, New York
	James W. Ellsworth House	Chicago
	Equitable Building	Atlanta
	Galt House (hotel)	Louisville, Kentucky
	S. E. Gross Stable	Chicago
	John C. Hately House	Lake Geneva, Wisconsin
	Immanuel Presbyterian Church	Chicago
	Marshall Field & Company Old Annex	Chicago
	Masonic Temple	Chicago
	Monadnock Building	Chicago
	Noyes Street School	Evanston, Illinois
	Perkins Apartment	Chicago
	Judge A. N. Waterman House	Chicago
	Western Reserve Building	Cleveland
	Woman's Temple	Chicago
1893	P. J. Kasper House	Chicago
	A. C. Farlin House	Chicago
	Gen. John A. Logan Monument (base)	Chicago
	Majestic Hotel	Chicago
	Peacock Cafe	Chicago
1894	Atchison Bank	Atchison, Kansas
	Crain Street School	Evanston, Illinois
	Charles Deering House and Boathouse	Evanston, Illinois
	Ellicott Club	Buffalo, New York
	Emmanuel M.E. Church	Chicago
	First Presbyterian Church	Evanston, Illinois

DATE	NAME	LOCATION
	Great Northern Theatre & Office	Chicago
	Reliance Building	Chicago
	Charles H. Schwab House	Chicago
	Tipton Bank	Tipton, Indiana
	Toledo Traction Company Power House	Toledo, Ohio
	Wyandotte Building	Columbus, Ohio
1895	C. H. Schroeder House	Chicago
1896	Fisher Building	Chicago
	Lake Shore & M.S. R.R. Station	Cleveland
	Majestic Building	Detroit
	Phillips Warehouse	Chicago
	Quadrangle Club	University of Chicago
	Silversmith Building	Chicago
	South Side Elevated Railway Company Power House	Chicago
	Theodore Thomas Studio	Chicago
	Union Station	Columbus, Ohio
1897	Illinois Trust & Savings Bank	Chicago
	Land Title Building	Philadelphia
	Spahr Building	Columbus, Ohio
1898	A. W. Green House	Chicago
	Hinman Avenue School	Evanston, Illinois
	Quincy R.R. Station	Quincy, Illinois
	Refectory Building	Chicago
	Reid, Murdoch & Company Warehouse	Chicago
	Union Trust Company	Pittsburgh
1899	Federal Building	Youngstown, Ohio
	Fisk Hall, Northwestern University	Evanston, Illinois
	Kent Memorial Library	Suffolk, Connecticut
	Red Oak National Bank	Red Oak, Iowa
	Simmons Memorial Library	Kenosha, Wisconsin
1900	Chicago Telephone Company Station(s) (5)	Chicago
	Continental Trust Company	Baltimore
	Lord Owen Building	Chicago
	Marshall Field & Company Warehouse	Chicago
	Merchants' Loan & Trust Company	Chicago
	Otis Elevator Company Plant	Chicago
	Ritchie Building	Chicago
	Union Savings & Trust Company	Cincinnati
	Union Station	Grand Rapids, Michigan
1901	Commercial Gazette Plant	Pittsburgh
	Frick Building	Pittsburgh

DATE	NAME	LOCATION
	West Pennsylvania Exposition Society	Pittsburgh
1902	Booth Fisheries Cold Storage Warehouse	Chicago
	Cincinnati Traction Company Building	Cincinnati
	Fifth National Bank	Cincinnati
	James B. Forgan Stable	Chicago
	Marshall Field & Company Store	Chicago
	Marshall Field & Company Wholesale Power Plant	Chicago
	Petoskey R.R. Station	Petoskey, Michigan
	Richmond R.R. Station	Richmond, Indiana
	Union Savings & Trust Company	Cincinnati
	Union Station	Pittsburgh
	Wood Street Building	Pittsburgh
1903	American National Bank	San Francisco
	Armour Square	Chicago
	Bessemer Park	Chicago
	Cornell Square	Chicago
	Davis Square	Chicago
	First National Bank	Chicago
	First National Bank	Cincinnati
	First National Bank	Uniontown, Pennsylvania
	Flatiron Building	New York
	Gimble Brothers Department Store (addition)	Milwaukee
	Hamilton Square	Chicago
	Heyworth Building	Chicago
	Hibernia Bank Building	New Orleans
	Joliet Public Library	Joliet, Illinois
	McCreery Store	Pittsburgh
	Marquette Park	Chicago
	Merchants' Exchange Building	San Francisco
	Ogden Park	Chicago
	Palmer Park	Chicago
	Pittsburgh Plate Glass Warehouse	Chicago
	Railway Exchange	Chicago
	Russell Square	Chicago
	Sherman Park Buildings	Chicago
	Stewart Building	Pittsburgh
	Union League Addition	Chicago
	Virginia Avenue Building	Pittsburgh
	John Wanamaker Department Store	New York
	Mark White Square	Chicago
1904	Bank of Commerce & Trust Company	Memphis, Tennessee

DATE	NAME	LOCATION
	Marshall Field & Company Warehouse	Chicago
	Third National Bank	Pittsburgh
	Indianapolis Traction Building	Indianapolis, Indiana
	Union Station	El Paso, Texas
1905	Edison Building	Chicago
	Fourth National Bank	Cincinnati
	Frick Building Annex	Pittsburgh
	Marshall Field & Company Stores	Chicago
	Marshall Field & Company "River" Warehouse	Chicago
	Mills Building Annex	San Francisco
	Orchestra Hall	Chicago
	Schmidlapp Memorial Library	Cincinnati
1906	Chicago & Eastern Illinois R.R. Freight House	Danville, Illinois
	Liberty Avenue Building	Pittsburgh
	Oliver Avenue Building	Pittsburgh
	Selfridge Department Store	London, England
1907	Henry C. Corbin House	Washington, D.C.
	Evansville R.R. Station	Evansville, Indiana
	San Francisco Chronicle Building	San Francisco
	Union Station	Washington, D.C.
	Vermont Marble Company Factory	Chicago
	Wick Building	Youngstown, Ohio
1908	Alms & Doepke Department Store (addition)	Cincinnati
	Commonwealth Edison Power Plant	Chicago
	First National Bank	San Francisco
	New Orleans Terminal Station	New Orleans
	Oliver Building	Pittsburgh
	R. Trimble Monument	Pittsburgh
1909	Board of Trade Building	Duluth, Minnesota
	Cedar Rapids National Bank	Cedar Rapids, Iowa
	Fleming Building	Des Moines, Iowa
	Ford Building	Detroit
	Gimble Brothers Department Store	New York
	Merchants' National Bank	Indianapolis, Indiana
	St. Louis County Court House	Duluth, Minnesota
	Scanlan Building	Houston, Texas
	Sioux Falls Savings Bank	Sious Falls, South Dakota
	John Wanamaker Department Store	Philadelphia
1910	Alworth Building	Duluth, Minnesota
	Black Hawk National Bank	Waterloo, Iowa

DATE	NAME	LOCATION
	Chicago Business College	Chicago
	Chicago Thread Manufacturing Company	Monticello, Indiana
	Crane Company Corwith Plant	Chicago
	Davis Manufacturing Company	Chicago
	Fuller Park Buildings	Chicago
	Highland Building	Pittsburgh
	Hotel Claridge	New York
	Illinois Tunnel Company 39th Street Station	Chicago
	Interurban Terminal Station	Columbus, Ohio
	Loft Building	Chicago
	Machinery Exchange	Chicago
	Marshall Wells Hardware Company Warehouse #2	Portland, Oregon
	Old Commercial National Bank	Oshkosh, Wisconsin
	Old National Bank Building	Spokane, Washington
	People's Gas Company Building	Chicago
	Putnam Building	Davenport, Iowa
	Scanlan Warehouse	Houston, Texas
	F. J. V. Skiff House	Winnetka, Illinois
	Southern Building	Washington, D.C.
	South Park Commissioners Administration Building	Chicago
	Union Station Plaza Improvements	Washington, D.C.
1911	Columbus Monument (base)	Washington, D.C.
	First National Bank	Hutchinson, Kansas
	Insurance Exchange Building, #2	Chicago
	U.S. Post Office	Washington, D.C.
	Rock Island Savings Bank	Rock Island, Illinois
	Union Station	Fort Smith, Arkansas
	Waldheim Building	Kansas City, Missouri
	Washington Park Buildings	Chicago
1912	Eighty Maiden Lane Building	New York
	Filene Store	Boston
	First National Bank	Pittsburgh
	Goddard Building	Chicago
	Hardin Square	Chicago
	Hill Building Loft	Chicago
	Marshall Field Retail Store	Chicago
	The May Company	Cleveland
	New York Edison Building	New York
	Otis Elevator Company Building	Chicago
	Society Brand Building (loft)	Chicago
	Stevens & Brothers Department Store	Chicago

Buildings designed before, but completed after, the year of Burnham's death

DATE	NAME	LOCATION
1913	W. D. Boyce Building	Chicago
	Butler Brothers Warehouse	Chicago
	Dime Savings Bank	Detroit
	Miners' Bank	Wilkes Barre, Pennsylvania
	Mt. Wilson Observatory	Pasadena, California
	Second National Bank	Toledo, Ohio
	Shillito Building	Cincinnati
	Starks Building	Louisville, Kentucky
1914	Continental & Commercial National Bank	Chicago
	Conway Building	Chicago
	First Wisconsin National Bank	Milwaukee
	Marshall Field & Company, Men's Annex	Chicago
1920	Field Museum of Natural History	Chicago

Appendix B

A Note on, and Index of, Comparative Building
Construction Costs, 1870–1970

The comparison of building construction costs between one year or period and another is a vulnerable adventure that must deal in approximate and suggestive rather than "precise" comparative figures. When
reading that a building of the 1870s, for example, cost x amount of
money, a natural (though virtually unanswerable) question frequently
involves a demand for some equation in terms of present dollar construction costs. First, one should realize that a building of the 1870s
would not, and most likely could not, be constructed in the 1970s (as it
was constructed in, and under the conditions of, the 1870s) except perhaps as an extremely expensive custom, educational, museum project.

The closest approximation, however, to a sense of comparative construction costs is provided in the "Construction Cost Index" of the *Engineering News Record* from 1903 to 1970 and from various indexes for
the pre-1903 (pre-ENR Index) period, based upon, and extrapolated
from, the *ENR Index*. The base year for the ENR and related indexes is
1913 (1913 = 100). In a detailed explanatory article ("News Record
Indexes: History and Use," *Engineering News Record*, September 1,
1949), the index is likened to "a surveyor's system of measuring altitudes
from fixed bench marks." The index was based on the 1913 costs of un-
skilled labor and of the basic building materials: lumber, cement, and
steel, materials "selected because they promised the most stable reaction
to the whole economy and to its price structure." (See entire article, as
cited, for a full explanation and rationale.) The figures since 1903 (the
year the *ENR* Index began) are taken from the "Construction Cost Index" as published in a supplement to the *Engineering News Record*,
March 23, 1972. The figures prior to 1903 (based on the ENR Index
formula) are taken from Appendix N of Miles Colean and Robinson
Newcomb, *Stabilizing Construction* (New York, 1952).

Construction Cost Index, 1870–1970
(Base Year, 1913 = 100)

Year	Index	Year	Index	Year	Index	Year	Index
1870	95.3	1895	69.8	1920	251.28	1945	307.75
1871	99.4	1896	68.3	1921	201.82	1946	346.04
1872	99.2	1897	66.5	1922	174.45	1947	413.16
1873	97.0	1898	67.5	1923	214.12	1948	460.72
1874	90.2	1899	74.4	1924	215.36	1949	477.02
1875	82.0	1900	79.9	1925	206.68	1950	509.62
1876	79.0	1901	83.6	1926	208.03	1951	542.62
1877	73.6	1902	83.8	1927	206.24	1952	569.40
1878	69.7	1903	93.90	1928	206.78	1953	599.99
1879	67.3	1904	87.40	1929	207.02	1954	627.96
1880	73.2	1905	90.55	1930	202.85	1955	659.72
1881	77.6	1906	95.10	1931	181.35	1956	692.37
1882	81.5	1907	100.55	1932	156.97	1957	723.85
1883	81.9	1908	97.20	1933	170.18	1958	759.16
1884	73.3	1909	90.92	1934	198.10	1959	796.91
1885	73.1	1910	96.33	1935	196.44	1960	823.55
1886	78.1	1911	93.43	1936	206.42	1961	847.05
1887	77.8	1912	90.70	1937	234.71	1962	871.84
1888	75.2	1913	100.00	1938	235.83	1963	900.96
1889	75.3	1914	88.56	1939	235.51	1964	936.38
1890	73.3	1915	92.58	1940	241.96	1965	971.22
1891	70.9	1916	129.58	1941	257.84	1966	1019.08
1892	70.9	1917	181.24	1942	276.30	1967	1070.40
1893	71.1	1918	189.20	1943	289.95	1968	1154.54
1894	69.2	1919	198.42	1944	298.72	1969	1269.20
						1970	1386.36

On Sources

A formal, alphabetized, tabular bibliography would involve an unnecessary duplication of the notes to the text. What follows here is an evaluation of the major categories of source material relating to Burnham's life and work. Readers desiring more specific citations should refer to the notes for the appropriate chapter and paragraph.

Manuscripts

Daniel H. Burnham Papers. Chicago Art Institute Library. As the notes will indicate, the majority of references for this study are primary sources. Most of them are manuscripts, and a sizable portion are from the vast Burnham Papers in the Library of the Chicago Art Institute. The four most important categories of material in that collection are: Burnham's outgoing letters, his unpublished diaries, his scrapbooks, and four large boxes of miscellaneous materials.

The letter-books include twenty-one bound volumes of personal and professional letters from Daniel Burnham to a wide variety of correspondents from 1890 to 1894 and 1901 to 1912. Burnham's letters from 1894 to 1901 have been inexplicably lost or destroyed. That loss is ameliorated partially by the fact that Burnham's unpublished diaries begin in 1895 and help to cover the period of the missing correspondence. The Art Institute owns the first thirteen volumes of Burnham's diaries for the years 1895 to 1907, and several small, pocket diaries covering various travels. The major diaries for the years 1908 to 1912 are in the possession of Daniel H. Burnham, III, San Diego, California, who made them available to the author, as cited below.

Burnham's incoming correspondence was not saved as systematically as the outgoing letters, with the exception of one volume of letters to Burnham from McKim, Mead, and White concerning the World's Columbian Exposition, February 11, 1890-April 4, 1893. Daniel Burnham, Jr., unfortunately (and for reasons not totally clear) destroyed, after his father's death, much of the incoming correspondence. Much of the nature of the missing incoming letters, however, can be interpolated from Burnham's responses in the outgoing correspondence. Daniel Burnham, Sr., moreover, preserved in his scrapbook several dozen of the incoming letters that he valued most highly, letters that proved extremely helpful in reconstructing his life, as the notes will indicate. Of Burnham's eight scrapbooks, four are organized along general chronological lines from approximately 1888 to 1910. The other four topical scrapbooks deal with the World's Columbian Exposition, Burnham's experiences and problems as A.I.A. president (1894-95), the origins of the Chicago Plan in Burnham's early scheme for the South Shore Drive and Lake Front, and the Burnham family's trip to Europe in 1907. The scrapbooks contain clippings, photographs, letters, and miscellaneous memorabilia that Burnham especially treasured or thought important. Four large boxes, labeled "Material By and About Daniel H. Burnham" include miscellaneous, loose, unaffixed items similar to the material in the scrapbooks and deal largely with the World's Fair, with aspects of Burnham's city planning, and with personal honors and memorials.

Of the four major categories of material in the Burnham Papers, Burnham's letters were unquestionably the most significant. Burnham was an avid and frequent letter writer. For the most part, his letters are tactful, but beneath the characteristic diplomacy, they reveal a candor, a passion, and a sense of commitment generally missing in the diaries. The letters are arranged chronologically in the bound letter books and are fairly well indexed. Of the more than nine thousand letter copies preserved, approximately three-fourths are typed and one-fourth are in Burnham's hand. The holograph copies have faded badly over the years and several dozen of them contain passages that are now illegible.

Burnham's diaries, both in public and in private collections, reveal less of his character and personality than do his letters, but they record faithfully the time, place, and nature of his personal and professional activities and pursuits. Though when taken alone, the diary notations often seem trivial and inconsequential, they frequently take on added significance when considered in aggregate. Burnham's obsession and fascinations with trains and transportation systems, for example, is revealed in his constant notations of the names and descriptions of the trains and rail companies as well as their times of departure and arrival, speed, efficiency, and general performance. The diaries are invaluable for placing and locating Burnham at any given time and for noting the names of people and institutions with whom he dealt in the course of each day for the last seventeen years of his life.

Burnham's scrapbooks and boxes of miscellaneous materials were less crucial than the letters and diaries in helping to reconstruct his life, with the exception of the important incoming letters that he pasted in the books. In addition to those letters, however, the books and boxes contain numerous obscure and useful clippings having to do both with Burnham's work and activities and with other ideas and enterprises that interested him but did not refer to him personally.

A more detailed breakdown of the Burnham Papers can be found in the card catalogue of the Chicago Art Institute Library. That catalogue also contains, in both original and printed form, a helpful though incomplete bibliography of journal articles and miscellaneous references that relate to Burnham and his work.

The Daniel H. Burnham, Jr., Papers, in the possession of Daniel H. Burnham, III, San Diego, California, contain a small, but rich array of sources relating to the senior Burnham. Like his father, Daniel, Jr., was an avid and efficient collector and diary-keeper. It is unfortunate for the historian that he destroyed or misplaced the letters and other materials he considered of no importance, but, on the other hand, he was probably also largely responsible for preserving the papers that have survived. After his father's death, in conjunction with his mother and his brothers and sisters, he deposited most of his father's papers in the Burnham Library at the Art Institute. At that time, however, he kept in his personal possession those diaries of his father's that related to the period of his own connection with the firm from 1908 to 1912.

In addition to the papers of his father, Daniel, Jr.'s, own papers have been valuable for the light they throw on the personal and professional life of the senior Burnham. Like his father, for example, Daniel, Jr., kept a diary of his daily activities. Unlike his father, he also wrote an autobiography late in life, a loosely constructed memoir that grows from but also supplements his diary notations. The most significant and engaging part of the diary is the first and isolated 1904 boyhood volume cited and utilized in Chapter XII of this text. There is a gap in the diaries from 1905 to 1909 when he apparently kept no journal, but the diaries resume in 1909 and continue without interruption to his death in 1961. The unpublished autobiography is Daniel, Jr.'s, summary of his life as he remembered and recorded it in 1960, the year before his death. It contains several choice anecdotes and appraisals of the senior Burnham and is especially valuable for the study of the last years of Burnham's life after Daniel, Jr., had entered the firm.

The papers of Daniel Burnham, Jr., also contain a small miscellaneous file of clippings and mementoes, but they add little to the larger file of such items in the Art Institute collection. The papers of Daniel H. Burnham, Jr., passed upon his death to his son, Daniel H. Burnham, III, who graciously opened them for the purposes of this research. This writer has encouraged Mr. Burnham to contribute the remaining diaries of his grandfather, Daniel H. Burnham, to the Chicago Art Institute Library, and he is considering such action at the date of this writing.

The Hubert Burnham Papers, in the possession of his daughter, Mrs. Cherie Burnham Morris, La Jolla, California, is a small collection that, for the most part, duplicates items in the larger Burnham collection in Chicago. Items of special interest include a copy of Daniel Burnham's will and a copy of the Reverend John Goddard's eulogy at Burnham's funeral.

The Charles Moore Papers, in the Library of Congress, Washington, D.C., include a number of primary manuscript sources that Moore assembled for his 1921 study: *Daniel H. Burnham, Architect, Planner of Cities.* Of particular interest are letters written to and from Burnham in his youth, letters and memoranda to Moore from Burnham's family and friends, and an autobiographical fragment, in Burnham's own hand, entitled "Biography of Daniel H. Burnham, Notes for Editor." Some of the materials Moore utilized in his study. Others he did not use at all. In still other cases, he used but seemingly misconstrued or failed to develop important aspects of his data.

The Augustus St. Gaudens Papers, Library of Congress, Washington, D.C., contain correspondence between Burnham and St. Gaudens, chiefly relating to the World's Columbian Exposition, the American Academy in Rome, and the improvement of Washington. Other letters deal with personal and miscellaneous artistic matters.

The Charles F. McKim Papers, in the Library of Congress, Washington, D.C., include correspondence between Burnham and McKim on the World's Columbian Exposition, the American Academy in Rome, and the improvement of Washington. Other letters deal with personal and miscellaneous artistic matters. Though dealing with virtually the same issues as the Burnham-St. Gaudens correspondence, the McKim letters are fuller, more explicit, and consequently more helpful to the researcher.

The W. Cameron Forbes Papers, Houghton Library, Harvard University, reveal a large, rich correspondence between Forbes and Burnham both before and after Burnham's work with Forbes in the Philippine Islands. Like his correspondence with both McKim and St. Gaudens, Burnham's letters to Forbes usually reflect him in his more introspective and contemplative moods.

The Edward H. Bennett Papers, in possession of Edward H. Bennett, Jr., Chicago, were especially valuable for their insights into Burnham's (and Bennett's) work on the San Francisco and Chicago plans. The papers include Bennett's personal unpublished diaries for the period of his association with Burnham and miscellaneous folders of letters and clippings relating to San Francisco and Chicago. Some of the material is duplicated in the Burnham Papers at the Art Institute, but much of it is unique and original, especially Bennett's diary observations of Burnham and his work.

The Harvard University Archives yielded brief but useful information on Burnham's Harvard connections, including the particulars of his honorary degree and his later role as a member of the University's Committee on Fine Arts and Architecture.

The archives of the Chicago Symphony Orchestra, Orchestra Hall, Chicago, were helpful in reconstructing the history of Burnham's connections with the orchestra and its two conductors, Theodore Thomas and Frederick Stock. Especially important were the manuscript "Records of the Board of Trustees, Chicago Orchestral Association," of which Burnham was long an officer. Several pertinent items are also contained in the Thomas Papers, Newberry Library, Chicago.

Interviews

Three personal interviews with Burnham relatives in the summer of 1969 were helpful in completing the more personal aspects of Burnham's story, particularly as treated in Chapter XII. The most productive interview was with Catherine Wheeler Burnham, Rancho Santa Fe, California. As the widow of John Burnham, oldest son of Daniel and Margaret, Mrs. Burnham was quite possibly the last surviving person who had actually known Daniel

Burnham, Sr., and was close to him for a considerable time. Catherine Burnham's clear and articulate recollections of her father-in-law stretched back ultimately to her earliest childhood memories of Evanston in the late nineteenth century when she visited the Burnham home as the child of friends and neighbors. She was a friend of all the Burnham children and ultimately entered the family herself as a quiet but perceptive daughter-in-law. Her description of D. H. Burnham was both critical and respectful and her willingness to answer personal questions was of immeasurable help.

Interviews with Cherie Burnham Morris, the daughter of Hubert Burnham, and Daniel H. Burnham, III, were also helpful. Though Mrs. Morris and Mr. Burnham never knew their grandfather personally, their recollections were useful in delineating the character of their grandmother, Margaret Burnham, and of their deceased fathers—Burnham's sons. They also related information about the elder Burnham as transmitted through their fathers.

Though not related to Daniel Burnham, Edward H. Bennett, Jr., Chicago, was helpful in discussing his father's relationship with Burnham. In passing on information gleaned from his late father, Bennett provided much the same kind of assistance as that provided by the children of Hubert and Daniel Burnham, Jr.

Burnham's Published Works

Burnham's published works are limited primarily to the printed versions of his city plans, but they also include several journal articles and part of a projected serial, coauthored with Francis Millet, that was cut short by the financial depression of 1893 and 1894: *The World's Columbian Exposition, The Book of the Builders, Being the Chronicle of the Origin and Plan of the World's Fair* (Chicago, 1894). The Washington Plan, drafted by Burnham as chairman of the commission and edited by its secretary Charles Moore, was printed as Senate Report No. 166, 57th Congress, 1st Session, and entitled *The Improvement of the Park System of the District of Columbia* (Washington, D.C., 1902). The short plan submitted to the City of Cleveland, by Burnham, John M. Carrère, and Arnold Brunner, was *Report on a Group Plan of the Public Buildings of Cleveland* (Cleveland, 1903). A more accessible reprinted version, used in this study was "The Grouping of Public Buildings at Cleveland," *Inland Architect and News Record*, XLII (September 1903). Edward Bennett supervised the preparation of the illustrations and Edward F. O'Day was editor of Burnham's *Report on a Plan for San Francisco* (San Francisco, 1905). Since most of the books were burned in the subsequent fire, the surviving copies of the plan are very rare items. Burnham's "Report on the Proposed Improvements at Manila," and "Report of the Proposed Plan of the City of Baguio, Province of Benguet, P.I." were written with the assistance of Pierce Anderson and were submitted to the government in typescript. Copies of the original typescript are in the Burnham Papers in Chicago and in the possession of the writer. They were published, among other places, in the *Proceedings of the*

Twenty-Ninth Annual Convention of the American Institute of Architects (Washington, D.C., 1906) and later as an appendix in Moore's *Daniel H. Burnham, Architect, Planner of Cities*. The *Plan of Chicago* (Chicago, 1909) was coauthored with Edward Bennett and edited by Charles Moore. Burnham's speech, "A City of the Future Under a Democratic Government," was published in the *Transactions of the Town-Planning Conference, Royal Institute of British Architects* (October 1910), 368-78. Burnham's biographical eulogy, "Charles Bowler Atwood," appeared in *The Inland Architect and News Record*, XXVI (January 1896), 56-57. His address at the University of Illinois, Urbana, "Principal Duty of the University to the People," was published in the same journal, XXVI (December 1895), 48-49. Burnham discussed the connection between the World's Fair and his later planning and identified himself with the "Progressive Movement" in "White City and Capital City," *Century Magazine*, 63 (February 1902), 619-20. "What An Architectural Association Should Be," *Inland Architect and Building News*, V (March 1885), 20-21, gave insights into aspects of Burnham's general view of his profession. "How to Set Up an Architectural Office Composed of Specialists," *Inland Architect and News Record*, XXXV (June 1900), 14-15, illustrates Burnham's managerial ideas. Burnham's presidential addresses before the A.I.A. have been noted in Chapter VI.

Published Memoirs and Autobiographies

Of the primary sources used in this study, memoirs and autobiographies were especially helpful in reflecting the atmosphere of time and place and in furnishing contemporary evaluations of Burnham and his work. The most significant works in this category were Louis H. Sullivan, *The Autobiography of An Idea* [1924] (New York, 1956), and Harriet Monroe, *A Poet's Life, Seventy Years in a Changing World* (New York, 1938). Sullivan's work, discussed in the Introduction to the present study, reflects its author's ambivalent, but largely negative, view of Burnham and his contributions. Becoming increasingly popular as Sullivan's fame has risen in the twentieth century, the book has undoubtedly influenced its readers' image of Burnham. My own study, I hope, both confirms and challenges the validity of Sullivan's assessment. Harriet Monroe's autobiography is more sympathetic to Burnham, but it does not eschew criticism of him. In addition to providing an informed evaluation of Burnham, the book supplements the same author's earlier biography of Root in giving useful information on Burnham's life and work. Augustus St. Gaudens, *The Reminiscences of Augustus St. Gaudens*, "edited and amplified" by Homer St. Gaudens (New York, 1913), was helpful but contained less information on Burnham than one might have expected from the closeness of the relationship.

Rose Fay Thomas's edition of the *Memoirs of Theodore Thomas* (New York, 1911) furnished insights into Chicago cultural life and into the history of the Chicago orchestra. William Dean Howells' *A Traveler From Al-*

truria (New York, 1894) describes Howells' impressions and evaluation of his visit to Chicago for the World's Fair, during which time he was Burnham's personal guest. Another significant view of the Fair is provided in Hamlin Garland's *A Son of the Middle Border* (New York, 1917), but the best and most famous interpretation is Henry Adams, *The Education of Henry Adams* [1918] (Boston, 1961), which also provides relevant information on St. Gaudens. Frank Lloyd Wright's *An Autobiography* [1932] (London, 1938) asserts that Burnham offered Wright an expense-paid education at the Paris Ecole des Beaux Arts to be followed by a position in the Burnham firm, which Wright refused.

Memoirs throwing light on the atmosphere of Burnham's Chicago include Carter Harrison, *Growing Up With Chicago* (Chicago, 1944), Adeline Hibbard Gregory, *A Great-Grandmother Remembers* (Chicago, 1940), and Caroline Kirkland, *Chicago Yesterdays, A Sheaf of Reminiscences* (Chicago, 1919). Paul Starett's *Changing the Skyline* (New York, 1938) is the revealing memoir of a former draughtsman in Burnham's firm, who went on to a notable building career of his own. Useful insights into Burnham's Chicago architectural milieu are also offered in John M. Van Oesdel, *A Quarter-Century of Chicago Architecture* (Chicago, 1898), and Henry Ericsson, *Sixty Years a Builder* (Chicago, 1942). Frederic C. Howe, *The Confessions of a Reformer*, [1925] (Chicago, 1967), was good on the atmosphere of Tom Johnson's Cleveland.

Two books that give information about the Burnham family's New Church Swedenborgian connections are George C. Field, *Memoirs, Incidents, and Reminiscences of the Early History of the New Church in Michigan, Indiana, Illinois, and Adjacent States, and Canada* (Toronto, 1879), and Ednah C. Silver, *Sketches of the New Church on a Background of Civic and Social Life, Drawn From Faded Manuscripts, Printed Record, and Living Reminiscence* (Boston, 1920). Though difficult to categorize, two official reports on the World's Columbian Exposition by leading participants, have the effect of contemporary memoirs. Daniel H. Burnham, "Final Report of the Director of Works" (1894), an elaborately bound and illustrated unpublished typescript in eight large volumes is located with an index file in the library of the Chicago Art Institute. H. N. Higginbotham, *Report of the President to the Board of Directors of the World's Columbian Exposition* (Chicago, 1893), is a good summary of the entire operation.

Biographies

Biographical studies of Burnham and his contemporaries were among the most significant secondary sources. The only existing biography of Burnham is Charles Moore, *Daniel H. Burnham, Architect, Planner of Cities*, 2 vols. (Boston and New York, 1921), written as an affectionate eulogy by a friend and colleague. In some places, the book is sketchy and superficial. In others, it is heavily overloaded with *verbatim* reprintings of Burnham's letters, speeches, and diaries. Moore was not a trained historian, and his work is indeed an uneven one, but it would be ungenerous and untrue to dismiss it as unimportant. It is, in fact, a valuable source of an almost primary nature. Moore knew Burnham well. He had access to the personal recollections of other friends, relatives, and associates who are since deceased. He also used various documents that have since been lost, and, in general, he recorded and preserved vital aspects of the Burnham story that might have not otherwise survived. It is hard to imagine that, in the absence of Moore's study, someone else would not have written a biography of Burnham, but the fact remains that since 1921, Moore's book has been the "standard" Burnham biography.

Many of the shortcomings of Moore's biography of Burnham were partially remedied some eight years later in his biography of his and Burnham's friend, *Charles Follen McKim* (Boston and New York, 1929). In the McKim study, Moore increased his speculative temerity and wrote a more attractive and unified book that further delineated Burnham and his association with McKim. Harriet Monroe's *John Wellborn Root, A Study of His Life and Work* (New York, 1896) is another key document in any study of Burnham, sharing with Moore's biography the status of a contemporary primary source. Monroe's book is essential for an understanding of Burnham's early career and for his part in the Burnham and Root relationship.

The best single study of Sullivan's contribution is still Hugh Morrison, *Louis Sullivan, Prophet of Modern Architecture* (New York, 1935), especially for architectural criticism. A good short assessment is Albert Bush-Brown, *Louis Sullivan* (New York, 1960). Charles E. Russell's *The American Orchestra and Theodore Thomas* (Garden City, N.Y., 1927) supplements Thomas' memoirs. Homer St. Gaudens treats his father and deals briefly with the Burnham connection in *The American Artist and His Times* (New York, 1941). Philip Jessup's *Elihu Root* (New York, 1938) touches on Root's long interest and involvement in the improvement of Washington. Elizabeth Stevenson's *Henry Adams* (New York, 1956) is a helpful companion to Adams' *Education* in filling out the story of his complex life and associations.

Carl Lorenz, *Tom L. Johnson, Mayor of Cleveland* (New York, 1911), sheds contemporary light on Johnson, but, like Johnson's autobiography, adds little to our knowledge of the Cleveland Group Plan. There is no modern or definitive biography of Johnson. Kermit Vanderbilt's *Charles Eliot Norton, Apostle of Culture in a Democracy* (Cambridge, Mass., 1959) studies another great "Roman" American and deals with Burnham's and Norton's numerous mutual interests. Fidelis Cornelius, *Keith, Old Master of California* (New York, 1942), deals with Burnham's friendship with the San Francisco painter. Information on Burnham and many of his contemporaries also came from such collections as *The Dictionary of American Biography* (New York, 1927), *The Encyclopedia of Biography of Illinois* (Chicago, 1892), and *Biographical Dictionary and Portrait Gallery of Repre-*

sentative Men of Chicago and the World's Columbian Exposition (Chicago, 1892).

Histories of Architecture

The classic one-volume history of modern architecture is Henry Russell Hitchcock, *Architecture: Nineteenth and Twentieth Centuries* (Baltimore, 1963), which deals with Burnham (and with almost every other architect of the times) judiciously and intelligently, if sometimes briefly. Sweeping over a broader period is the equally noted interpretation of the "Modern Movement" by Siegfried Giedion, *Space, Time, and Architecture, The Growth of a New Tradition* (Cambridge, Mass., 1962). Shorter but also excellent are Jurgen Joedicke, *A History of Modern Architecture* (London, 1959), and Vincent Scully, *Modern Architecture* (New York, 1960). Hitchcock, Giedion, and Joedicke are especially good on the skyscraper contributions of Burnham and Root, and to a lesser extent of D. H. Burnham and Company. A fine, recent study is William H. Jordy, *American Buildings and Their Architects, Progressive and Academic Ideals at the Turn of the Twentieth Century* (Garden City, N.Y., 1972). Though I occasionally disagreed with their conclusions, I was also stimulated by the articles in Edgar Kaufmann, ed., *The Rise of An American Architecture* (New York, 1970).

The standard survey of the history of American art is Oliver Larkin, *Art and Life in America* (New York, 1949), which contains short, lucid sections on the architecture and city planning of the Burnham era. The best and most recent surveys of American architectural history are John Burchard and Albert Bush-Brown, *The Architecture of America: A Social and Cultural History* (Boston, 1961), and Vincent Scully, *American Architecture and Urbanism* (New York and Washington, D.C., 1969). A shorter and more popular history is Wayne Andrews, *Architecture, Ambition, and Americans* (New York, 1955). Both the Burchard and Andrews volumes concentrate on the architecture of the late nineteenth and early twentieth century. Three earlier histories are slightly dated but still useful: Lewis Mumford, *Sticks and Stones, A Study of American Architecture and Civilization* (New York, 1924), Fiske Kimball, *American Architecture* (Indianapolis, Ind., 1928), and Thomas E. Tallmadge, *The Story of Architecture in America* (New York, 1936).

Especially good for the technical and structural aspects of American architectural history are Carl W. Condit, *American Building Art, The Nineteenth Century* (New York, 1960), and *American Building Art, The Twentieth Century* (New York, 1961). For the writings of the best contemporary architectural critic, who wrote extensively about Burnham and the Chicago School, see William Jordy and Ralph Coe's edition of Montgomery Schuyler's *American Architecture and Other Writings* (New York, 1964). A landmark in American art history is Lewis Mumford's *The Brown Decades, A Study of the Arts in America, 1865-1895* [1931] (New York, 1955). Carroll L. V. Meeks, *The Railroad Station, An Architectural History* (New

Haven, 1956) brilliantly chronicles and analyzes one important architectural genre and coins the label "Burnham Baroque."

William Aiken Starrett's *Skyscrapers and the Men Who Made Them* (New York, 1928) is an early treatment of the Chicago School and its influence. More recent and definitive is Carl W. Condit, *The Chicago School of Architecture, A History of Commercial and Public Building in the Chicago Area, 1875-1925* (Chicago, 1964). My frequent citation of Condit's work indicates my debt to him. Mark L. Peisch's *The Chicago School of Architecture, Early Followers of Sullivan and Wright* (London, 1964), deals with the residential and city planning adjuncts of the Chicago School and the Prairie School in addition to the familiar story of the business buildings. Published the same year as Condit's more heralded work, Peisch's book is, of the two, more favorable to Burnham's achievement. Three other useful general treatments of Chicago architecture are John Drury, *Old Chicago Houses* (Chicago, 1942), Thomas E. Tallmadge, *Architecture in Old Chicago* (Chicago, 1941), and John H. Jones, *A Half Century of Chicago Buildings* (Chicago, 1910). A contemporary source of great importance for any history of the early Chicago School is *Industrial Chicago, The Building Interests* (Chicago, 1891). Donald Hoffmann's edition of Root's architectural writings, *The Meanings of Architecture, Buildings and Writings by John Wellborn Root* (New York, 1967), also includes photographs of the major buildings of Burnham and Root.

Histories of Urban Planning

A good, general survey of the history of town planning is Frederick Hiorns, *Town-Building in History, An Outline Review of Conditions, Influences, Ideas, and Methods Affecting Planned Towns Through Five Thousand Years* (London, 1956). Magisterial and stimulating, though somewhat uneven, is Lewis Mumford, *The City in History, Its Origins, Its Transformations, and Its Prospects* (New York, 1961). The most recent surveys of American planning are John W. Reps, *The Making of Urban America, A History of City Planning in the United States* (Princeton, 1965), and Mellier G. Scott, *American City Planning Since 1890*. Reps' text is brief, but the collection of magnificent illustrations is not. Scott's treatment of the more recent period is thorough and informative. Another helpful overview of American urban planning, especially for its intellectual and theoretical history, is the unpublished 1967 Harvard dissertation by Jon A. Peterson, "The Origins of the Comprehensive City Planning Ideal in the United States." Peterson emphasizes the role of Charles M. Robinson in the City Beautiful Movement and rather underestimates Burnham's contributions. Robinson's own policy statements and contemporary surveys were also useful: *The Improvement of Towns and Cities, or the Practical Basis of Civic Aesthetics* (New York, 1902), and *Modern Civic Art, or the City Made Beautiful* (New York, 1903). The short essay in the Braziller series, "Planning and Cities," by Francoise Choay, *The Modern City, Planning in the*

19th Century (New York, 1969), is brilliant and provocative. Two older surveys that are still useful are Christopher Tunnard and Henry Hope Reed, *American Skyline, The Growth and Form of Our Towns and Cities* (New York, 1956), and Robert Averill Walker, *Urban Planning* (Chicago, 1941). An older, illustrated documentary of the City Beautiful mentality is Werner Hegemann and Elbert Peets, *The American Vitruvius: An Architect's Handbook of Civic Art* (New York, 1922). Charles Nelson Glaab and A. Theodore Brown's *A History of Urban America* (New York, 1967), contains intelligent discussions of urban planning and the City Beautiful Movement. Jane Jacobs, *The Death and Life of Great American Cities* (New York, 1961), is a bristling and occasionally brilliant attack on the legacy of Burnham and the City Beautiful planners. Her doctrinaire stridency is countered in an equally stimulating rebuttal by Lewis Mumford: "Mother Jacobs' Home Remedies," *The New Yorker*, 38 (December 1, 1962), 148-79.

The study of specific plans and planning projects in American and modern history is an open field for research. Useful for an important influence on Burnham is Howard Saalman, *Haussmann: Paris Transformed* (New York, 1971). The best study of the World's Columbian Exposition is still the unpublished dissertation by Maurice Frank Neufield, "The Contributions of the World's Columbian Exposition to the Idea of a Planned Society in the United States" (University of Wisconsin, 1935). Written during the halcyon days of New Deal optimism, the study has a curiously dated quality that is fascinating in itself. It is, however, a useful and stimulating piece of work for a study of the great fair of the 1890s. John W. Reps, *Monumental Washington, The Planning and Development of the Capitol Center* (Princeton, 1967), is a detailed and comprehensive work, as are Mel Scott's *The San Francisco Bay Area, A Metropolis in Perspective* (Berkeley and Los Angeles, 1959) and Harold M. Mayer and Richard C. Wade, *Chicago, Growth of a Metropolis* (Chicago and London, 1969). My debts to Reps, Scott, Wade, and Mayer are acknowledged more explicitly in the Notes.

Urban and Regional Histories

While there is a paucity of specific histories of city planning, numerous, more general histories of cities and regions were helpful in throwing light upon the planning dimension. The most useful histories of Washington, besides Reps' study, were Constance McLaughlin Green, *Washington, Capital City, 1789-1950* (Princeton, 1963), and Hans Paul Caemmerer, *Washington, The Nation's Capital* (Washington, D.C., 1932). Cleveland still lacks a full and comprehensive history but the most recent and useful portrait is George E. Condon, *Cleveland, The Best Kept Secret* (Garden City, N.Y., 1967). William Ganson Rose's *Cleveland, The Making of a City* (Cleveland, 1950) is a year-by-year chronicle of the major events in the city's history. In addition to Scott's work, cited above, the most helpful study of San Francisco at the beginning of the century was Walton Bean,

Boss Ruef's San Francisco (Berkeley and Los Angeles, 1952). For the same period in the Philippines, the most useful works were David P. Barrows, *History of the Philippines* (Chicago, 1925), and W. Cameron Forbes, *The Philippine Islands* (Boston and New York, 1928).

For Chicago, the standard history is Bessie Louise Pierce, *A History of Chicago*, 3 vols. (New York, 1937-57), the last volume of which deals with the early part of Burnham's era. Ray Ginger's *Altgeld's America* (New York, 1958), is a good example of an author's complete acceptance of Sullivan's image of Burnham and the consequent dichotomizing of the forces of good and evil. One of the most helpful and suggestive essays on Burnham's Chicago could well have been included under the category of collective biography: Ernest Poole, *Giants Gone, Men Who Made Chicago* (New York, 1943), which devotes separate chapters to sketches of Burnham, Marshall Field, Theodore Thomas, and other Chicago contemporaries. A sprawling and untidy, but frequently stimulating, study is Hugh D. Duncan, *Culture and Democracy: The Struggle for Form in Society and Architecture in Chicago and the Middle West During the Life and Times of Louis H. Sullivan* (Totowa, N.J., 1965). Chicago has been the subject of numerous popular histories and historical essays, some of which are uneven in quality. From more recent to older titles, the most helpful were: Emmett Dedmon, *Fabulous Chicago* (New York, 1953), Wayne Andrews, *Battle for Chicago* (New York, 1946), Dorsha B. Hayes, *Chicago, Crossroads of American Enterprise* (New York, 1944), Edgar Lee Masters, *The Tale of Chicago* (Chicago, 1933), Paul Thomas Gilbert and Charles Lee Bryson, *Chicago and Its Makers* (Chicago, 1929), Lloyd Lewis and Henry Justin Smith, *Chicago, The History of Its Reputation* (New York, 1929), John Moses and Joseph Kirkland, eds., *The History of Chicago, Illinois* (Chicago, 1895), and A. T. Andreas, *History of Chicago* (Chicago, 1886).

Histories of Chicago institutions with which Burnham was associated are: Philo A. Otis, *The Chicago Symphony Orchestra, Its Organization, Growth, and Development, 1891-1924* (Chicago, 1925), and Randolph Williams, *The New Church in Chicago, A History* (Chicago, 1906).

Contemporary novels with Chicago settings were also helpful in suggesting the ambience of the city during Burnham's lifetime. Especially stimulating were Henry Blake Fuller's *The Cliff Dwellers* (New York, 1893) and *With the Procession* (New York, 1895), Robert Herrick's *Memoirs of An American Citizen* [1906] (Cambridge, Mass., 1963), and Theodore Dreiser's *Sister Carrie* [1900] (New York, 1959).

General Histories and Monographs

The best one-volume surveys of the period of American history that encompassed Burnham's life are works whose very titles indicate their different viewpoints and approaches: Ray Ginger, *The Age of Excess, The United States From 1877 to 1914* (New York, 1965), and Robert Wiebe, *The Search for Order, 1877-1920* (New York, 1967). A useful collection of primary documents relating to the last quarter of the nineteenth century is Sigmund Diamond, ed., *The Nation Transformed, The Creation of An Industrial Society* (New York, 1963). Three volumes in the New American Nation series were also pertinent: John A. Garraty, *The New Commonwealth, 1877-1890* (New York, 1968); Harold U. Faulkner, *Politics, Reform, and Expansion, 1890-1900* (New York, 1959); and George E. Mowry, *The Era of Theodore Roosevelt and the Birth of Modern America, 1900-1912* (New York, 1958). Continually helpful in understanding this period is John Garraty's *Interpreting American History: Conversations with Historians* (New York, 1970).

More specialized histories of specific eras and cultural movements provided important background material and suggested ideas. Larzar Ziff's *The American 1890s, Life and Times of a Lost Generation* (New York, 1966) is stimulating literary and cultural history, especially useful for his treatment of Burnham's Chicago literary contemporaries. Ziff makes the likely suggestion that Daniel Burnham was the prototype for the architect, Tom Bingham, in Fuller's novel, *With the Procession*. Also excellent on the Chicago writers is Bernard Duffey, *The Chicago Renaissance in American Letters* (Lansing, Mich., 1954). Henry May's *The End of American Innocence, A Study of the First Years of Our Own Time, 1912-1917* (Chicago, 1964) covers a broader period than the title suggests and well deserves its reputation as a classic in American cultural history. Laurence W. Veysey, *The Emergence of the American University* (Chicago, 1965), suggests the influence of commercial and industrial managerial techniques upon the structure and organization of American universities, an influence that Burnham also imbibed and applied to a large architectural office. George E. Mowry, *The California Progressives* [1951] (Chicago, 1963), provided profiles of the San Francisco Progressives who sponsored Burnham's plan for their city and suggested ideas of a broader significance in my consideration of Burnham and the Progressive Movement.

Newspapers and Serials

Contemporary newspapers and periodicals provided helpful material for the most productive period of Burnham's life (1885-1912). Because they have indexes for important portions of those years, *The New York Times* and *The Chicago Record-Herald* were especially useful. The librarians of *The Chicago Tribune* and *Chicago Daily News* also allowed me access to their private "morgue" and clipping files and, in the case of the *Tribune*, to the paper's private, incomplete index. Also of use were particular issues of *The Washington Post, The Cleveland Plain Dealer, The San Francisco Chronicle, The San Francisco Bulletin, The Boston Herald,* and *The Evanston Index,* as cited in the notes.

Contemporary professional journals consulted for the same period (ca. 1885-1912) included *The American Architect, The Architectural Review, The Brick-builder, The Craftsman,* and most important, *The Architectural*

Record and *The Inland Architect*. The most important single issue of a contemporary journal was *The Architectural Record*, 38 (July 1915), devoted to a retrospective review of Burnham's work. The notes will also show that *The Journal of the Proceedings of the American Institute of Architects* was a valuable and much consulted source for this volume. Popular periodicals for the same period that yielded the most helpful articles and information (particularly on specific city plans) were *Century*, *The Nation*, *Outlook*, and *Collier's*.

More recent professional and scholarly journals containing relevant secondary materials, as cited in the notes, included: *The Architectural Forum*, *The Prairie School Review*, *The Journal of the American Institute of Planners*, *Proceedings of the Wisconsin Academy of Sciences, Arts, and Letters*, *The American Historical Review*, *Mississippi Valley Historical Review*, *The Pacific Historical Review*, *The Pacific Northwest Quarterly*, *The Journal of Southeast Asian History*, and *The Journal of the Society of Architectural Historians*.

Notes

Introduction

1. Henry May, *The End of American Innocence, A Study of the First Years of Our Own Time, 1912-1917* (Chicago, 1964), 30-51.
2. William Howard Taft to Ernest R. Graham, published in *The Architectural Record*, XXXII (August 1912), 184.
3. Cass Gilbert, "Daniel Hudson Burnham, An Appreciation," *The Architectural Record*, XXXII (August 1912), 175-76.
4. James Bryce to Charles Moore, December 8, 1921, Burnham Papers, Chicago Art Institute Library.
5. Frank Lloyd Wright, untitled note, *The Architectural Record*, XXXII (August 1912), 184.
6. A. D. F. Hamlin, in *The American Historical Review*, XXVII (January 1922), 596.
7. Louis H. Sullivan, *The Autobiography of an Idea* (New York, 1956), 286, 288, 291-92, 314.
8. The origins of the "Make No Little Plans" motto are ambiguous and difficult to document. Burnham apparently never wrote out or delivered the piece in the exact, and now famous, sequence quoted by Charles Moore in *Daniel H. Burnham, Architect, Planner of Cities*, II (Boston, 1921), 147. Moore's version, according to Daniel Burnham, Jr., was copied from the one used by Willis Polk, Burnham's San Francisco friend and junior associate, on Christmas cards that Polk sent out in 1912, following Burnham's death the previous June. Most of the statement was drawn directly from Burnham's address at the 1910 London Town Planning Conference, "The City of the Future Under a Democratic Government," *Transactions of the Royal Institute of British Architects* (October 1910), 368-78. Since Polk ascribed the entire statement to Burnham, the additional lines were probably drawn by Polk from conversations or correspondence with Burnham that are now lost. The entire statement is consistent with and appropriate to Burnham's views and values. Its sentiments, and frequently its phrasing, are reiterated throughout his correspondence, speeches, and published writing. Numerous examples are quoted and cited throughout this book. See also Henry H. Saylor, " 'Make No Little Plans,' Daniel Burnham Thought It, But Did He Say It?" *Journal, American Institute of Architects*, 27 (March 1957), 95-99.

Chapter I

1. Daniel Burnham to James Dredge, December 28, 1891, Burnham Papers, Chicago Art Institute Library.
2. Daniel Burnham, Manuscript Memorandum, "Biography of Daniel H. Burnham of Chicago, Notes for Editor," in Charles Moore Papers, Library of Con-

gress, Washington, D.C.; Walter J. Burnham, *Burnham Family Lineage Charts* (Pittsburgh, 1966), 42; Charles Moore, *Daniel H. Burnham, Architect, Planner of Cities* (Boston, 1921), 4-6.

3. Daniel Burnham, Memorandum, Moore Papers; Clara Burnham Woodyatt, Typed Memorandum, "Mrs. Edwin Burnham (Elizabeth Keith Weeks)," in Burnham Papers; "Daniel Hudson Burnham," in *The Biographical Dictionary and Portrait Gallery of Representative Men of Chicago and the World's Columbian Exposition* (Chicago, 1892), 86; Moore, *Daniel H. Burnham*, 7, 8, 10.

4. Woodyatt, Memorandum, Burnham Papers; Daniel Burnham, Memorandum, Moore Papers.

5. C. T. Odlmer, "New Jerusalem Church," *The New Schaff-Herzog Encyclopedia of Religious Knowledge* (Grand Rapids, Mich., 1953), 140-43; Frank Sewall, "Emanuel Swedenborg," *ibid.*, XI, 183-88.

6. Woodyatt, Memorandum, Burnham Papers; George G. Field, *Memoirs, Incidents, & Remniscences of the Early History of the New Church in Michigan, Indiana, Illinois, and Adjacent States, and Canada* (Toronto, 1879), 6, 7, 9; Ednah C. Silver, *Sketches of the New Church on a Background of Civic and Social Life, Drawn from Faded Manuscripts, Printed Record, and Living Remniscence* (Boston, 1920), 153, 154, 171.

7. Field, *Memoirs*, 10, 108, 109, 114; Woodyatt, Memorandum, Burnham Papers.

8. Woodyatt, Memorandum, Burnham Papers.

9. *Ibid.*; Elizabeth Burnham to Ellen Burnham, November 26, 1848; Elizabeth Burnham to Edwin Burnham, Jr., October 3, 1853; Elizabeth Burnham to "My Dear Children," June 7, 1864, Moore Papers.

10. Daniel Burnham to Harrison Montague, December 24, 1902, Burnham Collection; Woodyatt, Memorandum, Burnham Papers; Daniel Burnham, Memorandum, Moore Papers; A. T. Andreas, *History of Chicago, From the Earliest Period to the Present Time*, III (Chicago, 1885), 546.

11. Daniel Burnham, Memorandum, Moore Papers.

12. "Alumni Who Are a Credit, Noted Alumni of the Old Central High School," *Chicago Tribune*, December 29, 1895, 26; Daniel Burnham to Mary G. Cooke, n.d., 1901, Burnham Papers. Burnham's classmates at Chicago High School included such future notables as George B. Swift, later mayor of Chicago, and Melville E. Stone, later manager of the Associated Press, as well as his life-long friend, the realtor and businessman Edward Waller. The *Tribune* article also noted that "the records of the Old Central show his [Burnham's] average scholarship to be frequently as low as 55 percent, and 81 percent seems the highest he ever reached. Even his gentlemanly ways did not save his deportment. His restlessness never allowed this marking to go above 88 percent." Chicago public records, prior to the Great Fire of 1871, particularly for such institutions as schools and churches, are virtually nonexistent. The fire is as significant to Chicago historiography as to Chicago history, since the resulting loss of records has tended to obscure important aspects of the city's early development.

13. Andreas, *History of Chicago*, II, 348-49; III, 546; Daniel Burnham, Memorandum, Moore Papers; Woodyatt, Memorandum, Burnham Papers.

14. Burnham to his father, January 21, 1866, Burnham Papers.

15. Daniel Burnham, Memorandum, Moore Papers; Daniel Burnham to Secretary, Lawrence Scientific School, Harvard, July 5, 1905, Daniel Burnham, Jr., to Charles Moore, May 27, 1920, Burnham Papers; Moore, *Daniel H. Burnham*, 14-15.

16. The quotation re: "a long childhood" at the beginning of this chapter is from

the foreword to the first edition of Erik H. Erikson, *Childhood and Society* (New York, 1963), 17. There, without further elaboration or definition, Erikson uses "childhood" in its larger generic sense. Later on in his study, especially in the section "Eight Ages of Man," he uses "childhood" in a more specific clinical context. "With the establishment of a good initial relationship to the world of skills and tools," he writes, "and with the advent of puberty, childhood proper comes to an end. Youth begins." It should be clear from my discussion above that I am using the phrase in its larger, more general context and that I intend its meaning to be suggestive rather than clinically definitive or exclusive.

17. Daniel Burnham, Memorandum, Moore Papers. A later biographical sketch of 1890 (with data apparently obtained from Burnham, himself) noted that "it was while working with Mr. Hayward and having in the house where they lived together a library of 10,000 volumes, that the love of architecture was first developed, Mr. Hayward, who was a critic of the arts, rendering much assistance as did a family friend, W. P. P. Longfellow, a nephew and ward of the poet, since Professor of architecture at M.I.T." *Inland Architect and News Record*, XVI (September 1890), 19.

18. Burnham to his mother, April 27, May 11, 1868, Burnham Papers.

19. *The Daily Inland Empire*, October 4, 1870; Daniel H. Burnham, Jr., to Charles Moore, May 4, 1920, Burnham Papers. Edward Waller had apparently become enthusiastic over the Nevada expedition with the encouragement of a "Col. Cummings," whom he had met in Chicago real estate dealings. Cummings was the nominal "leader" of the group, which also included the young architect, Gustave Laureau. Searches in Nevada archives and newspapers of the period have failed to locate any additional information on Burnham's activities in the West.

20. Daniel Burnham to John Goddard, April 1, 1901, Burnham Papers.

21. Daniel Burnham, Memorandum, Moore Papers; Peter B. Wight, "A Paper Delivered at a Meeting Held at the Art Institute, Chicago, June 11, 1912," *The Architectural Record*, XXXII (August 1912), 176, 178.

22. Daniel Burnham, Memorandum, Moore Papers.

Chapter II

1. Daniel Burnham, undated memorandum entitled "Biography of Daniel H. Burnham of Chicago, Notes for Editor," Manuscript in Burnham's handwriting, Charles Moore Papers, Library of Congress, Washington, D.C.; Alan F. Mast, unpublished memorandum on the work of Burnham and Root, submitted to the Department of Art History, University of Chicago, 1962, p. 7, copy in possession of author. Mast's compilation of Burnham and Root's completed buildings lists 216 houses, 39 office buildings, 23 railroad stations, 16 apartment buildings, 10 hotels, 9 schools, 8 churches, 7 warehouses, 5 stores, 3 hospitals, and over 20 other miscellaneous structures.

It is important to note here that while the major portion of Daniel Burnham's personal and professional papers for the period after 1890 are available for study, practically none of the official firm papers of the Burnham and Root period have survived. The student of that earlier period must therefore rely on contemporary memoirs, critical articles, and various secondary sources since that time. Since relatively few buildings remain for personal observation, one must also depend upon photographs and plans of demolished works as the basis for analysis.

2. "John W. Root," in *Encyclopedia of Biography of Illinois* (Chicago, 1892), I, 256-58; Harriet Monroe, *John Wellborn Root, A Study of His Life and Work* (Boston and New York, 1896), or facsimile edition (Park Forest, Ill., 1966).

3. Monroe, *John Wellborn Root*, 22-24; Peter B. Wight, "Daniel Hudson Burnham and His Associates," *The Architectural Record*, XXXVII (July 1915), 4.

4. Monroe, *John Wellborn Root*, 25.

5. *Ibid.*, 25-27; Daniel Burnham, undated memorandum, published in Charles Moore, *Daniel H. Burnham, Architect, Planner of Cities*, 2 vols. (Boston and New York, 1921), I, 20-21.

6. Daniel Burnham to "my dear sister" [Ellen?], June 22, 1874, Moore Papers.

7. Margaret Sherman Burnham to Daniel H. Burnham, Jr., undated conversation, February 1918, in Daniel H. Burnham, Jr., to Charles Moore, February 21, 1918, Burnham Papers, Chicago Art Institute Library.

8. To Louis Sullivan, the Sherman house "seemed far better than the average run of such structures inasmuch as it exhibited a certain allure or style indicating personality. It was the best-designed residence he had seen in Chicago." Louis H. Sullivan, *The Autobiography of an Idea* (New York, 1956), 285.

9. Margaret Burnham to Daniel Burnham, Jr., in Burnham, Jr., to Moore, cited above.

10. Burnham to Margaret Sherman, September 20, 1875, Moore Papers.

11. Margaret Burnham to Daniel Burnham, Jr., in Burnham, Jr., to Moore, cited above.

12. Burnham to Margaret Sherman, cited above; Burnham, undated memorandum, in Moore, *Daniel H. Burnham*, cited above.

13. Monroe, *John Wellborn Root*, 122.

14. *Ibid.*, 123.

15. Louis Henri Sullivan, *The Autobiography of An Idea* (New York, 1956), 287-89.

16. Monroe, *John Wellborn Root*, 122-23.

17. Sullivan, *The Autobiography of an Idea*, 314; Mast, Memorandum, 3, cited above; Historian Thomas Tallmadge noted that Burnham and Root were "the first of the highly organized and efficient architectural organizations that carried on the great building enterprises of the last generation and are carrying them on today—offices that often have two hundred or more draughtsmen and superintendents in their employ. . . ." *The Story of Architecture in America* (New York, 1927), 186; Henry-Russell Hitchcock agreed but was more skeptical as to the results: "Root's partner, Burnham," he wrote, "developed the intricate organization of the American architectural office which has made of all but a few of our later architects not individual creative artists, but factory managers. . . ." *Modern Architecture, Romanticism and Reintegration* (New York, 1929), 109.

18. Sullivan, *Autobiography of an Idea*, 291.

19. John W. Root, "A Great Architectural Problem," *Inland Architect and News Record*, XV (June 1890), 67-71; reprinted in Donald Hoffmann, ed., *The Meanings of Architecture, Buildings and Writings by John Wellborn Root* (New York, 1967), 142; "Architectural Ornamentation," *Inland Architect and Builder*, V (April 1885, extra number), 54-55, reprinted in Hoffmann, 16-21; "A Few Practical Hints on Design," quoted by Harriet Monroe, *John Wellborn Root*, 64-75, from a subsequently lost manuscript, reprinted in Hoffmann, 145;

"Broad Art Criticism," *Inland Architect and News Record*, XI (February 1888), 3-5; reprinted in Hoffmann, 28.

20. John W. Root, "The City House in the West," *Scribner's Magazine*, VIII (October 1890), 416-34; reprinted in Hoffmann, *The Meanings of Architecture*, 223-33; Oliver W. Larkin, *Art and Life in America* (New York, 1964), 290.

21. John W. Root, "A Great Architectural Problem," *Inland Architecture and News Record*, XV (June 1890), 67-71; reprinted in Hoffmann, *The Meanings of Architecture*, 132-33.

22. Root, "Style," *Inland Architect and Builder*, VIII (January 1887), 99-101 reprinted in Hoffmann, *The Meanings of Architecture*, 159-68.

23. Root, "Architects of Chicago," cited above. Reprinted in Hoffmann, *The Meanings of Architecture*, 234-38; "A Few Practical Hints on Design," cited above; reprinted in Hoffmann, 143; "Architectural Freedom," *Inland Architect and Builder*, VIII (December 1886), 64-65; reprinted in Hoffmann, 194-99.

24. Vincent J. Scully, Jr., in *The Shingle Style, Architectural Theory and Design from Richardson to the Origins of Wright* (New Haven, 1955), 88, discusses the development of American residential architecture in terms that are pertinent to the progression of Burnham and Root: "In sum, the American house had now undergone a variety of changes adapting it to American conditions, functional requirements, and materials, which separate it, as an original style, from Norman Shaw's Queen Anne. The openness and flow of its space are American. So are the sheltering void of the piazza, the lightly scaled woodwork, and the rough shingles. By 1880 the American domestic development was clearly, for the time being, at least, on its own. It had assimilated its influences and according to the necessities of its own nature passed beyond them. American architects by 1880 had nothing more to learn from Norman Shaw. Although some of them continued to build Tudor mansions complete with half-timber, the original development continued to grow in its own right. One must recognize, therefore, a mode of building, approaching maturity around 1880, which was specifically American. That it should be called American has nothing to do with chauvinistic enthusiasms or with that piety of place which has corroded some historical studies, especially of the colonial. The term signifies a sensitive adjustment of materials, techniques, and sense of space to specific and newly evaluated conditions of American living."

25. J. H. Nolan to Burnham and Root, July 12, 1883, Burnham Papers.

26. "The lighting is accomplished," the journal stated, "by about seven hundred incandescent lights, fixtures for which being brass and copper. The main dining room is 60 by 100 feet. This is lighted by two main chandeliers of twenty-four incandescent lights each, and fourteen side brackets, of three lights each line the sides. The system is that of the United States Electric Light Company. . . . The plant is operated from an engine and dynamos placed four hundred and fifty feet from the main building. . . . Each light," it marveled, "is equipped with a separate attachment to turn the light off and on." *Inland Architect and News Record*, V (April 1885), 58.

27. The Kewanee station was for the Chicago, Burlington, & Quincy R.R.; the Aberdeen station for the Kansas City, Mobile, & Birmingham R.R.

28. Montgomery Schuyler, *American Architecture and Other Writings* (New York, 1964), 91-92.

29. Monroe, *John Wellborn Root*, 45; Montgomery Schuyler, "D. H. Burnham & Company," *Architectural Record*, V (December 1895), 62-64.

30. In its present marred condition and its increasingly crowded urbanized setting, the Lake View Church has lost many of its original attributes. The shingles have been painted and the larger surrounding buildings have tended to cramp it and to make it seem much smaller and shabbier than it appears in the early photographs.

31. Schuyler, "D. H. Burnham and Company," 64-66, cited above. The *Daily News* work by Burnham and Root consisted only of a new façade for an older existing building and a new, utilitarian addition at the rear.

32. Sullivan, *Autobiography of an Idea*, 285-86.

Chapter III

1. Sigmund Diamond, "Introduction," *The Nation Transformed, The Creation of an Industrial Society* (New York, 1963), 6-8.

2. Louis H. Sullivan, *Kindergarten Chats and Other Writings* (New York, 1947), 30; John Burchard and Albert Bush-Brown have also commented perceptively on the significance of the building in *The Architecture of America, A Social and Cultural History* (Boston, 1961), 190. Richardson's work, they believe, "came to fruition in the Marshall Field Warehouse. Here was his *chef d'oeuvre* and his swan song. It suggested to his successors how they might begin to make the details of a fine city of industrial buildings. It did not propose the larger truth that a great city must be more than a collection of fine individual buildings. There is nothing to suggest that this idea ever occurred to Richardson, much less to any other architect of the period. That revelation was saved for the age of reform and for Daniel Burnham of Chicago."

3. John Moses and Joseph Kirkland, eds., *The History of Chicago, Illinois* (Chicago, 1895), 554.

4. Sigfried Giedion, *Space, Time, and Architecture, The Growth of a New Tradition* (Cambridge, Mass., 1962), 206-9; Burchard and Bush-Brown, *The Architecture of America*, 134.

5. Burchard and Bush-Brown, *The Architecture of America*, 127, 135, 215.

6. *Ibid.*, 135-36, 153-54; Louis H. Sullivan, *The Autobiography of An Idea* (New York, 1956), 311.

7. Burchard and Bush-Brown, *The Architecture of America*, 152-54.

8. Carl Condit, *The Chicago School of Architecture, A History of Commercial and Public Building in the Chicago Area, 1875-1925* (Chicago, 1964), 52-54.

9. *Ibid.*

10. *Ibid.*, 52-55.

11. Thomas E. Tallmadge, *Architecture in Old Chicago* (Chicago, 1941), 142-44. Donald Hoffmann has questioned Tallmadge's weatherproofing story, asserting his own belief that Tallmadge was thinking of the all-season work on the foundations of the Rookery in 1885-86. I have not found further empirical evidence to prove or disprove either claim.

12. *Ibid.*; Condit, *The Chicago School of Architecture*, 55-56.

13. Harriet Monroe, *John Wellborn Root, A Study of His Life and Work* (Boston and New York, 1896), 259-60.

14. Henry Ericsson, *Sixty Years a Builder, The Autobiography of Henry Ericsson* (Chicago, 1942), 48-49.

15. Thomas E. Tallmadge, *The Story of Architecture in America* (New York, 1927), 184-85.

16. Montgomery Schuyler, "D. H. Burnham and Company," *Architectural Record*, V (December 1895), 50, 53.

17. Carl Condit, *American Building Art: The Nineteenth Century* (New York, 1960), 286-87.

18. *Ibid.*, 51-55.

19. *Ibid.*

20. There are rival claims for Holabird and Roche's Tacoma Building (1888) as the first all-steel framed structure. Apparently, however, the Tacoma's frame included iron as well as steel.

21. Donald Hoffmann, "John Root's Monadnock Building," *Journal of the Society of Architectural Historians*, XXVI (December 1967), 269-77.

22. *Ibid.*; Sullivan, *The Autobiography of An Idea*, 309.

23. Peter B. Wight, untitled "Paper Delivered at a Meeting Held at the Art Institute, Chicago, June 11, 1912," in *The Architectural Record*, XXXII (August 1912), 179-80.

24. Burnham to his mother, Elizabeth Burnham, n.d., Burnham Papers, Chicago Art Institute Library; Charles Moore, *Daniel H. Burnham, Architect, Planner of Cities*, I (Boston, 1921), 94.

Chapter IV

1. Ernest Poole, *Giants Gone, Men Who Made Chicago* (New York, 1943), 185; Maurice Frank Neufeld, "The Contribution of the World's Columbian Exposition of 1893 to the Idea of a Planned Society in the United States," unpublished doctoral dissertation (University of Wisconsin, 1935), 26.

2. Richard Schickel, *The Disney Version: The Life, Times, Art, and Commerce of Walt Disney* (New York, 1968), 46.

3. Daniel H. Burnham, "The Organization of the World's Columbian Exposition," delivered before the World's Congress of Architects, Chicago, August 1, 1893. Reprinted in *Inland Architect and News Record* (August 1893), 5; *Report of the President of the Board of Directors of the World's Columbian Exposition, 1892-1893* (Chicago, 1898), 7; Daniel H. Burnham and Francis D. Millet, *World's Columbian Exposition, The Book of the Builders* (Chicago, 1894), 7.

4. Report of the President, 8-9; Charles Moore, "Lessons of the World's Fair, An Interview with the late Daniel H. Burnham," *The Architectural Record*, 33 (January 1913), 36; Rossiter Johnson, ed., *A History of the World's Columbian Exposition Held in Chicago in 1893*, I (New York, 1897), 10.

5. Burnham, "Organization of the World's Columbian Exposition," 5; Burnham to A. W. Sawyer, October 30, 1890, Burnham Papers, Chicago Art Institute Library; Ben C. Truman, *A History of the World's Fair, Being a Complete Description of the World's Columbian Exposition From Its Inception* (Chicago, 1893), 31; Charles Moore, *Daniel H. Burnham, Architect, Planner of Cities*, I (Boston and New York, 1921), 31-32; *Report of the President*, 10-11.

Neufeld's study summarizes succinctly the intricate and complex administrative framework: "From the very beginning, with two independent agencies functioning, aware of their own importance, and each insisting upon ultimate authority, friction was inevitable." The Compact of November, 1890, however, corrected this by establishing "centralized control under a Director-General, appointed by the Commission with the consent of the Corporation, who administered the work of the sixteen great Departments created by the Compact. The corresponding Committees of the Corporation were subject to the decisions of the Departments." Burnham's ultimate chain of command was through the Corporation's Committee on Works and Buildings to the commission's Department of Works and Buildings to the commission's director-general and president. Despite this administrative complexity Burnham had wide powers and flexibility in his own large area of responsibility, and was little involved with the commission's formal administrative apparatus. Neufeld, "The Contributions of the World's Columbian Exposition," 23-24.

6. *Inland Architect and News Record*, XV (April 1890), 42.

7. Burnham, "Organization of the World's Columbian Exposition," 5; Rand, McNally, and Company, *A Week at the Fair, Illustrating the Exhibits and Wonders of the World's Columbian Exposition with Special Descriptive Articles* (Chicago, 1893), 31; Moore, *Daniel H. Burnham*, I, 33-34; *Report of the President*, 19-25. Burnham to William T. Baker, August 27, 1891, Burnham Papers; Burnham and Millet, *World's Columbian Exposition, Book of the Builders*, 10, 13.

8. Burnham, "Organization of the World's Columbian Exposition," 5; Moore, "Interview with . . . Burnham," 36; Burnham and Millet, *World's Columbian Exposition, Book of the Builders*, 24.

In deference to Root's memory and to avoid unnecessary confusion, Burnham's official version of the matter was that he and Root had resigned as consulting architects with Root being reappointed to act alone in that capacity and Burnham being appointed chief of construction. In a less guarded moment, however, Burnham gave a more precise version to the editor of the St. Louis *Post Dispatch*, displaying in the process his own increased egotism. The paper had offended him by implying in an article that Root had actually organized the Fair and that upon his death, Burnham had merely taken his place.

"After my appointment" as chief of construction, Burnham wrote the editor, "I suggested that Burnham and Root be allowed to resign as consulting architects and that Mr. Root be appointed to act alone in this capacity, but the committee having charge preferred to leave the matter as it was, and Burnham and Root continued to be the official consulting architects until Mr. Root's death in January last. He did not at any time have to do with the business of organization of the World's Fair, or that of our private firm and the company did not look to him in that capacity. By his death, they lost his great services as an artist, but were not hampered otherwise. My appointment therefore, was not to his place, as insinuated by your correspondent." Burnham to editor, St. Louis *Post Dispatch*, July 2, 1891, Burnham Papers.

9. Burnham, "Organization of the World's Columbian Exposition," 5-6; Moore, "Interview with Burnham," 37-38. William John Abbott, "Makers of the Fair," *Outlook*, 48 (November 18, 1893), 884; Johnson, *A History of the World's Columbian Exposition*, 43; Moore, *Daniel H. Burnham*, I, 34; *Report of the President*, 28. Burnham and Millet, *World's Columbian Exposition, Book of the Builders*, 28.

10. Burnham, "Organization of the World's Columbian Exposition," 6; Burnham and Millet, *World's Columbian Exposition, Book of the Builders* (Chicago, 1894), 17; Neufeld, "The Influence of the World's Columbian Exposition," 25; Burnham to John T. Dickinson, August 3, 1891, Burnham Papers.

11. Burnham to E. L. Corthell, October 4, 1890, Burnham Papers; Burnham, "Organization of the World's Columbian Exposition," 5; Fiske Kimball, *American Architecture* (Indianapolis, Ind., 1928), 166.

12. Burnham, "Organization of the World's Columbian Exposition," 5; Burnham

to Abram Gottlieb, November 25, 1890,. Burnham Papers; Moore, "Interview with . . . Burnham," 38; Moore, *Daniel H. Burnham*, I, 34.

13. Harriet Monroe, *John Wellborn Root, A Study of His Life and Work* (Boston and New York, 1896), 235; Moore, "Interview with . . . Burnham," 38.

14. Burnham, "Organization of the World's Columbian Exposition," 6.

15. Idem; Moore, "Interview with . . . Burnham," 38.

16. Burnham to Richard Hunt, *et al.*, December 13, 1890, in Burnham, "Organization of the World's Columbian Exposition," 6.

17. Moore, "Interview with . . . Burnham," 38-39.

18. Moore, "Interview with . . . Burnham"; unedited manuscript notes of interview cited above in Moore Papers, Library of Congress.

19. *Ibid.*

20. *Ibid.*

21. Harriet Monroe, *A Poet's Life, Seventy Years in a Changing World* (New York, 1938), 114; Ernest Poole, *Giants Gone*, 184.

22. Burnham, "Organization of the World's Columbian Exposition," 6.

23. *Ibid.*

24. *Ibid.*

25. Burnham to Sullivan and Adler, January 10, 1891, Burnham Papers.

26. Burnham, "Organization of the World's Columbian Exposition," 7; Burnham to James Windrim, February 7, 1891, Burnham Papers.

27. Burnham to James Windrim, February 9, 1891, Burnham Papers; Moore, "Interview with . . . Burnham," 41-42.

28. Moore, Interview with . . . Burnham; unedited manuscript notes of interview cited above in Moore papers, Library of Congress.

29. Burnham to Frank Sickels, January 29, 1891, Burnham Papers; According to Burnham: "The opportunity for gaining honorable distinction, however, made the duty of choosing men for the force comparatively easy, and in a very short time after the plans were finally adopted the following were on the field of action, working with one object—the welfare of the great enterprise: Charles B. Atwood, designer-in-chief, William Pretyman, director of color, E. G. Nourse, general engineer, Frederick Sargent, electrical engineer, J. C. Slocum, mechanical engineer, Wm. S. MacHarg, sanitary and water engineer, John W. Alvord, engineer of grades and surveys, Ernest R. Graham, assistant chief of construction, Rudolph Ulrich, landscape superintendent, and Dion Geraldine, general superintendent. Later the following changes occurred: Mr. Frederick Sargent assumed entire charge of all mechanical plants, Mr. Slocum going out and Mr. R. H. Pierce becoming electrical engineer, and in March of this year Mr. Sargent withdrew, leaving Mr. Charles F. Foster in charge as mechanical engineer, where he still remains. Mr. Gottlieb, the chief engineer, withdrew in the summer of 1891 and Mr. Edward C. Shankland took his place. Mr. W. H. Holcomb has since joined the force as general manager of Transportation, Mr. Pretyman resigned in May, 1892 and Mr. Frank D. Millet took his place. Col. Edmund Rice of the United States Army assumed control of the Guard in May, 1892. Marshall Edward Murphy took charge of the entire fire department in December, 1892, taking the place of Mr. A. C. Speed, who had been in charge until then. Mr. C. D. Arnold was made official photographer. Dr. John E. Owens was made medical director. Mr. Atwood came out to join me in my private practice in the spring of 1891. The needs of the Fair were so great he assumed the place of designer-in-chief instead." Burnham, "Organization of the World's Columbian Exposition," 6.

Chapter V

1. Daniel H. Burnham and Francis D. Millet, *The World's Columbian Exposition, The Book of the Builders* (Chicago, 1894), 30; Burnham to William T. Baker, August 28, 1891, Burnham Papers, Chicago Art Institute Library; Ernest Poole, *Giants Gone, Men Who Made Chicago* (New York, 1943), 184.
2. Burnham to Abram Gottlieb, November 25, 1890, Burnham Papers.
3. Burnham to Henry Ives Cobb, February 10, 1891; September 4, 1891, Burnham Papers.
4. Burnham to Messrs. Van Brunt and Howe, February 10, 1891, Burnham Papers.
5. Burnham to Frederick Law Olmsted, January 31, 1891, February 5, 1891; Burnham to Henry Codman, February 6, 1891, July 17, 1891; Burnham to Peabody and Stearns, June 6, 1891, June 8, 1891, and June 17, 1891, Burnham Papers.
6. Burnham to Richard M. Hunt, June 24, 1891, Burnham Papers.
7. Daniel Burnham, Statement to participants in "World's Fair State Buildings," *Inland Architect and News Record*, XIX (March 1892), 25.
8. Burnham to Thomas Smith, July 24, 1891; Burnham to Richard R. Kinney, November 18, 1891, Burnham Papers.
9. Burnham to George K. Davis, July 17, 1891, Burnham Papers.
10. Burnham to Messrs. Van Meter and Permain, January 5, 1892; Burnham Papers.
11. Burnham to John W. Woodside, December 4, 1891, Burnham to Phillipson Decorator Company, September 5, 1891, Burnham Papers; c.f. John Burchard and Albert Bush-Brown, *The Architecture of America: A Social and Cultural History* (Boston, 1961), 254.
12. Burnham to Mrs. Potter Palmer, January 14, 1891; Burnham to Sophia Hayden, n.d., March 1891; Burnham, "The Organization of the World's Columbian Exposition," Paper read before the World's Congress of Architects, at Chicago, August 1, 1893, published in *Inland Architect and News Record*, XXII (August 1893), 5.
13. Harriet Monroe, *John Wellborn Root, A Study of His Life and Work* (New York, 1896); David H. Crook, "Louis Sullivan and the Golden Doorway," *Journal of the Society of Architectural Historians*, XXVI (December 1967), 250, 257; Dimitri Tselos, "The Chicago Fair and the Myth of the 'Lost Cause,'" *Journal of the Society of Architectural Historians*, XXVI (December 1967), 259-68.
14. Burnham to Adler and Sullivan, July 31, 1891, August 5, 1891; Burnham to Louis Sullivan, February 11, 1891, Burnham Papers.
15. Charles Moore, "Lessons of the Chicago World's Fair, an interview with the late Daniel H. Burnham," *Architectural Record*, XXXIII (January 1913), 43-44.
16. Burnham to all Department Heads, July 13, 1891; Burnham to Geraldine, August 7, 1891, September 26, 1891, and November 18, 1891, Burnham Papers.
17. Burnham to Gottlieb, July 16, 1891, Burnham Papers.
18. Burnham to E. G. Nourse, August 11, 1891; Burnham to William T. Baker, August 12, 1891; Burnham to Edward Shankland, January 6, 1892; Burnham to editor, *St. Louis Post-Dispatch*, July 2, 1891, Burnham Papers; Edward C. Shankland, "The Construction of the Building, Bridges, etc. at the World's Congress of Architects at Chicago, August 1, 1893," published in *Inland Architect and News Record*, XXII (August 1893), 8-9.
19. "Strikes in the Building Trades in Chicago," *Inland Architect and News Rec-*

ord, XV (April 1890), 42; "Organized Labor and the World's Fair," *Inland Architect and News Record*, XVII (June 1891), 54.

20. Burnham to Lyman J. Gage, February 14, 1891, Burnham Papers.
21. Burnham to Charles Silber, June 15, 1891; Burnham to Dion Geraldine, July 23, 1891; Burnham to C. H. Cutler, September 17, 1891.
22. Burnham to William T. Baker, September 7, 1891, January 2, 1892; Burnham to F. O. Cloyes, January 6, 1892, Burnham Papers.
23. Burnham to Dion Geraldine, February 24, 1892; Burnham to A. F. Seeberger, August 3, 1891; Burnham to Geraldine, December 11, 1891, Burnham Papers.
24. Burnham, General Order to All Department Heads, June 29, 1891; Burnham to William T. Baker, July 22, 1891; Burnham to Dion Geraldine, July 29, 1891, December 24, 1891; Burnham to W. S. MacHarg, November 21, 1891, February 5, 1892, Burnham Papers.
25. Burnham to James Dredge, November 18, 1891, November 24, 1891; Burnham to Robert McCormick, November 24, 1891; Burnham to G. F. Watts, December 23, 1891; Burnham to C. D. Arnold, July 6, 1891; Burnham to R. E. A. Dorr, August 19, 1891, Burnham Papers.
26. Burnham to Oswald Lockett, December 2, 1890; Burnham to George R. Davis, December 8, 1890, August 11 [or 12], 1891; Burnham to William T. Baker, July 29, 1891, Burnham Papers.
27. Burnham to William E. Curtis, November 13, 1891; Burnham to Colonel Edmund Rice, November 13, 1891; Burnham to William T. Baker, November 14, 1891; Burnham to John James, February 17, 1892, Burnham Papers.
28. Burnham to Thomas A. Edison, May 12, 1891; Burnham to James Dredge, January 20, 1892, Burnham Papers.
29. Burnham to LeRoy Payne, June 11, 1891; Burnham to Milton W. Kirk, November 3, 1891; Burnham to Lyman J. Gage, November 16, 1891; Burnham to Charles Fuller, January 8, 1892, Burnham Papers.
30. Burnham to George R. Davis, October 26, 1891, Burnham Papers.
31. Burnham to Alex McKimmons, November 3, 1891; Charles Moore, "Interview with Burnham," April 26, 1908, original manuscript notes in Moore Papers, Library of Congress, 9; Poole, *Giants Gone*, 142. Charles Moore, *Daniel H. Burnham, Architect, Planner of Cities*, I (Boston and New York, 1921), 56.
32. Burnham to Frederick Law Olmsted, November 20, 1891; Burnham to George R. Davis, November 25, 1891; Burnham to W. I. Buchanan, December 29, 1891; Burnham to J. W. Collins, February 27, 1892, Burnham Papers.
33. Burnham to Frederick Law Omsted, February 5, 1892, Burnham Papers.
34. Burnham to Edward F. Lawrence, July 11, 1891, Burnham Papers.
35. *Report of the President of the Board of Directors of the World's Columbian Exposition, Chicago, 1892-1893* (Chicago, 1898), 7, 160-66; Robert Craik McLean, "Dedication of the Buildings of the World's Columbian Exposition," *Inland Architect and News Record*, XXII (November 1893), 33.
36. *Report of the President*, 28-29, 186-87; Burnham to W. I. Buchanan, October 21, 1891, Burnham Papers.
37. *Report of the President*, 185-87, 200-205.
38. "In Honor of Mr. Burnham," *New York Times*, March 26, 1893, 2.
39. *Ibid*.
40. *Ibid*.
41. *Ibid*.; McKim to Burnham, February 19, 1894, McKim Papers, Library of Congress.
42. Charles Eliot Norton, remarks quoted in Moore, *Daniel H. Burnham*, I, 78-79.

43. Burnham to Charles Eliot Norton, March 30, 1893, Norton Papers, Houghton Library, Harvard University.
44. Christopher Tunnard and Henry Hope Reed, *American Skyline, The Growth and Form of our Cities and Towns* (New York, 1956), 142.
45. Burnham, "Organization of the World's Columbian Exposition," 7; Henry Ericsson, *Sixty Years a Builder, The Autobiography of Henry Ericsson* (Chicago, 1942), 240.
46. Bessie Louise Pierce, *A History of Chicago, III: The Rise of a Modern City, 1871-1893*, 3 Vols. (New York, 1957), 511; Caroline Kirkland, *Chicago Yesterdays* (Chicago, 1919), 290-91; Emmett Dedmon, *Fabulous Chicago* (New York, 1953), 229-32; Hamlin Garland, *A Son of the Middle Border* (New York, 1917), 460; Henry Adams, *The Education of Henry Adams* (Boston, 1918), 341, 343; William Dean Howells, *Letters of an Altrurian Traveller, 1893-1894* (Gainesville, Fla., 1961), 22, 25-26.
47. Olmsted to Burnham, June 20, 1893, Olmsted Papers, Library of Congress.
48. "Resignation of Director of Works Burnham," *Inland Architect and News Record*, XXII (November 1893), 33; Louis Sullivan, *The Autobiography of An Idea* (New York, 1956), 321.
49. Burchard and Bush-Brown, *American Architecture*, 237; Adams, *The Education of Henry Adams*, 341-43; Howells, *Letters of An Altrurian Traveller*, 22-26; H. D. Lloyd to Burnham, March 26, 1895, Lloyd Papers, Wisconsin State Historical Society, Madison.
50. Montgomery Schuyler, "Last Words About the World's Fair," *Architectural Record*, III (January-March 1894), 271-301; Henry Van Brunt, "Architecture at the World's Columbian Exposition," *The Century Magazine*, XLIV (May 1892), 88.
51. Sullivan, *The Autobiography of An Idea*, 321-25.

Chapter VI

1. Records of the Overseers of Harvard College, XIII, September 30, 1891, through June 27, 1900, 111-12; *Harvard Degrees and Diplomas*, II; "Sparks to Eliot, 1849-1908," 187, Harvard University Archives. In 1905, Burnham also received an honorary doctorate from the University of Illinois; Burnham to W. L. Pillsbury, November 17, 1905, Burnham Papers, Chicago Art Institute Library.
2. *Proceedings of the Twenty-Eighth Annual Convention of the American Institute of Architects, 1894* (Providence, R.I., 1895), 8-10, 62.
3. *Proceedings of the Twenty-Fifth Annual Convention of the American Institute of Architects, 1891* (Chicago, 1892), 23-29.
4. *Ibid.*; "The Tarsney Act," *The Inland Architect and News Record*, XXX (August 1897), 4.
5. *Proceedings of the Twenty-Eighth Annual Convention of the American Institute of Architects*, 11.
6. Burnham to John G. Carlisle, February 14, 1894, Jeremiah O'Rourke to Alfred Stone, November 11, 1893, reprinted in *American Architect and Building News*, XLIV (April 7, 1894), 9.
7. Burnham to Carlisle, January 9, 1894, February 14, 1894, in *American Architect*, as cited, 10.
8. Burnham to Carlisle, February 14, 1894; O'Rourke to Stone, January 17, 1894, in *American Architect*, as cited, 10.

9. Burnham to Carlisle, February 14, 1894; Stone to O'Rourke, January 19, 1894; H. W. Van Senden to Burnham, February 6, 1894; Burnham to O'Rourke, February 9, 1894; in *American Architect*, as cited, 10.

10. Burnham to Carlisle, February 14, 1894, *American Architect*, as cited, 10-11.

11. Carlisle to Burnham, March 6, 1894; *American Architect*, as cited, 11.

12. Burnham to Carlisle, March 9, 1894, in *American Architect*, as cited, 11-12.

13. *Ibid.*; Carlisle to Burnham, March 12, 1894, in *American Architect*, as cited, 11-12.

14. "Compliments for Mr. Carlisle," *New York Times*, March 18, 1894, 1; McKim to Burnham, May 9, 1894, McKim Papers, Library of Congress.

15. "Mr. Carlisle and the Architects," *New York Times*, March 19, 1894, 4; *Inland Architect and News Record*, XXIII (April 1894), 26.

16. *New York Sun*, quoted in *American Architect and Building News*, XLIV (April 28, 1894), 37.

17. *Proceedings of the Twenty-Ninth Annual Convention, American Institute of Architects* (Providence, R.I., 1895), 9; *Proceedings of the Thirtieth Annual Convention, American Institute of Architects* (Providence, R.I., 1896), 28-41.

18. *Ibid.*; "Why the McKaig Bill Did Not Pass," *The Inland Architect and News Record*, XXV (March 1895), 13; "Secretary Gage and the Supervising Architect's Office," *The Inland Architect and News Record*, XXIX (March 1897), 11; "The Supervising Architect's Office Reorganized," "Regulations for the Enforcement of the Tarsney Act," *The Inland Architect and News Record*, XXX (August 1897), 3, 4.

19. Daniel H. Burnham, Diary, Burnham Papers, *passim*; Burnham to Thomas Rodd, August 29, 1902, Burnham Papers.

20. Burnham, Diary, May 7, November 4, 1898; December 29, 1897; January 7, 1899; January 24, 1901; May 9, August 18, 1899; December 27, 1900; May 2, 1901; October 13, 1897; July 4, 1900; June 9, 1897; January 20, 1901; February 10, 1900; May 7, 10, 1899; October 9, 1896; January 6, 1899, Burnham Papers.

21. Burnham, Diary, March 10, November 13, 1897; October 29, 1899; January 31, 1897; July 21, 30, 1896; July 10, 1898; July 1, 1900; August 29-September 6, 1896; August 1, 9, 16, 23, 1896; July 11, 1899, Burnham Papers.

22. *Ibid.*, February 4, 7, 8, 9, 1896.

23. *Ibid.*, February 11-February 23, 1896.

24. *Ibid.*, February 26-March 12, 1896.

25. *Ibid.*, March 14-March 24, 1896.

26. *Ibid.*, February 27, 1899; Burnham to William N. Sturgis, January 29, 1894, Burnham Papers.

Chapter VII

1. Charles Moore, "The Improvement of Washington City," *Century Magazine*, 63 (February 1902), 621-23; Christopher Tunnard and Henry Hope Reed, *American Skyline, The Growth and Form of Our Cities and Towns* (New York, 1956), 145-46; Henry James, *The American Scene* (Bloomington and London, 1968), 332-64. See also Mellier G. Scott, *American City Planning Since 1890* (Berkeley and Los Angeles, 1969), 31-57, and John W. Reps, *Monumental Washington, The Planning and Development of the Capitol Center* (Princeton, N.J., 1967), 26-29. Reps' volume is a thorough and scholarly study of the commission's work within the broader context of the entire

history of the capital city. My intention here is not to duplicate his highly detailed factual account but to focus on Burnham's part in the story within the context of his own life, largely as revealed in his personal papers.

2. Tunnard and Reed, *American Skyline*, 136; Constance McLaughlin Green, *Washington, Capital City, 1879-1950* (Princeton, N.J., 1963), 133; Scott, *American City Planning Since 1890*, 43-46.

3. Hans Paul Caemmerer, *Washington, The Nation's Capital* (Washington, D.C., 1932), 73; c.f. Reps, *Monumental Washington*, 70-93.

4. Caemmerer, *Washington*, 75; *The Improvement of the Park System of the District of Columbia*, Fifty-Seventh Congress, First Session, Senate Report No. 166, 1902, 7-10; c.f. Reps, *Monumental Washington*, 92-154.

5. Caemmerer, *Washington*, 74-75; Charles Moore, *Daniel H. Burnham, Architect, Planner of Cities*, I (Boston and New York, 1921), 135-40; 147-49; *Improvement of the Park System*, 13. Burnham to William H. Brown, October 7, 1901; Burnham to Charles Moore, August 24, 1901, Burnham Papers.

6. Charles Moore, *The Life and Times of Charles Follen McKim* (Boston, 1929), 182, 188.

7. Burnham to Frederick Law Olmsted, Jr., April 15, 1901, Burnham Papers.

8. Burnham, Diary, March 21, 22, 23, April 5, 6, 8, 19, May 1, 14, 17, 18, 19, 1901; Burnham to Lyman J. Gage, April 10, 1901; Burnham to Charles Moore, May 27, 1901, Burnham Papers.

9. Charles McKim to Wendell P. Garrison, April 10, 1901, in Moore, *The Life and Times of Charles Follen McKim*, 185; Burnham to R. A. C. Smith, April 10, 1901; Burnham to Lyman J. Gage, April 10, 1901; Burnham to Albert Wells, April 10, 1901, Burnham Papers.

10. Burnham to Frederick Law Olmsted, Jr., March 29, 1901, April 10, 1901; Burnham to Albert Wells, April 10, 1901; Burnham to Lyman J. Gage, April 10, 1901; Burnham to Charles Moore, May 27, 1901, Burnham Papers. Burnham to Charles McKim, April 10, 1901, in Moore, *Daniel H. Burnham*, I, 143; *Improvement of the Park System*, 15.

11. Burnham, Diary, April 19-24, 1901, Burnham Papers.

12. Burnham to Frederick Law Olmsted, Jr., March 29, April 10, 1901; Burnham to Albert Wells, April 10, 1901; Burnham to Charles Moore, May 27, 1901, Burnham Papers.

13. Moore, *The Life and Times of Charles Follen McKim*, 187; Burnham, Diary, June 13-June 21, 1901, Burnham Papers.

14. Burnham, Diary, June 21-June 30, 1901, Burnham Papers; Moore, *The Life and Times of Charles Follen McKim*, 190-91, 193; Moore, *Daniel H. Burnham*, I, 150.

15. Burnham, Diary, July 1-July 14, 1901, Burnham Papers; Moore, *The Life and Times of Charles Follen McKim*, 196.

16. Burnham, Diary, July 15-August 1, 1901.

17. Burnham to Augustus St. Gaudens, August 5, 1901, Burnham Papers; Moore, *Daniel H. Burnham*, I, 156; Moore, *The Life and Times of Charles Follen McKim*, 192; Scott, *American City Planning Since 1890*, 51-52; Burnham to Margaret S. Burnham, July 18, 1901, Burnham Papers.

18. Burnham to Charles Pugh, May 28, 1901; Burnham to Charles Moore, n.d., August 1901; August 23, 1901; Burnham to Frederick Law Olmsted, Jr., October 3, 1901, Burnham Papers; Senator James M. McMillan to Charles Moore, September 30, 1901, Charles Moore Papers, Library of Congress; Glenn Brown, "Personal Reminiscences of Charles Follen McKim; McKim and the Park Com-

mission," *The Architectural Record*, 38 (December 1915), 683; Green, *Washington*, 133; Charles Zueblin, *American Municipal Progress* (New York, 1916), 14-15; Tunnard and Reed, *American Skyline*, 150.

19. Burnham, Diary, July 18, 1901, Burnham Papers; Moore, *Daniel H. Burnham*, I, 155.

20. Moore, *Daniel H. Burnham*, I, 155; Green, *Washington*, 137; Thomas E. Tallmadge, *The Story of Architecture in America* (New York, 1927), 248-49.

21. Moore, *Daniel H. Burnham*, I, 158.

22. *Ibid.*, 166; Burnham to Charles F. Weller, August, n.d., 1901; Burnham to Charles McKim, August 3, 1901; Burnham to Charles Moore, August 23, 1901; Burnham to William T. Partridge, September 9, 1901; Burnham to Frederick Law Olmsted, Jr., September 9, 1901, October 15, 1901, Burnham Papers; Burnham's Diary noted August 16, 19, 20, September 15, 23, 26, 27, 28, 29, October 18, 19, 20, 21, 22, 23-26, December 3, 4-6 as days that Burnham spent in the east conferring with his colleagues; Reps, *Monumental Washington*, 99-107. I disagree with Reps' emphasis on McKim as the leading figure in the Washington project. He apparently drew this impression partly from Glenn Brown's account of the story, which had the same emphasis. I also disagree with Reps' conclusion that Olmsted and Moore wrote the report almost alone. Its ideas, I believe, were truly a joint effort similar to the pooling of ideas for the Columbian Exposition of Burnham, Root, Codman, and Olmstead. Burnham's diaries and letters indicate that he contributed substantially to the rough written draft of the report. In 1911, Burnham wrote: "I was chairman of the Washington Commission, and everything there was under my direction" (Burnham to H. A. Horwood, February 27, 1911, Burnham Papers).

23. Burnham to Charles Moore, August 23, 1901, Burnham Papers; Reps, *Monumental Washington*, 103-4.

24. Burnham to Charles Moore, August 30, 1901, February 1, 1902, February 10, 1902, Burnham Papers.

25. Burnham to Charles Moore, February 1, 1902, February 10, 1902, Burnham Papers; *Improvement of the Park System*, 58.

26. Robert W. Wrigley, "Daniel H. Burnham, Architect and City Planner," *Journal of the American Institute of Planners*, 35 (March 1961), 70-71; Moore, "The Improvement of Washington City," 623, 625-28; Daniel H. Burnham, "White City and Capital City," *Century Magazine*, 63 (February 1902), 20; Moore, *Daniel H. Burnham*, I, 168-70; Green, *Washington*, 135; *Improvement of the Park System, passim*.

27. *Improvement of the Park System*, 43-45; Green, *Washington*, 135-36; Moore, *Daniel H. Burnham*, I, 169.

28. *Improvement of the Park System*, 49-50; Green, *Washington*, 136; Moore, *Daniel H. Burnham*, I, 169.

29. Burnham, Diary, January 15, March 10, 1902, Burnham Papers; Moore, *Daniel H. Burnham*, I, 166-69; Green, *Washington*, 133; Burnham, "White City and Capital City," *Century Magazine*, 63 (February 1902), 20.

30. Reps, *Monumental Washington*, 139-54; Hans Paul Caemmerer, *The Life of Pierre Charles L'Enfant, Planner of the City Beautiful, The City of Washington* (Washington, D.C., 1950), 325; Philip Jessup, *Elihu Root*, I (New York, 1938), 279-80.

31. Green, *Washington*, 137-39.

32. *Ibid.*, 141-42; Moore, *Daniel H. Burnham*, I, 205-29.

33. Green, *Washington*, 141-42; c.f. Reps, *Monumental Washington*, 155-98.

34. John Burchard and Albert Bush-Brown, *The Architecture of America: A Social and Cultural History* (Boston, 1961), 275; *Improvement of the Park System*, 19.

Chapter VIII

1. Tom L. Johnson, *My Story* (New York, 1911), *passim*; Carl Lorenz, *Tom L. Johnson* (New York, 1911), *passim*; Edward W. Bemis, "Tom L. Johnson's Achievements As Mayor of Cleveland," *Review of Reviews*, XLIII (May 1911), 558-60; Frederick C. Howe, *The Confessions of a Reformer*, [1925] (Chicago, 1967), *passim*; Frederick C. Howe, "Cleveland, A City 'Finding Itself,'" *World's Work*, VI (October 1903), 3988-99; Charles N. Glaab and A. Theodore Brown, *A History of Urban America* (New York, 1967), 214-15; Hoyt Landon Warner, *Progressivism in Ohio, 1897-1917* (Columbus, Ohio, 1964), 75, 84-85; the Hanna and Steffens quotations are from Lincoln Steffens, *The Struggle for Self-Government* (New York, 1906), 183; the Howe quotation from *The Confession of a Reformer*, at the beginning of this chapter is from page 113 of the cited edition.
2. *Ibid.*
3. Howe, *The Confessions of a Reformer*, 80-81; Frank S. Barnum, "Architecture," in Samuel P. Orth, ed., *A History of Cleveland* (Chicago and Cleveland, 1910), 474; William Ganson Rose, *Cleveland, Making of a City* (Cleveland, 1950), 559; George E. Condon, *Cleveland, The Best Kept Secret* (Garden City, N.Y., 1967), 190, 351-53.
4. *Ibid.*
5. Herbert B. Briggs, "Municipal Improvement, Cleveland," *The Inland Architect and News Record*, XXXIV (August 1899), 4-5.
6. Daniel H. Burnham, Diary, July 15, 1902; Burnham to Edward A. Roberts, February 10, 1903, Burnham Papers; John M. Carrère, Untitled Remarks before the Thirty-Seventh Annual Convention, American Institute of Architects, October 15, 16, 17, 1903, in A.I.A. *Journal of Proceedings* (Washington, D.C., 1904), 111; Rose, *Cleveland, The Making of a City*, 629; Charles Moore, *Daniel H. Burnham, Architect, Planner of Cities*, I (Boston and New York, 1921), 182-83.
7. Burnham, Diary, July 24, November 20, 1902, January 16, 17, February 5, 20, 21, June 27, July 1, August 17, 18, December 12, 1903; Arnold Brunner, "Cleveland's Group Plan," *Proceedings of the Eighth National Conference on City Planning*, June 5-7, 1916 (New York, 1916), 15; Burnham to Edward Roberts, February 10, 1903, Burnham Papers, Chicago Art Institute Library.
8. Burnham, Diary, July 24, November 20, 1902; January 16, 17, February 5, 20, 21, June 27, July 1, August 17, 18, December 12, 1903; Arnold Brunner, "Cleveland's Group Plan," *Proceedings of the Eighth National Conference on City Planning*, June 5-7, 1916 (New York, 1916), 15; Burnham to John M. Carrère, December 19, 1902, Burnham Papers; *Cleveland Plain Dealer*, August 16, 1902, 10.
9. Burnham to Edward Roberts, July 14, August 21, 1903, Burnham Papers.
10. Arnold Brunner to Charles Moore, n.d., in Moore, *Daniel H. Burnham*, I, 202; *Cleveland Plain Dealer*, January 18, 1903, 4; February 5, 1903, 10; June 7, 1903, 9.
11. Brunner, "Cleveland's Group Plan," 19; Condon, *Cleveland, the Best Kept Secret*, 351-52; Daniel H. Burnham, John M. Carrère, and Arnold Brunner,

"The Grouping of Public Buildings at Cleveland," *The Inland Architect and News Record*, XLII (September 1903), 13-15. The official *Report on a Group Plan of the Public Buildings of Cleveland* was originally published in 1903. A second edition appeared in 1907. Because they are rare and difficult to obtain, the version copied in *The Inland Architect* is cited for the convenience of the reader.

12. *Ibid.; Cleveland Plain Dealer*, August 16, 1902, 10.
13. Brunner, "Cleveland's Group Plan," as cited, 15-16; Burnham, Carrère, and Brunner, "The Grouping of Public Buildings at Cleveland," as cited, 14.
14. Brunner, "Cleveland's Group Plan," as cited, 16.
15. Burnham, Carrère, and Brunner, "The Grouping of Public Buildings at Cleveland," as cited, 13-14.
16. *Ibid.*
17. Brunner to Moore, n.d. in Moore, *Daniel H. Burnham*, I, 202-4. The complicated story of how and why the site of the station was changed is discussed in detail in Condon, *Cleveland, The Best Kept Secret*, 189-92.
18. Burnham, Carrère, and Brunner, "The Grouping of Public Buildings at Cleveland," as cited, 15.
19. *Ibid.*
20. Carrère, Untitled remarks before . . . the A.I.A., as cited, 116; Unsigned editorial introduction to "The Grouping of Public Buildings at Cleveland," *The Inland Architect and News Record*, XLII (September 1903), 13; cf. *Cleveland Plain Dealer*, August 18, 1903, 14; August 20, 1903, 4; September 16, 1903, 1; September 20, 1903, 5; October 18, 1903, Part III, 7.
21. Brunner, "Cleveland's Group Plan," as cited, 19-20; Burnham, Diary, December 12, 1903; March 21, 1904; April 7, June 22, 23, 1905; May 7, 1906, July 30, 1907, Burnham Papers. Upon Burnham's death in 1912, he was succeeded on the commission by Frederick Law Olmsted, Jr. The influence of the Group Plan and the commission's aesthetic canon was especially notable in the later design of the art gallery and symphonic hall located in the park and university district on Euclid Avenue several miles east of the civic center.
22. Burnham to Tom L. Johnson, November 7, 1907, Burnham Papers.
23. Brunner, "Cleveland's Group Plan," as cited, 20.
24. Rose, *Cleveland, the Making of a City*, 700, 705; Burnham to Edward A. Roberts, July 18, 1911, Burnham Papers.
25. P. Abercrombie, "Cleveland, A Civic Centre Project," *The Town Planning Review*, II (April 1911), 131; Herbert Croly, "The United States Post Office, Custom House, and Court House, Cleveland, Ohio," *The Architectural Record*, XXIX (March 1911), 196.

Chapter IX

1. Herbert Croly, "The Promised City of San Francisco," *The Architectural Record*, XIX (June 1906), 425-30. Though published shortly after the earthquake and fire, Croly's article was written earlier in the spring. He appended a postscript, however, after the fire, stating that he was not changing the piece because he believed it was "as true under the new conditions as it was under the old."
2. *Ibid.*, 425, 427.
3. Mellier G. Scott, *The San Francisco Bay Area, A Metropolis in Perspective* (Berkeley and Los Angeles, 1959), 71-96, *passim*. I am particularly indebted

to Scott's excellent and detailed study of the growth of the bay area cities for much of the San Francisco background material.

4. *Ibid.*, 98-99; George E. Mowry, *The California Progressives* (Chicago, 1963 [1951], 23-28).

5. Mowry, *The California Progressives*, 86-104, *passim*; Samuel P. Hays, "The Politics of Reform in Municipal Government in the Progressive Era," *Pacific Northwest Quarterly* (October 1964), 157-69; c.f. Scott, *The San Francisco Bay Area*, 98-99.

6. *San Francisco Bulletin*, January 4, 1904; c.f. Scott, *The San Francisco Bay Area*, 95-97.

7. *San Francisco Bulletin*, January 4, 1904; c.f. Scott, *The San Francisco Bay Area*, 97-98.

8. *San Francisco Bulletin*, January 7, 1904, quoted in Scott, *San Francisco Bay Area*, 98.

9. Daniel H. Burnham to Willis Polk, October 27, November 21, 1903, in Burnham Papers, Chicago Art Institute Library.

10. Burnham to Polk, November 12, 1903, in Burnham Papers.

11. Scott, *The San Francisco Bay Area*, 98-99.

12. *Ibid.*; *San Francisco Chronicle*, January 16, 1904, p. 16; Excerpt from "Preface" in Daniel H. Burnham *Report on a Plan for San Francisco* (San Francisco, 1905), 7.

13. Burnham, Diary, May 1-17, 1904; *San Francisco Chronicle*, May 7, 1904, p. 9; c.f. Scott, *The San Francisco Bay Area*, 99.

14. *San Francisco Chronicle*, May 9, 1904, p. 6; c.f. Scott, *The San Francisco Bay Area*, 100.

15. Burnham to Willis Polk, September 1, 1904, Burnham Papers.

16. Interviews with Edward Bennett, Jr., Chicago, August 1968; Charles Moore, *Daniel H. Burnham, Architect, Planner of Cities*, II (Boston, 1921), 57; Burnham to Henry Schott, July 6, 1905, Burnham Papers.

17. Burnham to William G. Harrison, September 15, 1905, Burnham Papers.

18. Burnham, *Report on a Plan for San Francisco*, 35.

19. *Ibid.*, 67, 53.

20. Croly, "The Promised City of San Francisco," 430-31.

21. *Ibid.*, 431.

22. *Ibid.*

23. *Ibid.*, 434.

24. *Ibid.*

25. Burnham, *Report on a Plan for San Francisco*, 43-44; Scott, *The San Francisco Bay Area*, 104.

26. Burnham, *Report on a Plan for San Francisco*, 43, 180-84. It took San Franciscans over fifty years to implement Burnham's subway proposals, as work on the system began only in the 1960s.

27. Burnham did not cite Haussmann in the San Francisco report, but he did cite the work of Eugene Henard (p. 39), an important planning theorist of the Haussmann tradition. Henard's and Haussmann's work is placed in the larger context of nineteenth-century planning in the brilliant essay by Francoise Choay, *The Modern City: Planning in the 19th Century* (New York, 1969).

28. *San Francisco Chronicle*, September 28, 1905, p. 9. Thomas M'Caleb to Burnham, September 30, 1905, Burnham Papers.

29. Burnham to Edward Bennett, November 8, 1905, Burnham Papers.

30. Scott, *The San Francisco Bay Area*, 107.

31. *Ibid.*, 108-12; Burnham to Joseph Worcester, October 24, May 9, 1906, Burnham Papers.

32. Walton Bean, *Boss Ruef's San Francisco* (Berkeley and Los Angeles, 1952), 124-27.

33. *Chicago Record-Herald*, April 28, 1906, p. 5; Burnham, Diary, April 28, 1906; Burnham to Theodore C. Link, April 27, 1906; Burnham to Philip Sawyer, May 3, 1906, Burnham Papers.

34. Burnham to Eugene E. Schmitz, May, n.d. 1906, Burnham Papers.

35. Scott, *The San Francisco Bay Area*, 113-15. In addition to the big things, however, Burnham was also greatly concerned with details. "I take great pleasure," he wrote an inquiring housewife, in saying that "the 'window box' is one of the things that makes for goodness. It was urged upon the house-holders of San Francisco in addition to cultivation of flowers and shrubs in the front and back yards of all residences. The influence of this sort of thing is far reaching. It means thought and taste in the family life, and furthermore, a recognition of relationship to one's neighbors, in what should be a constant endeavor to make our common life lovely" (Burnham to Mrs. James H. Warner, n.d., 1907, Burnham Papers).

36. *Ibid.*, 116-17. Senator Francis B. Newlands to Burnham, July 12, 1906, Scrapbook Two, p. 64. Though Newlands was actually a senator from Nevada, he had vast commercial and personal interests in San Francisco. He was, in effect, California's "third Senator."

37. Burnham to Francis B. Newlands, n.d., July 1906. Burnham to Willis Polk, July 25, 1906, Burnham Papers.

38. Schmitz to Burnham, August 8, 1906, Scrapbook Two, p. 70, Burnham Papers. I disagree, of course, with Scott's assertion in *The San Francisco Bay Area* (p. 117) that when Newlands and Phelan asked Mayor Schmitz to support the new offer, he refused, because ". . . the mayor and his sworn political enemies, Phelan and Spreckels, could no longer maintain the pretense of collaborating in civic affairs. The hour of crisis—of civic prostration and acute human suffering—was over. . . . Under the circumstances it is not surprising that Burnham was not invited to head a new municipal commission [and] that no further thought was given to such a body. . . ." Apparently Scott did not have access to the Schmitz-Burnham correspondence discussed above.

39. Burnham to Schmitz, August 18, 1906, Scrapbook Two, p. 70, Burnham Papers.

40. James D. Phelan to Charles Moore, February 26, 1918, Moore Collection, Library of Congress; Scott, *The San Francisco Bay Area*, 104, 115-22, 154-60.

41. I am aware of the imprecision of the term "Victorian" in discussing a wide variety of late nineteenth century styles. I use it for convenience and because it evokes a generally consistent public image. There was, in San Francisco, a rich variety of nineteenth-century styles, both before and after the fire, ranging from the older revivals of exotic modes to newer, starker, incipiently "modern" forms. The spectrum ran, for example, in both original and rebuilt structures, from the "Second Empire" and "High Victorian Gothic" to the "Shingle Style" and "Craftsman" modes.

42. Croly, "The Promised City of San Francisco," 427, 430.

Chapter X

1. Robert M. Spector, "W. Cameron Forbes, A Study in Proconsular Power," *Journal, Southeast Asian History*, VII (September 1966), 74-75; Daniel H.

Burnham to W. Cameron Forbes, February 24, 1904, Forbes Papers, Houghton Library, Harvard University. I am grateful to Mr. David Forbes, Miss Carolyn Jakeman, and the Houghton Library for permission to use and quote from Forbes' papers. The quotation from "The Pro-Consuls," one of Burnham's favorite poems, is from *Rudyard Kipling's Verse* (New York, 1940), 108.

2. Burnham to Theodore Roosevelt, August 1, 1902; Burnham to Forbes, January 7, 1903, Forbes Papers.

3. Forbes to Burnham, February 17, 1904; Burnham to Forbes, February 24, 1904, Forbes Papers.

4. Forbes to Olmsted, March 11, 1904; Forbes to William Howard Taft, March 11, March 25, 1904; Forbes to Charles McKim, April 1. 1904, Forbes Papers.

5. Forbes to Burnham, April 1, 8, 1904; Forbes to Taft, April 6, 18, 1904, Forbes Papers.

6. Forbes to Taft, May 18, 1904; Forbes to Burnham, May 27, 1904, Forbes Papers.

7. Spector, "W. Cameron Forbes," as cited; Forbes to Burnham, September 1, 1905, May 28, 1906, October 10, 1907; Burnham to Forbes, June 9, September 23, 1905, Forbes Papers; David P. Barrows, *History of the Philippines* (Chicago and Yonkers-on-Hudson, New York, 1925), 267. Burnham was aware of the development of Simla as the British colonial summer capital in India. In part, he considered his work in the Philippines an American version of earlier British colonial examples.

8. Burnham, Diary, July 30, 1905, Burnham Papers, Chicago Art Institute Library; Daniel H. Burnham and Edward Bennett, *Plan of Chicago* (Chicago, 1909), 29.

9. Burnham to Charles McKim, September 14, 1904, reprinted in Charles Moore, *Daniel H. Burnham, Planner of Cities*, I (Boston and New York, 1921), 233.

10. Burnham to Henry C. Frick, August 8, 1904; Burnham to Richard W. Gilder, September 12, 1904, Burnham Papers; Forbes to Burnham, April 8, 1904, Forbes Papers. Burnham selected his junior partner, Anderson, for the trip because he felt the senior partner, Ernest Graham, should remain and run the office in his absence.

11. Burnham, Diary, October 13, 16, 19, 30, 31, 1904; November 2, 3, 7, 9, 11, 19, 23, 24, 27, 1904; December 1, 3, 1904, as reprinted in Moore, *Daniel H. Burnham*, I, 237-38. Burnham's travel diary for the 1904-5 trip to the Orient has apparently been lost since Moore had access to it and published much of it (ca. 1920). The original was not included in the collection of diaries and papers that the Burnham family later presented to the Chicago Art Institute.

12. Burnham, Diary, December 7, 8, 9, 11, 14, 18, 19, 20, 21, 22, 25, 30, 31, 1904; January 2, 5, 6, 8, 11, 12, 16, 1905, in Moore, *Daniel H. Burnham*, I, 238-41.

13. Burnham, Diary, January 16, 17, 18, 1905, in Moore, *Daniel H. Burnham*, I, 241-42.

14. Burnham, Diary, January 20, 21, 22, 24, 26, 27, 28, 29, 30, 31, February 2, 4, 6, 13, 19, 1905, in Moore, *Daniel H. Burnham*, I, 241-43.

15. Burnham to Charles Moore, March 13, 1905, in Moore, *Daniel H. Burnham*, I, 245; Burnham, Diary, September 14, 1906; Burnham to J. G. White, April 10, 1905, in Burnham Papers.

16. Burnham prefaced the plan with a concise statement of objectives: "(1) development of waterfront and location of parks and parkways so as to give proper means of recreation to every quarter of the city; (2) a street system securing

direct and easy communication from every part of the city to every other part; (3) location of building sites for various activities; (4) development of water-ways for transportation; (5) summer resorts." Daniel H. Burnham, "Report on Proposed Improvements at Manila," printed in *Proceedings of the Thirty-Ninth Annual Convention of the American Institute of Architects* (Washington, D.C., 1906), 135-51. Original copies of the official typescript report are in the Burnham Papers, Chicago Art Institute Library, and in the possession of the author. The printed source is noted for the convenience of the reader.

17. *Ibid.*, 136.
18. *Ibid.*
19. *Ibid.*, 137, 139, 140.
20. *Ibid.*, 141-42.
21. *Ibid.*, 148-49.
22. *Ibid.*, 151.
23. Daniel H. Burnham, "Report of the Proposed Plan of the City of Baguio, Province of Benguet, P. I." in A.I.A. *Proceedings*, as cited above, 151-56.
24. *Ibid.*, 152.
25. *Ibid.*, 152, 156; Burnham, "Report on Proposed Improvements at Manila," 151.
26. Burnham to War Department, Bureau of Insular Affairs, July 31, 1905; Burnham to Taft, October 6, 1905, Burnham Papers; Taft to Burnham, October 13, 1905, in Charles Moore Papers; *The Inland Architect and News Record*, XLIV (October 1904).
27. Burnham to Forbes, June 27, August 7, 1905; Pierce Anderson to William E. Parsons, Burnham Papers; William E. Parsons, "Burnham as a Pioneer in City Planning," *The Architectural Record*, XXXVIII (July 1915), 17-25; Moore, *Daniel H. Burnham*, II, 178.
28. Parsons, "Burnham as a Pioneer in City Planning," 17; A. N. Rebori, "The Work of William E. Parsons in the Philippine Islands," *Architectural Record* XLI (April 1917), 305-24 (May 1917), 423-34.
29. Writing of Manila in 1928, Forbes stated that Burnham's plans had been "in the main adhered to. The central park feature was immediately undertaken, and those improvements are already complete and a blessing to the inhabitants not only of the city, but of all the Islands. . . . Mr. Burnham's great conception called for a park area of nearly thirty acres, which was laid out upon a new area reclaimed from the harbor by the construction of breakwaters filled in by dredging an additional section of the harbor. To this new land was moved the new Luneta or park, where the evening band concerts were held and the population gathered for their evening stroll. A park was constructed in the centre of this so-called Luneta Extension to which the government gave the appropriate name of Burnham Park, and upon which a decorated flag pole has been erected in Mr. Burnham's memory. There was abundant room for beautiful playgrounds, and this new area was flanked on either side by impressive semi-public buildings."

Forbes was also enthusiastic over Baguio. Within ten years of its inception, the few original houses had "multiplied to several hundred buildings and the population of the city had increased with each season. The movement of the government to Baguio stimulated its growth very gently. Each year a slightly more ambitious programme was undertaken. Following the construction of the government centre, which was economically built of temporary materials around an open park or plaza, space was reserved for later construction of a permanent

group of government buildings to be built on a larger scale around the temporary central group. There were not lacking thoughtful Filipinos who felt, as did
General Aguinaldo, that Baguio ought ultimately to be the permanent capital
of the islands. A line down the main axis laid out by Mr. Burnham was cleared
through the pines, the hills terraced, and an artificial lake constructed in the
central valley. The park around the lake has been appropriately named for Mr.
Burnham. Buildings and stores sprang up along the line of the main street, and
in the business centre markets were built . . ." (William Cameron Forbes,
The Philippine Islands, Boston and New York, 1928, I, 404-05, 583). William
Parsons also noted, as early as 1915, that Burnham's Manila and Baguio "suggestions are being realized either in the acquisition of street areas or in actual
construction. In fact, much of the arterial framework has been constructed and
nailed down . . . with permanent public and semi-public buildings" (Parsons,
"Burnham As a Pioneer in City Planning," 24).

30. Burnham to Forbes, June 9, 1905, Burnham Papers; Forbes to Burnham, May
28, 1906, Forbes Papers.

31. Burnham to Forbes, n.d. 1906, Forbes Papers.

32. On the basis of maps, photographs, and the recollections of contemporaries,
American architectural influences in the Philippines were understandably more
obvious and dominant in the late 1930s than they were following the holocaust
of war and the subsequent postwar rebuilding. Though such structures as the
General Hospital, the Manila Hotel, and the older school buildings have been
poorly maintained in subsequent years, it is something of a tribute to Burnham,
Parsons, and other architects of the period that so much of their work was
restored and rebuilt in the postwar years.

Chapter XI

1. Edwin H. Blashfield, "Rome as a Place of Schooling for a Decorative Painter,"
Journal, Proceedings of the American Institute of Architects, Thirty-seventh Annual Convention, 1903 (Washington, D.C., 1904), 64-66.

2. *Ibid.*

3. Burnham to Charles L. Yerkes, July 17, 1905, Burnham Papers, Chicago Art
Institute Library; Charles Moore, *Daniel H. Burnham, Architect, Planner of
Cities,* II (Boston and New York, 1921), 75.

4. "Incorporation and Endowment of the Academy at Rome," *The Inland Architect and News Record,* XLV (April 1905), 22.

5. Charles McKim to John Mead Howells, October 23, 1894; McKim to Edwin
Blashfield, December 6, 1894, in Charles Moore, *The Life and Times of Charles
Follen McKim* (Boston and New York, 1929), 138, 161; McKim to Burnham,
May 10, June 8, July 5, 1894; April 6, 1895, McKim Papers, Library of Congress.

6. McKim to Burnham, March 13, 1905, in Moore, *Daniel H. Burnham,* II, 79-81;
Augustus St. Gaudens to Burnham, July 8, 1905, in St. Gaudens Papers, Library
of Congress.

7. Burnham to Charles T. Yerkes, July 17, 1905, Burnham Papers.

8. *Ibid.*

9. *Ibid.*

10. Burnham to St. Gaudens, July 17, 1905, Burnham Papers; St. Gaudens to Burnham, July 19, 1905, St. Gaudens Papers, Library of Congress. Yerkes died on
December 29, 1905.

11. Burnham to McKim, April 4, June 24, 1905, in Moore, *Daniel H. Burnham*, II, 83, 87-88; Burnham to James D. Phelan, June 12, 1905, in Burnham Papers.

12. Burnham to Phelan, June 12, 1905; Burnham to Willis Polk, July 5, 1905, McKim to Burnham, June 12, 1905, Burnham Papers; Phelan to Charles Moore, February 26, 1918, in Moore, *Daniel H. Burnham*, II, 2.

13. Burnham to Francis Millet, January 10, 1910, in Moore, *Daniel H. Burnham*, II, 94.

14. *Ibid.*

15. McKim to Burnham, n.d., in Moore, *The Life and Times of Charles Follen McKim*, 152; John Burchard and Albert Bush-Brown, *American Architecture, A Social and Cultural History* (Boston and Toronto, 1961), 262.

16. Burnham to George W. Breck, June 30, 1909, Burnham Papers.

17. Burnham, Diary, March 24, 1905; Moore, *Daniel H. Burnham*, I, 246-49; "Records of the Overseers of Harvard University," XIV (June 26, 1900-June 13, 1906), XV (June 27, 1906-January 11, 1911), Harvard University Archives.

18. Burnham, Millet, and members of the Committee on Fine Arts and Architecture, to Charles Eliot Norton, n.d., April 1905, Burnham Papers.

19. *Ibid.*

20. *Ibid.*

21. Burnham, Diary, July 17, 1906, June 29, 1911, Burnham Papers.

22. Burnham to Winslow Brothers Company, April 5, 1902; Burnham, Diary, January 19, 1904, Burnham Papers; Records of the Board of Trustess, Chicago Orchestral Association, June 6, 1912, 238, Chicago Symphony Orchestra Archives, Orchestra Hall, Chicago.

23. Burnham to Norman B. Ream, February 5, 1902, Burnham Papers.

24. Ernest Poole, *Giants Gone, Men Who Made Chicago* (Chicago, 1943), 289-90.

25. Burnham to Edward Ayer, February 14, 1903, Burnham Papers.

26. Burnham to John R. Hoxie, April 3, 1903, Burnham Papers.

27. *Ibid.*

28. Burnham to William T. Carrington, December 18, 1903, Burnham to Norman B. Ream, November 13, December 18, 1903, Burnham Papers; Poole, *Giants Gone*, 290; Philo A. Otis, *The Chicago Symphony Orchestra, Its Organization Growth and Development, 1891-1924* (Chicago, 1924), 145, 171.

29. Poole, *Giants Gone*, 290-91; Burnham, Diary, June 3, 1909; February 3, October 19, 1911, Burnham Papers.

30. Burnham to Mrs. R. A. Keyes, July 9, 1903; Burnham to W. B. Brown, April 30, 1908; Burnham to the Reverend Ferdinand S. Rockwell, n.d., November 1906, Burnham Papers.

31. Burnham to Lewis Burnham, October 7, 1901; Burnham to Margaret Burnham, June 30, 1911, Burnham Papers.

32. Burnham to Frederick Burnham, October 16, 1903, July 11, 1911; Burnham to Northern Trust Company, May 29, 1911; Burnham to Bertha Layton, December 10, 1906; Burnham to Lewis Burnham, July 6, 1911, Burnham Papers.

33. Burnham, Diary, February 1, 1904, July 27, 1909; Burnham to Margaret Burnham, April 18, 1903; Eda Lord to Burnham, March 8, 1910 (Scrapbook Three, p. 104); Burnham to John T. Williams, April 28, 1903; Burnham to Winifred Oliver, April 6, 1901; Burnham to Charles Deering, November 22, 1907; Burnham to Katherine Wyman, November 30, 1907, Burnham Papers.

34. Burnham, Diary, August 25, November 13, 1911, Burnham Papers. The inscribed Sullivan drawings are in the possession of W. R. Hasbrouck, Chicago, Illinois.

35. Burnham to Norman B. Ream, August 31, 1911, Burnham Papers.
36. W. Cameron Forbes to Gerrit Forbes, January 6, 1905, Forbes Papers, Houghton Library, Harvard University.

Chapter XII

1. Interview with Catherine Wheeler Burnham, Rancho Santa Fe, California, August 18, 1969; Burnham to Thresher and Glenney, July 11, 1902, October 27, 1906, Burnham Papers; Paul Starrett, *Changing the Skyline, An Autobiography* (New York, 1938), 29.
2. Starrett, *Changing the Skyline*, 33; Burnham to Sprague, Warner, and Company, July 16, 1904; Burnham to James P. Forgan, August 8, 1905; Burnham to Charles Deering, August 25, 1905; Burnham to Charles Wacker, February 10, 1907; Burnham, Diary, March 31, 1905, July 30, 1905, July 28, 1911, Burnham Papers.
3. Burnham to William Keith, April 14, 1902; Burnham to Fred Coleman, n.d., April 1902, Burnham Papers. Burnham enjoyed the luxury of servants. In 1901, he wrote Margaret from Europe: "An English valet is a great man, I can tell you. Everything about one's baggage is neat and clean; so are the clothes. He brings a bath early in the morning and makes things look as inviting as possible. Your razors are sharp, your shoes in order. Your shirts fixed. And so it goes until bed time. I just take a well-brushed hat and cane and walk about until noon . . . then I go on until I am ripe and ready to be put to bed, when he does it. He knows my habits already. I find the things I want at night and a lamp and book at the head of my bed . . . and I am covered up, tucked in, and bidden good night. He doesn't kiss me good night, but he does all the rest" (Burnham to Margaret Burnham, July 8, 1901, Burnham Papers).
4. Burnham to Forbes, July 20, 1905, Forbes Papers, Houghton Library, Harvard University; Burnham to Charles Moore, October 17, 23, 1905; Burnham to James D. Phelan, December 9, 1905; Burnham to Station Agent, Cable, Wisconsin, n.d., October 1905, Burnham Papers; Charles Moore, *Daniel H. Burnham, Architect, Planner of Cities*, I (Boston and New York, 1921), 255-56.
5. Interview with Cherie Burnham Morris, La Jolla, California, July 28, 1969; Burnham, Diary, September 1, 1901, July 30-August 1, 1907, February 13, 1908, March 18, 1909; Burnham to Jake Schmidlapp, September 5, 1901; Burnham to Albert Wells, May 5, 1909; Burnham to Willis Polk, August 2, 1909, Burnham Papers.
6. Burnham to William Cameron Forbes, March 31, 1905; Burnham to Albert Wells, March 27, 1901, Burnham Papers.
7. Burnham, Diary, June 28, 1903, March 12, 1912; Burnham to B. G. Sykes, June 20, 1905; Burnham to the Locomobile Company of America, June 3, 1905, Burnham Papers.
8. Burnham to Fred Coleman, July 11, 1906; Burnham to C. A. Coers, November, 13, 1907, Burnham Papers.
9. Daniel H. Burnham, Jr., unpublished autobiography, 26, typescript in possession of Daniel H. Burnham, III, San Diego, California; Burnham to Limousine Carriage Manufacturing Company, n.d., 1907, Burnham Papers.
10. Daniel H. Burnham, Jr., to Charles Moore, n.d., January 1918, Burnham Papers.
11. Burnham to A. C. McClurg and Company, October 14, 1908; Burnham to Frank Millet, July 27, 1908; Burnham to Duffield and Company, April 29, 1908; Burnham to Frederick Law Olmsted, Jr., December 24, 1907; Burnham to

Edouard Rahir et Cie, June 11, 1902, Burnham Papers; Moore, *Daniel H. Burnham*, II, 173.

12. Burnham, Diary, December 29, 1897, April 4, 1901, August 3, 1905, Burnham Papers.

13. Burnham to Samuel Mather, May 25, 1910; Burnham to Willis Polk, January 2, 1906; Burnham to Jules Guerin, January 8, 1906, Burnham Papers.

14. Burnham to Laurence Earl, January 9, 1907; William Keith to Burnham, n.d., Charles Moore Papers, Library of Congress.

15. Henry Adams, *The Education of Henry Adams* (Boston, 1961), 329. Burnham to Augustus St. Gaudens, July 9, July 25, 1903; Burnham to Mrs. Augustus St. Gaudens, October 23, 1908, Burnham Papers. Discussed in more detail in my unpublished doctoral dissertation "Daniel Hudson Burnham: A Study in Cultural Leadership," University of Wisconsin, 1971, 460-64.

16. Burnham to Dwight Perkins, February 13, 1908; Burnham to Theodore Roosevelt, May 24, 1904, Burnham Papers.

17. Burnham to Fred W. Upham, April 27, 1908, Burnham Papers.

18. Burnham to Samuel Bowles, June 13, 1905, Burnham Papers.

19. *Ibid.*

20. *Ibid.*; Burnham to Bowles, June 19, 1905, Burnham Papers.

21. Burnham to William E. Curtis, August 16, 1902, Burnham Papers.

22. *New York Times*, October 16, 1909; Burnham to C. D. Norton, October 14, 1909; Burnham to E. A. S. Clarke, October 25, 1909, Burnham Papers.

23. Burnham to Shelby M. Cullom, February 7, 1907; Burnham to James R. Mann, April 11, 1910, Burnham Papers.

24. Burnham, Diary, March 8, 1911, March 5, 1912; Burnham to Victor Lawson, March 13, 1912; Burnham to Daniel A. Campbell, March 1, 1907, Burnham Papers.

25. Daniel H. Burnham, Jr., unpublished autobiography, 36-37.

26. Burnham to Laurence C. Earl, October 2, 1902, Burnham Papers.

27. Burnham to Laurence C. Earl, October 14, 1902, Burnham Papers.

28. Burnham to Henry J. MacFarland, October 1, 1901, Burnham Papers.

29. Burnham, Diary, January 6, 1912; Burnham to House Committee, Union League Club, February 10, 1902; Burnham to Robert Critchell, October 5, 1903, Burnham Papers.

30. Burnham to Samuel Kirk's and Sons, August 12, 1904; Burnham to John M. Clark, September 2, 1904; Burnham to Hugh L. Burnham, April 22, 1910, Burnham Papers.

31. Burnham, Diary, March 2, 1903, April 21, 1903, February 20, 1908; Burnham to Arthur J. Eddy, February 12, 1902, Burnham Papers.

32. Burnham to John Whittaker, March 27, 1901, Burnham Papers.

33. Burnham, Diary, October 30, 1903, December 25, 1911; Burnham to W. L. Brown, August 8, 1905; Burnham to Captain Willard S. Brownson, April 2, 1904; Burnham to A. W. Houston, May 20, 1902, Burnham Papers.

34. Burnham, Diary, July 25, 1897, August 25, 1905, December 25, 1907, July 4, 1900, July 4, 1908, Burnham Papers; Ernest Poole, *Giants Gone, Men Who Made Chicago* (New York and London, 1943), 182.

35. Burnham, Diary, February 10, 1900, April 9-11, 1908, Burnham Papers.

36. Interview with Catherine Wheeler Burnham, Rancho Santa Fe, California, August 18, 1969; Burnham, Diary, December 27, 1907, Burnham Papers.

37. Interview with Catherine Wheeler Burnham, as cited; Burnham to Margaret Burnham, July 18, 1901, January 19, 1911, Burnham Papers.

38. Interview with Catherine Wheeler Burnham, as cited; Burnham to Lucy Elizabeth White, April 13, 1903; Burnham to Margaret B. Kelly, December 5, 1906; Burnham, Diary, December 23, 1903, Burnham Papers.

39. Interview with Catherine Wheeler Burnham, as cited; Burnham to Margaret Burnham, September 16, 1896, Burnham Papers.

40. *Ibid.*; Burnham, Diary, October 5, 1905; Burnham to H. C. Weaver, June 5, 1901, Burnham Papers.

41. Interview with Catherine Wheeler Burnham, as cited; Interview with Cherie Burnham Morris, La Jolla, California, July 28, 1969; Burnham, Diary, August 25, 1901; Burnham to "My dear Skiff," February 28, 1901; Burnham to Hubert Burnham, n.d., 1901, October 14, 1902, Burnham Papers.

42. Burnham to Hubert Burnham, January 13, 1903, October 14, 1903, Burnham Papers.

43. Interview with Cherie Burnham Morris, as cited; Burnham, Diary, July 10, 1905; Burnham to Hubert Burnham, August 9, 1906, Burnham Papers.

44. Burnham to Hubert Burnham, February 7, 1907, Burnham Papers.

45. Burnham to H. E. Wheelock, August 6, 1909; Burnham to Hubert Burnham, September 2, 1910, January 30, 1911, Burnham Papers.

46. Interview with Catherine Wheeler Burnham, as cited; Burnham to Frederick Winsor, April 20, 1903; Burnham to W. Cameron Forbes, June 5, 1901; Burnham to Alfred Worcester, n.d., August 1901, Burnham Papers.

47. Burnham to Frederick Winsor, December 13, 1901, January 25, 1902, February 1, 1902, Burnham Papers.

48. Burnham to Frederick Winsor, April 20, 1903, July 13, 1903, Burnham to Daniel Burnham, Jr., February 16, 1903, December 11, 1903, Burnham Papers; Interview with Daniel H. Burnham, III, San Diego, California, July 28, 1969.

49. Interview with Catherine Wheeler Burnham, as cited.

50. Daniel H. Burnham, Jr., unpublished diary, 1904, in possession of Daniel H. Burnham, III, San Diego, California.

51. *Ibid.*, January 6, 7, 13, 17, 19, 20, 22, 25, 27, 29, 31, February 29, 1904. Discussed in more detail in my unpublished doctoral dissertation, as cited.

52. Burnham to Secretary, Lawrence Scientific School, Harvard University, July 5, 1905, Burnham Papers.

53. *Ibid.*

54. Burnham to Daniel H. Burnham, Jr., August 4, 1905, Burnham Papers.

55. Daniel H. Burnham, Jr., unpublished autobiography, in possession of Daniel H. Burnham, III, San Diego, California, 5, 13-15.

56. Interview with Catherine Wheeler Burnham, as cited.

57. Burnham to Hubert Burnham, June 14, 1910, Burnham Papers.

58. Dora Root to Burnham, February 3, 1909, or 1910, Scrapbook Three, loose between pages 90 and 91, Burnham Papers.

59. *Ibid.*

Chapter XIII

1. Peter B. Wight, "Daniel Hudson Burnham and His Associates," *The Architectural Record*, XXXVIII (July 1915), 3. The name of the firm for a brief period following Root's death was listed simply as "D. H. Burnham," before it became the familiar "D. H. Burnham and Company." For the sake of clarity and convenience, the latter name will be used throughout this discussion.

2. *Ibid.*

3. *Ibid.*; A. N. Rebori, "The Work of Burnham & Root, D. H. Burnham, D. H. Burnham & Co., and Graham, Burnham & Co.," *The Architectural Record*, XXXVIII (July 1915), 34. Burnham to Joseph Worcester, n.d., April 1901; Burnham to Willis Polk, October 7, 1909; Burnham to George W. Perkins, July 15, 1909, Burnham Papers, Chicago Art Institute Library.

4. Burnham to Edward Probst, April 8, 1912; Burnham to C. D. Hilles, March 19, 1910, Burnham Papers.

5. Burnham to P. J. Weber, February 27, 1901; Burnham, Diary, June 4, 1911, Burnham Papers.

6. Burnham to Francis S. Swales, August 25, 1902, Burnham Papers; Carl W. Condit, *The Chicago School of Architecture, A History of Commercial and Public Building in the Chicago Area, 1875-1925* (Chicago and London, 1964), 208.

7. Frank Lloyd Wright, *An Autobiography* (New York, 1943), 125-27. Though I have found evidence that challenges the accuracy of other aspects of Wright's *Autobiography*, my ultimate conclusion is that this story is probably true. Even if Wright embroidered the details, it is logical that Burnham could and would have made the offer. He appreciated Wright's talent and he was able to pay whatever financial price was necessary. He left no record in his diaries or letters that I have been able to find, though he did mention social occasions with the Wallers and the Wrights about this time. Perhaps he could not bear to record such a blow to his ego.

8. *Ibid.*

9. Burnham, Diary, July 24, 1903, January 7, 1904, April 5, 1906; Burnham to James K. Vardaman, November 5, 1906, Burnham Papers.

10. Burnham, Diary, August 15-19, 1911, Burnham Papers.

11. For a detailed analysis, see William H. Jordy, *American Buildings and Their Architects, Progressive and Academic Ideals at the Turn of the Twentieth Century* (Garden City, N.Y., 1972), 62-63; and Condit, *The Chicago School*, 110-11. For contemporary analyses, see William Jordy's and Ralph Coe's edition of Montgomery Schuyler's *American Architecture and Other Writings* (New York, 1964), 198-99, and Charles A. Jenkins, "A White Enameled Building," *Architectural Record*, IV (March 1895), 299-306. There is considerable mystery and historical controversy about the actual design and building of the Reliance. No one knows, for sure, what the relative contributions actually were of Burnham and Atwood, and whether Root had anything to do directly with the final design of the upper floors.

12. The question of why the latter buildings of Burnham and of most other architects fell "below the level" of the 1894 Reliance is an important but difficult question to answer directly. The heavier classical pull from the other direction is discussed later in this chapter, but some of the answer lies in the Reliance Building, itself. To put it bluntly, most contemporaries, even the more sophisticated contemporary architectural critics, such as Schuyler and Rebori, simply did not like the building as much as later generations have. Long imbued with the importance of the "International Style," we have read back into the Reliance Building historical and aesthetic attributes that most contemporaries did not and could not see. Burnham and Atwood did the building in a spirit of experimental adventure, testing perhaps (1) just how far they could carry the idea of "wall-less-ness" made possible by the steel frame, (2) how much light they could get into an office building in the increasingly taller and darker canyons of the Chicago Loop, and (3) how economically spare and inexpensive they could make

the building. Some of the same considerations had gone into Burnham and
Root's earlier wall-bearing Monadnock, but that building, though spare and
clean, had had a "filled-out" look of aesthetic completeness that contemporaries
must have thought the Reliance lacked. For example, see Schuyler's discussion
in the Jordy edition, and the Rebori article, as cited below.

13. A. N. Rebori, "The Work of Burnham and Root, D. H. Burnham, D. H. Burnham and Company, and Graham, Burnham, and Company," *The Architectural
Record*, XXXVIII (July 1915), 69, 72, 81.

14. Burnham to Jake Schmidlapp, May 29, 1901, Burnham Papers.

15. Burnham to Henry G. Foreman, August 20, 1903, Burnham Papers.

16. Burnham to Theodore Starrett, June 10, 16, 1905, Burnham Papers.

17. Carroll L. V. Meeks, *The Railroad Station, An Architectural History* (New
Haven, 1956), 125-34. Meeks makes an illuminating analysis of that much dis-
cussed subject—the effects of the Columbian Exposition on American architec-
ture. He makes an interesting case, in particular, for the influence of Charles
Atwood's overlooked Exposition train station on the later stations of Burnham
and other architects. He cites, especially, the Union Station in Washington,
Reed and Stern's and Warren and Wetmore's Grand Central Station in New
York, and McKim, Mead, and White's Pennsylvania Station in New York.

18. Burnham to Edward Cullerton, January 8, 1902, Burnham Papers.

19. "Chicago's Most Massive and Costly Office Building," Supplement to *The Inland Architect and News Record*, XLVI (November 1905), 1.

20. *Ibid.*

21. *Ibid.*

22. *Ibid.*, 2.

23. Burnham to Henry C. Frick, n.d. 1901, June 10, 1904; Burnham to John La
Farge, June 4, 1901, Burnham Papers.

24. Burnham to J. P. Proctor, September 11, 1901, Burnham Papers.

25. Burnham to Frick, December 9, 1901, Burnham Papers.

26. Burnham to F. T. F. Lovejoy, May 29, 1901; Burnham to Harry S. Black, May
29, 1901, March, n.d. 1902; Burnham to Frick, February 5, 1902; Burnham to
Ernest Graham, May 25, 1903, Burnham Papers.

27. Burnham to Graham, February, n.d., 1903; Burnham to Frick, November 1,
1902, Burnham Papers.

28. Daniel H. Burnham, Jr., unpublished autobiography, 49-50, in the possession of
Daniel H. Burnham, III, San Diego, California.

29. Burnham to Fred W. Upham, December 21, 1911, Burnham Papers.

30. *Ibid.*; Daniel H. Burnham, Jr., unpublished autobiography, 48-49.

31. Daniel H. Burnham, Jr., unpublished autobiography, 48-49; Burnham to Theodore Ely, January 2, 1912, Burnham Papers.

32. "The Architect's Plaint," editorial, *The Boston Herald*, September 9, 1911;
R. Clipston Sturgis to editor, September 9, 1911, *The Boston Herald*, September 11, 1911.

33. Edward A. Filene to editor, September 12, 1911, *The Boston Herald*, September 13, 1911.

34. *Ibid.*

35. Rebori, "The Work of . . . D. H. Burnham and Company . . . ," as cited,
81-83; Burnham to George Maher, February 19, 1903; Wright, *An Autobiography*, 125. Burnham to James Parmelee, February 14, 1903, March, n.d., 1903,
Burnham Papers.

36. Burnham to Theodore Ely, January 22, 1902; Burnham to F. W. McKinney and S. H. Hodge, November 8, 1906, Burnham Papers.
37. Burnham to Committee of St. Paul's Cathedral, Pittsburgh, January 6, 1902; Burnham to the Rt. Reverend R. Phelan, Bishop of Pittsburgh, October 2, 1901; Burnham to Norman B. Ream, October 8, 1901; Burnham to Lyman G. Gage, May 16, 1902; Burnham to Sir William Van Horne, August 21, 1902; Burnham to Elihu Root, October 29, 1902, December 19, 1902; Burnham to Colonel A. L. Mills, December 6, 1902, June 19, 1903; Burnham to George Post, March 4, 1903, Burnham Papers.
38. Burnham to Stanford White, October 1, 1903; Burnham to Jake Schmidlapp, April 27, 1911, Burnham Papers.

Chapter XIV

1. Hamlin Garland, "The New Chicago," *The Craftsman*, XXIV (September 1913), 555-56.
2. C.f. Robert Averill Walker, *Urban Planning* (Chicago, 1941), 225-28.
3. Burnham, Diary, July 27, 1896, Burnham Papers, Chicago Art Institute Library.
4. Burnham to Charles Moore, April 26, 1908, in "Notes Taken at Meeting Held in the Office of the Railway Exchange Building, Chicago," in Moore Papers, Library of Congress; Burnham, Diary, November 24, December 6, 14, 18, 1896, Burnham Papers.
5. Burnham, Diary, February 6, 15, 1897, Burnham Papers.
6. Burnham, "The Commercial Value of Beauty," reprinted in Charles Moore, *Daniel Hudson Burnham, Architect, Planner of Cities*, II (Boston and New York, 1921), 101-2.
7. *Ibid.*
8. *Ibid.*
9. *Ibid.*, 111.
10. C.f. Richard A. Miller, "Burnham's Plans Shaped Modern Chicago," *Architectural Forum*, CXVI (May 1962), 110.
11. Burnham, Diary, January 26, 1901, Burnham Papers; "Proceedings of the First Meeting of the Chicago Plan Commission, November 4, 1909," Chicago Municipal Reference Library; Frederick A. Delano to Walter Moody, July 7, 1915, Moore Papers.
12. Delano to Moody, July 7, 1915, as cited above.
13. Burnham to Henry G. Foreman, August 28, 1903, April 21, 1904, Burnham Papers.
14. Burnham to Richard Watson Gilder, September 12, 1904, Burnham Papers.
15. Delano to Moody, July 7, 1915, as cited above; Burnham, Diary, September 21, 1906, Burnham Papers.
16. Burnham to Norton, October 13, 1906; Burnham to Delano, November 21, 1906, Burnham Papers; Edward H. Bennett, unpublished diary, November 12, 1906, Edward H. Bennett Papers, in possession of Edward H. Bennett, Jr., Chicago; "Chicago to Plan for the Future," *Inland Architect and News Record*, XLVIII (November 1906).
17. Burnham to J. G. Shedd, January 10, 1902; Burnham to Charles Moore, January 23, 1902; Burnham to A. A. McCormick, December 13, 1902, November 27, 1903; Burnham, Diary, October 22, 1903, January 30, 1904, Burnham Papers.

18. "Business Men's Clubs Merge to Boom City," *Chicago Record-Herald*, December 19, 1906. Not everyone was pleased with the merger, of course. The liberal reformer, William Kent, for example, wrote to Norton: "I deeply regret that the Merchants Club has resigned. It used to be public spirited and open-minded and useful and I used to be proud of my membership. I was only a little less proud of the fact that I never was asked to join the Commercial Club. . . . I am not and shall not be a member of the Commercial Club." William Kent to Charles D. Norton, January 25, 1906. C.f. Kent's letters to Norton on January 9 and February 1, 1907, Bennett Papers.

19. List of Committees, in Daniel H. Burnham and Edward H. Bennett, *Plan of Chicago* (Chicago, 1909), xv; Frederick A. Delano to Members of the Commercial Club, February 21, 1908, Bennett Papers.

20. Bennett, Diary, January 7, October 30, 1907; Charles D. Norton to Frederick A. Delano, July 9, 1908, Bennett Papers; Burnham, Diary, March 4, 8, April 1, 3, 4, 5, October 23, 29, 30, November 5, 16, 19, 26, 29, December 3, 9, 14, 20, 1907, Burnham Papers.

21. Burnham to Franklin B. Head, May 7, 1908; Burnham to American Civic Association, February 21, 1907; Burnham to Huntington Wilson, February 5, October 7, 1907, Bennett Papers, Chicago.

22. Burnham to Harbor Master, Lake Street Bridge, November 10, 1906; Burnham to the Anchor Line, November 9, 1906; Burnham to Joseph B. Strauss, November 26, 1906; Burnham to H. M. Sloan, December 18, 1907, Bennett Papers.

23. Burnham to Hubert Burnham, September 5, 1906, Burnham Papers; Burnham to Hubert Burnham, November 23, 1906; Burnham to Dr. Rollin Woodyatt, May 18, 1908; Burnham to Professor U. S. Grant, May 16, 1908; Burnham to Harry Pratt Judson, May 18, 1908, Bennett Papers.

24. Bennett, Diary, December 9, 1907, Bennett Papers.

25. *Ibid.*, December 4, 1907, October 13, 1908.

26. Bennett, Diary, March 18, May 5, 1908, Bennett Papers; Hugh Duncan, *Culture and Democracy* (Totowa, N.J., 1965), xiv.

27. Bennett, Diary, March 19, April 1, 12, July 13, October 21, 1908, Bennett Papers. There were, of course, complaints and grumblings about various details of the work in progress, usually from special interest groups or individuals seeking to protect property rights. For a discussion of such questions, see Michael P. McCarthy, "Chicago Businessmen and the Burnham Plan," *Journal of the Illinois State Historical Society*, LXIII (Autumn 1970), 228-56.

28. Burnham to Charles Moore, June 19, 1908, Burnham Papers.

29. Burnham to Richard Kiehnel, July 23, 1907; Burnham to Albert Wells, September 30, 1907, Burnham Papers; Bennett, Diary, January 17, 25, February 26, March 5, 1908; Frederick Delano to Commercial Club Members, February 21, 1908, Bennett Papers.

30. Burnham to Ernest Graham, July 8, 1909; Burnham to Charles Moore, July 24, 1909, Burnham Papers. In speculating on Moore's part in the writing of the finished plan, several historians have suggested that he contributed more than he did. The notes and drafts for the Plan, in Burnham's own handwriting, in the Burnham papers, Chicago Art Institute Library, tend to confirm Burnham's substantial authorship. Moore helped to shape the report and to polish Burnham's occasionally inelegant syntax and Burnham insisted that his support be acknowledged on the title page. In spirit and rhetoric, the Chicago Plan is similar to other examples of Burnham's writing, with which Moore was not connected.

For a discussion of Moore's similar role in the preparation of the Washington Plan, see Chapter VII.

31. Burnham and Bennett, *Plan of Chicago*, 1, 2.
32. *Ibid.*, 4.
33. *Ibid.*, 32.
34. *Ibid.*, 32, 33.
35. *Ibid.*, *Passim*; see also William E. Parsons, "Burnham As a Pioneer in City Planning," *The Architectural Record*, XXXVIII (July 1915), 27-31; Robert L. Wrigley, Jr., "The Plan of Chicago: Its Fiftieth Anniversary," *Journal of the American Institute of Planners*, XXVI (February 1960), 31-32; "Burnham's Plans Shaped Modern Chicago," as cited, 109-11.
36. Burnham and Bennett, *Plan of Chicago*, 80.
37. *Ibid.*, 51-52.
38. *Ibid.*, 109, 123.
39. *Ibid.*, 61-62.
40. *Ibid.*, 78.
41. Carl W. Condit, *American Building Art, The Twentieth Century* (New York, 1961), 212-13.
42. Burnham and Bennett, *Plan of Chicago*, 8.
43. *Ibid.*, 81-82.
44. John Alvord to Burnham, July 27, 1909, Scrapbook Three, p. 20, Burnham Papers.
45. Theodore N. Ely to Burnham, October 29, 1909, Scrapbook Three, p. 70, Burnham Papers.
46. Walker, *Urban Planning*, 235-41; Walter D. Moody, *What of the City?* (Chicago, 1919), 329-33; Lloyd Lewis and Henry Justin Smith, *Chicago, The History of Its Reputation* (New York, 1929), 315-22; Miller, "Burnham's Plans Shaped Modern Chicago," as cited, 111-12; Wrigley, "The Plan of Chicago, Its Fiftieth Anniversary," as cited, 33-37.
47. For a good, short, discussion of the early years of the plan's implementation, see Mellier G. Scott, *American City Planning Since 1890* (Berkeley and Los Angeles, 1969), 138-41; for a longer, illustrated, and more detailed treatment, see the excellent study by Harold M. Mayer and Richard C. Wade, *Chicago, Growth of a Metropolis* (Chicago and London, 1969), 290-315, and 315-465, *passim*.
48. *Chicago Record Herald*, January 14, 1911, 1.
49. Burnham to Henry Foreman, August 14, 1909, Burnham Papers.
50. Burnham to W. Cameron Forbes, November 25, 1911; Burnham to Owen Aldis, December 18, 1911, Burnham Papers.

Chapter XV

1. Burnham to James S. Evans, July 31, 1905; Burnham to Francis S. Swales, September 29, 1909, Burnham Papers, Chicago Art Institute Library.
2. Burnham to J. Frank Decker, April 3, 1905; Burnham to B. H. Pendleton, July 31, 1905; Burnham to James W. Swayne, July 23, 1906; Burnham to W. B. Bell, August 2, 1906; Burnham to Mayo Fesler, October 30, 1906; Burnham to Mrs. Andreas Weland, February 20, 1908; Burnham to Rollan Adelsperger, February 12, 1910; Burnham to William Van Horne, n.d., August 1910; Burnham to Robert L. Burch, March 18, 1911; Burnham to E. S. Shannon, April 6,

1911; Burnham to E. H. Crump, February 8, 1912; Burnham to John Ihlder, March 13, 1908; Burnham to Roy S. Smith, April 1, 1908; Burnham to Edmund C. Hill, February 25, 1910; Burnham to C. B. Merrick, December 18, 1909; Burnham to Lewis L. Gillette, n.d., 1909; Burnham to W. L. Abbott, July 30, 1909; Burnham to Elizabeth Askew, May 11, 1911; Burnham to J. C. Dana, November 15, 1911; Burnham to W. P. Flynn, January 13, 1912, Burnham Papers; Edward H. Bennett, Diary, March 30, 1909, February 19, 1910, Bennett Papers, in possession of Edward H. Bennett, Jr.

3. Burnham to Joseph Millet, March 5, 1912, Burnham Papers.

4. Burnham to Newell D. Hillis, December 1, 4, 1911; Burnham to J. H. Friedlander, December 7, 1911, Burnham Papers; Edward H. Bennett, Diary, May 21, 1910, Bennett Papers.

5. Burnham to Nicolas Murray Butler, December 7, 1911; Burnham to Wisconsin State Capitol Commission, July 11, 1906; Burnham to Richard Lloyd Jones, December 20, 1911, Burnham Papers.

6. Burnham to Cass Gilbert, May 15, 1911; Burnham to Lorado Taft, July 12, 1911, Burnham Papers.

7. Burnham, Diary, September 10-24, 1910, Burnham Papers.

8. Burnham, Diary, September-October 1910, *passim*; Burnham to John W. Scott, September 6, 1910; Burnham to Edward B. Butler, April 23, 1910; Burnham to Ian MacAlister, May 26, 1910, June 30, 1910; Burnham, "The City of the Future Under a Democratic Government," *Transactions of the Royal Institute of British Architects* (October 1910), 368-78.

9. Burnham, "The City of the Future Under a Democratic Government," as cited.

10. *Ibid.*

11. *Ibid.*

12. *Ibid.*

13. "The Town Planning Conference," *Journal of the Royal Institute of British Architects* (October 22, 1910), 795-96.

14. Burnham to Werner Hegemann, July 19, 1910; Burnham to Charles D. Norton, June 20, 1910, Burnham Papers.

15. Burnham, Diary, *passim*; Burnham to E. B. Wilkerson, May 14, 1909, Burnham Papers; Charles Moore, *Daniel H. Burnham, Architect, Planner of Cities* (Boston and New York, 1921), *passim*; John W. Reps, *Monumental Washington, The Planning and Development of the Capitol Center* (Princeton, 1967), 144-54. The commission's ultimate goal was to eliminate from the Mall all buildings not of a neoclassical character. In 1904, for example, Burnham wrote that he planned eventually to "wipe out the present Smithsonian Institution." Burnham to H. M. Pettit, June 30, 1904, Burnham Papers.

16. Reps, *Monumental Washington*, 154; Burnham to Charles Moore, June 17, 1910; Burnham to Francis Millet, June 25, 1910, Burnham Papers.

17. Burnham to Charles D. Norton, July 27, August 8, 1910, Burnham Papers.

18. Burnham to Francis Millet, January 24, 1911; Burnham to Daniel Chester French, March 6, 1911; Burnham to Charles D. Hilles, April 17, 1911, Burnham Papers.

19. Reps, *Monumental Washington*, 154-59.

20. *Ibid.*

21. *Ibid.*

22. *Ibid.*; Burnham to Francis Millet, April 12, 1912, Burnham Papers.

23. Burnham to Charles Moore, August 2, 1911; Burnham to Henry Bacon, August

16, 1911; Burnham to William Randolph Hearst, January 20, 1912, Burnham Papers.

24. Reps, *Monumental Washington*, 159.

25. Burnham to Allan K. Pond, April 21, 1911, Burnham Papers.

26. *Ibid*.

27. Burnham to Allan K. Pond, January 29, 1911; Burnham to R. Clipston Sturgis, January 29, 1912, Burnham Papers.

28. Burnham to Theodore Ely, August 15, 1911, Burnham Papers.

29. Burnham to Lewis T. Burnham, November 13, 1911, Burnham Papers.

30. Burnham to John W. Root, Jr., February 6, 1912, Burnham Papers.

31. Burnham, Diary, April 12-22, 1912. This last of Burnham's travel diaries has been lost since Moore had access to it and reprinted parts of it in the early 1920s. I therefore quote from the diaries as reprinted in Moore, *Daniel H. Burnham*, II, 153-57.

32. Burnham, Diary, April 15-21, 1912, in Moore, *Daniel H. Burnham*, II, 154-55.

33. Burnham, Diary, April 22-May 23, 1912, in Moore, *Daniel H. Burnham*, II, 155-57.

34. "Daniel H. Burnham Dead," *The Evanston Index*, June 8, 1912. The ashes were returned to Evanston on July 8, 1912. Burial took place on October 27, 1912, on a small wooded island in Graceland Cemetery, Chicago. A large, simple boulder marked the grave. The island was then reserved for exclusive use of the Burnham family to include children and their spouses. Daniel H. Burnham, Jr., Diary, in possession of Daniel H. Burnham, III, San Diego, California.

35. See, for example, the tributes cited in chapter one and "Daniel H. Burnham Dead," *The Evanston Index*, June 8, 1912.

36. John Goddard, "Address . . . at the Funeral of Daniel Hudson Burnham. . . ." Typescript in Hubert Burnham Papers, in possession of Cherie Burnham Morris, La Jolla, California.

Index